1950

Marinaro, *A Modern Dry Fly Code*, 1950

Charlie Fox, *Advanced Bait-Casting*, 1950

Harrisburg Fly-Fishers present Phillippe rod to PA State Museum, 1955

1960

Marinaro fishes Michigan's Au Sable River, meeting with George Griffith, Art Neumann and George Mason, c.1960

Charlie Fox, *This Wonderful World of Trout*, 1963

Charlie Fox, *Rising Trout*, 1967

1970

Marinaro's 2nd edition of *A Modern Dry Fly Code*, 1970

Marinaro meets Tom Maxwell and Tom Dorsey, c.1970

Marinaro meets Hoagy B. Carmichael, 1973

Marinaro, *In The Ring of The Rise*, 1976

Marinaro travels to England to fish the Rivers Test and Itchen, 1976

Carmichael's *A Master's Guide to Building a Bamboo Fly Rod*, 1977

1980

Marinaro, Maxwell, Beck, Harvey, Robbins, Leiser and Shenk visit President Carter at Camp David, 1980

Excursions to New Brunswick for Atlantic Salmon, 1975-1983

Vincent Marinaro, deceased, March, 1986

Split & Glued By Vincent C. Marinaro

Bill Harms and Tom Whittle

Foreword by Hoagy B. Carmichael

Paintings and illustrations by Kim Mellema

Published by Stony Creek Rods
Harrisburg, Pennsylvania

Copyright 2007 by Bill Harms and Tom Whittle
All illustrations and paintings copyright 2007 by Kim Mellema
Foreword copyright 2007 by Hoagy B. Carmichael

ALL RIGHTS RESERVED. No part if this book may be reproduced
in any manner without the express written consent of the publisher,
except in the case of brief excerpts in critical reviews and articles.

Published in collaboration with the Pennsylvania Fly Fishing Museum Association by
Stony Creek Rods
6530 Leo Drive
Harrisburg, Pennsylvania 17111
www.stonycreekrods.com

Trade Edition   ISBN 978-0-9796532-0-9
Limited Edition   ISBN 978-0-9796532-1-6

Design by
Christina Lauver
Peacock Graphics
1841 Clarks Valley Road
Dauphin, Pennsylvania 17018

Printed and bound in the United States of America by Jostens Printing and Publishing

With kindest regards
Bill Harris
Tom Whittle

CONTENTS

FOREWORD vi
Hoagy B. Carmichael

PREFACE viii
Bill Harms and Tom Whittle

A BAMBOO ROD-MAKING PRIMER 1

CHAPTER ONE *Working Back To Vince's Beginnings* 6
   Lost, But Found 8
   Questions And Propositions 14
   Vince's Beginnings 24

CHAPTER TWO *Learning To Build* 32
   "But of Any Of These Mongrels We Will Have Naught" –*George Parker Holden* 35
   Robert W. Crompton: Another Mentor 42
   College, Married, Then Abroad 50

CHAPTER THREE *Heyday In The Cumberland Valley* 56
   Dawn Of An Era 57
   "The Pennsylvania Boys" –*Sparse Grey Hackle* 66
   To Deal With A Limestoner 74

CHAPTER FOUR *Those Pesky Phillippes* 80
   The Phillippe/Marinaro Connection: Questions Of Provenance 82
   Who Said What? 89
   A Search For Precision 94

CHAPTER FIVE *News From Other Makers At Mid-Century* 108
   The Holden Associates 109
   In Praise Of The Humble Panfish 120
   Grumblings About Rod-Makers 127

CHAPTER SIX *Good Times Beyond The Valley* 134
- Roughing It At Poe Paddy 136
- Specters On The Hampshire Downs 139
- Another Camp David Accord 146
- *Salmo Salar* 149
- Telling Tales Out Of School 155

CHAPTER SEVEN *At The Master's Bench* 158
- Shall We Dance...? 159
- We Build A Rod: Part I 169
- We Build A Rod: Part II 175
- Getting It All Together 182

CHAPTER EIGHT *It's All In The Design* 190
- From Shooting-Boards To Roof-Rods 192
- The Well-Tempered Taper 198
- Theoretically Speaking.... 204
- Reading The Graphed Rod 209

CHAPTER NINE *A Selection Of Vince's Rods* 218
- Our Picks 220
- Measuring The Tapers 220
- Meet Our Experts 222
- Let's Cast Some Rods 225

CHAPTER TEN *Picking Up Where Vince Left Off* 258
—By Tom Whittle
- How I Met Vince.... 259
- Don't Know 'Bout The Other Guys, But.... 263
- Beyond Mere Tweaking 265
- A Not-So-Radical Example 270
- Tapers by Whittle and Harms 275

NOTES 282
APPENDIX 287
INDEX 293

Foreward

Vince:

When I first picked up a fly rod in the 1960's there were few newly published books from which one could find guidance. The old-timey wisdom of men like Edward Hewitt and Ray Bergman, mixed with the exactitude of Ernest Schwiebert's florid *Matching The Hatch*, seemed awkward to a young man who had taken the no-nonsense legacy of the Beatles and The Yardbirds seriously, yet who was searching for information that would blanket the seemingly out-of-reach question, that of how to hook a rising trout on a dry fly.

And then, in 1971, I saw the bright azure cover on the Crown Co. reprint of a book called, *The Modern Dry Fly Code*, on a shelf in a small fly shop in Vermont. A new book to curl up with, written by an author who was not familiar to me. Although I had only recently reached the cusp of fly-fishing sophistication, I could not put the book down, rapidly digesting the carefully placed words that so easily held my interest. The Spartan, close-to-the-bone, style of writing forced me to think about the ideas on the pages, many of which I soon found worked well on rivers far from the limestone streams of Pennsylvania. Rivers like Vermont's Battenkill, Michigan's Au Sable, and the legendary Beaverkill River in the Catskills, none of which had seen the unusual silhouette of a poorly tied pontoon hopper, succumbed to many of the ideas that lurked in those hallowed pages.

I finally met the author of *The Code* at the hands of my great friend, Chauncey Lively, one of the most innovative fly-tier-fishermen in the history of the sport, on Pennsylvania's Falling Spring Creek in 1975. It was several years before my rod building book was on the stands, so, with no credibility in my back pocket, I stood within Chauncey's long shadow, hoping that I would not have to make an awkward cast, or pull the fly away from a rising trout, in the presence of Mr. Marinaro. We met again at a fly fishing show in Harrisburg, Pennsylvania a year after my book was published, and he greeted this new-kid-on-the-block with a studied reserve, followed quickly by a well thought out rod building question. Was he testing me, a stumper maybe, or was he baiting a trap, patiently waiting for an answer that would scratch Vince's peevish notion that the phalanx of authors who had recently come over the hill, responsible for the late '70's avalanche of new fly fishing books, were often only moderately versed? I stood my ground that evening, robust in the security of my sophomoric knowledge. I must have shown a willingness to also listen, which was the currency I later learned he was looking for.

Vince Marinaro was a man of many stripes. He was cautious, often unyielding, vain, somewhat distrustful, and shy, with a soft, self-deprecating wit that was normally shielded from people other than his close friends. Always well dressed, Vince was often the center of attention at gatherings of fishing folk, and it was from that vantage point that I was able to watch my new friend, usually the shortest man in the circle, parry questions about his rod tapers that he didn't want to answer, or avoid those in the crowd that he felt needed to do their homework. "Too many statements, not enough statesmen," I heard him say one evening. While it can be said that Vince was usually cautiously open-minded, one had to be able to prove an idea before it gained passage with him. His great book, one of the three greatest American books written on the sport of fly-fishing in my opinion, was testament to that belief.

My early time with Vince led me to respectfully ask, almost demand, some answers to the suppositions that he routinely raised in his new book. I had recently read *In the Ring of the Rise*, and I wanted answers to why he was not more specific about tapering dimensions, and numerous other key points that I was to so boldly reveal in my own book. It was not easy going, as the answers I wanted came slowly. Was he being coy, maybe just dastardly intransigent, or just waiting for the moment to let me in? Like an acolyte, I had to wait for the answers.

After his wife, Martha, died in 1978, Vince lived alone and he was often lonely. Unexpectedly, he phoned one evening to ask if he could come to my house for several days, bring some rods, so that we could have a "session," as he called it. I picked him up at Penn Station, cradling his well-appointed overnight bag like a grateful station porter. Several of us hosted a welcoming party for Vince, inviting a group of like-minded people who would be glad to meet him and talk angling. He asked if he could cook an Italian meal, pasta mostly with a rich Italian sauce, which led us to spend the better part of two hours in the local A&P sifting the stores numerous shelves for just the right ingredients. He took forever, looking at labels, weighing ingredients, loading the cart with the freshest they had, and generally wearing my patience to the bone. His approach to cooking, writing, or his dress was one of precision.

Nothing was left to chance, and when one of the guests walked by the boiling pot of pasta, tasted it, and threw a handful of salt into the mixture just as Vince walked in, I thought I was going to witness a brawl.

We had many such weekends over the years, earmarked by my cat, "Miles," who liked my new rod-making pal, and always curled up on his bed late at night. In time, Vince became a real friend, almost a confidant, which finally led to his invitation for me to spend a weekend at his Marble Street house in Mechanicsburg. I was very excited. I knew that it might lead to my learning how he made his rods, see his tools and planing jigs, and maybe even swipe a taper or two, so I was a bundle of energy as I rang the door bell at his modest ranch-style home. Vince's lifework was everywhere. He had asked me to bring down several of my most select culms of bamboo (one never left Vince's presence without having given up something), which I did, but I swapped those pieces of bamboo for the license to wander through Vince's store of rod building tools and tapers like a dog at a picnic. I had given him several old Thomas rod blanks that were made from solid pre-war cane, and was surprised to find that he had removed the varnish and laid the sections on his earthen basement floor, thus allowing the microorganisms to feast on the hide glue that held the strips together. The grin on his well-shaven face cast little doubt as to where the idea had come from, as he held the clean bamboo strips in his hand, ready for reshaping. We cast every rod in the house, some with actions that suited my taste, which later led to my designing and making several rods that had the letters "T.M.S." on the shaft. The Marble Street experience was a trip to the center of eastern fly-fishing's inner circle. I learned a lot that weekend, as well as confirmation that Vince had opened his well-guarded door, and let me pass.

Hoagy B. Carmichael
November, 2006

Preface

The subject of this book is Vincent Marinaro—his life as a fly-fisherman, but with a particular focus upon his career as a maker of bamboo fly rods. With the 1950 publication of *A Modern Dry Fly Code*, Vince's reputation began to grow and by the time of his death in 1986, he was lionized as the dean of central Pennsylvania's famous limestone streams; the man who revolutionized anglers' perspectives about trout feeding habits, terrestrial patterns and fly-fishing itself. *A Modern Dry Fly Code* was based on Marinaro's long years of research on trout feeding behavior, an interest that continued through all his following decades. In 1976 he published his second book, *In The Ring of The Rise*, and this book, too, became a staple in every fly-fisherman's library. Among the many other remarkable things in its pages, here, for the first time, Vince devotes a chapter to the design and construction of his bamboo fly rods. [1]

Even so, Marinaro's interest in rod-making remains a great mystery. While he had been building since he was a very young man, few but his local friends knew him to be a maker—despite the ubiquitous inscription on his rods: "Split & Glued by Vincent C. Marinaro." Vince never boasted publicly of his rods, never sold them or gave them away—although one went to Sparse Grey Hackle (Alfred W. Miller) in the late 1940s, and another to Barry Beck in the 1970s. In fact, he spoke little about his rods even among friends. He allowed few people to handle them; guarded his tapers jealously; wrote only two, brief articles in the 1950s about gluing the bamboo rod, and nothing after. There are explanations for this secrecy, however, and we will come to those in our first chapter.

It always seemed strange to those of us who knew Vince that he would work so hard to make his findings about tying flies and fishing known, while actually working against being recognized as a builder of bamboo rods. In the 1970s, when Vince was teaching me to build rods, his frequent explanation was always dismissive: "Nobody's interested in bamboo any more." In one sense, Vince was entirely correct, for the revolution in fiberglass fly rods already had come and gone—sweeping away the large, commercial, bamboo rod market—and by the mid-1970s the newer mania for graphite rods was already well under way. I would mention, too, that as of the early 1970s, neither Vince nor I knew any amateur makers. We knew of Hoagy Carmichael's work with Garrison, and earlier, Vince had also befriended Tom Maxwell and Tom Dorsey (soon to form Thomas & Thomas), but our awareness of other independent makers ended just about there. Certainly, as we discovered later, it wasn't that these did not exist, but that in those days rod-makers had little-or-no knowledge of one another and information did not circulate.

Yet, Vince was also (and most pointedly) not correct, because a decade after *The Ring* was published, there emerged an entire, new generation of amateur, bamboo rod makers—anglers who would have sold their firstborn to lay hands on one of Marinaro's cane creations. Such was his soaring reputation, that it preceded everything he did. But the new wave of interest in bamboo rods did not come about because Vince suddenly became influential as a rod-maker. Indeed, he was never influential at all and kept his work entirely private. Instead, the real impact upon independent makers came from Vince's good friend, Hoagy

Carmichael, who, in 1977, published his seminal work on Everett Garrison, *A Master's Guide To Building A Bamboo Fly Rod*. Other notable authors had preceded Carmichael on the subject of rod-making, but the time was ripe and it was Hoagy's book that fully captured the imagination of the amateur rod-maker.

From the 1980s to the present, the isolation of earlier days turned around fully, and amateurs and independent professionals alike found themselves part of a large, rod-making community. Where, before, there was only the odd maker working alone in his garage or basement, now we have computers in nearly every home and one can peruse scores of web sites featuring hand-made bamboo rods, advice on restoration work, chat-rooms and lengthy descriptions of the rod-making process. Nobody could possibly estimate how many amateur makers may have emerged in recent decades, but there are now a dozen or more annual "gatherings" hosted in different regions of the U. S and Canada, each drawing 50-100 makers. Added to this, are the several rod-makers' forums on the Internet, all suggesting that there could be a thousand or more independent makers in North America, with additional hundreds emerging throughout Europe and Japan.

Neither Vince nor I saw the movement coming, but because of the scale of renewed interest among makers, collectors and historians alike, Tom Whittle and I felt encouraged to turn our attention to Vince's career. We have undertaken this book jointly, discussing the many issues, interpretations and problems of its presentation. Tom's role in our project was to oversee all matters of graphics, photography and technical interpretation, to compile data from Vince's rods, and to provide research information from the holdings of the Pennsylvania Fly Fishing Museum Association (PFFMA). I took on the job of writing, recalling my years of friendship with Vince and explaining his principles of rod design and construction. (Accordingly, when one reads the plural form of authorship "we," the implication is concurrence between Tom and me. On the other hand, the singular form suggests either my own experiences or certain views that came to me only as I wrote. Tom might agree or disagree: He didn't always say.)

The larger purpose of this preface is to explore the problems of writing about another man's work, and what follows may serve as a useful point of departure. All writers must worry about questions of accuracy and authenticity, of interpretation and sufficiency. But we are even more concerned for their alter-egos—conjecture, innuendo and approximation. As something of a disclaimer, we would say that our estimations of Marinaro's life and his many contributions are based on the best knowledge we could find. At a minimum, readers would have a right to expect as much, but concerns lurk even in the midst of our assurances.

To illustrate what we mean and its connection to our work on Marinaro, consider how (just a few years back, in *The American Fly Fisher: Journal of the American Museum of Fly Fishing*) an old debate about the origins of dry-fly fishing in America arose with renewed vigor. The magazine published three noteworthy articles, each with the shared intention to explore connections between Frederic Halford and Theodore Gordon. In "History and Mr. Gordon," Paul Schullery writes about Gordon's questionable role in introducing the dry fly to America. Andrew Herd's article, "Frederic M. Halford: The Myth and the Man," traces Halford's exaggerated and often misrepresented reputation even in England. And Ken Cameron, in "Rigor Without Mortis," writes about the insidious creep of fiction into what is taken to be history. [2]

Among many other things, all three writers point to John McDonald's 1947 publication of Theodore Gordon's collected notes and letters, and an assertion that led the general fishing public to accept Gordon as "the one who introduced and adapted the dry fly to the U.S." [3] McDonald's introductory essay explains:

> Two disparate traditions that today make up the central course of our fly tying and fly-fishing were then operating independently of each other. The first of these was the long line of English fly-fishing from the time of Berners, which was then making its greatest turn with the development of the dry fly. The other was American fly-fishing, which was then still locked in the wet fly, used mainly either in indigenous fancy patterns or in imitation patterns tied on British models. *Gordon brought about the juncture of these traditions* [italics added]. [4]

This conjoining, as McDonald would have it, happened on account of one, momentous letter in February of 1890 from Halford to Gordon—a response to Gordon's earlier inquiry about the advisability of using Halford's dry flies on American waters. As McDonald put it, Halford's letter enclosed "a paper into which he clipped a full set of his dry flies, each carefully identified in pen and ink, *and the dry fly winged its way to the New World*" [italics added]. [5]

An apocalyptic moment, indeed, except the problem with this historic event is that its consequences may be more spellbinding than factual. Schullery, in particular, raises some serious questions about the Gordon-Halford legacy, both in his article and in his 1987 book, *American Fly Fishing*. Schullery's writings document numerous American magazine articles appearing in the 1880s—articles instructing readers how to tie and fish the dry fly—and these, nearly a decade prior to Gordon's receipt of Halford's flies. Although it's true that those earlier flies had little in common with Gordon's signature, "Catskill" patterns, still, they were meant to be floated and fished dry.

Schullery explains further that Halford-style dry flies were available even as early as 1888 from both Orvis and William Mills. Additionally, two volumes of Halford's own writings had been published in America before his gift to Gordon. Schullery emphasizes that, by contrast, Gordon's own writings didn't appear in America until 1903. During the 1890s Gordon published, not in America, but exclusively in England, and even in this, his contributions were only in the form of notes and letters to the British *Fishing Gazette*. In America, on the other hand, Schullery reminds us there was John Harrington Keene. Throughout the 1880s and '90s, Keene published numerous American magazine articles on tying and fishing the dry fly, and in two of his books (*Fishing Tackle, Its Materials and Manufacture,* 1886, and *Fly-Fishing And Fly-Making*, 1887) we find additional advice on the dry fly—again, all prior to Halford's 1890 gift to Gordon, and well before Gordon's own writings reached the American public. [6]

But, what to do about this controversy—this myth-making and the perils of authorship? The collective point of Schullery, Herd and Cameron is that *all* writers—for better or worse—are writers of history, but they also argue that the problem of writing history is one of keeping it separate from fiction, issuing a strong warning to any would-be author. Their suggestion is that Theodore Gordon's reputation came about because, somehow, it is what we have wanted. That is, among both writers and readers, the collaborative need for legend is often stronger than our attention to facts. We believe it is so.

For our part, Tom and I might apologize that we are merely writers of a casual fly-fishing history and that our efforts were never meant to measure up to the mark of "History." We could beg for mercy, pointing out that History is more official and significant than one's dabblings in the doings of the odd fisherman; that History flows from different springs, engaging in scholarly discourse with congressional records, national leaders, wars and treaties, economic boom and crash, the rise and fall of class-structures and so forth. We would be mistaken. Although perhaps unjustified, everything that's written comes to balloon in significance, and even though the writer may not have intended to write history with a capital "H," if it's printed for the public, it begins to function as such.

To illustrate how powerful is the attraction to myth and legend, consider one, pointed example of the fiction-making impulse at work. Following, are a few sentences from McDonald himself as found on the dust-jacket flyleaf to his 1st edition of Gordon's letters:

> I was curious [about the origins of the Quill Gordon fly] and convinced my co-editors at *Fortune Magazine* that we should do a story on trout flies. After working on it for a few weeks I did not think there was going to be a story. A lot of charming but isolated facts about flies did not make much sense and the origin and distinctive character of the American dry fly seemed to be beyond explanation. I took to reading old periodicals in search of a clue. There, lost in the *Fishing Gazette* [British] and *Forest & Stream* [American, now extinct], I first came across Theodore Gordon's writings. I read much of his fleeting work, and then talked to some of his old friends. Among Gordon's personal papers, to which I was given access through the courtesy of his old friend, Roy Steenrod, I came across the actual flies which the great English angling writer, Frederic M. Halford, had sent to Gordon in 1890—*the first, I believe, in the U.S. and the ones from which Gordon fashioned the first American dry flies. The search thus ended with treasure. It was not hard to see that Gordon was the missing link between the central tradition of English fly-fishing and the similar, yet distinctive, American methods of today.... Gordon's writings, I believe, are the most significant, historically, in American fly-fishing literature....* [italics added]

This is certainly a fascinating personal account, but we're left asking why McDonald wasn't able to encounter the research materials available to Schullery—the numerous, earlier articles on the dry-fly, Keene's contributions, Halford's own American publications, and the Orvis and Mills catalogues with Halford-style dry flies. McDonald was a skilled researcher and historian and surely nothing was hidden from his view, able to be discovered only later by Schullery. Why would McDonald say that all he had found were "charming but isolated facts about flies *[that]* didn't make much sense?"

We also wonder what McDonald meant by his claim to be looking for "the distinctive character of the American dry fly." If, by "distinctive," he really meant the Catskill patterns all along, of course that trail would lead back to Gordon. But, regardless of how definitive Halford's influence was upon Gordon's own fly-tying, this does not justify asserting that American fly-fishers came to learn of the dry fly because of Halford's gift. May the good Lord forgive our impudence, but in introducing the dry fly to America, Gordon himself appears to have been out of the loop.

One possible explanation for McDonald claiming exclusivity in the Halford-Gordon legacy may be that the connection he had just "scooped" was simply too compelling for his imagination to resist. In McDonald's own, telling words, his "search" had uncovered a "treasure," the "missing link." What he had in Halford's flies was a hidden cache, booty, the completed DNA sequence, and a fabulous story! McDonald must have felt like Robert Lewis Stevenson and Charles Darwin, all rolled up into one.

While I do apologize for being flippant and disrespectful here, our purpose really is not to discredit Mr. McDonald, for his collection of Gordon's notes and letters will always deserve a position of highest prominence in every fly-angler's library. Our true intention was to satirize the powerful attraction that legend has upon us all, even when we work in earnest. Often, its appeal is as irresistible for the writer as for the reader. We love stories; mystery, complication and suspense. We love lost-and-found, damsels and knights in distress, perilous journeys, miraculous discoveries and foes overcome. And best of all, we love to see justice and resolution, kingdoms and treasures restored to their rightful trustees–you know, Cinderella's slipper and all that. But this is the stuff of myth, legend and fable, not ordinary that of history.

Even so, Gordon's personal history remains a riveting account, and the irony is that it does indeed supply what the imagination wants. In Gordon, we find a truly mysterious and solitary figure, a sort of invalid-hermit, bereft of family and disappointed in career—a mere wisp of a man, a misanthrope who had all the credentials of good society, but who squandered and shunned its legacies. He's a man obsessed, an innovator seemingly unmatched in skill and dedication. He becomes a legend in his own time, yet none really knows him. He goes his own way. Rumor has it he may be forlorn of love. He is tubercular, dying alone in near-wilderness squalor, and too soon. He leaves behind few friends, some boxes of notes and letters, feathers, hooks, thread and dust—his stove is cold. And, as of McDonald's writing, no one even knows where he lies buried.

Gordon's story has everything for a novel, yet most interestingly, these elements of his personal life are all, apparently, quite true. To our point, however, Schullery, Herd and Cameron marvel at what both writers and readers have done with Gordon's biography and why: Why would we persist in a fly-fishing history that assigns Gordon a position he never quite occupied, "elevating this man to messianic status," as Schullery puts it? [7] How could so many of Gordon's contemporaries (earlier and more public participants in the development of American dry-fly fishing) have been ignored while we fetched the untouchable Gordon from their midst? Why, like McDonald, have readers wished to dream of this eccentric person at the expense of a clearer view of his contemporaries? Perhaps we conscript Gordon because he seems to possess, in spades, all those larger-than-life American proclivities for self-sufficiency and suffering, accomplishment and failure, tenacity and vulnerability. And, too, like a melancholy Huck Finn, Gordon actually lived our dream of "running away from it all."

Tom and I want to emphasize that we don't believe McDonald sought to deceive either his readers or himself. On the contrary, we think he truly believed he had found "the unicorn in the garden"—to put the myth another way. We do not wonder that the discovery became so compelling for McDonald, but we do wonder why he seemed bent, throughout, to see just one unicorn when there stood before him, a field of perfectly good horses.

This is just one, curious pattern in the history-making process. The other, more unsettling part is a species of "inadvertency" attending even the writings of the scrupulous scholar: The conscientious historian becomes mythmaker. Schullery, Herd and Cameron suggest that the annals of history are rife with inaccuracies, omissions and fictions, and we know it is so. As an antidote, Cameron insists that writers (even of fly-fishing) need to engage in a form of fastidious research he calls "rigor," or elsewhere, "comprehensiveness." Continuing, Cameron states, "Mythmakers... don't apply rigor. Historians do. However, for their rigor to work properly, it has to leave a trail for us to follow. This trail is made, not of bread crumbs, but of notes." [8] Cameron appears to say the divisions between history and myth, fact and fancy can be called out, and that confusing one with the other can be avoided through rigorous scholarship, a trail of footnotes and documented sources.

Up to this point, we had been doing well with the essays of these three men. On this particular issue, however, we part company with Cameron. Although rigor is necessary, its practice remains inadequate to render history fully recoverable. Nor are we comfortable that even its primary records are necessarily factual, revealing or reliable. Reconstructing cause-effect relationships is a tenuous exercise at best, and in the end, even the most rigorous scholar resorts to probability in discerning who played exactly which parts—with what hidden motives, or with whose awareness. Even calculated estimations are interpretations.Conjecture joins with innuendo and point-of-view. And with any of these, arrives the possibility for fiction—notes or no notes, inadvertently or otherwise.

History, we would insist, is never more than someone's *version* of history—something to be considered and wondered at. And then, re-written. When seen in this light, none of us seems likely to avoid leaving fictions in our wake. Nor can we hope, ultimately, to be saved from ourselves merely by applying Cameron's standards of rigor and comprehensiveness. As these exist only in degrees, so our writing can never be more than relatively acceptable. We want to be fair to Cameron's position, however, for his idea is that, while the writer may not attain perfect accord with TRUTH, at least he can at blaze an identifiable trail to be followed by others... so, fair enough.

Here, I could write that Tom Whittle and I promise to exercise Cameron's high standards, but we must also admit that our text has been selective and that we've not found it possible either to explain or to document everything. So, can our account be called rigorous and comprehensive? Probably not. Further, I should point out that although I knew Vince very well, I was hardly his constant companion over the years of our friendship. I cannot attest to all his comings and goings and didn't become familiar with each of his acquaintances or their conversations. Moreover, even from the years of our collaboration, I've been unable to resurrect all the rod-making information that Tom and I really would have wanted. You see how easily even a firsthand account is set on it's ear?

Do we write of Vince and his career as a fly-fisher because, along some grand, canonical scale, we believe his contributions now must become fully known? No, we don't know about such lofty matters. Instead, we offer this book simply because we knew Vince, because we value his work as a maker of fly rods, and because we remember him fondly. We believe there are many readers of fly-fishing history who, while they know Vince's writings on fly-tying, stream entomology and fishing strategies, do not know him as a maker of fly rods. We hope they would like to. So, we have pursued this study simply because we wanted to—Vince and his rods are of interest to us.

We offer our perspectives as we believe we have come by them, possibly seasoned with the odd insinuation, inflation or slur, and perhaps with unaccountable inclusions or exclusions. There may be disguised shades of some personal agendas as well. We apologize in advance if we engender fictions in this manner, for this would be the creep of willfulness. But, put on guard, we hope readers will recognize such infelicities even where we do not.

In the opening paragraph of his introduction to Theodore Gordon's notes and letters, John McDonald writes what has come to be a much-loved quote: "Time moves slowly in fly-fishing. The last time it moved appreciably in the U.S. was with Theodore Gordon." [9] While this statement, even in its inflation, may have been true of Gordon, it also seems to be true of Vince Marinaro. Certainly, we all know a great number of writers who have gone on record as thinking so.

Is it merely ironical that we should have expended so many earlier paragraphs debunking the myths surrounding Theodore Gordon, now only to appropriate MacDonald's hyperbole in our own appreciation of Marinaro? ("But wait!" says the boy, caught with his hand in the cookie jar, "I can explain!") Yes, it's ironical, though we hope not merely so. Rather than explaining the comparison away, we would indulge it, but with some important differences.

As with Gordon, Marinaro too, was reclusive, driven and highly opinionated. He was somewhat disappointed in career, obsessed with fly-fishing, entomology and fly-tying. He was cranky with strangers and loath to divulge his secrets. He suffered no fools, went his own way, revered English chalk-stream traditions and, particularly, the contributions of Frederic Halford. Marinaro was also a fly-tying innovator, and in his day, a man whose skills and dedication seemed almost without match. Finally, like Gordon, Marinaro, was an author whose works and personality have been elevated, for better or for worse, to near-messianic status by writers and fly-fishers alike.

On the other hand, the differences between Marinaro and Gordon are equally significant: Unlike Gordon, Vince had the good fortune to live in an age when transportation became swift and information was quickly and efficiently circulated. Secondly, while Vince was by nature a solitary man, he did not remove himself from communal life, seeking seclusion in remote surroundings as did Gordon. The consequences of both these differences are that Vince came to enjoy the acclaim issuing from his work during his own lifetime. He had repeated opportunity to reflect in public upon the many results of his findings. Also unlike Gordon, the community of fly-fishers did not need to speculate for long upon the kind or the extent of Marinaro's influence. There is no mystery and nothing of the "lost-and-found" about Marinaro's career—no decent into obscurity.

That said, there remains one aspect of Marinaro's career where his accomplishments remain unexamined and almost unknown—his work as a bamboo rod-maker. Actually, it's almost amusing to note that, even in these long shadows of obscurity, Vince seems to have had it his own way. Like Gordon, Marinaro left behind almost nothing but his tools and a handful of rods, some rudely stuffed into a barrel. There remain no builder's notes, no taper graphs, no mathematical calculations, no personal records of how many rods he built, when, why, or what he thought of them. In his later years, he retained much of his correspondence, but scarcely any letters are from other makers.

Apart from two, early and brief articles published in *The Pennsylvania Angler*, Vince made nothing public about his fly rods until that one, teasing and compelling chapter in *In The Ring Of The Rise*. Hence, the memory of my years of association with Vince is about all we have as our "authority" to organize our later chapters on rod-building and design. Drawing upon what I shared in Vince's career as a maker, plus what Tom and I discovered from friends, relatives and the remaining rods themselves, we have put these chapters together. We hope Mr. Cameron will understand....

We cannot play "McDonald" to Marinaro's lost influence as a rod-builder, for although there is much news to interpret and relate, it would be impossible to reclaim an influence that never existed. We have his tapers now, and while this is certainly interesting information, the news cannot be regarded as even remotely similar to McDonald belief that he had discovered a "missing link." Personally, of course, I wish Vince had been more influential, since it was he who taught me to build rods, and I know there could not have been a more capable master. Additionally, because Tom and I have remained believers in Vince's principle of the "convex taper," we wish that other makers had been able to read, all along, his many ideas about fly rod design and construction.

Still, just as Theodore Gordon's letters had to wait for McDonald, so the study of Marinaro's bamboo fly rods had to wait for time to play itself out. But, again, the two cases are vastly different. While Gordon is said to have slipped unaccountably into the ether of lapsed memory, it was Marinaro himself who requested his family not to give his rods and tapers general circulation. During Vince's life, and shortly after, there were a few reasons for that request, and we wish to explain in our first chapter the conditions that led the Sebastian Marinaro Estate to permit our exploration of his work. For the present, let us say only that the "Marinaro Collection," held by the Pennsylvania Fly Fishing Museum Association, has been made available for our evaluation and publication through the grace and generosity of Vince's surviving family members. And so, we are finally able to present details of the rods he built.

Marinaro's reputation has long since been established, and this book will do little to add to that. We hope, nonetheless, that fly-fishers may come to appreciate what may be a last, unwritten chapter in Vince's already distinguished career. Vince will always remain something of an enigma, but while the mystique continues to surround the private man, there are very few unanswered questions about the meaning and position of his work.

Everyone we know in this neck of the woods has one or two tall, "Marinaro Tales" to spin, and we shall pass along more than a few ourselves. Vince was, indeed, a man who altered the direction of fly-fishing in America, and was fairly treated as royalty by the prestigious Fly Fishers' Club of London when, in 1976, he paid a visit to England and the storied waters of the Rivers Test and Itchen. So, of Vince Marinaro, it might truly be said that he, too, moved appreciably the fly-fisher's very slow clock.

Photo by Tom Whittle

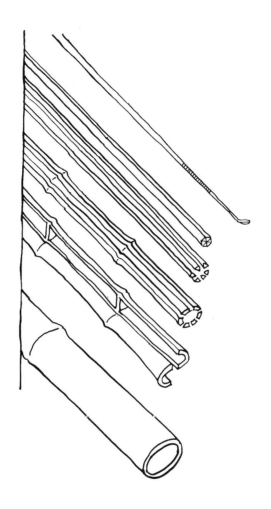

A Bamboo Rod-Making Primer

*For those unfamiliar with the process,
the following photo-essay illustrates the basic
steps in building a hand-planed, bamboo fly rod.*

A Bamboo Rod-Making Primer

1. A bamboo culm is first split in half; then into six, equal segments.

2. Internal, node "dams" are chiseled flush.

3. Smaller strips are split from the six, larger segments—18 for a 2-piece rod (with 2 tips) and 24 for a 3-piece rod.

4. Strips are selected for each rod section. Nodes are staggered to the maker's pattern and strips are cut a 6" longer than the sections' final lengths.

5. The external "lip" on each node is filed flat.

Split & Glued by Vincent C. Marinaro

6. Strips are "squared" by planing their sides, and a portion of the pith is removed from their inner surface.

7. Crooked nodes and larger bends are straightened over an alcohol lamp (or heat gun).

8. The squared strips receive a 60-degree bevel. Bevels are shaped only along a strip's interior surfaces. No taper is introduced at this stage.

9. Triangular strips for each section are bundled together and placed in an oven for a regimen of "heat-tempering."

10. The "V-groove" of the planing form is adjusted to a desired rod taper.

A Bamboo Rod-Making Primer

(Bamboo Rod-Making Primer, continued)

11. "Enamel" is scraped from the external surface of each strip prior to tapering. This outer surface is made smooth and flush, but without disturbing underlying power fibers.

12. Strips are planed to their tapers within the form. Power fibers are protected by alternating the outer surface from one side of the groove to its other.

13. Glue is brushed along the strips for each section. The node-staggering pattern has been re-established, secured with tape, and the strips are placed, apex-up, on wax-paper.

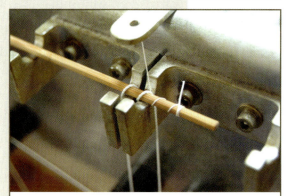

14. Glued strips are rolled together and passed twice through the binding machine—first, rotating in one direction, then counter-wrapped in the other.

15. Each section is straightened by eye before the glue begins to set. (Photo omits the binding-string for clarity.)

16. After curing, binding-string is removed and residue glue is filed away. All six outer surfaces are then sanded smooth, using 320 or 400-grit paper.

Split & Glued by Vincent C. Marinaro

17. Cork rings are glued on the butt section (or on a separate mandrel), clamped together, and the grip is given its shape on a lathe.

19. A wooden reel seat is mounted on the exposed, rounded shaft.

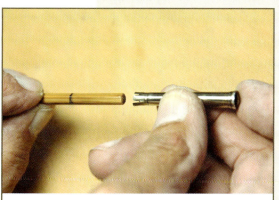

18. Ferrules are mounted on each section.

20. Guides are located at appropriate spacings and wrapped in place with silk thread.

21 (A and B). Several coats of varnish are applied to the guide wrappings and sanded. Then the entire rod is finished either by brush (example "A"), or using the dip-tube method (example "B").

A Bamboo Rod-Making Primer

Chapter One

Working Back to Vince's Beginnings

I can recall my first conversation with Vince Marinaro on the subject of bamboo fly rods. It was the summer of 1973. Unschooled and new to the topic, I was very much surprised to learn that an amateur could actually construct his own split-bamboo fly rod. Surely, there would be satisfaction in such a project, but my assumption was that one's results could hardly measure up to those of a professional maker. "Not so," said Vince, happy, I'm certain, with the opportunity to hold forth on the merits of going it alone. "Once you learn what you're doing, you can build a rod to tighter tolerances than the best commercial makers."

Well, I was mechanically handy too and had spent much of my life working with wood, but this statement taxed my credulity to its limit. After all, the required tolerances we're talking about in a fly rod are mere thousandths of an inch—thinner than the smallest gap of light one can "pinch" between thumb and forefinger. Often, Vince would simply choose not to discuss a topic, but once struck by the mood to hold court, he was rarely modest about his accomplishments. Even so, his claim turned out to be perfectly true.

I'm not at all sure why Vince became willing to discuss rod-making with me, but the two of us quickly struck up a friendship, and eventually he also agreed to teach me to build bamboo rods. Vince was an "odd duck" with many eccentricities, but I like that in a person, so before long we were fishing regularly on the Letort, Penn's Creek, the Tulpehocken and Falling Springs—joking, smoking piteous cigars and talking endlessly about fly rods and design. Those early days were filled with work, fishing and nonsense, and they led to a friendship lasting until Vince's death in 1986, a span of time when he taught me nearly everything I needed to know about being a good friend and a rod-maker.

Four Marinaro rods

photo by Tom Whittle

Working Back to Vince's Beginnings

More than half a century has passed since the fly-fishing public first learned about Marinaro. He had written a few magazine articles by 1950, but at the time, was largely unknown outside Pennsylvania. His first book, *A Modern Dry Fly Code*, was published in 1950, almost simultaneously with Charlie Fox's *Advanced Bait Casting*, and Marinaro's career before the public was under way. Over the next five decades Vince's persona would grow to near-legendary status, and the public's fascination with his compelling and difficult nature only redoubled an appreciation of his many original discoveries. All, that is, except his fly rods—about which the public knew nothing.

Marinaro's prescriptions for terrestrials and midges have long been among the first to arise in any discussion about fly-fishing techniques, and his tying innovations—(the cut-wing, thorax pattern and the hackle-wing spinner)—were of equal importance. Marinaro's stream-side discoveries helped anglers understand what trout experience, and the work he and a dozen other men undertook in the late 1940s along the Cumberland Valley's numerous limestone trout streams remains unchallenged. Indeed, *A Modern Dry Fly Code* is as pertinent today as when it was first written. Yet, despite the fact that Vince's book was written in the midst of his most productive years as a rod-maker, Marinaro declined to mention his life-long fascination with bamboo. Strangely, apart from passing mention by Charlie Fox in his *Advanced Bait Casting* and Vince's own, two, brief articles on gluing (*The Pennsylvania Angler*, 1952-53), Marinaro's skill as a builder of bamboo rods was unknown.

Vince on Falling Springs

In fact, Vince had been building rods since he was a teenager in 1928 or '29, but even among those of us who knew him, his involvement with bamboo rods remained a mystery. We knew they were of his own manufacture—each one clearly displaying the inscription, "Split and Glued by Vincent C. Marinaro"—but rod-making was a topic Vince just didn't care to divulge. At long last, he broached the subject in his *In The Ring of The Rise* (1976) and the public was finally offered a glimpse of Marinaro's design and building objectives. Yet even those pages fail to offer more than a brief overview—interesting, informative and revealing, but still achingly incomplete. Alas, not during Vince's lifetime, nor since his death in 1986, has the public learned more. Until this present project, Vince's building techniques and tapers have never been explored.

Lost, But Found

Our story of Marinaro and his rods begins in the 1970s when I first met Vince, but his own experience goes back to formative decades from the early 1930s onward. Following his relocation from Butler to Harrisburg, Pennsylvania, the 1940s and '50s became Marinaro's halcyon days, a time when he first met with success in his fly-rod tapers and similarly began systematic studies into the hidden life of trout and the "bugs" along Cumberland Valley's limestone streams. He also fashioned a dozen new tying patterns, published *A Modern Dry Fly Code* (1950) and several magazine articles. Those were wonderful, active years for Vince, with large groups of friends joining in his work. But nothing stays the same for long, and there also came a time when Vince's passion faded—earlier friends moved on to other pursuits, common interests became splintered and fishing conditions themselves began to change.

So it was, during the 1960s, that Vince became greatly disheartened about the future of trout fishing in Pennsylvania, especially on his beloved limestone streams. Having already witnessed the demise of Cedar Run, Hogestown Run and Silver Springs, he grew increasingly soured by the unenlightened trout management of Pennsylvania's Fish Commission—especially its misguided trout stocking policies and a reluctance to look at stream habitat improvement. Meanwhile, Big Spring, among the best brook trout fisheries in the East, was being decimated by a small commercial fish hatchery's pollution.

His exasperation was sharpened during visits to Michigan's Au Sable watershed, where Vince witnessed a stark contrast between the energetic trout programs there and his own state's lethargy.

Marinaro relates in *The Ring* how the idea for the nation's first Trout Unlimited chapter was conceived in the late 1950s along the Au Sable River by George Griffith, Art Neumann, George Mason and others—how its habitat protection ideas were supported by the Michigan Department of Conservation. Throughout the 1960s, and '70s, early spring would find Marinaro, Bill Fritz and Wayne Leonard visiting Grayling, Michigan to fish the Hendrickson hatch. There, they were regularly joined by Griffith, Neumann and several of their friends.

Although Pennsylvania's own Cumberland Valley Chapter of Trout Unlimited was the second such chapter formed within this organization (with Charlie Fox as its first President), Pennsylvania's Fish Commission had a long and undistinguished record of providing only lip-service to stream conservation. More recent Fish and Boat Commission policies have changed somewhat for the better, and just a few years ago, the agency began a new brook-trout habitat program, setting aside many miles of

Au Sable "longboat."

Vince with a Tulpehocken rainbow

prime headwaters on some of the state's best freestone streams, specifying no-stocking and no-kill areas within these waters.

Despondent over the Cumberland Valley's worsening conditions, Vince fished here little during the 1960s. His interests in the fall turned back to archery and the wing-shooting of his youth, while summertime was given largely to golf. Perhaps it's not surprising to learn that he soon began making his own bows, fashioning stocks for his guns and split-bamboo shafts for his clubs. Vince always said those years were spent well enough—he had some great adventures and developed many new friends—but he also told me it was a sad time for him. He just couldn't get over his love of limestone trout fishing and the camaraderie he once knew.

Vince didn't know it, but the "good old days" were about to return. In 1970, while fishing on Falling Springs near Chambersburg, Pennsylvania, Marinaro made the acquaintance of Tom Maxwell and Tom Dorsey. Falling Springs, at that time, was very much in its prime, full of burly, stream-bred, brown and rainbow trout, and its "Trico" hatch in particular, a marvel to behold. Maxwell and Dorsey lived nearby and though they were recently out of college, they had been making rods together for several years. Vince was immediately impressed with their work and heartened to discover that there were, once again, others sharing his passion for fine fly fishing and bamboo craftsmanship. Vince befriended Maxwell in particular, and the two maintained a close relationship lasting until Vince's death in 1986.

Working a good brownie on Falling Springs

Split & Glued by Vincent C. Marinaro

Vince and Hoagy—1976

Early in the 1970s, several additional friends entered Vince's life, and all helped to renew his interests in rod-building and angling. There was Ted Sutsos, an affable young lawyer and avid bamboo rod-collector from the Washington, D.C. area. Sutsos bought the Yellow Breeches Fly Shop (Boiling Springs, Pennsylvania) in the beginning of the 1970s and quickly gathered around him a group of able and knowledgeable young men—Billy Skilton, Tom Baltz and Bobby Hauser in particular. Soon, others from just outside the area began to frequent the shop. These included Frank Thompson, another collector and accomplished fly-tier from Beltsville, Maryland and Rick Robbins, also from the D.C. area. As it happened, Maxwell was teaching rod-making to Robbins, just as I was about to begin with Vince. So, Rick, with his plane in one hand, his old copy of Kreider's book in the other, and Maxwell running his phone bill to oblivion, began to master the process. I'm sorry not to have known Tom well myself, but we met only after Thomas & Thomas bought the Sewall Dunton holdings in 1972 and moved their operation to Massachusetts. Unfortunately, at that point, the two Toms were no longer "locals." Maxwell was surely among the most gifted makers during the last decades of the century and a nicer fellow was not to be found.

It was also during these years that Hoagy Carmichael, Jr. entered the picture, introduced to Vince one day in 1975 along Falling Springs by Chauncey Lively. Hoagy's video on Everett Garrison had just been completed and the project to write *A Master's Guide To Building A Bamboo Fly Rod* (1977) was already under way. So, with strong, common interests, these two quickly became friends as well.

The 1940s and '50s may have been Vince's heyday, but the 1970s became similarly rich and productive years. Heartened by his new friends and the long-overdue acclaim coming from Crown Press' 1970 re-issue of *A Modern Dry Fly Code*, Vince seemed to gain new footing, and the fly-fishing community was about to witness another chapter of the "Marinaro mystique." Vince was in his seat once again and, with fire in his belly, the old spark was back in his eyes. No longer a feisty, young upstart, he was now the crusty, venerable oracle. Before, he could only argue a case, now he would truly hold court.

Wayne Leonard assists Vince

photo by Dick Henry

Working Back to Vince's Beginnings

My Lord, what a performance he gave though those remaining years. And, Oh! how we relished every chance to drizzle a little rain on his parade. Many of Vince's friends during these latter times were several years his junior, so, with affection and respect (and following the lead of Wayne Leonard), we all began calling him "Pappy." Each fish missed or lost would draw a whoop or a shout from one of us: "Jeez, Pappy! Didn't you tell him who you are?" or, "Hey Pap, you're just standing there. Get over here and net this one!"

My own fly-fishing in the Cumberland Valley began a few years after moving to Carlisle, Pennsylvania in 1968 and taking a teaching position at Dickinson College. I had been involved with racing sailboats for much of my life, but in the early 1970s my best friend, Joe Lauver, cleared my head and turned my attention back to fly-fishing. I didn't know Vince as yet, but exploring the Letort in that first summer, I met Ed Shenk one evening while fishing the Sulfur hatch. This was my first experience on the stream, so I just drove to an area I had heard of near the Bonny Brook quarry. Soon, I struck up a conversation with "some guy." We introduced ourselves, but being a new kid on the block, no bell went off at the mention of Ed Shenk. There would be little reason for him to recall that meeting, but I surely do. Ed was very kind and offered to show me the waters. During the course of the evening, he told me about the small fly rods he loved to make, the techniques of fishing cress-bugs, sculpins and grasshopper patterns, and most usefully, he explained how the silky Letort waters work. Ed also gave me a few of his Sulfur patterns, took me in tow, and treated me to a little tour of the hatch—first up in Trego's Meadow, and then downstream near a favorite spot below an abandoned railroad trestle.

I honestly don't recall if I caught anything that evening, but anyone familiar with how the Letort receives its new guests can imagine I would have been summarily skunked—and not for the last time. Because Ed haunted the Letort regularly, we ran into one another on many more occasions. Ed had been fishing the stream several times each week ever since the 1930s, and by the '70s there would have been no fisherman better acquainted with its secrets. Kind, gentlemanly and good-natured, Ed always impressed me a great deal more than he could know. But, for some reason, the thing that continued to fascinate me was his idea of re-making fly rods. Ed wasn't a bamboo rod-maker as such, but he loved to resurrect those gangly, old, three-piece rods, discard the butt section and try to work up a more responsive two-piecer by remounting the grip or perhaps trimming back through the ferrule areas. Ed worked with the older fiberglass rods too, but it was the idea of bamboo that stuck with me.

"Trego's meadow" no longer a meadow

"Rails-to-trails" bridge over Letort

Bamboo got into my blood at once, although I still wasn't aware that a fellow could make his own fly rod starting from just a culm. That was for Vince to reveal. Almost at once, and following Ed's lead on small rods, I acquired my first cane rod as an adult—a little 6-foot, 4-weight, Thomas & Thomas "Individualist" with transparent, lemon wraps. I couldn't possibly have been more proud, for it was a lovely thing to behold. Couldn't wait to show it to Ed! But, before that happened, I met Vince.

Fishing again with Lauver on the Letort, (one fine day in 1973) we were working a stretch less than a mile below the Bonny Brook quarry. Although Joe didn't know him well at the time, he recognized Vince making his way along a path, was eager to say hello and to introduce me. We meandered in Vince's direction, and I can still hear Joe saying, "You're gonna like this guy. He's a crank like you. Doesn't like anybody, and he makes his own fly rods." Well, that didn't exactly describe either of us, though there may have been more than a grain of truth in it.

Joe Lauver and Harms: Catskill Gathering—2004

photo by Chris Bogart

I don't recall a great deal about our first conversation, except that Vince seemed to be in a very good mood, and after the manly handshakes and obligatory "please-ta-me-chas," he noticed my little Thomas & Thomas, fitted with a wonderful "Baby" St. George reel. I told him I recently purchased the outfit from Barry Beck—then operating his father's fly shop in nearby Berwick, Pennsylvania. Vince brightened, saying he knew Barry very well, so I supposed he may have thought that, although I was surely a neophyte, at least I was starting out with some of the right credentials. Emboldened, I asked about the rod he was using. He simply said it was one of his own. Playing dumb, I asked what he meant by that. Perhaps it was because Vince recognized I was a "newbie" and my questions were naive and free from ulterior motives (naive, true; but certainly not free from ulterior motives), or perhaps it was just because we had a nice day and Vince was feeling expansive that he told me he had been building his own split-bamboo fly rods for most of his life.

Vince also said he had been on something of a hiatus for nearly a decade, but recently began building again. At the time, I was unaware that he did not care to discuss rod-making—hearing only later that this was because he had little patience with those who didn't share his drive to discover things the hard way. Had I been up to speed on that issue, I expect I would have been too intimidated to pursue our first conversation. Vince was an extremely proud man, understanding well what he'd accomplished under his own steam, and he had no truck with camp-followers or small talk. He never wasted his time on folks who took the easy path or who were merely impressed with the discoveries of others. So, a conversation about rod-making was no casual indulgence for him and he just wasn't going to get into it with someone who wasn't already "there." Lord knows, I wasn't there at the start, but I was both appreciative and eager. Maybe that was good enough to get us off on the right foot. Although nothing was apparent to me, Joe said later, he believed I was "in."

Most of our friends assumed that because Vince eventually taught me to build, and because we became close companions for many years, he must have provided me with his taper information as well. But this was never the case.

Indeed, it was quite the opposite. Vince worked endlessly to help me evolve a few good tapers of my own, but in this he never did more than demonstrate how to set up useful graphs and explain *ad nauseam* his principles—offering critiques of my progress as we went along. Tedious trial and error had been his only path to a successful fly-rod taper, and he insisted that if I were going to be a rod-maker, it should be so for me as well.

Marinaro on the Letort

Vince never built to anyone else's dimensions, and he believed firmly that nobody could call himself a rod-maker unless he had worked out his own set of tapers. No doubt, there remains something to it from one point of view, but while I would no longer insist on Vince's maxim, at the time, I took his opinion entirely to heart. Later in the 1970s, Maxwell, Carmichael and I each wrapped and finished a few of Vince's rods, but in all cases we were expressly directed not to mike the rods' dimensions. Knowing Tom and Hoagy, I'm sure they would have honored that request, and I know I did.

Marinaro's opinion on this issue strikes us as a little harsh and restrictive because Whittle and I recognize that there always have been dozens of superb rod-makers working in shops owned by others, and building rods whose tapers were designed by others. But Vince reserved his highest respect for original work and paid little attention to accomplishments that, to him, seemed merely derivative. We might wonder where one draws that line, considering that everybody's work is based in large or small measure on the contributions of others. Nevertheless, although construction techniques might be one thing, in the matter of taper-design, Pappy's voice was both loud and clear. To him, the genius of a good rod was a proper taper—the rest being "mere" craft.

QUESTIONS AND PROPOSITIONS

Howell Raines, in *Fly Fishing Through the Midlife Crisis* (1993), rumors that Marinaro "died an embittered man, feeling he never got the recognition he deserved. He left orders for his hand-made bamboo fly rods to be burned."[1] Raines' book, an okay read overall, is often flamboyant, noisy, and chocked to the gills with new-found opinions, breezy generalizations and a transparently showy cast of political and fishing luminaries. It's also more than a little reckless in several assertions. Raines' assessment of Vince's last days in particular is both untrue and a great unkindness.

Vince's family and friends recall that he died with peace and dignity in March of 1986. Living, briefly, in a local nursing facility, Vince grew very ill in his last months from the leukemia he developed some years earlier and was often sad that more of his old friends did not stop by for a visit. His youngest son, Sebastian, and daughter-in-law, Maggie, lived just down the road and other family members visited frequently. However, no longer able to fish, tie flies or get about to enjoy the many activities that used to fill his days, it's true, as might be expected, that Vince became lonely, depressed and frustrated. But there was no bitterness, no feeling that he had been slighted, and most certainly, no thought about destroying his rods.

Marinaro's remaining rods, building equipment, flies, library and fishing paraphernalia were passed on to his son, Sebastian. Then, in 2000, two years after Sebastian himself passed away, the entire collection (including 13 rods) was acquired from the Sebastian Marinaro estate by the Pennsylvania Fly Fishing Museum Association (PFFMA). Two additional fly rods (to the best of our knowledge) are currently owned by private individuals, but apart from these, Marinaro never sold, gave away or promoted any of his own rods. Vince, at some time prior his

"Vince's fishing gear"

death, requested of Sebastian that the taper information not be given general circulation, the rods not be sold, and Sebastian himself wished for the collection to remain intact.

Vince nets one on the Tulpehocken

Since 1986—all these intervening years—further exploration of Vince's rods and building experiences remained impossible. After the purchase of the "Marinaro Collection," however, a limited agreement was arranged between the PFFMA and the Marinaro Estate whereby Tom Whittle (PFFMA President) and I would be granted permission to release Vince's taper information, but within the context of this present project only. Additionally, the PFFMA stipulated that any use or attribution of the "Vincent C. Marinaro" name shall be strictly forbidden either in the construction or in the sale of any fly rod resulting from a Marinaro taper.

Happy beyond words with our arrangement, Tom and I are now free to investigate the many questions and mysteries surrounding the work of this remarkable man. We've been planning this study for more than a few years, pondering at length how to proceed and hoping that, with luck, we might do justice to this long-neglected part of Marinaro's career. We want to discuss Vince's life and times, his many fishing experiences and misadventures, and his local waters. But mostly, we mean to account for Marinaro's path to becoming a rod-maker, to document his building practices and objectives, and to explain his design principles. In Chapter Nine, we will submit a selection of his rods to a series of casting evaluations and present the tapers of all existing rods.

Strangely, Marinaro left behind no charts, graphs or notes on construction, so I must rely upon memory while Tom was left with the challenge of deriving exact data from the rods themselves, then creating a range of photographs and some useful graphics.

I was not a rod-maker myself when I met Marinaro, although I was surely eager to learn about it. I must have bugged Vince nearly to death before he softened at last and began to explain some of the basics. But I didn't want

Beautiful stream-bred brownie

basics—I wanted the real deal, the particulars. I wanted to be a maker. Vince remained hesitant for many months, and eventually explained it was because, over the years, he had been approached by several folks who were eager to make a rod, each occasion resulting in failure once the neophyte realized the work that would be involved. Vince was never particularly flexible in his views nor accommodating of other folks' inabilities, and he did not wish to waste time on something that seemed unlikely to succeed. He had always worked alone, nearly in isolation, and he knew that any other amateur maker in the 1970s would have to do the same.

But bamboo rod-making has undergone an enormous change since those days back in the 1970s—a most unanticipated explosion, and in proportions unlike anything Vince ever saw or could possibly have imagined. The fascination that Marinaro created with *The Ring* was not responsible for this sudden growth of interest in bamboo rods, but his book surely increased a desire among amateur makers to learn more about his designs. And it is this renewed love affair with bamboo fly rods—plus a growing interest among collectors and historians—that sparked our desire to present a more complete picture of Marinaro's contributions to rod-building. Hence this book.

Readers might wonder about Vince's personal motives and why he never sought to make his discoveries public. Why was he so secretive, seemingly even nonchalant about rod-making while being so expansive and forthcoming about, say, stream entomology, fly-tying and materials, photography and fishing techniques? The disparity wouldn't appear to make sense. Some folks have even suggested perhaps making fly rods was incidental—not really of central importance to Vince. Or, perhaps the rods themselves were actually something less than wonderful.

Early in the 1970s, when Vince and I became friends, I learned with certainty that neither of these was true. Yet, so many unanswered questions remain. How long had Vince been serious about making rods? How many did he make? Have people seen or used them? What do they look like and how do they cast? Where are they now? What were his building practices? Why was he so fussy about his tapers? Are the rods really different from those of other makers? And perhaps most of all, considering the wide respect accorded to Marinaro's life of research, why have not all these questions been answered, long since?

In fact, there were some compelling reasons why the public failed to hear much about Vince's rods—two of which I learned at once, as they seemed almost self-evident. The others, Tom and I believe we discerned only after the PFFMA purchased the "Marinaro Collection." We'll offer our explanations of these matters in what follows, but as we begin, it would seem useful to describe a little of the rod-making "culture" that Vince inherited—essentially, one of secrecy and insularity.

From the 1800s up through the present, nearly all rod-makers learned their trade through some sort of direct apprenticeship. Hiram Leonard, for example, had already become famous by the beginning of the 20th century, but the acclaim came not only from his rods—it was equally because of the many first-rate makers emerging from his shop, including E. F. Payne, F. E. Thomas, E. W. Edwards, George Halstead, the Hawes brothers and George Varney. All were employed at the Leonard factory in one capacity or another, and shortly after 1890, all set up their own operations. Many partnerships evolved and dissolved among these men, and between them and their offspring (plus independent makers like "Pinky" Gillum, Everett Garrison, Nat Uslan, Sam Carlson and others), two generations of the finest independent rod-makers along the East Coast soon came to be.

The first, large manufacturer of bamboo fly rods and hardware was Thomas Chubb in Post Mills, Vermont—a highly successful business that was purchased by Montague in 1890 after Chubb's building was destroyed by a disastrous fire. Shortly after the turn of the century, Montague found manufacturing competition in the likes of the Cross Rod Company, South Bend and Horrocks-Ibbotson. Montague continued to build rods of good quality, while the latter companies focused on mass-production, with greater emphasis on quantity than quality. It's revealing that, of the numerous makers and production managers within the large, eastern companies,

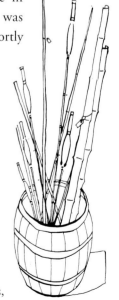

Working Back to Vince's Beginnings

few are remembered—George Varney of Montague and Wes Jordan of Cross, South Bend and (most notably) Orvis being the exceptions.

Additional hotbeds of rod-making activity in the early decades of the 20th century were southern Michigan, Colorado and the West Coast. Among the more successful, Heddon, Paul Young, Lyle Dickerson, Granger, Winston, Powell, and Weir & Sons were all offering rods by the late 1930s. Of these, only Heddon, Granger and Winston were larger production companies, and while nearly everything Winston built was of excellent quality, Heddon and Granger also turned out several very fine tapers. In all, however, nearly every professional rod-maker emerged from some existing shop, and only the smallest handful was self-taught.

Whether running large operations or small, rod-makers had become fiercely secretive from the late 1800s on, carefully guarding their materials, construction techniques and taper dimensions. Inevitably, a great mystique evolved around the craft, initially promoted by the makers themselves. Despite it being damnably difficult and time-consuming to become a good maker, and despite stiff competition and the number of personal livelihoods at stake, this mystique swelled to absurd proportions—and especially so, once a public eager to swallow inflated marketing claims came into the picture. Many commercial makers went so far as to place limited-access restrictions (even for their own employees) on rooms containing their beveling machines and mills. The secrets of the trade simply were not available to the public, and no amateur was going to learn to build a fly rod by snuggling up with a professional.

Such was the culture of bamboo rod-making that Marinaro inherited. In his day—so very different from our own—the particulars of building a rod were not discussed by those who had wrestled with the beast. Marinaro, himself, beginning to build in the late 1920s, had to unravel this project on his own with only a couple books at his disposal, a difficulty that was compounded both by his youth and by his geographical isolation from other makers.

We'll describe Vince's earliest years as a builder in the final section of this chapter, but we return to our former questions about Vince's reluctance to discuss rod-making: The first and most obvious explanation is that, ever since the 1950s and the advent of fiberglass, bamboo fly rods had fallen out of favor with the public. And when graphite arrived, even fiberglass was made obsolete. By the 1970s, the public's interest in bamboo fly rods had disappeared almost entirely and that segment of the industry fell into near-total collapse. Vince knew there never had been more than a small handful of craftsmen capable of building their own rods, and now that bamboo seemed a thing of the past, he wondered what purpose would be served by discussing a matter that so few people even remembered.

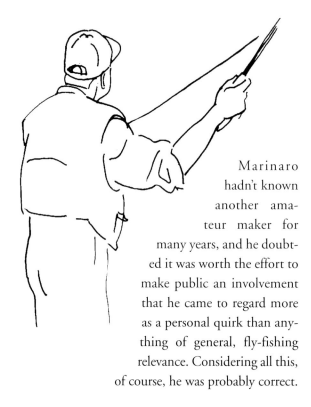

Marinaro hadn't known another amateur maker for many years, and he doubted it was worth the effort to make public an involvement that he came to regard more as a personal quirk than anything of general, fly-fishing relevance. Considering all this, of course, he was probably correct.

A second explanation was related, but a bit different. Vince considered the process of rod design and construction too complex, too exacting and too time-consuming for would-be amateurs to benefit from mere written information. Hands-on instruction might be one thing, but to Vince, discussing the matter in print seemed futile. Well he remembered what he had overcome in the long, lonely process of working out advice from Dr. George Parker

Holden's little book, *Idyl* [sic] *of The Split-Bamboo* (1920). Certainly, by the 1970s, there was little reason to imagine that other amateurs were inclined to follow this same path. Vince believed that after having invested more than 45 years himself as a rod-maker, it seemed preposterous to suppose that an amateur would be willing (or able) to follow in his footsteps merely by reading some prose on the topic. His attitude may seem condescending, but truly, the prospect of elaborating on rod-making struck Vince as disingenuous—self-serving on the one hand, while holding out only false encouragement for the beginner on the other. By contrast, writing about fly-tying or entomology was an altogether different matter. These topics had always been popular with fly-fishermen and great numbers of the brethren had attained high degrees of proficiency on both counts.

In the longer view, however, an unexpected twist of history proved both these explanations to be entirely unfounded because, from the early 1980s forward, a renewed interest in bamboo rod-making began, the likes of which had never before been seen. This occurred within a few short years following the simultaneous publication of two 1977 books—*How to Make Bamboo Fly Rods* by George Barnes, and Hoagy B. Carmichael's *A Master's Guide to Building A Bamboo Fly Rod*—and before long, the number of amateur rod-makers virtually exploded. Ironically, very few of us were aware of the scale of public interest back then. Indeed, in the 1980s, even while the movement was fully upon us, most of its participants— including myself— failed to realize it was happening.

Interestingly, the brotherhood of amateur rod-makers, as such, did not begin in the eastern U.S. where bamboo rod-making had its first start, but began quietly in 1988 in the far-northwest with Jon Bokstrom and Don Anderson. Their bright lights led to the very first gathering of amateur rod-makers, hosted at Corbett Lake, British Columbia. In the meantime, I doubt any of us back in the East knew enough amateur makers to fill a teacup. Not that they weren't here, Lord knows, but that most of us hadn't even thought to look around.

In 1990, however, Ron Barch and Wayne Cattanach—a pair of insightful and enterprising young makers from Michigan—learned of the great success at Corbett Lake. Quickly, they put out some inquiries and made their own arrangements for a small group of amateur makers to come together in Boiling Springs, Pennsylvania, along the banks of Yellow Breeches Creek.

Catskill Gathering

Everyone was eager to learn how and when the others began, with each person popping-out names of additional makers around the country. This little, eastern gathering proved to be a seminal event, but not without a certain measure of discomfort. Previously, I suppose, each of us had rested smug, isolated and satisfied in our delusions that we were unique geniuses of the basement—each being the last, hidden vestige of a noble and dying breed. I mean, Vince was gone, so, apart from myself, how many "Grand Potentates of The Planing Form" could there be? Surely, these others were imposters! So, our egos chastened and subdued, some of us almost felt disappointed to learn how widespread amateur rod-making already had become.

Soon after the Boiling Springs gathering, Ron Barch began to publish his informal newsletter, *The Planing Form*, certain there were many other makers hidden among the folds of the countryside. About that same time, computers and the Internet became affordable for most households, and down in Texas, Jerry Foster devised a new web site for

Ron Barch and Wayne Cattanach

amateur rod-makers, soon to host Mike Biondo's discussion forum as well. By the mid-1990s, and for the first time ever, dozens of amateur makers across the US emerged, came to know each other and were eager to share information, sources and building techniques. No one currently knows how many hundreds of amateur rod-makers there may be, but a new fascination with cane among both amateur and cottage-industry makers has taken hold in North America, and is spreading as surely through Europe, Australia and Japan.

Certainly, there remain several, first-rate, professional makers, but by far, the greatest number of custom-built, bamboo fly rods (and of the finest quality) now come from the many independent, cottage-industry and amateur makers. Not every independent maker can build an excellent rod, but the best among us certainly do. (To mention only a tiny selection of first-rate makers we happen to know, Ron Kusse, Bobby Taylor, Per Brandin, Walt Carpenter, Mark Aroner, Al Medved, Bill Fink, John Zimny, Willis Reid, Tom Smithwick, Harry Boyd, Tim Abbott, Rick Robbins, Jeff Wagner, Robert Kope, Dana Gray, Bob Maulucci, John Pickard, Jim Bureau, Wayne Cattanach and Dave Van Burgel come immediately to mind.) Most of these men will sell a rod; some will not. Some build privately or only for friends, while others have turned openly to the retail market, and the distinction between "amateur" and "professional" becomes blurred indeed. Among the independent makers we've mentioned, however, the issue of quality does not hang in the balance.

Our brotherhood seems to consist of a great many "geezers"—Whittle and me as perfect examples—perhaps with the explanation that a nostalgia for quieter days finally caught up with those of us who survived the Porsches, Harleys or divorces of mid-life crisis. Nearly all of us grew up using cane, but after a flirtatious tryst with graphite we returned where loves and loyalties were strongest. It is curious to note, however, that in our youth probably no more than the smallest handful of fly-fishers was lucky enough to own a truly first-rate rod, the rest of us reveling in childhood memories of only garden-variety cane rods. My own first rod (as a 13-year-old) was a hand-me-down South Bend of dubious pedigree, and I was just as happy chucking nightcrawlers with it as casting a fly. So, it isn't exactly as if we just couldn't wait to get back to our Paynes, Dickersons, Garrisons and the like.

The prospect of casting to trout with a hand-built, bamboo fly rod has a charm in one's later years that, for most of us, is simply irresistible. And the possibility exists, too, that for the more diligent among us, we could actually build the equivalent of a Payne, Dickerson or Garrison—or better. Meaning no disrespect to the Old Masters, nowadays this happens with regularity.

New rods at "GrayrockGathering:" —2004

Carole and Al Medved with Clara, our mascot

Happily, not all the Brethren of Bamboo are codgers. Many are talented young fellows in their 30s and 40s. In the East, we're thinking of Al Noland, Russ Gooding, Bill Taylor, Bob Maulucci, Bob Williams, the Dietrich brothers or Tim Zietak, who wouldn't have known the good old days; Midwesterners include Jeff Wagner, John Pickard, Jimmy Chang, Todd Talsma, Jeff Shaeffer and Brett Reiter, to name just a few. And still larger groups of young makers exist to the West and South, whose many names we couldn't begin to compile.

Rod-making books, materials, tools, planing forms, milling-machines, heat-treating ovens, ferrules, reel seat hardware, guides, cork, glues, varnishes and endless lists of published tapers are all readily available for the intrepid amateur who wishes to have a go. Vince, alas, was already gone by the time this resurrection began. He could never have anticipated its development. Considering this, we can easily understand why he would have held the views he did just a decade before.

A third reason Vince was reluctant to discuss his fly rods—one that became known to us only after the PFFMA acquired his collection—is that apparently, at some point between the publication of *In The Ring of The Rise* and his death in 1986, Marinaro intended to make arrangements with one of the few, remaining, commercial bamboo rod makers to issue a series of his own rods. While Vince was closed-mouth about making rods in general, he was particularly chary about discussing his tapers. His secrecy had always been connected to the idea that every good rod-maker should evolve his own design principles and data, but even knowing this, we wonder if pursuing a commercial endorsement of his rods might have become a factor in later years as well.

We have no direct evidence of what might have been on Vince's mind regarding such a venture, but in the PFFMA's "Marinaro Collection" archives, Tom Whittle located a draft of a letter written to Thomas & Thomas by Vince's son, Sebastian. In that letter, Sebastian proposes a series of "Marinaro tapers." The letter is a partial draft, hand written, not dated, and no reply exists. Yet we know from its contents that in some measure Vince and Sebastian were discussing commercial possibilities for the rods.

In a conversation I had with Tom Dorsey just over a year ago, I learned that, at some point after Vince's death, Sebastian did indeed contact Thomas & Thomas to explore a limited edition of Marinaro rods. Certainly, from the early 1970s forward, Vince's reputation was considerable, and his fly-rod tapers would have been valuable property to himself and his family. Dorsey admitted that, at the time, he was powerfully tempted to pursue Sebastian's offer, but believed the more prudent course would be to rely upon Thomas & Thomas's own line of bamboo rods. In any case, considering these developments, there can be little wonder at Marinaro's later years of secrecy.

Harms and Al Medved with the "Medved Beveler."

photo by Jim Wilcox

Whittle and Chris Bogart

In a final and more recent twist, Whittle discovered, upon measuring several of the existing rods in the "Marinaro Collection," that the perfected casting characteristics of Vince's "convex taper" (as described in *The Ring*), may not have been worked out entirely to his satisfaction until his last decade of building. All this will be explained in a later chapter, but for now we're wondering if perhaps a last reason Vince avoided discussions on rod-making and design was that he always thought of his tapers as works-in-progress and did not want others to regard any existing rods as representing his best efforts. Had Vince been trying through all those decades to achieve an ideal set of tapers, only reaching that goal to his satisfaction in the years surrounding the publication of *The Ring*? And, might the chapter on rod design in that book have been written partly as a "market teaser" for some commercial production of his rods? Such questions are pure conjecture, admittedly, and the latter smacks uncomfortably of cynicism. Still....

Catskill Gathering—2004

Working Back to Vince's Beginnings

Marinaro tests a "roof-rod."

During the 1970s, when Vince was teaching me the craft, he never mentioned exactly what his current rods represented to him. Naive and absorbed with my own new experiences as I was, I merely assumed that "the perfect convex taper" was what Vince had always built, and it never really occurred to me to inquire what he was up to with his most recent designs. But I surely do recall the day he showed off one of his new, three-piece, 9-footers. What a day of self-congratulation was that! After standing well back and shooting his entire leader directly over the roof-beam of his house—always his test to determine if he had a good rod, a "roof-rod," as he would call those that passed muster—Vince beamed with pride, waved his rod about in the air and danced a little victory jig for my amusement. He was insufferable, really. And, oh, how he loved to rub it in!

So, finally, Tom and I can't help but wonder if those long conversations Vince and I were having about taper design weren't, in another way, his continuing effort to perfect his own. Those of us who knew him will vouch that obsessiveness was nothing out of the ordinary for Vince, but he certainly was a man possessed during those years. So we're greatly tempted to believe that, while the earlier explanations would account for Marinaro's more general unwillingness to discuss rod-making, our last suggestions might offer the most compelling reasons for his refusal to discuss taper design.

VINCE'S BEGINNINGS

The bamboo fly rods built by Vince Marinaro during the 1970s represent a lifetime of pondering and experimentation. Yet all owe their beginnings to a single source—the idea, first conceived when Vince was a teenager, that he might build his own bamboo rods. Vince describes these beginnings with additional details *The Ring*, "I was finally, some forty-five years ago, induced to become an amateur rod-builder. Actually, it was something that I undertook under a kind of duress." Similarly, a 1974 letter to Kevin Leibold describes these beginnings, "My rod-building efforts go back many years—maybe 45 years ago—when I was in High School. I was dedicated to the dry-fly at an early age."[2]

Although Vince graduated from high school in 1929, there's no way to know exactly when he attempted that first rod, but it was an undertaking of his own and devoid of practical assistance. Rod-making is difficult enough to learn even with a master at one's side, but Vince's attempts as a teenager living in western Pennsylvania's hills strike us as heroic. Those were distant times and places, and while it's difficult to think what rural life might have been like back then, it was certainly not as we now find it. Few of us have cause to imagine life in the 1920s, but a glimpse suggests an understanding of Vince and his world:

In 1920, women had just been granted the right to vote. The first Postal Service airmail delivery started in 1923. Laundry hung on the lines every Monday, water was pumped daily from the well, kerosene lamps lit the dark of night, an outdoor privy graced each backyard and coal fueled behemoth furnaces in the basements. Rural transportation was by rail, horse-and-buggy, and bicycle, but at less than $400 a pop, Henry Ford's "Tin Lizzy" soon came within reach of many families. Radios blessed urban homes fortunate enough to have electricity, but wind-up phonographs were popular in every parlor. Sand-lot baseball provided the major source of public entertainment, although silent movies were falling a close second. (The first, fully-synchronized, talking picture, Al Jolson's *The Jazz Singer* didn't come until 1927.) But the "Roaring Twenties" also brought us Prohibition, "speakeasies," the "Tommy Gun" and the rise of organized crime.

T. S. Eliot agonized over Western civilization's growing, post-war disillusion in perhaps the century's most significant poem, "The Waste Land," (1922). But Charlie Chaplin, Duke Ellington, Eddie Cantor, Bix Beiderbecke, Betty Boop and the "Charleston," balanced that somberness and everyone rolled into the "Jazz Age." And, while any garden-variety bamboo fly rod could be bought at the local hardware store for $5, a truly first-rate fly rod came in at something close to $40.

In 1924, Clarence Darrow was defending the infamous Leopold and Loeb against murder charges, and just a year later, Darwin's theory of evolution in the Scopes "Monkey Trials." F. Scott Fitzgerald's *The Great Gatsby* and Ernest Hemingway's *The Sun Also Rises* arrived nearly together in 1925. This was the age of the "Harlem Renaissance," the famous Cotton Club, Langston Hughes and Zora Neale Hurston—all contrasting to the toxic ignominy of a rapidly-growing Ku Klux Klan.

By the end of the decade, "Lucky" Charles Lindbergh had flown solo across the Atlantic: "Babe" Ruth hit 60 home runs, a record that stood for 30 years, and America fell in love with Hoagy Carmichael's "Stardust." And, although it couldn't have been the first thing on anyone's mind, some might have noticed that from 1923 to 1929, "Silent Cal" Coolidge was President.

But, first with a slide and then with finality, it all came crashing down one very black Thursday in October of 1929. Within a short time, the world was never the same again. It's hard to imagine what a teen-aged boy living in the remote hills of northwestern Pennsylvania might have had on his mind during the late 1920s, but for Vince it was not Betty Boop, the Charleston or Babe Ruth. Vince was only a high school student, but ever his own man, he was thinking about fishing for trout, spying on insects, developing new fly patterns and making bamboo fly rods. Drawn to a somewhat solitary existence with something like an inborn love of the natural world, Vince began fly-fishing as a child, often saying that he cannot recall a time in his life before he was fishing.

Clockwise from top-center: Grandfather Alfonso Marinaro; Uncles Carmen, Anthony, Vincenzo, Nicola, and Vince's father, Giuseppe

Vince's mother, Rosina

Vince's father, Giuseppi

His family reports that for days on end he would wander about the little streams near his childhood homes, first in Reynoldsville, then Butler, Pennsylvania. During his high school years, he'd hike out, bicycle or hitch a ride—take a little food, perhaps a bedroll, such basic fishing gear as had been given to him, and simply explore his world on his own. During many summers, there were weeks on end—day and night—when Vince was more likely to be found on the local streams than anywhere around his neighborhood.

Vince was born in Reynoldsville in 1911 to an industrious family of Italian immigrants, and although life in those early years was difficult, his father gradually became a successful businessman. Vince's eldest daughter, Vincentia and husband, Ted Czotter, retain all the old, family records and genealogies, and over the course of a few weeks, the three of us spent a few hours talking on the phone and comparing notes. On the other end, "Vincie" and Ted pulled out all their old boxes and folders, sharing the lead as we reconstructed the old stories. Jabbering away with questions and tales of my own experiences with Vince, neither of us seemed able to bring our conversations to a close.

Through the family records, we learn a heartening story. Perhaps it's a variant of the American Dream, but not in the sense that we see only a rosy picture. On the contrary, Vince's history is compelling because it seems typical—a sequence of family immigrations from Italy, beginning back in the 1890s, and the efforts of his father, Giuseppi, and five siblings to make a new start. Beginning with Carmine Marinaro in 1892, one-by-one, five boys and one girl supported each of the others to make the journey from Italy to America. All the brothers but one arrived in Reynoldsville, Pennsylvania to work the surrounding coal mines, while Vincenzo Marinaro, a priest, was assigned to a parish in Butler, not far distant.

Working the coal mines was always a miserable proposition, but the brothers were bright, ambitious, and determined to find success. In a short time, three of them abandoned the mines and joined their resources to pursue a number of business interests in town. Vince's father, Giuseppi, seems to have been particularly industrious and may have been the one responsible for the brothers' success. All the enterprises began small, but within a few years the brothers owned a general store, a cigar factory, a bottling company, a pasta manufacturing business, a bank and a modest hotel. Each of these prospered, and soon the brothers were sending money back home to Italy, supporting remaining family members and providing help to relatives and friends who wished to make the trip to America. Giuseppi managed the various enterprises, but also became a notary public, a banker, even the local sheriff.

Giuseppi married Rosina Fero, a fellow Italian immigrant, at age 26, when she was just 16 years old. Rosina was living with her parents in Butler, working in a general store, and as we might have expected of the times, the marriage was arranged by her father. Also typical of those years, Vincentia's family history reports that the following day, Rosina went back to work—this time, managing the brothers' small hotel in Reynoldsville. But Rosina was capable and energetic, and she, too, had dreams of success. Their arrangement worked well, and within a few years, she and Giuseppi were busily raising five children—Vince being the next-to-youngest.

Rosina's family home in Butler, PA—1930s

Vince's family had not exactly become wealthy, but they seemed well on their way down that road when Giuseppi died in October of 1921. Vince's father was just 49 years old, and Vince himself had not yet turned 10. Shortly after, Rosina moved the brood from Reynoldsville back to her hometown of Butler where her family and Vince's uncle, Father Vincenzo, helped with their care.

Vincentia tells us that her father's high school years were entirely ordinary and good grades came easily, but fly-fishing was always first in his heart. It was also in his last years of high school that Vince began to explore rod-making. Lacking experience and guidance in those first years, however, Vince later reported that most of his early rods led to disappointment. Soon, he would begin undergraduate studies at Duquesne University, and while one might suppose that college would interrupt his rod-making, it appears that most of Vince's early progress occurred during those years.

Being one of the youngest children, Vince must have learned independence and self-reliance at an early age, perhaps because he had to, but his temperament seems a more likely explanation. We also suppose his mother and uncle would have doled out the usual chores and responsibilities to Vince's older siblings. So, with his consuming interest in nature, he wandered the woods and streams to his heart's content and without much cause for anyone's concern. In nearly everything, Vince was on his own. No one in his family seemed to share his interests, but neither did he seek companionship—always preferring to spend his free time alone, fishing and hunting.

Vince: Butler high school graduation—1929

Summertime always meant fly-fishing, yet back on the water and dissatisfied with the rods available to him, Marinaro began to investigate the problems of building his own fly rod—"under a kind of duress," as he described the matter in later years. Again, from *The Ring*, we read:

> Perhaps the most severe limitation placed on all of us at that time was in the matter of tackle, in just about every department, particularly, proper dry-fly rods. The rods available in those days were long–nine feet or more, heavy, very slow to respond, and extremely tiresome under the burden of the numerous false casts that a dry-fly-fisherman must make in a long fishing day.... So, my impatience with existing and available rods induced me to try my hand at rod-building.[3]

Even as a very young man, Marinaro quickly developed his own standards, objectives and reasons for preferring one fly rod to another. The problem, as he explained it to me, was that his earliest rods were hand-me-downs, built with the older, "wet-fly action." But Vince was interested in dry-fly fishing, and he sought quicker and more responsive action from a rod. Certainly, these were available, but that would have meant buying a new rod from one of the better makers. Vince may have been aware of such rods (though I couldn't say), but even if he were, as a teenager living out in the sticks, it seems unlikely he would have had the opportunity to become familiar with them.

Consequently, when Marinaro denigrates "the rods available in those days," we might temper his view by recalling his age, circumstances and location. It's not as if Vince could have tested a wide range of the finest rods of his time—those by Leonard, E. W. Edwards, F. E. Thomas, E. F. Payne, and so on. Had Vince been familiar with the mahogany and leather showrooms of New York's Abercrombie & Fitch or Chicago's Von Lengerke & Antoine, his assessment might have been different. But even if the idea to locate an excellent dry-fly rod had occurred, the notion would have been dismissed out of hand. How would he search out these makers? Where would he find the money to pay for their services? And by the early 1930s, his resources were even fewer—a poor college student during the Depression simply does not buy expensive fly rods. Making his own rods, then, was Vince's only path toward getting what he wanted. (Indeed, the high price tags on the best rods have always been motivators for amateur rod-makers.)

While we're not suggesting that Vince misled us on his motives for beginning his rod-making, we do believe it's unlikely that he would have had access to the best dry-fly rods of his day, and it's certain that the rods he *did* use left him unhappy. I never learned which rods those were, but most likely, they would have been by Heddon, Cross, South Bend, Horrocks-Ibbotson or Montague. A few of these companies, to be perfectly fair, offered some very good tapers, but these were largely "bread and butter" tackle manufacturers whose profits came from supplying the market with inexpensive, serviceable rods—the least distinguished of these circulating in the greatest numbers throughout rural America. Considering Vince's growing love for dry-fly fishing, it is not difficult to imagine why he became dissatisfied with ordinary rods.

Even so, what measure of expertise and sophistication could have led Vince to such strong opinions? Readers should recall that, even in the late 1920s, dry-fly fishing in America was still in its infancy. As Vince reminds us in *The Ring*, those earliest, pioneering books of Gill, LaBranche or Rhead were then little more than a decade old, and both the fly-fishing public and tackle manufacturers were still finding their way into this new notion of casting and fishing. Vince was no different. Yet, even as a teenager, he was quickly convinced, had already begun developing and fashioning his own flies and was constantly prowling for better fishing techniques. Given Vince's nature, it's no wonder that he quickly came to sense what a dry-fly rod should do for him—how he wanted it to feel and perform.

All practical considerations aside, probably the most compelling force behind Vince's decision to build rods was his own nature—his curious mind, skepticism and fierce sense of self-reliance serving as the prime motivators. Those of us who knew Vince marveled at his relentless need to understand everything through his own experiences. He had a demanding temperament and a large measure of audacity—this latter, not ordinarily regarded as a positive attribute, but one that typified the most fruitful pursuits of his career. We believe Vince undertook building his rods, not so much because he had to, but because he *wanted* to; because the prospect fascinated him; because he needed to know if he could do it. Vince was blessed with strong and intuitive mechanical skills, and even as a young man, he had spent many years working with wood, so it wasn't exactly as if he were entertaining a range of challenges entirely outside his expertise. He wanted to build his own fly rods, never mind why, and that's all there was to it! Readers may well consider this to be "a kind of duress."

Vince's first years as a maker were strictly trial-and-error, and except for what he could make of a couple old books on rod-making, no guidance was at hand. The earliest of these books was Henry P. Wells' *Fly-Rods and Fly-Tackle* (1885), an enjoyable and informative book on all aspects of fly-fishing tackle, but of the two chapters dealing with fly rods, only one focuses on rod-making and the emphasis here is on building with hardwoods. Wells is a wonderful read for anyone having an interest in the era, but it's hard to imagine his book could offer much practical assistance to a beginning bamboo rod maker. Nevertheless, Wells gave Marinaro the inspiration and courage to believe he could succeed.

A second book was somewhat more detailed, Perry Frazer's *Amateur Rodmaking* (1914). Frazer offers a survey of the many types of fishing rods available—varieties of bait casting rods for fresh or salt water, as well as bass, salmon and tournament rods. The book also contains a chapter on the history of the bamboo fly rod, followed by two chapters attending to the bamboo building process. Frazer says "Tonkin" bamboo is certainly best for a fly rod, but warns against the difficulties of managing this material in construction, strongly advising the amateur to begin with wood and to avoid bamboo until some expertise has been attained. In some ways, Frazer's work might have been useful for the beginner (notwithstanding the primitive planing and gluing techniques), but both chapters lack the depth and detail necessary to succeed with the modern bamboo rod. Most notably absent, is any help in the matter of designing a fly rod's taper, and one finds no mention of rods for the dry fly.

A third, more useful inspiration for Marinaro was only discovered a few years after he had begun making rods—Dr. George Parker Holden's *Idyl of The Split-Bamboo* (1920). Dr. Holden was by far the most influential of all early writers upon amateur makers; a fact well documented in Hoagy Carmichael's *A Master's Guide to Building A Bamboo Fly Rod* (1977). Dr. Holden, Camichael points out, lived in Yonkers, New York, and was also responsible for teaching master-maker, Everett Garrison (who lived nearby) the craft of rod-building.

Nevertheless, while recognizing Holden as excellent company for his instruction, Vince was also painfully aware that, as a very young man living in western Pennsylvania, no real assistance would be at his side. Unlike Garrison, Vince would not have the priceless benefit of first-hand experience at a master's bench. He would have to go it alone, find his own sources for cane, guides, ferrules, cork, reel seat hardware and glues. No market for amateur rod-making supplies existed in the early 1930s, so Vince had to make his own equipment. He had to learn how to construct his own steel, planing forms, make the binding machine, drying cabinet and various other jigs and fixtures.

Nowadays, all this has changed, but a similar dearth of supplies and information existed for the amateur maker even in the 1970s when Vince was teaching me to build. There was a period, however, from 1935 through the 1950s, when mail-order catalog magnate, George Herter, offered amateur rod-makers both a range of supplies and a manual on bamboo rod construction—this, a response to the growing market spawned by Dr. Holden's book. But when fiberglass fly rods began to sweep the marketplace in the 1950s and Herter's catalogues were no longer available,

A gaggle of old rods

photo by Tom Whittle

the amateur maker once again faced all the old difficulties of locating building materials and equipment.

Additional assistance for the amateur arrived in 1951—two books, *The Wise Fisherman's Encyclopedia*, edited by A. J. McClane, and *The Bamboo Rod And How to Build It* by Claude Kreider. *The Wise Encyclopedia* includes a concise, 60-page article on rod design and construction—together with drawings and illustrations—and was compiled by J. Deren, Lew Stoner (the genius behind R. L. Winston Rod Co.) and Lou Feierabend (the inventor of the "Super-Z" ferrule and a colleague of both Robert Crompton and Nat Uslan). McClane's *Encyclopedia* was both current and relevant, but at mid-century, it was Kreider's book that served as the only truly practical guide for the amateur builder. Kreider was up-to-date with all the latest techniques and advice, and the entire book was devoted, step-by-step, to making the modern bamboo fly rod.

Significantly, Kreider expresses his deep gratitude to Robert Crompton, the man who became heir to George Parker Holden's influences and the common denominator between so many makers (professional and amateur) of that time. It was Crompton who had designed the binding machine and planing boards available through Herter's catalogs, and from the 1930s onward, it was also Compton who became Marinaro's trusted friend, confidant and mentor.

Kreider's book covers every step of the design and building process, but its timing in the market was most unfortunate. For one thing, the work made its appearance just as the public was turning its attention to new and less expensive fiberglass fly rods, while other blows came from the growing craze for spin-casting and the Embargo against trade with China—including, of course, the import of bamboo. All this created a fast-fading interest in the bamboo fly rod market, and the help offered by Kreider, the *Wise Encyclopedia* and Herter's *Manual* was short-lived.

The Wise Encyclopedia remained available longest, probably because its contents are diverse. Kreider's book, however, was soon out of print, although remaindered copies were available on the discount market for a few years. But when Herter's *Manual* also disappeared, independent makers were once again abandoned to their own devices. Amateur builders were unable to be of much help to one another (except strictly on a local basis), no network of communication existed and rod-making information simply did not circulate. Meanwhile, the professionals barely talked even among themselves.

Working Back to Vince's Beginnings   31

Chapter Two

Learning to Build

Marinaro's earliest attempts at rod-making brought great disappointment, not for lack of talent or motivation, but because in the late 1920s, useful information was scarce and difficult to locate, particularly for a boy living far from any center of fly-fishing activity. Today, it's easy to learn what help is available and how to access it—knowledge quickly gathered by home computers able to tap a network of resources. But the search for information would have been altogether different in Vince's early days.

We learn from *The Ring* that Marinaro's first efforts at rod-making were with various sorts of hardwoods, his first experiments employing local materials. He mentioned hickory and ash to me, but in his book he says he used a few traditional woods as well—greenheart and lemonwood. This seems odd, Tom and I think, and we don't know exactly why Vince would have begun building with wood. Hardwood fly rods were common in former days, but even as early as the 1880s bamboo had become the preferred material. And Vince's own, first rods, however disappointing they may have been for fishing the dry fly, were also of bamboo. Marinaro writes of his first, frustrating experiences as a dry-fly fisherman:

> I had become enamored of the dry fly very early in life, but it was a time when very little was known about it. It was only a few short years before my own involvement that the books of Gill, La Branche, and Rhead had been published. They were helpful but I did not realize how very much they were limited until later years, when in the light of my own experience I was able to overcome many difficulties, mostly on my own initiative. Perhaps the most severe limitation placed on all of us at that time was in the matter of tackle, in just about every department, particularly, proper dry-fly rods. [1]

Indeed, although "proper dry-fly rods" were being developed by the second decade of the 20th century, Vince couldn't have known much about the particulars of their construction. There was little-or-no literature on the topic of dry-fly tapers, and none that Vince had discovered at the time he began building. But we wonder what he could have meant in decrying the fly rods of his early years. More to our point: If he were already thinking about how a dry-fly rod should perform, what hope could he have in building with wood? Wood was handy, of course, and it had been a satisfactory material for several centuries, but certainly it was never desired for the newer dry-fly rods. Still, while this is common knowledge now, what would a teenager living out in Butler, Pennsylvania in the 1920s have known about all that?

Vince on the Letort in 1947

Several older rods

"But Of Any Of These Mongrels We Will Have Naught"
—*George Parker Holden*

Advice to begin rod-making with hardwoods came from both Wells and Frazer, who took considerable pain in their books to warn the amateur against building with bamboo—not because of shortcomings in the material itself, but because of the great difficulty in construction. Not yet aware of Holden's *Idyl of The Split Bamboo*, Vince regarded Frazer as the most current source of information. So, perhaps Marinaro's first attempts at rod-making were only meant to familiarize himself with his tools and the process. It's likely Vince was only heeding Frazer's strong warning when he read:

> Without question split bamboo is the best material known to-day. If you can obtain the material in butts, joints, and tips, glued-up, so that the "making" consists merely in finishing it and fitting handgrasps, ferrules, and trimmings, if care is exercised a very good rod will be the result. But I would strongly advise the novice not to attempt to make a split bamboo rod complete; at least not until he has had ample practice in making all-wood rods. Instead, pay a visit to some professional rod-maker, if this be possible, at a time when he is making split bamboo rods, and ask permission to watch him at work for a little while. If you do, my word for it, you will go away a wiser if not a sadder man, for you will be convinced that you lack the skill necessary to finish the six slender strips and fit them together perfectly, even if you can secure bamboo that will prove to be worth cutting up. [2]

Tom and I found still another (but odd) book in Marinaro's library, Harlan Major's *Salt Water Fishing Tackle* (1939)—odd, because its subject is salt water fishing and Vince never had much interest in this. Yet Major's book also contains several pages on amateur rod-building, again, mostly directed at hardwoods and similarly advising against bamboo. We doubt Major's work could have influenced Vince because it was published 10 years after he began building. Yet, the book is of interest to us because, even as late as 1939, Major estimates that building with bamboo is beyond the skills of an amateur maker. Major's concerns aren't directed at construction difficulties, but at the unmanageable crap-shoot involved in obtaining good cane. He believes the path to making a bamboo rod is one of uncertainties, and the prospects for one's success, dubious at best:

> If there are any amateur rod makers who enjoy almost insurmountable difficulties as a game and a challenge to their stick-to-it-iveness and luck, they can find no better pastime than making split-bamboo rods from the rough cane into the multi-splined finished article. But if the fisherman wishes to be reasonably sure that he can enjoy using, as well as making, his rod, he had better purchase a glued stick and confine his efforts to its finishing and mounting.... I've seen many sweet-actioned rods, split and glued by an amateur, but the problem is like jay-walking through automobile traffic during rush hour–the odds are bad. The problem is not lack of skill. The rod-making hobbyist can be as expert as a professional and may be more so than most of them.... The difficulties he must face cannot be surmounted by great effort, but instead much of the trouble is at the source of supply. [3]

Major laments the dearth of good building materials, in particular, the uncertain quality of bamboo. Its suitability for rod-making is influenced, he tells the reader, by how it is grown, harvested and shipped, and these variables create a litany of problems in quality control. While it's true that authors before Major often found fault with Calcutta (India) cane—a species more likely to yield kindling and garden stakes than good fly rods—Major was actually writing about the more recently discovered Tonkin (Chinese)

Marinaro on the Letort in the 1960s

cane. Tom and I are not aware of the exact state of affairs of Tonkin cane imports during the 1930s, but it is highly unlikely that the quality was as grim as Major reports.

What we do know is that, by 1939 when Major's book was published, fine bamboo rods were being turned out by the thousands (both by independent makers and production companies) and Charles H. Demarest, Inc. was able to supply Tonkin cane in almost unlimited quantities. Still, the point Major wishes to make is that professional makers know how to select good culms from their supplies, while amateurs, with their tiny stock and lack of experience, do not. This could be true by degrees, but Holden's *Idyl of The Split-Bamboo* addressed that problem nearly 20 years earlier, offering lengthy instructions to the amateur on how to select good cane. We're aware that information circulated slowly in those days, but not so slowly that in the course of two decades, Major would have had difficulty catching up with Holden's advice. But whether Major's assessment carried validity or not, our point is that his book represents what amateurs **believed** they were up against even a decade after Vince had begun building.

Only a deeper commitment and more thorough familiarity with the building process itself would have motivated Vince to seek out Tonkin cane. All this came soon enough once he discovered Holden's book, but Vince began simply with only Wells and Frazer as his guides. Both authors advised the amateur to build with wood, so we suppose Vince simply followed suit: first trying his locally available materials. Marinaro describes the results of those earliest experiences in *The Ring* writing:

> Eventually, I had to abandon these woods because they were unsatisfactory on many counts. The experience was valuable. I learned a great deal about rod action. Without training as an engineer, the knowledge acquired is gained through the empirical process. It is a matter of trial and error: sensing and feeling the changes needed, requiring, of course, the ability to execute those changes in order to improve each new model. I learned two important things in those days: The length of a rod had to be held within proper bounds and a suitable material must be used.... It was apparent to me that the only suitable material was bamboo. Accordingly, I made the giant leap into the making of split-bamboo fly rods. [4]

We heard those were the good old days

I don't know exactly when Vince discovered Holden's *Idyl* and began using bamboo, but because Holden died in 1934 and Vince told me they had corresponded often, his conversion to Tonkin cane couldn't have been more than a couple years after he began building. In Marinaro's earlier-mentioned letter to Kevin Leibold (then, a 17-year-old admirer), Vince writes, "I found a book in the Public Library, by Dr. George Holden called *The Idyl of The Split-Bamboo*. It inspired me to try to make the kind of a rod that I wanted. I did not realize then what a huge undertaking it was, but I persevered."

Holden's influence provided the "giant leap" Vince needed and put him on the right path. Through Holden, Marinaro learned about the very special properties of Tonkin bamboo, how to select a proper culm, how to split and prepare strips for planing and how to manage the difficulties of gluing and binding—this latter, rather on the primitive side, but good enough to get a start. Also present in Holden's book is an analysis of the flexing characteristics of various rod types, including, for the first time ever, a discussion of dry-fly tapers.

Holden's work remains a treasure trove of wisdom and information, a classic for rod-makers. Despite today's extraordinary range of information, better tools, machines and jigs, slicker techniques, superior materials and a full spectrum of taper designs, Holden's book was the first to bring the prospect of building one's own precisely-tapered, bamboo rods within the grasp of the amateur maker. The process became truly realistic and manageable, the results reliable and repeatable. As to Vince's quick conversion to bamboo, we wonder how it possibly could have been otherwise after reading the following words by Dr. Holden:

> The British manufacturer has a penchant...for combining different woods in individual rods, as a greenheart butt- and second-joint with a bamboo top, or an ash or hickory butt with greenheart and bamboo for the other sections. *But of any of these mongrels we will have naught*; as for us we pin our faith and fealty to the silk-wound hexagonal rod cunningly yet simply devised of its subtle, individual triangular strips of cane throughout, and *we can but view with compassion that angler who suffers a permanent perverted attachment to some one or other of the monstrosities mentioned above* [italics added]. [5]

We just have to love a guy who knows his mind and will mince no words, and I'm sure even a very young Marinaro would have recognized his own kind in the good Doctor. Prose like Holden's, alas, is dead and gone. Continuing his encouragement for the amateur rod-maker, Holden writes:

> The making of a split-bamboo rod is readily within the accomplishment of anyone who can handle a few of the simpler carpenters' tools, with patience—and your true angler already has this quality well developed. A little time, a little absorbingly interesting work, a small outlay for rod fittings or mountings, and forty-cents' worth of bamboo in the rough is transformed into the most beautiful of all sporting implements, that the owner could not have duplicated by a professional rod-maker for forty dollars. Almost any manual labor, especially if diverting and concentrating the attention into novel paths, is balm for the jaded or worried mind. This work is light and innately fascinating. The reader is assured at the outset that by careful attention to and the following out of the very explicit directions contained in the chapters immediately following, he can construct not merely a passably-good split-bamboo rod, but a high-grade article that any expert angler would be glad to own—a rod that will have balance, action, finish, and distinction, and the possession of which will give infinite satisfaction to its creator.[6]

All wonderfully inspirational, yet Vince explained that Holden's greatest assistance came from his detailed instructions to build the adjustable, steel planing form. We don't know for certain that this was entirely his own invention, although on page 85 of *Idyl* Holden suggests it was: "I had worked out the details of my steel planing-mold and had used it with great satisfaction...." Whatever the case, it's interesting to learn from Hoagy Carmichael's book (1977) that it was Holden who taught Everett Garrison how to construct this same, flexible, planing form.[7]

The new device provided Marinaro with a tremendous advantage in his search for accuracy, for previously, the only means of tapering bamboo strips was the humble planing-board, or "shooting-board," as it was also called. The shooting-board was just serviceable, but far from satisfactory. It was crude and lacked all measure of control. Actually, the device was little more than a hardwood board (in later years, steel) into which four, 60-degree grooves had been cut along its 48-inch length. Each groove was tapered from deep-to-shallow, and each established its initial depth at the point where its neighbor left off.

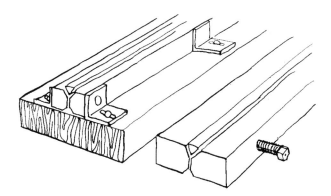

Holden's planing form (left) and Garrison's improved version (right)

Learning to Build 37

Marinaro Fishing on Penn's Creek—1947

Pack-Saddle Bridge over PA's Brush Creek

photo by Bill Harms

Now, Holden did not work in thousandths-of-an-inch, but in his determination to control even fractional dimensions more exactly, he knew the adjustable, steel form had to be the answer. Consider: One 64th of an inch equals 0.0156" (about the thickness of four sheets of paper), but only half that thickness carried through the upper section of a fly rod will make the difference of one, full, line size. More to our point, distributed here and there through various areas of a tip section, even a mere 0.004" (the thickness of a single sheet of paper) can have much to do with the particulars of a rod's action. So, hanging in the balance, to put the matter as succinctly as possible, is the question of whether one is to build a fine fly rod or not. The precision of one's tools and the maker's ability to "hit the numbers" are crucial. Holden writes:

Vince told me that he, too, first began with the old shooting-board, but said he doubted, even back then, that it could ever produce the rods he wanted. One-by-one, he would lay his bamboo strips into the largest groove, plane them to a triangular shape, then shift them through the series of grooves until all strips were reduced to the desired taper. When finished, the six strips for a rod section would be similar, but they never matched each other identically. Only by luck, Vince said, could he obtain a set of strips that approximated the fly rod he had in mind. But approximation was not the goal Vince sought, and at once, he constructed Holden's flexible planing-mold from the steel bars.

As to the question of accuracy, when Vince was learning to build, tapers were still designed and executed in 64ths of an inch, plus-or-minus. "Close enough," some wet-fly fishermen might have groused, but for Vince, this lack of precision was altogether unacceptable. It was probably Everett Garrison, an engineer by training, who first began to think and to work in thousandths-of-an-inch, and with certain improvements to Holden's flexible steel form and the application of machinists' measuring instruments, Garrison was among the first to obtain these new and precise tolerances. I don't know when Vince began this same practice, but my guess is it may have happened later in the 1930s—the years when he was corresponding with Robert Crompton regularly, and first heard about Garrison's methods.

> For further preliminary planing and tapering, the author still makes use of the wooden mold, acceptably and quickly constructed, for this work, of any soft wood such as pine or cypress; *but he never succeeded in turning out joints of satisfactory excellence until he adopted a steel mold or planing-board for the last, fine planing-down of the strips to their ultimate dimensions* [italics added].... This steel mold is adjustable for the full length and varying calibers of the joints of any rod, from one having a diameter up to one inch or more at the extreme butt, if so desired, and a width at the tip of anything from a scant one-sixteenth of an inch upward. Also, the mold being made in independent halves, of not excessive rigidity, it may either be sprung apart or compressed along the middle—the ends first being secured—to produce a joint having either a convex or concave taper; or with it you may turn out simple straight-tapered joints or those having double or combined straight tapers. [8]

Holden's writing kindled a whole new interest in amateur rod-making, and responding to this burgeoning new market, in 1948, George Herter began to publish his often-revised *Rod Building Manual and Manufacturer's Guide*—a

Learning to Build

A dandy 20" Letort brownie

She goes back home

work that continued through the late 1950s. Rod-building materials and supplies had long been available through Herter's mail order catalogue, but of greater assistance to the amateur, Herter's *Manual* contains a brief history of the bamboo fly rod, useful demonstrations of the construction process and a selection of rod tapers. The *Manual* also includes sample drawings and descriptions of a few planing forms developed by earlier amateurs. But, strangely, while Herter devotes nearly a full page of graphic and verbal attention to Holden's steel-bar forms, he fails to credit its inventor or mention Holden by name. Quite to the contrary, Herter seems more concerned to explain why he thinks the device is actually ***unsatisfactory*** for building bamboo rods, writing:

> As the use of wooden V blocks went out, the use of steel V blocks came in. Adjustable steel V blocks were at first used to some extent but were soon abandoned for the following reasons: 1. They were very expensive to make, as they required a great deal of skilled machining if they were to be made accurately. 2. They could not be used as measuring devices for straight tapered rods, as had first been anticipated. It was found that it was impossible to plane the strips accurately enough in the planing form without measuring the strips carefully. [9]

None of these remarks is true, of course, but it doesn't take long to guess Herter's likely motive. Immediately following his criticism of the Holden-type planing form, Herter launches an eager promotion of his own, steel version of the old shooting-board, touting his product as the one "the hand made rod makers have all come to use...." [10] For all we know, this may have seemed true to Herter, for his world revolved around his catalogues, and his own planing forms would have been the only ones seen leaving his shipping dock. By contrast, Holden's steel planing form was never available on the commercial market, but we would wager that any maker who used one would never again attempt to build a rod on something as chancy as a shooting-board.

That Herter would have slighted Holden is more than ironical, for Herter was only supplying the market in the first place because of amateurs' response to Holden's book. Indeed, Holden, during the 1920s and '30s, seems to have accomplished on a smaller scale what Carmichael's book on Garrison did for amateur makers from the 1980s onward.

But as significant as Holden's adjustable planing form was, it wasn't the only new idea to catch Marinaro's attention. Vince loved to point out that it was also Dr. Holden who first made mention of the "convex taper." Apparently, Holden was not instrumental in developing this taper, but he did have a number of encouraging things to say about its casting characteristics.

Even into the 1920s, dry-fly fishing was a new concept, and designing new rods for this purpose was still in the experimental stage. Different tapers were required and Holden was very much interested, but the convex taper is only one among several new, dry-fly designs he discusses. Preferring not to present actual data or charts, Holden explains that his descriptions of fly-rod tapers (whether for the wet fly or dry) are meant only to estimate the casting characteristics of each—hoping to encourage amateur makers to carry out experiments of their own. Holden tells us this was a fundamental motive behind his entire project, for he believed that amateur makers should be as involved in a rod's design as in its actual construction.

This latter, in particular, caught Vince's attention. He often said that Holden's lack of dogma both intrigued and stimulated him—that, even as a young man, he too, believed both design and construction should be goals of a true rod-maker. He began thinking, later telling me that when he read Holden's discussion of the promising flexing-properties of the convex taper, he became convinced this was the way to go—no doubt eager, even then, to generate dogma of his own. Consider Holden's own words on the convex taper:

> For a rod for fishing with the fly, good results may be obtained in one having a straight or even taper throughout, from butt to tip; and by varying the caliber of such a rod, almost any degree of stiffness or flexibility of practical purport may be obtained. *But a rod may be built on a swelled or convex-taper that will have a superior action* [italics added]; and by looking at the diagrams below, showing just what is meant by a straight, a compound-straight, a concave, and a convex-taper, one will immediately recognize that *the lines of the latter are the same as those which experience has proven most acceptable for flagstaffs and ships' spars—which also are subjected to persistent bending strains* [italics added].
>
> It is very important for best results that the fullness at the butt of the top-joint be carried well forward until about the outer half of the joint is reached, when the caliber may fall away pretty sharply from there on to the very tip.[11]

That first reading of Holden's explanation became a defining moment, influencing Marinaro's entire career as a maker. He reports in *The Ring* that, at one time or another, he tried nearly every known taper design, but returned again and again to the principle of the convex taper. We'll discuss the particulars of Vince's own design criteria in Chapter Eight, where Holden's contributions will become more apparent

Vince said that he and Dr. Holden corresponded often during the few years before Holden's death in 1934. Indeed, as I came to notice after Vince was gone, both the terms and the ideas he used to explain his designs were those first introduced by Holden. I didn't realize this at the time because I had not yet read the good Doctor, but when I opened his book shortly after Vince died, their like-mindedness—in terminology as in principle—became clear.

Month after month, Vince would remind me of the lengthy advice Holden had offered, but it's both unfortunate and a great disappointment to Tom and me that Vince retained none of that correspondence. That's the way Vince was—he kept some records, while simply discarding a great many others. To be fair, though, the period of his collaboration with Holden spanned only a very few of those earliest years in the 1930s when Vince was starting out, and surely he anticipated neither Holden's nor, indeed, his own later significance.

Learning to Build

ROBERT W. CROMPTON: ANOTHER MENTOR

Through Holden, Vince discovered a second mentor, Robert Crompton. Crompton was a most unusual and talented man who, like Holden, learned his craft the hard way. Although it was Holden who first wrote about the convex taper, it was the younger Crompton who seems to have been its "inventor." It was because of Crompton, too, that Vince learned to manage its design potential, certainly the most important objective in all his rod-making to follow. Crompton, something of a professional maker by the time Vince came to know him in the 1930s, soon became a legend within the industry, providing invaluable theoretical and practical help to both amateur and professional rod-makers everywhere.

Crompton's image loomed large over every rod that came from Vince's workbench. Yet, working behind the scenes, it's probably because Crompton did not openly pursue a commercial market that his legend is largely lost to history. I hadn't heard of his influence at the time I was learning to build, and except in Claude Kreider's *The Bamboo Rod And How to Build It* (1951), little mention of his name appeared in the literature I was accumulating. However, hearing Vince sing Crompton's praises almost daily, in my mind the man soon morphed into a monument. Frankly, I could kick myself for lacking the foresight to question Vince more pointedly on his relationship with Crompton because, today, almost no information survives. But I was more full of myself in those days, I suppose, and gave little thought to what needed to be preserved. Crompton, for his part, although he had a great many friends and associates among the prominent makers of his time, left almost no paper trail—no personal correspondence, no data, no books and only a handful of magazine articles.

It's a most peculiar thing, too, that while a few of our contemporary writers refer to Crompton and his contributions, no one we've contacted seems to be aware of exactly how they came by their information. In a conversation I had a few years back with the late Ernie Schwiebert, I learned that even he couldn't recall exactly how he put together his information on Crompton—saying that, while at work on his 1978 *Trout* he, too, had been unable to locate primary sources. Writers will often pass information along from one person to the next, having reasons of their own to trust that somewhere "back there" were sources who knew, first-hand, what they were talking about. Certainly there is no cause to call Schwiebert's references to Crompton into question, yet it's a most unfortunate thing that we have been able to document so little. No doubt, there are a great many letters written by Crompton stashed in the attics and garages of a great many people. But, how to find them...? Again, as was the case in his relationship with Dr. Holden, Vince kept none of his own correspondence.

Even so, we did find something—a February 19, 1928 newspaper article, "*Fisherman Finding Way to Robert Crompton for Fancy Equipment,*" by Julian Sargent of the *St. Paul Pioneer Press*. It's a rare and wonderful little feature story and was provided to us through the St. Paul Public Library in Minnesota:

A man with a pipe in his mouth may be glimpsed doing some little home-making job about the place, clad in Outer's *[an outdoorsman's]* costume of moccasin boots, khaki trousers and flannel shirt. And if the man is seen, there will be a brown Springer spaniel racing about, snapping at the snow, tossing it into the air with its nose, and tearing back to its master from time to time to report progress.

There is a story in this odd and artistic house, a philosophical study in the man, a reverie of contentment in the dog, and in the three of them a rounded tale of life in which its beauty triumphs over its bumps.

Robert W. Crompton of New York, artist, bond and security salesman, outdoor writer, fisherman, roamer of the Northern woods, and former drawer of humorous cartoons, slipped and fell one day three years ago while cranking an automobile. A slight paralysis of the left arm and leg resulted. It was sufficient, however, to cut off his power to earn money by the methods previously used. He was then 37 years old.

His first step toward a solution of the problem was to come west and place himself under the observations of the Mayos of Rochester, leaving in her New York studio his wife, Edna L. Crompton, one of the foremost women illustrators, widely known for her cover designs for *Red Book*, the *Saturday Evening Post* and the *Pictorial Review*....

So he began putting his revised program into effect—a man of strange mixtures entering middle-age with his earning power at a standstill, the product of a farm at Prairie Center, Ill., of two years in his early twenties on the art staff of the *Chicago American*, of the life of a painter in Chicago and New York, and lately of the business life of Gotham....

Next in Mr. Crompton's program of setting up a new life came the fish rods. And right here let it be said that there is considerable to making a six-strip fly rod. Tapering six bamboo segments down to a tip no ticker than a match, with a fit so accurate that the dividing lines are invisible to the naked eye, calls for workmanship as fine as that of a watchmaker. Mr. Crompton rigged up special machines of his own design to cut the strips, finish them and gauge them. He called experts from nationally known tool-making firms to help him with his mechanical problems.

But the workmanship was not the only thing he demanded should be right. He knew there must be some one curve in the taper of the rod that would give greater stamina, for minimum weight, than any other. To find this curve he put the problem before engineers and mathematicians of the University of Minnesota, University of Wisconsin, Boston Institute of Technology and Armour Institute. Thus the diameter of his rods at every point was established to a thousandth of an inch.

And as in the case of the man who builds a better mouse trap, the world of fishermen is beginning to be aware of Mr. Crompton. It is not exactly wearing a rut to his hand-hewn door, but here and there people are beginning to speak of "that fellow who makes the fish rods."

He is now tooling up to make a five-strip rod, which he has a geometrical idea will throw the flexing more into the fiber and less into the glue; and these rods will run from $110 to $120.

As to whether he thinks his partial paralysis will eventually wear itself out, all Mr. Crompton will say is "one of us is going to."

A portly Falling Springs rainbow–1970s

Crompton died on August 8, 1949, at age 61 and suffered badly during the last year from his expanding paralysis. Although unable to work in his shop, he remained active—on better days pecking out large numbers of letters.

Not to dispute Sargent's article, we know that Crompton's experience building the five-strip fly rod dated back in time much farther than the clipping suggests. Crompton, in one of his rare appearances in print, wrote an article for the 1938 *Fishing Annual*, reporting an incident of uncanny happenstance. He was drift-fishing, one day, down Wisconsin's St. Croix River, searching out some nice smallmouth bass, but finding treasure instead:

> On my first trip down the river, about ten miles out of Gordon *[Wisconsin]*, I saw a boy of about fifteen or sixteen about a hundred yards ahead of my boat, wading hip deep and casting a rather neat fly. The boat was edged over to his side of the stream for a better view of his altercation with a nice two-pounder. This over, I engaged him in conversation, intently eyeing his rod the while. I openly admired it, much to the boy's wonderment as it certainly was a tough looking old tool, though to all save me. He could tell me little of the rod save that someone had given it to his brother. When I offered him a couple of dollars for it he looked at me with suspicion. He just KNEW that anyone offering such a sum for that old "pole" couldn't have all his buttons. The deal was soon closed. *I had bought and again possessed my original five-strip rod!* This rod recovery took place just ten years ago and the rod was then about twenty years old. This rod's performance and stamina, plus many laboratory experiments, again plus all that had been brought to light during the past ten years have all contributed to my firm conviction as to the merits of five-strip construction.[12]

Some quick math reveals that, because Crompton wrote his article in 1938 and recovered his rod 10 years earlier when it was already 20 years old, this original five-striper was built about 1908, a time when Crompton himself was just 20 years old and living in Yonkers, New York. In any case, from the day that rod was recovered, Crompton remained ever after, a powerful advocate of five-strip construction, imploring all who would listen to heed his advice.

Many listened, even while Everett Garrison took particular and lengthy exception. Garrison was an engineer of great insight and ability, and no disagreement with him should be undertaken casually. Yet it was Nat Uslan who soon carried out the command, with Crompton providing guidance in the design and construction of Uslan's new milling equipment. Ironically, and despite Garrison's compelling theory describing the inherent vulnerabilities of five-strip design, in practice, the five-striper's casting ability and longevity might persuade us to give the nod to Crompton. Apparently, the five-strip rod is a case rather like the bumblebee that doesn't know it lacks the ability to fly.

Vince never became convinced of the need for a five-strip rod, although I recall him saying that Crompton often suggested he give it a try—strange, perhaps, considering the respect Vince had for every other piece of Crompton's advice. At the time Vince and I were building, he was not yet aware of Garrison's objections to the five-strip rod and seemed, instead, to be voicing his own reservations from a more general view of aesthetics or tradition. On the other hand, I also remember him expressing concern for the likely difficulty he would have in obtaining accurate measurements on a rod whose pentagonal cross-section could be miked only between a given flat, across to its opposing apex.

It was this apex that caused Vince's skepticism, since the precise edge of these outer corners will waver ever so slightly—just as they must when corners of fine, triangular strips are joined, sanded and finished. Would the measured stations truly represent cross-sectional mass, or might those measurements be compromised by minute dips and rises along that apex? Vince's rod-making was entirely trial-and-error, and one of his habits was to "tweak" the design for each new rod from the dimensions of one of his existing rods. In short, Vince wondered how he could know if a finished, five-strip rod had hit the design numbers he was after, and doubted that a pentagonal cross-section could permit reliable measuring. Still, perhaps all these objections were only excuses, for it is certain that many hundreds of excellent five-strip rods have been built since Crompton's day, even by makers less skilled than was Vince.

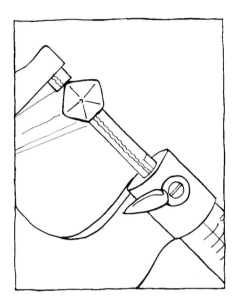

Of greatest significance to his rod-making career, it was Crompton whom Vince credited for helping him to develop the convex taper first described by Dr. Holden. Crompton was many years Holden's junior, but these two men had become fast friends in the early decades of the 20th century. Each was a self-taught rod-maker, and for several years prior to Crompton's 1925 departure for St. Paul, Minnesota, they were also fellow New Yorkers—living not too far apart in Yonkers. The two men compared notes frequently and, because the convex taper was one of several "causes" Crompton promoted, so it seems likely that Holden's strong endorsement of the convex theory in *Idyl* came directly through his friend.

Dr. Holden, in the early 1930s, advised Vince to correspond directly with Crompton. But, because Holden died only shortly after Vince had his start as a rod-maker, it was Crompton (through the following years until his own death in 1949) who provided Vince with both general guidance and specific advice in building. We find, in that 1974 letter from Vince to Kevin Leibold, a strange and oblique reference to Crompton's very early influence:

Learning to Build   45

> Eventually I made contact with a professional rod-builder who taught me the finer points of the craft. He is dead now but I shall always remember his wonderful kindness to me.... My rods are more powerful than usual because I want them to be able to lift a long line off the water–to hold my back cast off the weeds behind me–and to handle the heavier lines for wind-bucking qualities. Such rods can be made light and stiff by utilizing convex tapers–like so...*[Vince's drawing]*. Older rods and even most modern one *[sic]* use a straight taper-like so...*[Vince's drawing]*. I learned this from my dead friend. The real trick is to get just the right amount of convexity without making the rod clubby or heavy. It must have delicacy as well as power.

In addition to our insistence that Vince's obscured mention would lead back only to Crompton, another issue in this correspondence is perhaps noteworthy: Vince, writing to Leibold, seems to imply that the particular requirements he developed for his fly rods would date all the way back to the 1930s and Crompton's early influence. Our awareness of Vince's rod-making career, however, suggests that he is actually citing a set of criteria that evolved only over time, needs that a rod must satisfy to fish the limestone streams of the Cumberland Valley—as he explains at greater length in *The Ring*. The point here is that Vince only wished to attest to what he learned from his "dead friend" about the convex taper; not fully realized initially, perhaps, but surely understood before the time of his correspondence with Leibold.

Dusk on Boiling Springs Lake

Marinaro said his earliest successes came with mid-sized rods up to 8 feet in length, but his real objective always had been to design a lightweight and powerful 9-footer. That's an interesting claim because, of the 13 rods in the PFFMA collection, three measure less than 6' 8" and only one comes in at 7' 6"—all built in the 1970s. All Marinaro's other surviving rods are longer than 8 feet. Where, oh where, are all those early, "successful," mid-sized rods?

Vince determined he needed longer rods to fish his local limestoners, and designing a good one presented a series of problems that he welcomed heartily. Like Houdini, Vince dearly loved to tie himself up in chains just to see if he could get out.

Designing a good 9-foot rod is especially troublesome because the "lever weight" of a long rod quickly accumulates to produce a clumsy feel in the hand. Even at a mere 4 ounces, a 9-footer can hang on one's wrist and, in casting, soon tire the arm and shoulder—the problem only growing worse, should the rod's weight be distributed any farther down its length than absolutely necessary. Nor can the action of a long rod be as "crisp" as a shorter rod because their greater lengths cannot be moved sharply. A faster rod is always purchased at the cost of greater mass,—inevitably, a self-defeating exercise in a 9-footer.

When faster line speed is desired from a short rod, the caster merely gives it more rapid and stronger strokes ("hauling," notwithstanding). But powering-up the long lever-arm of a 9-footer with stronger casting strokes takes a toll on the fly-fisher in short order. At the same time, while long rods must be moved more slowly, they do have the advantage of generating good line speed on their own, merely by virtue of their tips being at a greater distance from the grip. This creates a broader casting arc and causes the tip of a long rod to travel both farther and faster than its shorter counterpart. Still, although the long rod must be moved more gently, dry-fly fishermen surely do not want a soft action. The challenge here is to design a rod that's powerful enough to deliver sharp and accurate casts, but one that's lightweight

Vince preferred a long rod even on small streams

and without soft action. Obtaining maximum strength at minimum weight was always Marinaro's objective, but the difficulties in working this out for the perfect 9-foot rod would be doubled and redoubled. We'll explore Marinaro's design theories in Chapter Eight—at that point, offering an explanation of how he worked around these problems.

Vince experimented with every possible combined shape to minimize the hindrance of weight, and briefly describes some of his successes in *The Ring*. Here, Marinaro also presents some useful insights concerning the problems of excess weight—an important issue not reserved only for the rod itself. We read Marinaro railing adamantly against the quest for "balance" in one's casting rig, insisting on the need to minimize weight everywhere, at all costs, even including the reel seat. Of course, because a reel seat intended for ordinary trout fishing requires very little strength, one's design considerations are in no way worrisome. Vince frequently used simple balsa or cork for his reel seats and narrow, aluminum, sliding bands for the hardware. These latter were cut from very thin-walled tubing, allowing the rings to be pinched slightly to fit up and over the foot of the reel and gripping it securely.

Of greater importance than any other single issue, Marinaro always believed that weight is the caster's greatest enemy, regardless of its location. His concerns went even beyond the rod and its reel seat—extending to the reel itself. And so, indulging one of Tom's and my own favorite rants, we harken back to Marinaro's strong objections to using a heavier reel. Always believing the advice to balance a rod with its reel as being useless and seriously counterproductive, once again, Vince seems to have learned his lesson from Robert Crompton. In another of Crompton's rare magazine articles, we read his own exasperated insistence that:

> The word "balance" should be barred by law from use in tackle description. The oracle is yet to be born who can PROVE that any rod should "balance" at any certain point. To contend that all rods of a certain weight should be balanced, with a reel of this or that weight is just as absurd. ... Our rod "balances" with, say 25 feet of line out. The cast is then lengthened to 50 feet. This lightens the butt while adding to tip weight, plus water friction. Our "balance" has gone with the wind. Re-cap—even though a "balance" could be effected it can not be maintained. Forget it.[13]

The question of balance, of course, is a bogus issue, despite the seemingly endless clamoring from rod and tackle manufacturers—and despite, too, similar concerns even as expressed by skilled, contemporary makers. Balance, if needed at all, is useful only when a rod is being held in a state of repose—as, for instance, when strolling with the rod to or from the stream, or when lolling about with rod-

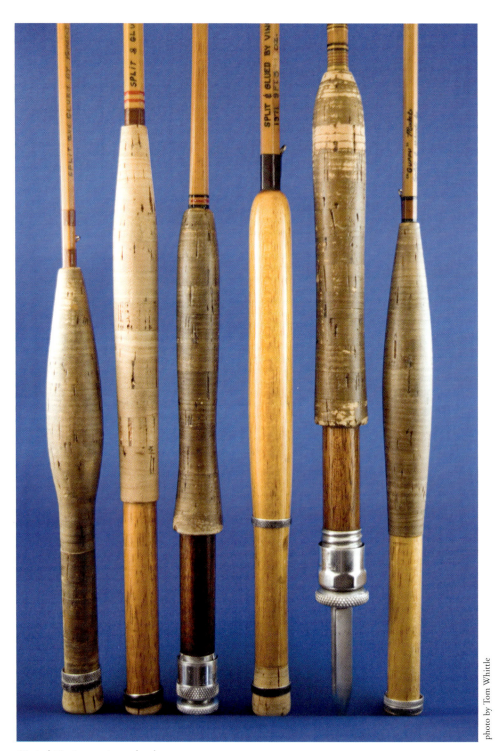

Typical Marinaro grips and reel seats

in-hand, lighting a cigar or picking one's nose. But if this were the extent of the fishing public's concern, we should have enforced, long since, an overdue end to a most silly discussion. Just grab the damn thing wherever it happens to balance, and you're good to go!

Unfortunately, both fly-fishers and the marketing community alike have gotten the notion into their heads that, for a trout rod to **cast** well, it must be balanced by a reel of adequate weight. Rubbish! A rod's performance is affected by a wide variety of dynamic factors, but the most killing in every casting situation is the effect of extra weight, whether located in the fly, the leader, the line, the knots, the rod itself or the reel. When casting, many laws of physics are put into play, but especially those of inertia on the one hand and momentum on the other with every gram of added weight inviting both of these to affect the cast adversely. All weight, wherever it is located, must be set into motion, stopped, then moved again in an opposite direction. And with more weight, still more physical effort must be exerted and dissipated, all functioning negatively to dampen the rod's performance exactly in the manner of an increasingly heavy pendulum. The initially clumsy rod now becomes loggy with the addition of a heavier, "balancing" reel.

Even so, it has been argued that, because a reel is located at the fulcrum of one's casting motion, any weight pivoting through this neutral position will not come into play. If this were true, there would be a good case for the "balancing reel," but the argument has no merit. Watch someone cast: There really is no identifiable pivot-point, and the wrist certainly does not remain "neutral." Only smaller, bamboo rods of 7 feet or less (having no need for a balancing reel in the first place) can be cast, or pivoted, with the wrist alone, but even then, usually only for close-up fishing.

Actually, a number of pivots (or points of articulation) show up as a rod is cast. "Pivoting," if it can be traced at all, flows dynamically over a wide area, from one's waist, to the shoulder, elbow, wrist and fingers—then it "springs" to somewhere down the length of the butt. These motions effectively negate the idea of a fulcrum entirely because the entire rod and reel, along with one's arm and shoulder, are all fully engaged in the casting motion. Thus, any reel exceeding the minimum possible weight will begin to function more like a ball-and-chain than anything else, deterring the rod from performing up its design potential and tiring the caster. Tournament casters have known this for a very long time, often discarding their reels entirely—an unacceptable solution for the fly-fisher, of course, although we would insist that the basic principle of physics remains true. Crompton was quite correct in his objections, as was Vince. All unnecessary weight is an enemy to every good rod taper, just as it is to every good cast.

Learning to Build

COLLEGE, MARRIED, THEN ABROAD

One might have supposed from much of the above that Vince's earlier years consisted of nothing but tying flies, fishing and building rods. There may be something to that view, but surely not to the extent we have thrust upon him. Except for his extreme self-reliance and the obsession with fishing, in all other ways Vince's early days were like those of any other ordinary, young man. He had all the usual dreams and aspirations, even becoming proficient at playing the violin at a young age. His outdoor activities were certainly important, but so was his future. As was frequently the case among immigrant families, expectations for the sprouts were held particularly high, and Vince's parents were determined that each of them should pursue a professional career of one sort or another.

Vince's father died in 1921, but even in those early years the family businesses were successful and his parents were able to set aside substantial trusts for the children's education. However, an important condition was placed upon each child to access those funds—none was to marry until their education was complete. Vince's sister, Marietta, took degrees to become a piano teacher and assistant principal in the local school system. His oldest brother, Alfonso, began studying for the priesthood, but left the program and turned his attention to the business world. Another older brother, Nicholas, became a physician and director of a sanatorium in Connecticut. Theodore, the youngest in the family, also began medical school, but found it not to his liking, and instead, started a successful carpentry business.

But times were hard in the 1930s, and life in western Pennsylvania, as elsewhere, was devastating for many families. In the counties surrounding Pittsburgh, rural economies had long been dependent upon either agriculture or coal mining, but by the late 1920s, farming had become a desperate proposition, and several major coal seams were nearly worked out. With the onset of the Great Depression, coal mines either down-sized their operations to skeleton crews or simply shut down, causing an equally devastating impact on the manufacturing and commercial sectors. Up and down the main streets in nearly every small town, hardware and dry-goods stores, bakeries, five-and-dimes and farm cooperatives sat empty, with boarded doors and shuttered windows. Countless families were left destitute. Many of the younger folks eventually found work at various Civilian Conservation Corps projects, while others scrounged coal from the fields at night to sell among friends and relatives for whatever they could get—called "bootlegging." Saddest of all, were the many shattered families who just packed up what they could and wandered off to parts unknown.

Vince's home in Butler:—1930s

We don't know how Vince's mother managed the ravages of the Depression, but between her own family in Butler and a little financial help from Vince's uncle, Father Vincenzo, there must have been adequate assistance to keep the family going. Vince's daughter, Vincentia, reports that Rosina's relationship with her deceased husband's side of the family in Reynoldsville deteriorated in the years following Giuseppi's death, so help was not sought there. But Vincentia also reports that one of Rosina's sisters had a farm nearby where the Marinaros often helped out, so, with a regular source of food from the farm, they found their way. No one in the family knows how the money for the children's education might have been protected during the "Panic of '29," but somehow those funds remained secure.

Prior to "Black Thursday," Vince's older siblings already had left home, several had received their education and were married. In some measure, Rosina's load must have felt eased, but both Vince and his younger brother, Theodore, were still at home. Soon, Vince would leave for college, but not until a full year after his 1929 high school graduation, and Theodore would remain home still longer. The years of the Great Depression ground on and on....

Ever since Vince had been a child, his parents expected him to become a lawyer, very likely in response to certain of his father's friends who had become successful in the profession. So, in 1930, Vince headed off to nearby Pittsburgh where he began college life at Duquesne University—receiving his B.A. in business in 1934. All very industrious and admirable, but it's likely he devoted as much attention to fishing and rod-building as he did to studying. At the very least, he had access to a good research library and would have had ample opportunity to pursue his correspondence with Holden and Crompton. In fact, Vince told me that, although he still hadn't developed satisfactory tapers, he had become a pretty good maker by the time he graduated from college.

In 1936, Vince entered Duquesne's three-year program leading to a degree in law, but, technically, although he had completed college, he was not yet free from the terms of his trust fund. Nevertheless, always headstrong and determined to do things his own way, Vince tip-toed behind the trustees and, in a private ceremony before a Justice of the

Peace, he secretly married his young love, Martha Symons. Given the closeness of the family, we can't imagine that such a thing would have been kept secret for long. Apparently it wasn't, because the two held a proper church wedding some months after, and their first child, Vincentia, was born toward the end of the following year. Vincentia says she doesn't know what happened to the stern conditions of the trust, but admitted that, as rumor has it, lawyers will sometimes find it fruitful to redress such annoyances.

The whirlwind marriage took everyone by surprise and caused something of a scandal within the family, yet in my conversations with Vincentia, I learned that Martha loved to tell the story of her first meeting with Vince—it's just so typical of him, really "vintage Vince." Martha had recently completed her training in Lancaster, Pennsylvania to be a nurse and was working at her first job in Pittsburgh. Vince had only just begun law school, and the two met while living in the same chaperoned boarding house near Duquesne University. Although they were somewhat acquainted, no courtship had begun, but then, one ordinary evening as they happened to be passing on the staircase, Vince simply said to Martha, "I think you're the girl

Learning to Build

One of Vince's old Kodak cameras

I'm going to marry." Presumably, Martha would have had something to say about the matter, but Vince was not entirely without charm among the ladies, so in 1936, they slipped off to a Pittsburgh Justice of the Peace.

Cocky and brash as we all knew him to be, it was common for Vince to hold strong opinions even before investigating a topic, and in later years we loved to tease him when he'd conjure some elaborate theory right off the top of his head. But more often than not, these would be borne out by experience.

By 1939, Marinaro had completed his law degree at Duquesne and returned with Martha and Vincentia to Vince's family home in Butler—Vince struggling to find work and Martha with a second child on the way. Then, debilitating health problems suddenly struck both of them. Immediately following the premature delivery of their second child, Alphonse, Martha lapsed into a coma that lasted for several months. Vince, coping with this and his inability to find work, sank into a deep depression. The care of Vincentia and the newborn infant was spread among family members, but when Martha emerged from the coma, she was taken back to her parents in Minnesota for a long period of recovery.

Nearly two years passed, constituting the blackest of black holes for the Marinaro family, but Martha finally became well enough to return to Butler. The family lacked an income, but at least the four of them were reunited. Vince, still not well and still without work, was able to do little but build rods. We might think that making fly rods under such desperate circumstances would be a frivolous waste of time with little consolation, yet, as Vincentia explained, the opportunity for her father to do something he loved probably served as a kind of therapy and gave him the peace of mind to endure.

At long last, came a job offer. An old friend of the family had been successful in locating a position for Vince within Pennsylvania's Department of Revenue, so in 1942, the Marinaros (Vince, Martha, Vincentia and Alphonse) moved to Harrisburg.

By all family reports, Vince was always grateful for the opportunity to attend college and to practice law as well, even while his deepest sense of fulfillment was in the out-of-doors. Hunting and fishing were not interests shared by his brothers or other family members, and it was no secret that, despite his vocational path, Vince had been blazing his own peculiar trail from the start. Career pursuits and his involvement with outdoor activities had always run down something like parallel tracks, and this same dual-existence continued throughout his professional life and into the years of retirement.

Interestingly, Vincentia told us that her father was never especially eager to become a lawyer, wishing instead he had been free to study archeology or geology. Along with other early interests, Vince remained fascinated with Native American artifacts and studied several of the Pennsylvania and western New York tribes—the Lenni Lenape, the Susquehannocks and the Erie. He could identify their arrowheads, axes and pottery, and following their lead, even hunted with his own bows built from local Osage Orange—the most successful of which remains with his daughter-in-law, Maggie.

It's useful to consider these two stories of Vince's life extending into the 1940s. On the one hand, there was the fiercely independent and introverted side of his personality, involving all his solitary obsessions with hunting, fishing, fly-tying, rod-making and his frequent correspondence with Holden, Crompton and others (not to mention those lonely years of sickness, isolation and depression). On the other hand, there was his more public life—involvements that included college, obtaining a law degree, marriage, beginning a family, and meeting professional

Martha Marinaro and baby Vincentia

Vince in Butler: 1950s

Vince enjoying his old pipe–1984

expectations in his field. We mention this not as a mere observation for, truly, Vince seems to have lived his entire life torn between his private world and his communal responsibilities. As Vincentia explained to me, her father "was a man who lived two lives," never really striking a comfortable balance between them.

The world of "grown-ups" would have it that family and public duties should come first, of course, with photography, stream entomology, wing-shooting, rod-making, fly-tying and so forth being satisfied to pull up the rear of the line. It's not that Vince would have disagreed: After all, he and Martha *did* successfully raise a family of five bright children, and he did become both accomplished and highly respected in his profession. But Vince was simply Vince—never at peace living quite the way the world prescribed. Martha knew this from the start. It was not easy, but she accepted, understood and was tolerant of Vince's many excursions and the gangs of fishermen and hunters traipsing through the house.

Indeed, had Marinaro's devotion been only for family and community and his genius directed only at the practice of law, life could have been simple. Grown-ups would have smiled their approval and Norman Rockwell may have painted his portrait. But Vince was a deeply complicated man, eccentric and divided in his devotions, and the "gift" of genius comes at a far higher cost than most would suspect. Marinaro's personal interests were not mere hobbies, but profound and consuming needs, and although I did not know him until after his retirement from Pennsylvania government, I believe his personal pursuits always absorbed the better half of his attention.

We have no idea how many rods Marinaro may have built during his early years (nor, shudder, what became of them)

but Vincentia says that, both before and after the family's 1942 move to Harrisburg, she recalls seeing one after another emerge. One of her earliest memories from Butler—when she was just 5 years old, and before the move—is how she thought of herself as "daddy's little girl" and always wanted to be at his side. One evening, when Vince said he was going to work on fly rods, she begged to be allowed to help, and was, surprisingly, invited to join him. However, she was also told that, because he was going to prepare strips and glue up some sections, she was not to touch anything. (Hot, hide glue is damnably messy stuff and the gluing process is critical.) Vincentia remembers fondly that she and her daddy wiled-away the entire night in the kitchen—Vince, working at the table, patiently explaining every step he was taking; she, perched on the old, coal stove with her blanket, alternately begging to help, but fighting desperately to stay awake.

Vincentia also remembers her sixth birthday, shortly after Martha and Vince relocated their family to Harrisburg—the only time she ever got a little swat across her behind! Vincie said her daddy had just finished a rod and she was given permission to play with it. She was also instructed to be careful, not to damage the rod in any way. Delighted and eager to play, she skipped down the hall, waving her new toy. You know the rest of the story.... Alas, she tripped and fell, the rod buckling beneath her and shattering, irreparably, into splinters. Birthday or no, Vincie says she got her little behind paddled.

As to all those missing rods from the early years, we suppose that, because Vince was not a pack-rat—perhaps worrying, too, that his tapers could fall into the hands of others—he may simply have destroyed the rods that no longer suited him. Vince kept nothing that was not of immediate use. In later years he lamented to me that, back in the early 1960s, when he and Martha moved across the river from Harrisburg to Mechanicsburg, he simply stuffed his excess culms rudely into a trailer and hauled them off to a local dump. But this wasn't just cane. It was the treasured, "pre-Embargo" cane! So, Tom and I wonder if, however ignominious, his early rods may have met with a similar fate.

CHAPTER THREE

HEYDAY IN THE CUMBERLAND VALLEY

The year was 1942. Vince was 31 years old and had just accepted his first job in Harrisburg with Pennsylvania's Department of Revenue. Within a decade, he would become a corporate tax law specialist in that agency, a position he held until his retirement. Charlie Fox, in a 1989 interview with Eugene Macri, Jr., recalls meeting Vince for the first time and how they began a lifelong friendship:

> Vince loved this stream *[the Letort]*, but I took him other places. He was a stranger in these parts. I took him to a lot of different places on the *[Yellow]* Breeches. We would hook up every evening. The way this thing started, well I believe it was in 1942, and I was the editor of the *Pennsylvania Angler*. And in came Vince unannounced. He said, "I'm interested in an article you wrote about a yellow mayfly." Well, we talked and talked, and I found out that he had no car. He lived up on Penns Street and had access to the bus. He travelled *[sic]* back and forth by bus. I said, "Do you want to go out fishing with me?" And he did, I don't remember where we went first, but he was all tickled. He said, "I'll talk to Martha, and set it up so that you could come up and have dinner with us. You bring your stuff along in the car and as soon as dinner is over–we'll take off!" That's how Vince got around here. Hell, if I hadn't done that I don't know how he would have fished.[1]

Later, Vince bought a car, but he absolutely hated to drive, and through the years a great many of us continued Charlie's stream-side, chauffeur service. In every important way, Fox's recollection begins at the beginning, but in my recent conversations with Vince's daughter, Vincentia, I also learned that Marinaro spent some time in the Cumberland Valley about eight years prior to moving his family here in 1942. Now, either Vince never spoke to me of those first experiences in the area, or for some reason, I just wasn't paying attention, but when Vince died, I remember being surprised to read an obituary reporting that he took his law degree at Carlisle's Dickinson School of Law in 1937. I simply thought the information was mistaken because I knew that degree had been awarded by Duquesne University in 1939, and put the matter out of my mind. Well, it was mistaken, but not entirely.

Apparently, Vince first came to Carlisle in 1934, just after receiving his B.A. from Duquesne. He entered Dickinson's law school and was scheduled to graduate with the class of 1937, but following his first year, family difficulties caused him to withdraw from the program. So, in 1936, Vince began law school once again, this time back at Duquesne. Nothing of his Cumberland Valley fishing experiences can be resurrected from those earliest years, but I'm sure Vince would have given it a shot. It's true that the local limestone streams slept quietly in those times, but Vince could sniff a trout a mile off, and it's impossible to imagine he was so absorbed with studies that he never poked his nose into the wind.

Dawn of an Era

Fox and Marinaro became the greatest of friends almost as soon as they met—nearly inseparable fishing companions—yet the two were as different in temperament as the otter from the badger. Within only a year or so, they joined their love of Cumberland Valley fly-fishing to studies on trout-feeding habits, habitat protection, entomology and

Charlie and Vince get into a good one on the Letort—1960s

They get a first look

Charlie lands it for Vince

fly-tying patterns. In the early 1940s these local, limestone streams were little known beyond the surrounding areas, but by the start of the next decade, Fox, Marinaro, and a dozen compatriots would change all that. In fact, their work began a fly-fishing revolution. Perhaps this is something difficult to appreciate in these jaded days of instant access to information and overnight experts, but their new studies (particularly in the case of Marinaro) eventually attained international acclaim. Countless experiments and investigations by these several men resulted in a dozen books and scores of magazine articles, and in short time, Marinaro, Fox and the local limestoners had become legendary.

September "Tricos"

From the late 1940s onward, Pennsylvania's chalk streams began to enjoy a cachet, and their champions left behind a literature equal in significance (if not historical depth) to Pennsylvania's Brodheads or New York's Catskill streams. Not that the legends emerging from the Cumberland Valley fishery boasted the venerable, old clubs or social prominence of other areas, but the quality of fishing, the rich local history and the many stream-side discoveries truly put these limestoners on the map. Happily, class privilege, snob-appeal and exclusivity were never the order of the day among these fishermen, but everything else about fly-fishing here created a tradition as remarkable as could be found anywhere. Most importantly (and unlike the best waters in the Catskills, the Berkshires or the Poconos), the limestone streams of the Cumberland Valley have remained, to this day, free from privately-managed clubs and posted property. Spotted here and there, a few landowners occasionally restrict trespassing, but public access to fishing has never been impacted in anything but the smallest way.

These prime, trout-fishing waters, just to the west of Harrisburg, were never regarded by urbanites and their families as a primary vacation destination—the perfect area for lengthy, rustic getaways. Certainly, there has always been a great fascination among tourists for the many little towns like Carlisle, Boiling Springs and Newville with their log and limestone architecture. Throughout the area, too, tourists can trace a centuries-old trail of history, dating back to the first settlers and the Revolutionary and Civil Wars. One finds both charm and a sense of peace in the old-world appeal of an almost manicured, agricultural landscape, but the inhabitants of New York, Philadelphia, Baltimore or Washington, D.C. typically chose the crisp mountain air and remote, wooded settings over the bucolic (and humid) farmland of Cumberland Valley.

Thus, the patterns of socially prominent vacationers to other areas had a certain, negative impact on the attention these limestone fisheries received. Well, it wasn't "negative," exactly. It was only that the local streams escaped wide public attention—and that can't be all bad. Prior to the 1950s, most trout-fishing literature in the East focused on the romance of waters in more secluded places—the Catskills, the Adirondacks, or Maine's Rangeley Lakes, all accessible by a day's train ride from large, urban centers. Acclaim and news of favorite family destinations tend to follow leisure and wealth.

Manistee brookie to the fly

As a first, noteworthy exception to the pattern, however, we read in the letters of Theodore Gordon that this most famous of all American fly-fishermen recalls spending some summers of his youth near Carlisle, exploring the Cumberland Valley's streams. Gordon doesn't elaborate on the matter but, by golly, he was here! Surely, to be able to say "Theodore Gordon Fished Here" remains a fine point of local pride, but of greater attraction are those notes of his that carry our imagination back to the 1860s when limestone brook trout reigned supreme. Gordon makes only passing mention of those early years, but we can't help wondering what it must have been like to creep through the meadows, to peer into crystal springs or mill ponds and spy the fish below—brilliant, native brookies, maybe up to two pounds or more, dapping the surface. To be among the first to cast a fly on those innocent, glassy currents must have seemed like a gift from the gods.

But most interestingly, because we know that fly-fishing literature on these limestoners actually reaches back many decades prior to Gordon's youth, our query is answered in other writings, still more compelling than those nostalgic wisps of Gordon's presence as a boy. During the late 1820s (as Paul Schullery notes in *American Fly Fishing,* 1987) George Gibson became one of America's first fishing journalists. Although Gibson claims to have fished the Cumberland Valley's streams regularly even before 1800, the first news of his piscatorial adventures appeared in 1829 when he became a "fishing correspondent" for the newly-founded *American Turf Register and Sporting Magazine*. Schullery writes that this Baltimore-based magazine was the nation's very first periodical dedicated to sporting events and activities. Its chief concern was the race track, but it also had regular sections dedicated to hunting and fishing. Schullery gives George Gibson and Pennsylvania's earliest fishing literature even greater attention in his *Royal Coachman*.[2]

Certainly, a few local fishermen had always been aware of Gibson's entries in *The Turf Register*, but it was Charlie Fox who first made some of Gibson's fascinating articles fully public. These were delivered to the Fly Fishers' Club of Harrisburg in a 1947 paper. Local pride and love for the history of fly-fishing literature are reasons enough to quote Gibson's charming first entry of September of 1829 at length:

Sir,—-You ask me for a paper on trout and trout fishing in Pennsylvania. This you shall have with pleasure, but as I am no more than a practical man in such matters, you cannot expect much.

Although I commenced wetting flies in times long gone by, my experience extends only to Cumberland County; but trout were formerly found in all the limestone springs in the state. Owing, however, to the villainous practice of netting them, they are extinct in some streams and scarce in others. *[Gibson's comment pertains to brook trout. Browns and rainbows were not introduced to these waters until nearly a hundred years later.]*

In Cumberland there are three good trout streams. Big Spring, west of Carlisle, runs a distance of five miles and turns six flouring mills and affords fine sport almost the whole distance. A law of the state makes it penal to net in this stream and forbids the taking of trout between the months of July and April. It is the only spring branch in the state protected by law; the good effect of which is so apparent that it is hoped other streams will receive the same like protections.

The Letort, which flows past Carlisle, is another good stream. It runs about four miles through meadow grounds and turns three flouring mills. It formerly afforded excellent sport, but owing to the infamous practice of netting and setting night lines, the fish have been much lessened in numbers and size.

Silver Spring, east and north of Carlisle, runs half a mile and turns two flouring mills. This stream breeds the best and largest trout of any in the state—they are from one to three pounds; and it requires nice tackle and an experienced hand to land them.

The rod used is fifteen or sixteen feet long, very delicate, and throws from twenty to thirty feet of line—and in all these streams the fisherman is most successful with the artificial fly. The color used in April is black or dark brown; in May, dun or red hackle; in June and July imitations of the millers or candle flies are found best.

The habits of this fish are soon told. In winter they seek the deep calm pool, and seldom or ever change their position or go abroad. In spring and summer, they delight in rapids. They feed on flies, worms, water snails, and prey on small fish. They spawn in September; and for that purpose select ripples and shoal water, with gravel and sandy bottom. When the spawn or young trout is brought out, it approaches close to the shore, or gets into very shoal water to protect it from larger fish, for it is a fact that the large trout will kill and eat the small ones. As he gains strength and size he returns to deep water, and in time becomes the monarch of his pool.

In conclusion I will give you my first evening at Silver Spring. It was long since with a party of five, and all bait fishers except myself. The proprietor of the ground advised me to use bait. He had never been successful with a fly. I would not be advised. The evening was fine, a cloud obscured the sun, a gentle breeze rippled the water, and such was my success, that in less than one hour, I landed twenty trout, from one to two pounds each. The proprietor cried "enough"—I asked for the privilege of another cast. I made one, and hooked a large trout with my bobbing fly, and in playing him, another one of equal size ran at, and was hooked by my tail fly, and both were landed in handsome style. The last throw was fatal to my sports in that pool—for I never afterwards was a welcome visitor; but many is the day I have met with nearly as good success in the other millpool.[3]

Gibson's accounts of those early days of fishing seem almost too good to be true, but imagine the fun he might have had with a dry fly and a little 7 1/2-foot Garrison! It is true, as Gibson reports, that early netting practices had all but decimated brook trout populations in many Cumberland Valley streams. But even though the practice was not tolerated later in Gibson's century, the once-famous brookies never returned in anything like the numbers witnessed during his day.

Two noteworthy exceptions, however, beg our attention—Cedar Run in New Cumberland and Big Spring in Newville. In these two streams, native brook trout continued to thrive even in the midst of intimidating competition from brown trout, first stocked in local waters during the 1930s. Cedar Run had always been a perfect little jewel of a stream and one of the county's favorite fisheries from Gibson's time forward, as all local fisherman "of a certain age" will attest. Today, sadly, the stream suffocates under the influence of suburban sprawl—the ignominy of its death throes escalating since the 1950s. Some stretches of Cedar Run were channelized to fall between the parking lots of a mall, a prison, a used car lot, and the like, while still other areas weep herbicides, pesticides and fertilizers, thanks to the many lovely, green lawns rolling down to its banks. No doubt, many folks in our modern age boast these as the fruits of progress.

Meanwhile, 30 miles west, Big Spring continued to be regarded as among the most productive of the Cumberland Valley's spring creeks. Despite heavy poaching, the uppermost mile or so of the stream retained its original strain of brook trout well into the 1960s—in earlier years, holding fish in numbers that rivaled any other watershed in the eastern U.S. (certainly, excepting Maine's Rangeley Lakes and the Rapid River). It's interesting that even though local netting practices are thought to have ended during the late 1800s, our 1890 photograph tells a different story. Though the fish are not large, that's a nice haul of Big Spring "contraband."

But Big Spring, too, eventually fell. The stream first became damaged through its middle and lower stretches after the 1953 introduction of a small, commercial fish hatchery—bitterly opposed by Marinaro, Charlie Fox and many others. The 1968 closing of this smaller hatchery might have returned lower portions of the stream to health, but in 1973, the Pennsylvania Fish Commission constructed its own, state-managed hatchery. This facility was built atop the river's spring-fed source and spewed

Netted brookies at McCracken's Mill—1890

Laughlin's Mill—1890

a nitrogen- and phosphorous-rich stew of effluents directly into the headwaters—eventually decimating the fishery below.

The Fish Commission would point with pride, however, to "the ditch," a 300-yard stretch at the headwater that remained artificially rich with food from the hatchery and supported several hundred strong trout. But immediately below this short area, the once-healthy ecosystem became overwhelmed—its oxygen-depleted water running nearly barren through the remaining, four, downstream miles. The State never admitted culpability, but the hatchery was finally shut down in 2001, thanks to tireless efforts by Dr. Jack Black, a senior research scientist at the Roswell Park Cancer Institute, Gene Macri, Ralph Shires, the Cumberland Valley Chapter of Trout Unlimited and a greatly incensed public.

Unlike the county's other limestoners, Big Spring is most fortunate in that it flows through an entirely rural area with only the small village of Newville situated along its downstream end. Understandably, local folks are very protective of the rich heritage of this little stream and the charm of its

Laughlin's Mill today

history. Indeed, the livelihood of an entire community depended upon it ever since the early 1700s when Scottish immigrants first populated the area and began to farm—soon building several flouring mills along the stream.

In the 1730s Newville, like Carlisle, had been an Indian trading post—both villages occupying strategic locations at the crossings of major east-west and north-south trails. From those days forward, and particularly when its mills

Heyday in the Cumberland Valley   63

became active, Newville played host to a constant flow of settlers, travelers and merchants. Soon, there were rooming houses, and in the later 1800s, a comfortable hotel at the railroad station as well. But those early travelers and fishermen were also able to find accommodations at a few of the water-powered mills. In addition to room and board, mill guests could catch all the brookies ever imagined—fishing in the stream or casting to lunkers sulking deep in the millponds. Local lore has it that some of the mills derived greater income from their guests than from the flour.

The most popular "trout mill" was Irwin's (halfway up the stream from Newville), serving as a social hub through the latter part of the 19th century for locals and travelers alike. No one seems to know if its great popularity came about because the owners were more affable and sought the business, or if it was just better suited to fishing and guests. Perhaps they served a high tea or piped each fish to the net...or maybe their pond was easily accessed and held the choice trout.

McFarland's, Irwin's, Piper's and McCracken's. All six mills produced flour, although at the time of the Civil War, McFarland's was producing paper—still later, becoming a mechanized knitting operation. McCracken's, at the top of the chain, was the largest, most powerful and profitable of the six. When rail service finally reached west to Newville, McCracken's enjoyed its hour of fame and was specially commissioned to grind flour for Queen Victoria and her court in England.

The four mills upstream from Newville were all connected by a one-lane, dirt, access road (amusingly called the "Newville Turnpike"), featuring a toll house at the one location where the road crossed the stream. To avoid the inconvenience and cost of traveling to and from Newville, most of the workers and their families from the upper mills lived near the headwaters in a thriving, little hillside-village adjacent to the stream, called Springfield. Although the community has long-since disappeared, many generations of millers were born, went to school and passed to their

Big Spring brookie—1950s

Ginter's was the last of the six mills downstream (established by the ancestors of astronaut and Senator, John Glenn). Just upstream and within Newville itself, lay Laughlin's, the only surviving mill, now beautifully restored to its original state. Between these and the upper end of Big Spring, four additional mills were built—

reward in that little settlement. Where, once, there were more than 50 houses, a school, post office, smithy, bank, church, barrel factory, general store and a cemetery, now there is only a brambled hillside, the old barrel factory, a couple foundations and, set back, an attractive group of newer homes.

Piper's Mill—1890

Spinner's Fording—1890

Springfield was of primary importance to the upper area, but spotted here and there, the houses of mill-workers, farmers and townspeople were built all along both sides of the stream. Since the road crossed only one bridge, fords were located where the stream was shallow, and a number of footbridges spanned the creek as well—all safe from flooding because of a low gradient in this small valley and manageable, surface runoff.

It's sometimes said that technology is fate, but so is geography. By the beginning of the 20th century, Big Spring's water-powered mills—too small to satisfy increasing demands, and too distant from convenient distribution points—were fast becoming an anachronism. All were closed by the first decades of the new century, and all but Laughlin's, either destroyed by fire or wrecking crews. Flour production passed to more accessible locations, and Newville folded once again into its quiet landscape. Although McCracken's was the last to be razed (in 1960), it had been abandoned for decades. As with the others, its dam was removed and the stream restored to its original channel—the mill site now occupied by a fishermen's parking area. Today, only Laughlin's mill, the oldest of the six (and restored by the village), remains in Newville. Though hard to verify, the locals believe this to be one of the most frequently-photographed historical sites in the state.

Lass on East Main Bridge—1890

Following the 2001 closing of the State-run hatchery, Big Spring's struggle to return to its natural condition seems promising, with signs of renewed life already apparent. But, because the stream meanders so very gently downstream through meadows and flats, the flushing-action needed to cleanse years of pollutants and sediment takes place only gradually. More time must pass before a full prognosis can be made, but six years after the hatchery ceased its operations, the upper and middle reaches of the stream are again showing evidence of the old insect hatches, together with promising numbers of stream-bred rainbows and brook-trout fry. And so, with good stewardship from the recently-formed Big Spring Watershed Association and the Cumberland Valley Chapter of Trout Unlimited, it's likely we may soon see the healthy population of native brook trout that Gibson, Gordon, Marinaro and Fox once enjoyed. Big Spring is being watched closely, and already its 2-mile, protective corridor with a no-kill policy is yielding results.

"THE PENNSYLVANIA BOYS"

— *Sparse Grey Hackle*

The happiest times for Cumberland Valley's fishery, its true acclaim, came from the late 1940s forward—this, because Vince Marinaro and Charlie Fox had the foresight to pull together an upstart group of local fly-fishermen who called themselves "The Fly Fishers' Club of Harrisburg." Marinaro coined the club's name, intentionally fashioning it after the Fly Fishers' Club of London and its namesake in New York, but the group became more commonly known as the "Harrisburg Fly-Fishers" (HFF). Its agenda was to hold regular luncheon meetings at which papers would be read and current research shared. Marinaro and Fox, eager to assemble the best efforts of the best fly-fishermen in the area, formed the association early in 1947 and the group quickly began its efforts to study and preserve south-central Pennsylvania's limestone streams.

They understood the heritage of this resource well, knowing that without the kind of attention a group of conservation-minded individuals could muster, the fishery was not likely to survive. Already, patterns of suburbia were stretching west from Harrisburg, reaching deep into rural areas

Vince spies for Charlie—1957

Comparing notes

and endangering some of the finest streams. For decades, livestock had been breaking down the banks, while newer agricultural practices, heavily reliant on chemicals, also began taking a toll in certain locations. Fish-harvesting needed to be controlled; stocking practices enlightened; land-management undertaken. A larger and more public education was required. Interesting, how this group's efforts anticipated, by more than a decade, the formation of Trout Unlimited and similar, national organizations. Still, the demise of both Cedar Run and Big Spring happened very much despite the bitter wars waged by this group—the same, sad result of countless other battles, nationwide.

In their fascinating book, *Limestone Legends* (1997), Norm Shires and Jim Gilford edit the full account of The Fly Fishers' Club of Harrisburg, giving lengthy exposure at last to the many papers and studies undertaken through the years. Paul Schullery was kind enough to write the introduction to this volume, having lived and fished in the Harrisburg area himself for many years. Schullery's introduction makes a particularly interesting point as he acknowledges the unique character of this group and its projects:

> When I consider the most productive and creative fishing clubs in the United States—by which I mean the ones that best combine good company with a nationally influential study of the fishing and its needs—the Fly Fishers' Club of Harrisburg strikes me as different from the rest. Of all of these groups, "those Pennsylvania boys" (as Sparse Gray Hackle called them) seemed to spend a higher percentage of their time fishing right in their own back yards.... Most of the other clubs were based in a city that was, at best, on the edge of a fishing country. Harrisburg is surrounded by its club's fishing country....
>
> I suspect that this immediacy—this sense of being close to the water, even when convened for a club meeting—is one of the things that bring a special neighborliness to the narratives in this book....

The group had no bylaws, no officers, no dues and no requirements for membership other than one's dedication to fly-fishing and nature conservation. We may have created the view that its purposes were only serious-minded, scientific and political, but this wasn't entirely the case. As with any bunch of schoolboys who never quite grew up (pillars of the community or not) there was regular hilarity, practical joking and no small measure of insobriety. The episode of "the noble rock" was one such silly caper (referenced by Gordon Wickstrom in *Notes From An Old Fly Book*, 2001).

Vince told me there was really nothing special about the rock, but on one of his fishing trips to Michigan's Au Sable River (and with his mind on geology or archeology) quite incidentally, he noticed a large stone along the stream that seemed a bit different from others around it. He picked it up and said he just started musing on its origins. One fanciful notion led to the next, and before long, the rock bloomed with emblematic significance, implicating the whole geographical history of Michigan and its social development. The mood passed, Vince said, but as he returned to fishing, he stuck the rock in a vest pocket and carried it home.

Shortly after returning to Pennsylvania, Vince was fishing with his good friend, Bill Fritz, when he pulled the rock out and began to lapse into his former revery, spinning his tale of this "noble rock" and its significance. Then, he gave the rock to Bill. Well, however sincere Vince may have been, "Fritzie," always the joker, wasn't buying *that* malarky! Yet, he pretended to go along with the ceremony and took the rock with him. Each year, ever after, the rock went back and forth between the two, but always when unexpected, and always with a long and inflated speech before an audience of friends. Shortly after Vince died, Bill held a little stream-side ceremony along the Letort where Marinaro owned a piece of property and awarded the noble rock its final resting place in Vince's home water.

Informally, the most important meetings of the HFF took place along the banks of the Letort on the meadows owned by Charlie Fox. In 1945, Charlie purchased a lengthy stretch of property on the creek, just upstream from the southern edge of Carlisle, and eventually built his home at

Bill Fritz on Marinaro's meadow explaining the "Noble Rock"—1986

Fritz offers the benediction

The "Noble Rock's" final resting place in the Letort

its lower end. Because of his boundless hospitality and magnetic personality, Fox was always regarded as the group's ringleader, and for the next couple decades, Ed Koch, Ross Trimmer, Lloyd King, Gene Craighead, Bill Bennett, Ernie Schwiebert, "Bus" Grove, Bob McCafferty, Ed Shenk, Jim Kell, Chauncy Lively, Vince and many others belonging to this "new generation" of fly-fishers, could be found somewhere in the vicinity of Charlie's meadow. Some came to fish; some would work in the stream; still others would do the cooking, and, of course, there were those who showed up to imbibe the sweet nectar of Kentucky and just "fart around." As Jim Gilford explains it:

> Charlie's water on the Letort was a rendezvous.... His meadow was their laboratory, classroom, and conference center. It was there Marinaro experimented with his opaque silhouettes and unraveled the mystery of imitating Jassids and other terrestrials. Fox's meadow, with its selective surface feeders, also was the testing ground for various prototypes of Japanese beetles, ants, and grasshoppers.... And it was the site Charlie chose to experiment with man-made redds and to test some of his management ideas.[4]

Vince was certainly the most frequent visitor to Charlie's meadow, but he usually preferred working either alone or with Fox, Gene Craighead or Bill Bennett. Indeed, much of the stream-side research we read in *A Modern Dry Fly Code* and *The Ring* was carried out on banks of the Letort all along Fox's meadow.

Vince loved to recall, especially, the delights of a little fishing hut that Charlie and others constructed shortly after purchasing the land. The hut was located at the upstream boundary of Fox's property, just at the edge of the stream, and was meant to be reminiscent of the Cotton/Walton arrangement in England—providing perfect, rustic harbor for gentlemen fly-fishers. Unlike Walton's prototype, however, Fox's structure had no architect, lacked the elegant masonry and certainly added nothing by way of property value. Basically, it was a crudely built Quonset hut of wood, tar-paper and an old door and windows. But it was more than serviceable, provided good shelter and ample room for some fly-tying and fishing equipment. Vince often camped-out for long weekends in the little hut—

Heyday in the Cumberland Valley 69

Charlie's fishing hut in the 1950s

sometimes just because he liked being there, but also because he was conducting experiments for his first book. In "A Backward Look," Marinaro's introductory essay to the 1970 edition of *A Modern Dry Fly Code*, we read:

> It was during this early period that Charles Fox acquired his holding on the Letort and set up a fishing hut before he built his home there. We were constant companions in those days, brought together by a common bond, our total devotion to the wonderful world of trout and fly-fishing. I spent a lot of time in that hut, on weekends and vacation periods. In it there had been placed, by Bob McCafferty, a professional flytier and mutual friend, a rather large and elaborate chest containing a wealth of fly-tying materials–a really fine gift.... It was a fine arrangement. The water was only a few feet away from the hut and the fly-tying bench. The trout rose steadily to the daily fall of beetles. I had only to tie a fly, rush out, and give it an immediate trial. Constantly goaded by repeated refusals from the trout, I continued to fashion numerous unsuccessful models of the beetle.... [5]

Those were the good old days, but as expected, the hut and most of its old friends are no more. The site is now spanned by I-81's bridge over the troubled Letort, and those old regulars have passed on to deeper pools. But, even while Charlie's meadow and the fishing hut became holy ground for Vince and the rest of the gang, similar activities took place along the banks of other streams, and all fueled the dozens of luncheon papers to follow.

Among the group's many experiments, there were several early attempts to stock the Letort and Cedar Run with the eastern Green Drake mayfly (*Ephemera guttulata*). Expert advice on the best methods was sought from stream entomologists as well as from Edward Hewitt, who had written extensively about his own, similar efforts on the Neversink. The first attempt, in 1945, involved capturing emerging Green Drake duns from Stone Creek, about 70 miles distant. Alas, although several hundred mayflies were transported back to the Letort and released, none was seen again.

In the following year, the group traveled to Honey Creek to gather mating spinners. The flies were netted and placed in large tubs of water where they deposited what must have been hundreds of thousands of eggs—these, becoming attached to layers of burlap placed on the bottoms of the tubs. The tubs were taken back to Carlisle, and the egg-laden cloths then placed at selected spots in the stream. It seemed like a good technique, but met with only brief and limited success, and within a few years the Drake was again absent from the Letort. Indeed, the method was sound because such transplants had been successful in other water, but for some reason, conditions on the Letort simply wouldn't support Green Drake propagation.

Gladys and Charlie Fox (r), Vince, and guest along the Letort

In a different experiment, Charlie and others built a few spawning beds for the Letort's browns. The trick was to identify stretches that were of proper depth and flow, but these areas also had to be near roads because of the need to move tons of round, river gravel into place. One ideal location happened to be at the end of a lane directly adjacent to Fox's home, while another was just upstream near the Bonny Brook quarry. Here, truck-loads of gravel were evenly distributed to create a solid layer along the stream bed, and in the very first season, dozens of spawning trout took advantage of their new quarters. Fox noted, however, that the fish were highly competitive, chasing each other fiercely, and in their efforts to find the right mate and create redds, they often destroyed existing nests.

Fox's solution was simple: Construct a series of open "stalls" along the bottom, where mating fish would be unseen and undisturbed by the others. Quickly, several sub-surface, rock walls were built in the spawning areas, and the once-open and brawling free-for-all was converted to a steamy bordello with corridors of discrete rooms. None of this could remain effective in a freestone creek, but like Big Spring to the west, the Letort flows across a low gradient, is fed entirely by springs, and while the stream occasionally swells its banks, it never experiences the surges of flooding. Now, decades later, the Cumberland Valley Chapter of Trout Unlimited continues with regular touch-up work, and the redds in front of Charlie's former home remain a popular gathering spot for late fall's *Salmo trutta* revelers.

Stream-work aside, from the late 1940s on, the group's more "official" meetings took place in the old Harrisburger Hotel, at first, with weekly luncheons scheduled year-round. Frequently, one or another of the members prepared a paper that would be read before the group. More than 20 such studies in the first year alone, these were intended to be collected for future binding into a complete library. A great many of the papers were indeed preserved, and several provided the impetus for subsequent books or articles published in prominent fly-fishing magazines. Yet the papers were never bound into a single publication until Shires and Gilford's 1997 initiative.

Ross Trimmer "advises" Vince

Heyday in the Cumberland Valley

Speakers were never in short supply, and the group's enthusiasm for discovery grew to be infectious. One of the earliest papers was prepared by Sparse Grey Hackle (Alfred W. Miller), who, after fishing the limestone waters with Marinaro and Fox during the previous summer, delivered an essay he titled "The Pennsylvania Boys." We do not have that paper in its original, but Sparse later read a somewhat altered version in its entirety to the Anglers' Club of New York, and in 1948, the piece finally appeared as an article in the *Journal of the Anglers' Club of New York*. Contained in that article, are some of Sparse's prophetic words:

> Those who think that the center of angling progress and sophistication is in the Catskills would change their minds if they were to spend a week fishing around Harrisburg, Pennsylvania, as I did this summer. They would be convinced, as I was, that the angling progress of the future will come from there, in part at least....
>
> But they also have a sizeable group of fishermen who, for expertness, sophistication, and sporting idealism, at least equal anything we can boast of and for activities far surpass us....
>
> These Pennsylvania boys laugh at the idea that the pattern doesn't matter if you handle it correctly and insist that it is necessary to imitate exactly the hatch on the water, use fine gut, and fish delicately and far off to achieve consistent success. They read Halford and believe what he says. Their average knowledge of stream entomology would put the average Anglers' Club member to shame, and they keep emergence tables, either mental or written, as a matter of course. And they put their fish back. It is not surprising that such men are conservation minded. They lug big boulders to build deflectors; they cut trees to anchor in the stream; they pile in brush to harbor insects....
>
> It may sound a bit sour to say so, but it seems to me that these are the men we used to be, carrying on from the point where we left off doing things and began merely talking about them. They are breaking new ground, and if they do not rise from it a fine crop of new advances and increased knowledge, I will be much mistaken.[6]

As it happened, Sparse was entirely correct in his prediction. Consider the outpouring of literature from the following writers—all either directly involved with the work of the HFF or on intimate terms with the limestone waters and their local champions: Charlie Wetzel's *Practical Fly-Fishing* (1943) and *Trout Flies, Naturals and Imitations* (1955), Vince Marinaro's *A Modern Dry Fly Code* (1950) and *In the Ring of the Rise* (1976), Alvin "Bus" Grove's *Lure and Lore of Trout Fishing* (1951), Charlie Fox's *This Wonderful World of Trout* (1963) and *Rising Trout* (1967), Ed Koch's *Fishing the Midge* (1972), Ed Shenk's *Fly Rod Trouting* (1989), and Don Holbrook and Ed Koch's *Midge Magic* (2001). We were also tempted to include the works of Ernest Schwiebert (despite his many publications carrying far afield from the Cumberland Valley) because, from the late 1950s onward, Ernie and the limestone gang remained thicker than thieves. In addition to books, we could also include the dozens of major, magazine articles by these and other writers.

Edward R. Hewitt

After its first year, the HFF suspended its weekly luncheons and began, instead, a series of annual banquets (these continue), including formal presentations by well-known, fly-fishing authorities. The first, featured, guest speaker was Edward R. Hewitt, "The Dean of American Fly-Fishing," as he was introduced by Charlie Fox. No stranger to the region, Hewitt had explored the area's limestone streams in earlier years with George LaBranche, continuing his more recent visits to fish and compare notes with Marinaro and Fox. So, in 1947, Hewitt and Sparse jumped a train in New York, traveled to Harrisburg and joined in the premier, banquet celebration. What a pair these two must have made—the imperious, privileged and highly-opinionated Hewitt, and the jocular, populist, chocked-with-tall-tales Sparse! Who wouldn't love to have a recording of their conversations to and from Harrisburg?

Hewitt, during those years, was conducting a variety of experiments on the Neversink with his "window box"—a device that allowed the viewer to look into a volume of water and inspect a floating fly in the same manner as might the trout. Vince was enormously impressed with this work, and soon undertook his own similar studies, devising photographic experiments through his specially constructed "slant tank." Vince's contraption enabled him to peer through the slanted glass at the underside of the surface film and to record the effects of refracted and mirrored light. In this manner, the peculiar visual patterns created by both natural and artificial flies could be documented—the purpose of which was to create sight-patterns in his artificials resembling what a trout would see in the naturals. Most especially, Vince became fascinated with the manner in which a floating fly first entered a trout's "cone of vision." Although early results from this research formed a basis for much of *A Modern Dry Fly Code*, Vince's work continued off and on for many more years, finally receiving full and detailed attention in *The Ring*.

While times have changed greatly for both the Cumberland Valley fishery and the old HFF, the tradition of annual banquets continues uninterrupted. The list of guest speakers is long, indeed, but a selection includes: Lou Fierabend, Joe Brooks, Lee Wulff, George Harvey, Charlie Fox, Lefty Kreh, Arnold Gingrich, Alvin Grove, Charlie Wetzel, Fred Everett, Ed Shenk, Eric Leiser, Ed Zern, Joe Humphries, Carl Richards, Dave Whitlock, Art Flick, Leonard Wright, Leon Chandler, Jim Bashline, Barry and Cathy Beck, Dick Talleur, Ed Jaworowski and, of course, Ernie Schwiebert.

Although the original, weekly luncheons had been abandoned early, the many studies and papers carried on—no longer read before the full group, but finding their way into various publications. In 1988 the luncheons resumed, but as annual events at which papers would be read once again. Without question, the HFF continues to good purpose, but over the many years it has become a large and disparate group and the once-singular focus of that tightly-knit group found along Fox's meadow is no more.

The efforts of those old fellows were, no doubt, repeated in many other areas across the country—the best intentions of gentlemen coming together with a mutual trust, a common purpose, and a deep and patient respect for the natural world. Looking back, Tom and I can't help but lament the passing of that old comradery and the excitement of new discoveries, but we suppose such changes are a sign of our times. How different was then from today—now, with newly-equipped fly-fishers sporting high-end equipment and every possible gadget; satisfied to read a couple fish-and-tell magazines; fly in, hire a guide; power-up the "blackberry" (gotta stay in touch with the office), and breeze in and out of some stream for a quick fix. For such people, the idea of personal discovery, patience and habitat protection would seem entirely a thing of the past.

Vince plays a good fish on the Letort—1971

TO DEAL WITH A LIMESTONER

Within the enormously fertile atmosphere of this new era, Marinaro began the most prolific work of his fly-fishing career. Immediately upon his 1942 arrival in the Cumberland Valley, Vince began to reckon with spring creeks that were vastly different from the hardscrabble, freestone, mountain streams where he learned to cast a fly. This new opponent required him to face-off with a different kind of water. Here, he found eight, meandering, low-gradient, meadow brooks with alkaline-rich, spring-fed water, teaming year-round with insect life. Cedar Run, Silver Spring, Hogestown Run, the Letort, the Yellow Breeches, Big Spring, Green Spring and Falling Spring all provided superb fishing for the public, while two or three others remained small, secret treasures. None but the 35-mile-long Yellow Breeches flows over a course of more than 7 miles, and all present the same maddening challenge of highly technical fishing.

Temperatures in these spring creeks are moderated throughout the year by a limestone aquifer that provides both large and minute honeycombs of seeping springs—sources of water that emerge at less than 60-degrees. Consequently, these creeks warm only slightly in summer, and cool but little in winter. Along certain stretches, a stream's flow will open out somewhat as it sweeps around bends or stumps, while through other areas one finds beds of silt and smaller, silky currents braiding a tangle of channels through mats of elodea, duckweed and watercress. Many swampy areas lie adjacent to these spring creeks, just as do tall grasses, bushes and banks of willow trees overhanging the water's edge.

The streams are also very different from one another, but in ways one may not expect. It's odd, but a few of the creeks, like Silver Spring and Big Spring, have always been somewhat shallow (the old millponds notwithstanding), showing large expanses of rock, sand and gravel with some deeper holes downstream. Others, like the Letort, contain deep runs nearly throughout, only a little gravel, and broad, silted beds covered with elodea. The Yellow Breeches, on the other hand, ranges widely between these extremes—changing back and forth along its length from one formation to the other.

Trout love to establish feeding lanes among the gentler weed channels, and because most of these are undercut deeply (or have sheer boundaries), the fish are provided with perfect cover and an inexhaustible food source. On the other hand, it's also because sub-aquatic "critters" are in such plentiful supply within the vegetation that trout in these limestone waters are not as likely to respond to the prospecting dry fly might their more opportunistic brethren of the freestone. Shrimp, cress-bugs and crayfish thrive in the alkaline-rich waters, a food chain replete with all sorts of delicacies. This is wonderful for fish, but except during prolific hatches (or when probing, later in August, with a fat grasshopper), a wise fisherman will realize that these trout have no need to be looking up in search of their dinner table. Even so, the ever-optimistic dry-fly fisher encourages himself, knowing that, because these springs support a head of trout far greater in number (and size) than any freestone counterpart, the law of averages may tip once again in his favor: You're probably gonna get skunked, but you know what's in there and you just can't resist.

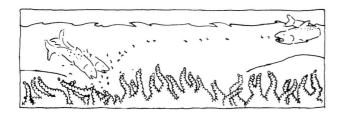

Still more spectacular, at daybreak on the Letort, it used to be common to see fat, highly-colored, brownies cruising the shallow water atop beds of elodea. We're talking about big bruisers in plain view, in just inches of water, dorsal fins and tails often exposed. These trout are not waiting passively for the current to deliver the odd breakfast snack; they're actively hunting for "bugs," and they've worked out some pretty clever measures to get them. One technique is to poke their heads into the elodea, then to shake vigorously side-to-side—their thrashing dislodging cress bugs that drift haplessly along the top of the weeds. Next, the trout does a lazy, downstream pirouette to greet the bounty of bugs once again, delighting as they backstroke, one-by-one, into his gaping mouth. Neat.

The naive fly-fisher might think he need only insert one of his own imitations into the mix and reap a harvest. But just try to fool one of these fish, even with your favorite tie, finest tippet and stealthiest cast. The instant your leader touches the water (or before), every trout within 40 yards is gone, and you're muttering your way back to the car for a shot of coffee—or something stronger!

Tight fishing—1970

New to the area, Marinaro was unaccustomed to fishing in these conditions, but he found the challenges both exciting and boundless. Different fly patterns needed to be developed; rod actions needed to be altered; new fishing techniques had to be worked out. Leaders must be longer, the tippets finer, more supple. Back casts must be held high above underbrush and grass. Stealth was required in taking up a fishing position, often with casts reaching far across weed beds. And tricks must be devised to overcome drag in the uncertain, marbled currents and channels. All these became issues of endless concern, a challenge that appealed enormously to Vince and his love of what he came to call "problem angling." Consider Marinaro's careful attention to the difficulties of fishing these new waters in *A Modern Dry Fly Code*

> Let the angler take his position directly across from the trout in such a way as to face the opposite bank squarely. Aim the cast high above the weeds and deliver it far beyond the trout, over the land on the opposite bank for perhaps ten feet, bringing it to a halt with a decided abruptness that will cause it to recoil sharply toward the angler, thereby achieving a series of close-packed loops on the surface of the backwater and allowing the fly just barely to clear the weedline. Theoretically it is a successful cast, since the series of loose coils pay out slowly into the fast current, allowing the fly to pursue a natural and leisurely drift in the backwater....
>
> One more observation in connection with this cast is worthy of note; that is, in order to obtain maximum benefit from the slack line, the forward cast must be delivered with considerable force, stopping its forward motion sharply, thereby causing it to jerk backward and fall in loose curves on the water. I have never been able to do it properly with soft rods and light lines. In recent times, I have resorted to heavier lines and stiffer rods in order to accomplish my purpose....
>
> Such is the character of the fish and the fishing on the Letort and other limestone waters—exacting to a high degree, where tackle and technique must be finely adjusted and, above all the artificial pattern must be correct.... [7]

Vince reaches across grass and weed beds

Some may have thought that casting conditions such as these would apply only to the limestoners of Pennsylvania—that freestone creeks tumble more directly and are relatively unaffected by tangled currents and weed beds. But this would be a mistake, for many productive stretches along freestone streams present similarly difficult fishing conditions. Really, anywhere one finds a low-gradient flow, one also finds gentle and complicated currents moving with boils and shifts sometimes too subtle for the eye to discern. Delicate flows merge with stronger ones to form "seams," or they make their way over and around in-stream obstacles, often including grassy islands, stumps, sub-surface boulders or fallen trees, and all these conditions conspire to spoil a free drift for the fly.

Even on freestone streams that roll more forcefully, there will be areas near the banks or behind rocks that present the fly-fisherman with equally compromised casts. In all these cases, the "puddle-cast, as Vince liked to call it, will help to obtain a clean float. On Michigan's Au Sable and Manistee Rivers, particularly, where currents are often delicate, fishermen are fond of flicking a dry fly downstream as they work through tangles of cedar "sweepers" along the stream banks. Here too, the well-delivered puddle-cast becomes a highly effective weapon. In all these cases, however, one must use a proper rod with a proper taper to accomplish that task as intended.

During the 1940s, Marinaro's rod-making blossomed. He became determined to discover tapers and lengths that would help overcome these new fishing difficulties. Again, we don't know how many rods might have been made or what they were like, for unfortunately, all but two rods from those earlier years seem to have met their end. These two will be of special interest to us later—especially because one of them is a bait-casting rod.

Marinaro began his most concentrated work on the convex taper in the 1940s, but that was a process never really brought to its conclusion, for no matter how many rods he may have built, Vince was never entirely satisfied. Those of us who've cast his rods can't think this would have been a result of deficiencies, but only that Vince had particular objectives in mind and his demanding temperament would accept nothing less than precisely what he intended.

Sweepers on Au Sable's "Holy Water"

Tangled currents on Michigan's Jordan River

A Modern Dry Fly Code was, in large part, the result of Vince's many late-1940s stream-side collaborations with Fox, Gene Craighead, Bill Bennett and others. Certainly

Passing the tradition along

among the most significant American fly-fishing books of the 20th century, this work bears the fruits of many years' labor. Yet, it is in Charlie Fox's two books from the 1960s (*This Wonderful World of Trout* and *Rising Trout*) where we read the many fascinating anecdotes lying behind those early years of research. In all, between Fox, Marinaro and others in the HFF, we encounter a record of some of the most interesting work ever undertaken in the history of American dry-fly fishing—certain, later writers even calling Marinaro and Fox the "Halford and Marryat of Cumberland Valley." Howell Raines, gushing in his *Fly-Fishing Through the Midlife Crisis* writes, "In short, in Marinaro, Schwiebert and Fox on the Letort, you had something like the fly-fishing equivalent of Hemingway, Fitzgerald and Dos Passos in Paris." Although decidedly hyperbole, Raines is correct in attributing significance of the highest order to a body of work essentially destined to set on its ear one's understanding of dry-fly fishing to date.

Marinaro awakened the fly-fishing world to terrestrial insects, including detailed information on tying the Jassid, grasshopper and ant. He discovered the unique, visual impressions made on the surface film by a spent imago. He exposed the habits of trout feeding upon tiny *Baetis, Tricos,*

Diptera, minuscule flying ants and numerous other "weensie" critters—collectively, "midges," or what Ed Shenk loves to call "fishing with next to nothing." Marinaro's revolutionary and compelling cut-wing and hackle-point, thorax patterns (which, owing to their critical proportions and time-consuming details, few tiers have mastered) are among the cleanest-floating and most effective dun imitations ever devised. Yet they've never been available in fly shops, so if you want to fish them, you'll need to master the recipe yourself. Certain writers have complained that the cut-wings spin excessively, that they don't always alight on the water correctly, or that they take too long to fashion. While these complaints carry a measure of validity, they're usually heard from tiers who simply don't understand what the patterns entail, or who are impatient and prefer no-fuss fly tying.

One can read *A Modern Dry Fly Code* again and again, each encounter seeming as fresh as the last, and each charming us with fly-fishing experiences and research not found in

A cut-wing, thorax tie from Vince's fly box

other works of the day. Vince's stream-side discoveries are both detailed and documented, and these he evaluates within the larger context of conventional wisdom gathered by authors from home and abroad. To us, however, the only peculiar thing about *The Code* is what's absent. That is, despite Marinaro's equally-extensive experiences as a rod-maker during those same years, not a word about these endeavors is to be found. Certainly, no book can contain everything and perhaps Vince thought he might turn his attention to rod-building matters at some future point. Even so, Marinaro is one of America's most well-read, articulate and insightful writers—offering page after page of information in precise, literate prose that is at once forceful and compelling, anecdotal and comfortable. How strange it seems, nowadays, when we reflect that we didn't always know what Vince and others in the Cumberland Valley taught us.

Even more strange is that Marinaro's findings remained unfamiliar to the public for a great many years following *The Code*'s initial appearance. Our present estimation of Vince's work is nothing like the dismal reception his book suffered during the 1950s—not that it was rejected, but worse, it was simply ignored. But how could this be, given the significance we now attribute to Marinaro's work? Some folks surmised the problem was G. P. Putnam's vastly misguided and inadequate marketing scheme: Others argued the book simply was too far ahead of its time. Both explanations are probably true but, of the thousand or so copies in that 1st edition, most were remaindered within a year. As a result, Marinaro's revolutionary discoveries languished on the shelf for decades before his work eventually emerged again—this time brought out in 1970 by Nick Lyons at Crown Publishers. Tom and I can't help but believe the public's renewed interest in Marinaro was largely due to the positive reception of Fox's two books, published just a few years earlier in the 1960s. Indeed, it seems likely that Vince himself meant to acknowledge a certain indebtedness to Charlie, as his 1970 introduction recalls "our total devotion to the *wonderful world of trout....*" [italics added].

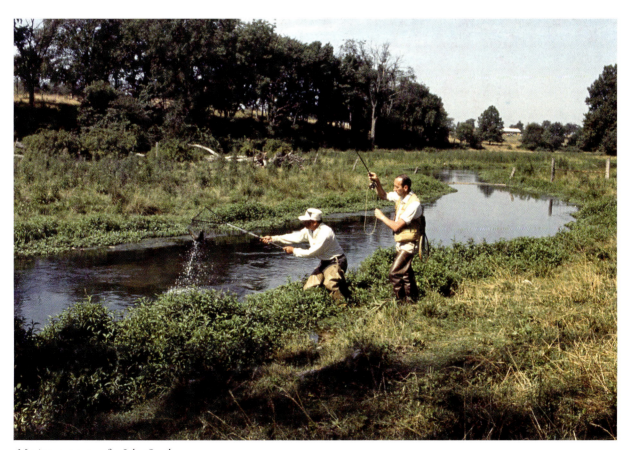

Marinaro nets one for John Snyder

Chapter Four

Those Pesky Phillippes

There's yet another episode to relate about Marinaro and the Harrisburg Fly Fishers. A wonderful occasion arose not long after the HFF's formation—an opportunity for the group to view a Phillippe fly rod, one of the earliest demonstrating six-strip construction and with all three sections built of bamboo. Tom and I began our account simply enough, but for a variety of reasons the story quickly implicated issues of larger historical significance, and soon we found ourselves deeply mired in puzzles and tales about the first American, bamboo fly rods.

Marinaro and others from the club gathered in the spring of 1954 for a special banquet to examine this rod from the collection of Asher J. Oldenwalder, an occasion Ernie Schwiebert thought marked the rod's 100th anniversary. Schwiebert and several others believed the rod had been built by Samuel Phillippe shortly after Phillippe began incorporating six strips of bamboo into all three rod sections. The rod itself had been uncovered several years earlier when Marinaro and his friend, Mahlon Robb, were doing a little research into the history of the six-strip fly rod. In the course of their inquiries, they happened to learn of a Phillippe rod in Easton, Pennsylvania, and at once, Marinaro and Robb contacted Mr. Oldenwalder for permission to view the rod at his home. Sometime later, they also arranged for it to be donated to the Pennsylvania Historical and Museum Commission (the agency operating the State Museum).

While experts in the field are now certain that six-strip, bamboo construction was not practiced as early as 1854 (with some historians also wondering if Phillippe actually has the distinction of building the first six-strip rod with all three sections of bamboo), the Oldenwalder rod remains one of America's most historically significant, fly-fishing artifacts. Indeed, only five or six Phillippe rods have ever been located. The rod is in excellent condition: Its craftsmanship is impeccable, lavish in decorative details, and it survives as one of the finest, documented examples of its kind. The rod is held within a recessed, silk-lined, walnut case, and is accompanied by a tiny, 2-inch reel of German silver with side plates fashioned from mother-of-pearl. This latter is unmarked, but considering that Samuel and his son, Solon, were also skilled gunsmiths, it seems certain that one or the other would have built the reel as well. Several months after their banquet, and on behalf of Mr. Oldenwalder, the HFF presented the Phillippe rod to the Pennsylvania State Museum.

Marinaro and friends examine the Phillippe rod—1954

The Phillippe/Marinaro Connection: Questions of Provenance

There is no way to know for whom the Phillippe rod was built or through how many hands it may have passed before coming to Mr. Oldenwalder, but judging by its appearance, it must have been a very special commission, used little and never traveling far from Easton and the Phillippe shop. In our desire to understand this rod more completely, Tom and I made arrangements to inspect it at the museum and similarly began a search for more details of its provenance. This was of particular interest to us, for if the rod were actually constructed by Samuel Phillippe sometime around 1854 as Schwiebert and others thought, not only would it be one of our earliest examples, but in fact, the oldest, all-bamboo, six-strip rod ever documented. Among a variety of other surprises, however, we soon discovered (in truth, re-discovered) that the rod as presented by the club was not built by Samuel Phillippe at all, but by his son, Solon Phillippe—and not in 1854, but perhaps 1862, or more likely, still later. However, if this were true, then the Phillippe rod would not be quite the artifact that Marinaro, the Harrisburg Fly Fishers and several later authors presumed it to be.

We'll review some contesting opinions in a moment, but whichever views may hold true, the rod is one of our most important representatives of those earliest days. More than merely exemplary, the Phillippe rod appears to be state-of-the-art. But it's partly because of the rod's perfection that it seems unlikely to have been built before other makers began using similar construction techniques. The Phillippe rod is both rare and noteworthy, and Tom and I will spend a good deal of time discussing our discoveries. Still, to us, of greater importance than the artifact itself is what this rod came to signify about a particular moment in the history of bamboo, fly-rod construction.

Collectors and makers all love to ponder how bamboo fly rods have been built, and in pursuing this, they often find themselves moving back through time to discover what earlier makers were thinking, what they were trying to accomplish and how they went about it. The Phillippe rod was built a long time ago—so long, in fact, that those days might seem unrelated to our present concerns. But the more Tom and I began to understand this rod, the more we realized that it stands just at the brink of several developments responsible for our modern fly rods. Technical advancement in every field is an evolutionary process, often with each new contribution standing on the shoulders of something that came just before. Yet, every now and again, we also see that a sudden, quantum leap of some kind has taken place, and we wonder why. What happened to make this possible?

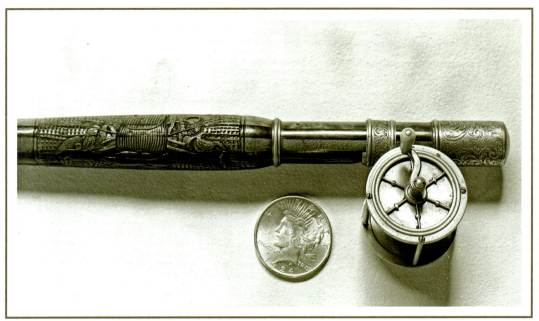

Phillippe rod and reel—1954

The Phillippe rod does not, in itself, represent such a leap. More teasingly, the rod seems perched just at that last, seminal moment, almost making the quantum leap that followed inevitable. It was to be the leap responsible for our "modern" fly rods and the legacy that Marinaro and others inherited. Indeed, although all-bamboo, six-strip rods had been built by Solon's father and others somewhat earlier, and although building with bamboo itself prepared the way to our modern rods, of far greater importance to the legacy of the modern fly rod is the question of *what to do with* that new material. Historically, what we will be discussing is the quick trip leading from Ebenezer Green, Charles Murphy, William Mitchell, Robert Welch, Thaddeus Norris, John Krider and the Phillippes in the 1860s (all huddled between Philadelphia and Manhattan), to the Maine builders, H. L. Leonard and Charles Wheeler, and their bamboo rods of the later 1870s. That trip crosses little more than a moment in time, yet lies an entire world of rod-making away.

A. J. Campbell, in his *Fly Fishing Tackle* (1997), describes this change as a transition from the "smith" to the "production" age of fly rods. Perfectly true, but in our present focus, production issues themselves are not our concern. Instead, we want to draw attention to the path rod-makers took shortly after the Phillippe rod was built—how those makers came to realize exactly what bamboo is and how that material would be manipulated to yield fly rods of precision. Precision certainly had been achieved by the Phillippes and others in terms of aesthetics, hardware and the mechanics of joining strips to one another, but before the 1870s, bamboo fly rods had not been precisely-designed as *casting* instruments. As we consider the Phillippe rod, we want to explain its construction, then trace the critical changes responsible for the "leap" to the modern rod.

Back in that "smith age," makers like Phillippe had come to appreciate the flexing superiority of bamboo (its lighter weight and greater strength), but they had not yet realized exactly what design implications lie hidden within those strips of bamboo. It's not as if Phillippe and others longed for more precise tapers, but just didn't know how to go about getting them; rather, it was that the contribution of a fly rod's taper, in its own right, was little more than a primitively-held concept. To build the modern fly rod, makers needed to discover new and more appropriate ways for shaping their bamboo strips, but *wanting* to do so relied on something still more fundamental—a recognition that the "old" shaping techniques were actually destructive of bamboo's greatest promise. At last, with the achievement of new and precise planing techniques, makers were in a position to begin thinking about designing optimal action into their rods. The Phillippe rod, as beautifully built as it is, was constructed just at the edge of the "modern" era, but falling short by less than a decade.

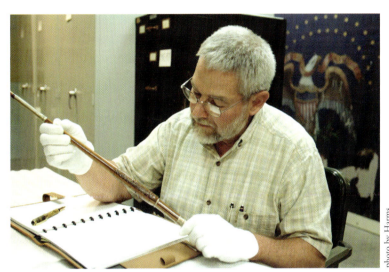
Whittle inspects the Phillippe rod

A full explanation of these developments will emerge as the final section of this chapter, with important implications for Marinaro and other makers of the modern fly rod. For the present, however, let's begin our tale of the Phillippe rod itself at the moment it was first brought to the attention of the public in 1954. It's a strange and convoluted story, and because so many eyes have been focused on the rod through the years, our account is replete with twists and turns. Assumptions of its provenance range far and wide. In a November 1955, *Field & Stream* article by A. J. McClane, we find one of the first reports of the Phillippe rod after Marinaro and Mahlon Robb uncovered it several years earlier. Whether McClane's information is accurate or not, what he presents in that article seems to have been forgotten or overlooked by later writers.

Learning to Build

"Last spring," McClane writes, "105 members and guests of the Harrisburg Fly Fishers Club gathered at a formal dinner to examine a split-bamboo fly rod made by Solon Phillippe in the year 1862." But, how had McClane determined Solon to be the maker, and how did he decide on 1862 rather than the 1854 date Schwiebert asserted? After all, later writers decided that Samuel and 1854 was the right combination. Unfortunately, all those early explanations seem to have been lost and the museum itself has no records to account for the claims. McClane, a few lines down, characterizes the 1954 ceremony writing, "...the Harrisburg unveiling and formal totemization of Phillippes, *pere et fils*, is sharply nostalgic." Perhaps McClane only meant to imbue his piece with a certain literary turn, but he does suggest here that both Phillippes were under consideration in some measure—with what questions in mind, he doesn't say.

Curiously, the catalog description in the Pennsylvania State Museum also pronounces Solon to be the maker, but neither does the museum know when its description was written nor does the curator know how the author came to decide upon Solon. Further, while the catalog information correctly estimates the rod's construction to fall between 1848 and 1870, a range of that magnitude is not edifying. Many other details in the catalog are absent or somewhat in error, and the museum does not hold much in the way of supporting literature. Most odd, its existing records reveal no reference to Asher Oldenwalder, the rod's actual donor. The gift seems to have been presented without accompanying documents. We wonder how it could happen that Mr. Oldenwalder, a respected collector of fishing memorabilia, would have failed to contribute any information about the rod's provenance—surely, some accident of fate.

Part of the initial confusion as to whether the rod's maker had been Samuel or Solon will come into focus when we observe that Samuel seems to have had no middle name, or if he did, we doubt anyone could corroborate his use of it. Tom Kerr, an ardent fly-rod historian, holds copies of both Samuel's and Solon's interment records and tells me that no middle name appears on Samuel's document. Solon, however, did have a middle name. It began with the initial "C" and was used with frequency.

The point is this: A beautifully engraved maker's mark on the rod's hardware reads, "S. C. Phillippe, Maker, Easton"—a detail that can be viewed with perfect clarity in the accompanying photograph. Fishing-tackle historians at

Phillippe ferrule showing the maker's mark

Opposite view of ferrule showing fishing scene

mid-century seem not to have suspected that Samuel lacked a middle name, and because the given names of both *pere et fils* begin with "S," the mistake in identity was quick and natural. Regardless, identifying Marinaro's "find" was never an ordinary undertaking, for less than a handful of Phillippe rods have ever been verified—none displaying a signature.

As our final thought on this matter we note that, up through the 1950s, Solon's name rarely came to mind anyway since most fly-fishing literature attending to the Phillippe surname centered on questions of which American first made use of bamboo, or who developed the first four- and six-strip fly rods. Solon was never proposed to be in the running here, and when mentioned at all, he's usually assumed to be somewhere in the back of the shop, learning the trade and coming along later.

Perhaps we can appreciate the persisting confusion over the Phillippe name when we note that even as recently as 1997, A. J. Campbell, in his *Fly Fishing Tackle*, includes the following reference, "Born in Reading, Pennsylvania, on May 25, 1801, Samuel C. Phillippe moved to Easton in 1817-1818...." [1] The birth date is in error, but also Campbell's assumption that Samuel had a middle name beginning with "C." And, in one of our old, PFFMA photos of the 1954 ceremony, we see a gentleman pointing directly to the maker's mark, almost as if to say: "You see? It says right there, 'S[amuel] C. Phillippe.'"

During the 1860s, the Phillippes were primarily gun-makers (although Samuel also built violins earlier in his career), and neither of them seems to have produced many fly rods. Actually, considering the low number of rods coming from their shop, one wonders if history would have remembered the Phillippes at all were it not for Dr. James Henshall's desire to lionize their work in the second edition of his *Book of The Black Bass* (1904).

Conflicts over the Oldenwalder rod's provenance began not long after the rod's 1954 debut, including speculation that it might be a match to a very similar item described in Henshall's book. Henshall's description (originally written as an article for *Outing* magazine in May of 1902) mentions an exhibit he carried to Chicago's 1893 World's Columbian Exposition where he says he displayed "an oil portrait of Samuel Phillippe, together with several of his rods." We also read that one of Samuel's six-strip rods "was a very finely finished and handsome rod with solid silver mountings, neatly engraved; it was accompanied by a reel of mother of pearl, the only one I have ever seen. This last was doubtless one of his later rods." [2] Although there's no way to know what dates Henshall had in mind in referring to Samuel's "later rods," more recent writers believe he ceased building shortly after 1865.

Could the rod that Henshall describes be our specimen? Jeffrey Hatton, antique rod aficionado, author and friend, pointed out to me that the photographs of the Phillippe rod I supplied (as well as those seen on the dust-jacket of Martin Keane's 1976 book, *Classic Rods and Rod Makers*) indeed do seem to yield a match, but with few details and no photographic evidence of that original rod, the connection is impossible to verify. Still, it's difficult to imagine there could be more than one six-strip, Phillippe rod meeting Henshall's description—one that's engraved and accompanied by that unique reel of mother of pearl. But, should "his" rod be the one in our museum, we wonder how Henshall could have missed Solon's name on the maker's mark, or mistaken Solon's initials for those of his father—especially considering Henshall's claim that he knew Solon and the Phillippe family well.

For our part, we would state that everything in Henshall's description of the rod and reel corresponds to the museum artifacts that Tom and I examined. This is not to affirm that we have a match, only to say that the similarities are more than striking. So, we believe that either Henshall's assertion about the rod's maker was simply a mistake or there are at least two rods and reels matching his general description—one by the father (once in Henshall's possession at the Chicago Exposition, now lost), and another by the son (unknown to Henshall, now in Pennsylvania's State Museum). More will emerge in a moment, but for the present, Henshall's mistake about the maker is a far more likely explanation.

In addition to the confusion over which Phillippe had been the maker, there are similar disputes about the rod's date of construction—even about its physical features. Lew

Dignitaries verify the maker's mark

Stoner and J. Deren, writing in *The Wise Fisherman's Encyclopedia* (1951), George Herter, in his *Rod Building Manual and Manufacturer's Guide* (1958), and Ernest Schwiebert, in *Trout* (1978), all seem to have repeated an identical set of errors. All mistakenly state that Mr. Oldenwalder's rod was built by Samuel, that it features an all-bamboo butt-section with a swelled, bamboo grip, and that this grip is decorated with gunstock checkering. We'll continue with the rod's physical details in a moment, but first, the likely date of its construction.

Schwiebert (in describing Samuel Phillippe's rod-making skills) writes in *Trout*: "The Oldenwalder rod was calibrated by Vincent Marinaro, himself a skilled rod-maker and author of *A Modern Dry Fly Code*, when it was exactly a century old." A few pages later, Schwiebert compares this rod to one built by Charles Murphy in 1867 for Samuel Kauffmann, noting, "...but the Oldenwalder Phillippe rod had used six-strip construction throughout its length fifteen years earlier...." [3] Both statements would date the Phillippe rod to sometime around 1854, but most notably missing are Schwiebert's reasons for determining that year. Failing explanations, it seems just as likely that the rod's presumed age could have been the result of accumulated lore—a guess made to Mr. Oldenwalder, perhaps, and simply passed along.

Now, all these issues may be interesting for collectors and historians to consider, but what about the more casual bamboo-rod enthusiast? To be perfectly blunt, for all Tom and I care (philistines, though we may be), the Phillippe rod could be the product of either the father or the son. Yet its date and physical attributes remain of concern. That is, if we're going to trace the path leading from the "smith age" to our modern fly rods, it matters greatly to know when a rod was constructed and how. That path is a sequence of developments, but for our purposes here, it matters less who made them than what those developments were.

The harder we searched, the more certain we became that the Phillippe rod would not have been built prior to 1869—thus, dating it at least five years after Charles Murphy and others also began building six-strip, bamboo rods. Evidence for our date comes from Jeff Hatton and Tom Kerr, both of whom pointed to a photograph of the Phillippe rod on the dust-jacket of Keane's *Classic Rods*. The photo depicts a fishing-scene carved into one side of the grip, and is almost identical to an illustration first seen in Genio Scott's *Fishing in American Waters* (1869), carrying the strong suggestion that the former would have derived from the latter. [4]

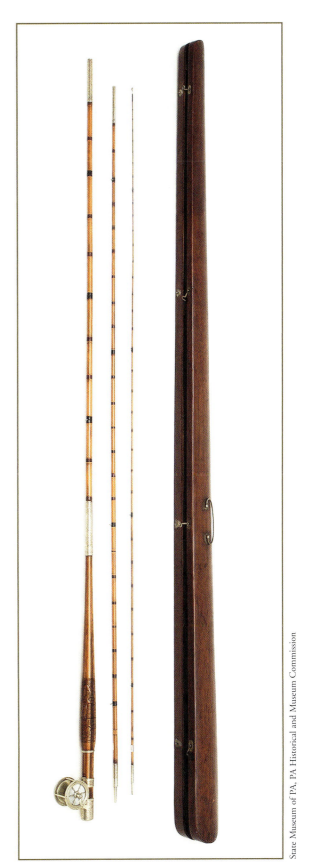

The Phillippe rod, case and reel

Fishing-scene carved on grip

Sketch by Genio Scott

Then, flipping through the pages of Scott's book myself, I noticed that its title page features a decorative, still-life sketch depicting a creel, rod, fish, net and other paraphernalia arranged in neat symmetry. Our own examination of the Phillippe rod revealed this same design carved on the reverse side of the its grip. Not proof-positive, for it's just possible that both Solon Phillippe and Genio Scott could have used art-work created at an earlier time by some third party. But, as Jeff Hatton also pointed out, Scott writes a wonderfully cryptic *apologia* in the "Preface" to his book, assuring us that he had a great time creating all the book's drawings himself.

It now seems almost conclusive that Phillippe's carved designs derived from Scott's book. But, with something of a proprietary bias for "our" rod, and with hopes that its date of construction might fall as early as possible, we wonder (in a last gasp) if perhaps Phillippe and Scott were acquaintances. Maybe Solon had become familiar with Scott's drawings long before that book's 1869 publication. Alas, this too, seems unlikely, for Scott was considerably older than Solon, lived in New York City, was not at all known for art-work, was deeply involved with fashion design and the garment industry, and he fished chiefly on Long Island and along the St. Lawrence River. Solon, on the other hand, was principally a gunsmith in the mid-1860s, little-known as a rod-maker, lived in then-remote Easton, Pennsylvania, and at age 21, left his area for 3 years to fight in the Civil War. More conclusively, while Scott writes rather extensively in his book about the best contemporary fly rods and their casting characteristics, we notice that he recommends rods by Robert Welch and includes no reference whatever to the Phillippes.

Although many details remain unclear, one thing seems certain: Samuel's son, Solon, could not have built the rod as early as 1854, for he was then only a 13-year-old boy. But even if it were built in 1862 (as thought by McClane), how could Solon gain access to Scott's original drawings 7 years before the book's publication? On the other hand, if it were actually the elder Phillippe who built the rod, surely he would have known that, on such an elaborately conceived and decorated rod, it would do him no good to have his son's name engraved in the maker's mark. Besides, how might Samuel have obtained Scott's sketches for the grip before the book's appearance? Finally, then, we believe the only likelihood is that it was Solon who built the rod, and no earlier than the 1869 appearance of Scott's book.

Carving on opposite side of grip: creel & paraphernalia

Sketch by Genio Scott

WHO SAID WHAT?

In our search for the "truth" about the Phillippe rod, Tom and I discovered that not only is its provenance mired in confusion, but later descriptions of its physical attributes are equally muddled—almost as if its several champions were not referencing the same rod at all. A. J. Campbell, writing as recently as 1997, says of the rod held in Harrisburg:

> By 1848 the Pennsylvanian *[Samuel Phillippe]* had produced versions with four-strip tips and mids. The example in the Pennsylvania Historical Museum in Harrisburg shows this style of construction, the butt section mortised of light and dark hardwoods. *[italics added]* [5]

Well, now what!? Is the Oldenwalder rod ***not*** of six-strip construction after all, revealing only the older, four-strip design? Again, was it built by Samuel or Solon? And is the butt section really made of mortised hardwoods, and ***not*** bamboo, as Schwiebert and others had attested? Confusion runs rampant, and, alas, poor George Herter, in his *Rod Building Manual*, would seem to have been hoisted with his own petard when he writes:

> The father of modern complete four and six strip bamboo fly rod making, however, was Samuel Phillippe.... Many authors and would-be-historians have confused the facts about Samuel Phillippe through lack of knowledge.... The sportsman among them should have hung their heads in shame. This also applies to his present day critics.... Mr. Asher J. Odenwalder *[sic]*, 45 South 4th Street of Easton, Pennsylvania, a noted present day collector of fishing rods, has a six strip bamboo rod made by Phillippe. The cigar shaped Phillippe grip is even made from bamboo on this rod, and it is beautifully checkered. Because this grip swelled from the rod, itself, people who observed the rod thought the butt was made from wood, not bamboo. This is not at all true, but shows the class of people who take it upon themselves to be authorities on rods. [6]

Oh dear...! My mother loved the familiar homily: "Make your words soft and sweet, lest one day you should need to eat them." Indeed, despite Herter's unfortunate self-condemnation, the swelled grip of the Oldenwalder rod is not at all made of bamboo, but fashioned of 12 strips of laminated (or mortised) hardwoods. The strips are sequenced with alternately light and medium-colored ash, with every third strip taken from darker walnut—impossible for anyone who had seen the grip to confuse with bamboo. Even Schwiebert repeats Herter's error in *Trout*. But neither is the grip of this rod made of bamboo, nor is it checkered. The grip area displays, instead, the two, 4 1/2-inch, elaborately-carved, fishing scenes mentioned above, each surrounded by a stippled background—in all, impossible to mistake for gunstock checkering.

While we cannot account for all the disagreements about the rod's attributes, problems may have begun when writers misinterpreted an original document provided by Mahlon Robb to his friend, Charlie Fox—a document first made public in Fox's *Advanced Bait Casting* (1950). Here, Robb offers his account of how he and Marinaro first uncovered the Phillippe rod:

> I was joined in my search for historical data relative to the conception of the bamboo rod as it is constructed today, by Vincent C. Marinaro, fisherman deluxe, and Colonel Henry W. Shoemaker, who is the chief in charge of the Pennsylvania archives. The Colonel, who writes a very interesting column on Pennsylvania folklore in his paper, the *Altoona Tribune*, had written on several occasions concerning Samuel Phillippe of Easton as the inventor of the split-bamboo rod…. Colonel Shoemaker had given credit to Phillippe in his column; however, he was taken to task by some who claimed credit should go to the late Hiram Leonard of Central Valley, N.Y.
>
> The Colonel contacted the Northampton County Historical Society *[Easton, PA]* and was advised that there was a Phillippe rod in the hands of a local citizen. The private collector turned out to be Ashler J. Odenwalder *[sic]* Jr., an Easton banker and friend of the Colonel. Vince Marinaro and I journeyed to Easton to talk with him and examined the rod. Mr. Odenwalder was a gracious host and he permitted us to make measurements of the rod. We found it to be of six-strip construction and instead of having a wooden butt as we had been advised, it was all split bamboo. The reason that some observers did not notice that it was all bamboo was because Phillippe made the butt section with a swelled grip. He had autographed the rod with a checkering tool of a gunsmith just as plainly as if he had written his name on paper with ink. Two points were proved. First, the rod was made by Phillippe, and second, it was six-strip bamboo in each of its three joints. [7]

Robb and Marinaro were the first to examine the Phillippe rod, but Robb's last sentences are puzzling to us—confused and ambiguous. Robb does not explain exactly what he and Marinaro were hoping to learn, but if there were a question in their minds as to the rod's maker, it couldn't have been whether that was Phillippe, for the name is vividly engraved within the maker's mark. Instead, their question must have been whether the maker had been the father or the son. Whatever the explanation, the "checkering" on the grip leading them to pronounce Samuel as the maker should never have been regarded as conclusive. For one thing, the pattern on the grip is not at all that of gunstock checkering (as various of our photos demonstrate), but we also note that, regardless of the nature of the pattern, Solon was also a skilled gunsmith and was just as capable as his father in matters of fine craftsmanship.

The pattern on the grip is just one erroneous point about the Phillippe rod. The construction of the butt section itself is yet another, and Robb's account only adds to this confusion. Although finished as a permanently-fixed piece, the butt section is actually constructed of two parts, joined in the middle. There is the six-strip, bamboo, rod shaft itself, but there is also a long, gently-swelled, wooden "hand-piece." This latter is permanently attached to the bamboo shaft within a rolled-and-soldered sheathing of German silver (looking like a ferrule and containing the engraved maker's mark), but being fixed in place around those two, joined parts. The length of the wooden hand-piece, including its engraved silver sheathing, is just shy of 20 inches, while the bamboo shaft portion, including the female ferrule at its outer end, is 28 1/2 inches.

It seems likely that the confusion about the "bamboo grip" would have evolved unwittingly from Robb's descriptions. After looking at the rod, Robb expresses surprise to discover that "instead of having a wooden butt as we had been advised, it was all bamboo." No doubt, he and Marinaro expected to see a butt-shaft entirely of wood because, ear-

Bamboo shaft joined to wooden hand-piece

photo by Tom Whittle

lier, that was how the 20-inch, wooden hand-piece (called the butt) had been described. In similar fashion, when Robb and Marinaro demurred and identified the butt as being "all bamboo," they were probably referencing only the 28 1/2-inch shaft portion, for the question of whether Phillippe ever built butt-shafts of bamboo was also a matter of some dispute. Pandora's box is open, and we see that misunderstandings happen so quickly that one hardly dare state anything.

Perhaps, if readers consider the following, they can understand why Stoner, Deren, Herter and Schwiebert would have departed in so many similar ways from the history and construction of the Phillippe/Oldenwalder rod: For one thing, it is very clear to us that none of these writers actually viewed the rod. Secondly, their writings suggest that each of them imposed Dr. Henshall's general information about the Phillippes upon Robb's later description of the rod. Thus, in believing Samuel to have been the builder, Herter and Schweibert (particularly) seem satisfied to end all discussion by referring to Henshall. Indeed, on this topic, many authors have believed Henshall's authority to be above reproach. Apparently, researchers often ended their quest for the Phillippes once they worked back to that presumed, first-hand evidence. Even Perry Frazer, writing his *Amateur Rodmaking* in 1914 (and nearly Henshall's contemporary), places utmost confidence in Henshall's information, assuring us that:

> In the revised and extended edition of the *Book of the Black Bass* (1904), there is much additional information on the subject, and the date of Phillipe's [sic] first rods is established as 1845 on the testimony of contemporaneous fellow-townsmen, friends, and fishing companions. From the evidence now in my possession, Phillipe was undoubtedly, indubitably, and manifestly the first to make a four-strip or six-strip split bamboo rod. [8]

It may go hard to challenge an endorsement of such finality, but, unfortunately, Henshall is in error on a number of issues concerning the history of bamboo fly rods. Several problems in Henshall's writings have been uncovered by more current research, and a few of these are given brief appraisal by A. J. Campbell (*Classic and Antique Fly-Fishing Tackle*)—who does not withhold his opinion of the matter.[9] In addition to Henshall's several odd omissions and biases, historians also remind us that much of his information about the Phillippes (while presented as first-hand, and presumably, irrefutable) was derived through the perceptions and memory of his contributors. It's not that these sources meant to mislead, only that other records call some of their recollections into question. Even Samuel's son, Solon, in volunteering his own account of his father's accomplishments, seems to have recalled earlier years with something less than complete clarity. And apparently, Henshall, too, had highly questionable motives and opinions of his own. Consequently, we cannot know which of his contentions is reliable and which may have been improvised to suit his own purposes.

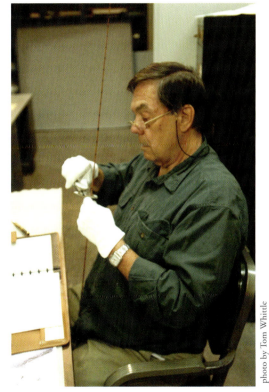

Harms mikes the Phillippe rod tip

We hope the accompanying photographs, taken during our own examination of the Phillippe rod in May of 2006, will account for its construction and ornamental details.[10]

First to note: The assembled rod measures 11 1/2 feet. The butt section is 48 1/2" long, including its ferrule; the mid-section is somewhat shorter at 46 1/2", including both its upper ferrule and the spiked, male ferrule; and the sole, tip section measures nearly the same at 46 3/8", including its tip-top and spiked, male ferrule.

There are three, hanging-ring guides on the butt—the first located 8 inches below the outer end of the female ferrule, the second at 15 1/4" and the third at 23". The mid-section has four such guides, these located at 6", 17", 28 1/4" and 40" below the end of the female ferrule. The tip-section, similarly, has four guides—the first at 6 1/4" below the tip-top, the second at 16 3/4", the third at 27 3/4" and the last one at 38 1/4".

More importantly: We confirm that all sections of the rod (tip, mid-section, and the 28 1/2-inch, shaft-portion of the butt) are, indeed, six-strip construction, and all of bamboo. The naked eye could determine this with ease, but we examined still more closely under magnification. Nodes were visible throughout all three sections, but their distribution around the circumference seems to follow no pattern—often with two (but as many as four) nodes lying adjacent. Additionally, we thought that either the strips were not all taken from the same culm or they had been shifted up or down in assembly, for adjacent strips show distances between their nodes of unequal measurement. Finally, the shafts of all three sections are fully rounded in cross-section.

In contrast to the bamboo shaft-portion of the butt, the 20-inch, swelled hand-piece is constructed of 12, full-length strips of mortised hardwoods—exact sequences of light and dark ash, alternating every third strip with darker walnut. We also took note of the little rows of markings that form a background for the grip's carvings. Contrary to Robb's and Schwiebert's descriptions, the pattern of these markings is totally different from the field of pointed diamonds cut by "the checkering tool of gunsmith," and were created, instead, by a square punch-tool and hammer (an embossing technique called "stippling"). Marinaro had checkered a few gunstocks himself, although it seems clear he would not have done so prior to the time he inspected the Oldenwalder rod.

We assumed the hand-piece and butt-shaft would have been joined to one another by means of a scarfed glue

Close-up of stippling technique

joint—the decorative sheathing being used merely to hide the joint—but we were surprised to discover this was not the case. Within the German-silver sheathing (just at the area where it surrounds the end of the hand-piece), glue had deteriorated entirely and turned to a fine powder. There, the hand-piece was loose and when it slipped away from its sheath we saw that the two segments of the butt met only end-to-end. Each had simply been glued within its own half of the sheathing. This struck us as a remarkably uncertain method of joinery in an area asked to carry such high stress-loads, but for some reason, Phillippe thought the arrangement might be strong enough. Actually, except for the glue break-down a 135 years later, it was. And so, as George Herter might say, our quibble just "shows the class of people who take it upon themselves to be authorities on rods."

Elaborate, scrolled engraving covers all elements of the rod's hardware, and the particular patterns were easily recognized as identical to engraving found on the best guns of the day. Certainly, there's no reason to imagine that the Phillippes were also engravers, for such decorative work has always been the specialized provence of artisans attached to the jewelry or firearms trades. Thus, it seems certain the rod's engraving was jobbed-out by Phillippe, just as would have been customary for finer guns.

Other decorative elements on the rod include its intermediate wraps and tipping. It's true that intermediates were thought to be necessary in those days, but typically, these wraps were not also decorative. In an unusual detail for the

Detail of reel-seat hardware

time, both the hanging-ring guides and the intermediate wraps are tipped with just three turns of deep, red silk—each tipping being perfectly separated from its primary wrap by an open space of barely 1/32". The original colors would have been far more vivid, but the guide wraps appear to be an extremely dark maroon (perhaps initially black), while the intermediates and tipping remain a lighter shade—showing somewhat rosy hues, a bit deeper than those seen on the Leonard "Hunt" series. The intermediate wraps are located on 1 1/2-inch centers throughout the mid-section, but on the tip-section, spacings narrow progressively to less than three-quarters of an inch. The bamboo portion of the butt section shows intermediates located on 2 1/2-inch centers, but the 20-inch, wooden hand-piece has no wraps at all.

Of greatest surprise to Tom and me, however, was the excellent condition and the delicacy of the Phillippe rod. We had seen photographs earlier, but because pictures so often lack a sense of real-life scale, we expected to be looking at another of those large, clumsy, old rods. No such thing, for despite its 11 1/2-foot overall length, the Phillippe rod seemed almost diminutive. The tip-top comes in at an extremely fine 0.059" (over-the-varnish measurement); the grip area and reel seat, combined, measure just less than 9"; and the rod's all-up weight is only 8.6 ounces—with half of that concentrated through the 20-inch hand-piece.

Tip-top and intermediate wraps

Also remarkable, is the quality of the rod's construction. We expected to find glue-lines, but there are none. We expected to see a heavy, wrinkled and cracked finish, but although it is somewhat marred, the finish is thin, smooth and intact. The varnish on the hand-piece is only barely dulled through the grip area, but the rest remains in nearly perfect condition, and the carvings meant to be grasped by one's hand show no sign of wear. Nor could we find evidence that anything had been restored or repaired. Although some guides are missing, and several tippings, similarly, have left for parts unknown, all fittings and existing wraps appear undisturbed from their original state. There is only one tip, however, and because the specially-made carrying case reveals spaces for two, we suppose the other tip was lost or destroyed.

As a last observation, we note that the only element of the Phillippe rod perhaps calling its c.1869 date into question could be the construction of its ferrules. Well before the end of that decade, most rod-makers had begun to include shoulders ("steps") on the male or the female parts, also adding hoop-strength for each female part by soldering a small "welt" (a circular band of metal) just at the outer end of its barrel. But the Phillippe rod does not use such ferrules—revealing, instead, the earlier, straight-tube construction with neither shoulders nor reinforcing welts. Puzzling, for the rod, the reel and the carrying case are all elaborately executed, and in every respect, their construction appears to be state-of-the-art for the period. Experts in the field will need to determine what this may mean.

As to the many erroneous descriptions of the Phillippe rod cited above, it seems that Deren, Stoner and Herter were mistaken simply because they repeated earlier sources of information (Henshall and Robb). These three, more-recent writers were all far-removed from the East Coast and never saw the actual artifact. But Schwiebert lived nearby, had been a friend of Marinaro for many years, and claimed that he personally examined three Phillippe rods.[11] One of these had been held by the Anglers' Club of New

York (a rod some believe to have been among those destroyed in the tragic January 1975 bombing of an adjacent restaurant). But, among the other Phillippe rods Schwiebert says he knew is the one from the Oldenwalder collection, still believing in his 1978 *Trout* that it is the work of Samuel and dates to 1854. It's hard to imagine why Schwiebert persisted in this, but it seems apparent that, like the other writers mentioned above, he, too, had not actually seen the rod.

Rolled-and-soldered German silver ferrules

photo by Tom Whittle

As we stated earlier, Tom and I often wondered if these several parties might have been writing about some other rod, yet each of the sources we've cited specifically identifies the rod in question as "the Oldenwalder rod" that Marinaro measured—now held in the Pennsylvania State Museum. There has never been but one such example. So, not only do we continue to wonder about the history of the Phillippe rod, but, for the present, the contributions of the Phillippes themselves lie obscured in the archives of time.

A Search for Precision

What did Tom and I mean when we stated, earlier, that the Phillippe rod represents a last, preparatory stage to our modern fly rods? We'll explain this in what follows, but we need to emphasize first, that we do not judge a fly rod to be "modern" because it may be shorter and lighter, or because its action is delicate and crisp, or because its details may satisfy more current and refined aesthetic tastes, or, indeed, even because it's now used to cast the dry-fly. All these are only personal or cultural preferences.

On the contrary, to us, what makes a rod "modern" is a set of construction techniques that allows the rod-maker to predict and obtain exactly the action he has chosen. He accomplishes this confidently and repeatedly, both because he understands precise sets of design parameters and because he knows how his specialized tools will yield the expected results. The process of building the modern, hand-planed fly rod is demonstrated in our Primer (preceding Chapter One), but in what follows, our purpose will be to explain why this process does not at all represent what bamboo rod-making meant in Phillippe's day.

We referred to a rod's "action" just above, but this is a most untidy concept to describe how a fly rod casts: The word says everything, yet nothing. Explanations of a rod's action have been around for a very long time and always mean to estimate how a rod's weight and motion feel in one's hand—how the rod responds when we impart flexed energy along its length, or how it feels when playing a fish. Still, although a rod's action is palpable and very real, the ability to verbalize that "feel" escapes us almost entirely.

For present purposes, however, it's not a fly rod's action (or feel) that will be of interest; instead, our focus is on the construction practices themselves that makers have used to obtain the action they wanted. To begin, we point out that nearly all current estimations of a fly rod's action are understood to be a function of its taper. Inevitably, the rod's length and weight are factors as well, but within these parameters, contemporary fly-fishermen and builders alike consider a rod's particular action to result from its designed taper—even to the extent that this connection is now taken for granted.

But, how different from Phillippe's time when makers determined "action" through the choice of building materials, the rod's length and its ferrule sizes. In Phillippe's day, a rod's feel and casting characteristics were determined by construction procedures very different from those used in the modern fly rod, but more importantly, design implications of the taper itself remained largely unsuspected.

Phillippe reel

Indeed, to the Phillippes and others, a rod's "taper" simply did not mean what makers came to understand only the briefest moment in time later.

Tom and I will explain the transition to the modern rod (the exact legacy inherited by Marinaro and others), but we anticipate our conclusions by saying that it arrived suddenly and without precedent with H. L. Leonard and his kind in the mid-1870s. Certainly, other writers have made this same observation, but none has demonstrated exactly what this change means from the rod-maker's perspective—and the change wasn't one of subtle evolution. Specifically, three important lessons still had to be learned from the Phillippe era, and in the following order: Someone had to; 1) realize, fully, that it is necessary to preserve the hexagonal shape of a six-strip rod—thus, retaining ***all*** outer fibers to capitalize on bamboo's full potential; 2) discover planing techniques able to remove material ***only*** from each strip's interior surfaces and to yield precisely identical strips, and; 3) discover what manipulating the shape of a taper, ***in itself***, contributes to the action of a bamboo fly rod. Only upon realizing these three objectives would the "smith" age pass and the modern era of precision (and "production") begin. The Phillippe rod was poised just at the precipice of these discoveries, but rod-makers in his day had not yet thought to take that plunge.

These statements are freighted with questions and require explanation, so let's follow the trail. We begin with our case-in-point—the Phillippe rod and its actual construction. Marinaro gave the rod its "official" measurements at some point prior to 1954, but the odd thing is that he obtained those diameters (historically, called "calibers") in sixty-fourths of an inch. Perhaps a strange practice to apply as late as the 1950s, but we suppose the explanation is that Marinaro wished to use the same measuring system that had been standard in Phillippe's time. Also reminiscent of that antiquated practice, the calibers were obtained at just three locations for each of the sections—one at each end and another at midpoint. Marinaro's measurements are cited by others, but they seem to have appeared first in Herter's *Manual*:

> three sections of six-strip bamboo; length 11 feet; swelled-grip checkered bamboo; diameter of swelled grip at largest diameter 1 inch; butt section above checkering 34/64; middle of butt section 25/64; top of butt section 23/64; middle joint 19/64 - 18/64 - 14/64; tip 12/64 - 10/64 - 5/64; dovetailed ferrules size 19 and 12. The six strips are so finely worked that after gluing you cannot see the joints with a 10-power magnifying glass.[12]

Earlier, Tom and I explained that the rod is actually 11 1/2 feet in length, but we were surprised to discover that certain other measurements had been taken more coarsely than expected. Perhaps, when Vince first examined the rod, his notion to gather measurements was only an impulse and he lacked adequate instruments. As to those three, distant, measuring points for each section, Lord only knows what dimensions Phillippe may have been shooting for between the 23 inches (or so) separating the stations, but building across such broad increments seems to have been standard back then. The point here is that, somehow, early rod-makers obtained the action they were after, but their methods were more "by the seat of the pants" than through any carefully controlled design. Why?

There are a couple possible answers—one having to do with the common fishing practices in those days, and the other, implicating limitations in rod-construction techniques themselves. First, to the latter issue and an 1883 magazine article written by T. S. Morrell (a writer of popular sporting literature) for the *American Angler*. Describing the usual practice to determine a taper, Morrell admits he's only an amateur maker, but he says he learned his techniques a couple decades earlier from his Newark, New Jersey friends, E. A. Green and Charles Murphy—decidedly, no better company for any rod-maker to keep back in the 1860s. Morrell seems not to have realized it, but his procedure to establish a taper was already obsolete by the 1883 date of his article. Still, despite his crude and imprecise techniques, the methods Morrell learned from Green and Murphy remained common even into the early 1870s. Morrell explains how to derive a rod's taper as follows:

> The manner of getting the size *[of the six strips]* correctly is to take the male ferrule for the thick end of the joint, and the female ferrule for the small end; stand each on end on a piece of paper and make a circle outside; then with a pair of small compasses measure the circle into six equal parts, and draw a line from point to point across the circle, so that all the lines meet in the centre. This will show the size and taper of each piece (strip), and the exact shape.[13]

The result, if Morrell describes the entire process, would be a dead-straight taper—beginning at one end of a section and increasing in a uniform, linear progression to its other. It's possible there could have been additional tapering considerations, but Morrell suggests none. Nor have we discovered more sophisticated explanations of early tapers in the writings of others. Thus, it would seem that all one required for a taper was an initial choice of rod length, followed by additional choices of ferrule size. In this latter, Morrell offers no advice for the maker's deliberations—doubtless, because choosing ferrules was thought to be a rudimentary kind of decision. His larger intention was only to explain how to use one's ferrule tubes to determine the end-dimensions for his six, individual strips, knowing that, when finished, the end-to-end taper will simply fall into place between these points.

In an earlier paragraph, we questioned how precisely Phillippe may have controlled his tapers, but there's little reason to suppose his practices differed from those of Green, Murphy and Morrell. More about rod-construction in a moment, but we realize, too, that for the sort of fly-fishing practiced in the mid-to-late 1800s, subtleties of precise measurement would not have made great deal of difference. The length, weight and action of those old rods were so completely different from anything preferred today that it's barely possible to imagine fly-fishers in the 1860s would have noticed subtleties in a taper. Subtleties mean everything to the lighter and shorter, modern, dry-fly rod, but they just don't have much effect in rods measuring 12 feet or more in length, and before Murphy, Mitchell and the Phillippes, these usually weighed over a pound. Moreover, in slinging wet flies across a pool with rods of that magnitude, fishermen were not worried about taxing their energies with false-casting. Apparently, false-casting as we know it today wasn't practiced at all, and a rod's action was usually expected to deliver a brace of flies directly to its target with a single, swooping back-cast.

Fly-fishing in the 19th century was a far cry from our current methods, and because of those differences, our earliest rod-makers probably had little cause to fuss about designing precise tapers. The question of "action" was answered well enough through Morrell's methods, plus some external tweaking to follow. What fishermen wanted was a long and supple rod, and most discussions of those early rods focus less on its feel when casting than on its ability to hook and play a fish.

In 1864, Thaddeus Norris wrote his treatise, *American Anglers' Book*, and between this work and Genio Scott's *Fishing In American Waters*, late 19th century readers were provided with what they regarded as definitive information on the topic of American sport-fishing. The following selection from Scott's book contains his view of the best composite trout rods with the best actions:

> Rods made from split bamboo are unquestionably the best in use; but a Robert Welch rod, of ash for the butt and second joint, lancewood for the third, and split bamboo for the fourth or tip joint, is the best rod that I have ever owned for general fly-fishing.... I prefer a single action rod to the one of double action or a "kick in the handle," though the latter may send a fly farther, and deliver it more gracefully, but it lacks the snap of the single action to strike.... Neither rod should be to withy, but have snap or elasticity enough in the top to hook a fish without yielding enough to permit the sinner to disgorge. One of the pleasures of fly-fishing is to use a rod which will responsively hook a trout without an effort of the angler. The sport consists in delivering a fly neatly on a straight line–seeing the trout rise gushingly to the surface and accept the lure–and playing a trout gracefully.[14]

(Two incidental queries come to mind: In learning of the "double action" rod, do we assume we're reading about the nascent stages of "parabolic" action—built somehow by intention before the 1860s, only to be "invented" 80 years later amidst the spokes of a bicycle and a French *hotelier?* And, in reading "the trout *[rising]* gushingly to the surface *[to]* accept the lure," are we to understand that, back in the 1860s, this fisherman regularly tormented his brookies with the floating fly? How rude... Halford had not yet been published!)

Continuing our look into 19th century fly-fishing, it is always a delight to read Henry P. Wells' elegant, persuasive and charming prose, but particularly on his requirements for a rod's length, weight and action. Even toward the end of Wells' century—when there was a concentrated effort to reduce length and weight—the question of optimal action was far from settled. Here, in his 1885 *Fly-Rods And Fly-Tackle*, Wells addresses a rod's flexing needs:

Genio Scott's "The Angler and his Gaffer"

> All will admit that comfort in use, efficiency in casting the fly, and power to control and land the fish after it is fastened, are the desiderata; strength to withstand the incidental strain, and elasticity to recover on the removal of the deflection caused thereby, being in all cases presumed.
>
> When the fly-rod is under discussion, we not unfrequently hear it urged, as the highest of encomiums, that some particular rod can be so bent with safety that the tip will touch the butt....
>
> If the prime object and sphere of usefulness of a fly-rod was to tickle the butt with the tip, there would be nothing to be said. But this is not the case. To cast the fly with fluency and precision, and without a sense of dread in the caster when his line exceeds the length of his rod, lest on the back cast he fasten his flies in his own ears–this, and the power to control at will the course of the struggling fish with an implement adequate to any possible emergency, yet imposing on its user not one ounce of superfluous labor–these are the desiderata in a fly-rod.
>
> Give your rod nerve–backbone–so that when you take it in hand it feels as if the tip were absolutely under your command, even when weighted with forty feet of the line it is proposed to use. It should be pliable, and when swung horizontally, holding the handle quite still, it should work evenly from the butt, and with a constant and even increase of uniform action quite to the tip. Look first to this, then give it as much lightness as the material you use will permit.[15]

While Scott's and Wells' explanations of fly-rod action typify what was wanted in the 1880s, their "desiderata" bear little resemblance to what fly-fishers prefer today. On the other hand, although a dry-fly fisherman wouldn't care for the action Wells prescribes, at least we can see that his mind is just at the edge of accounting for flexing characteristics in the more concrete terms we look for nowadays. It's not that earlier writers were unable to express themselves on the topic of action with words that might please us more: It's simply that they were not thinking about flexing needs in the way we do. It's not power of expression that was wanting, but awareness and purpose. Wells' book is fascinating in a number of ways, and we will be dealing with a few of his additional ideas in just a moment—a set of explanations that emerges both unannounced and unanticipated.

In the meantime—returning to the Phillippe rod and our questions about its construction—we mentioned that early building techniques commonly yielded a straight taper. But a minimum of math applied to Marinaro's dimensions reveals that the tapers in Phillippe's rod sections do not progress uniformly at all. To be more particular, we offer a sidebar of the dimensions Tom and I took at the Pennsylvania State Museum. Consistent with our current practices, these were obtained in thousandths-of-an-inch and at 5-inch increments along each of the three sections—the diameters measured over varnish probably no more than 0.004" thick. Although the rod maintains surprising concentricity throughout its length, we found a few, small anomalies, and in those areas we averaged our readings around the circumference.

When plotted on graph paper, the Phillippe rod's taper increases through each of the 5-inch stations we assigned, but the surprise was to see erratic jumps and dips throughout. That is, while a constantly increasing taper is there, that taper appears to have been determined almost randomly—modeled less with any sort of plan than with a jumping-bean. Even allowing for possible inaccuracies in measuring or plotting, when I smoothed-out certain extreme deviations, the graphed taper remained far from uniform in its progression and its trajectory does not describe anything like the straight taper suggested in Morrell's writings. What was Solon thinking in arriving at the action he wanted?

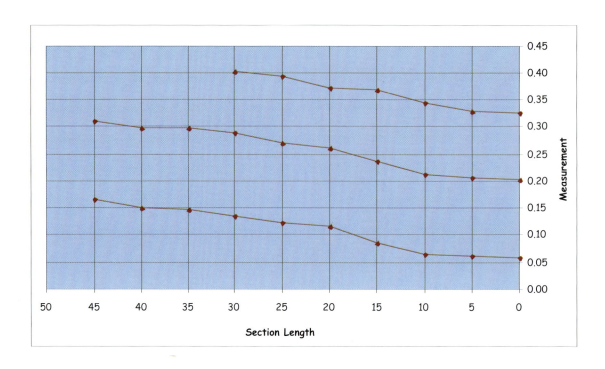

Station	Butt	Mid	Tip
0	0.326	0.202	0.058
5	0.328	0.206	0.061
10	0.345	0.212	0.065
15	0.368	0.237	0.084
20	0.373	0.260	0.116
25	0.395	0.270	0.124
30	0.402	0.289	0.135
35		0.297	0.147
40		0.298	0.150
45		0.312	0.167

The Phillippe rod's measurements

No documentation exists to explain the building practices employed in the Phillippes' shop, but Solon was not lacking in craftsmanship. So, despite eccentricities in the taper of this rod, we can expect its overall action must be close to what he was after. Still, our questions remain: What action *was* that and how was it obtained? What did a taper mean to him and how critical was its construction? Nowadays, a rod's final taper is planed directly into the interior surfaces of its strips, but apart from Morrell's article cited above, little evidence exists to document how bamboo strips were prepared in Phillippe's day. How did Phillippe and other makers shape their strips?

Readers would seem to get a peek at those early methods through Fred Mather's *My Angling Friends* and his own, early encounters with Phillippe's better-known contemporary, Charles Murphy. Mather was not reporting as a rodmaker himself, but only wished to recall certain conversations to which he was privy back in 1865—those between Murphy and his rod-making friends at Conroy's, down on lower Manhattan's "Tackle Row." Mather registers his early appreciation for the accuracy involved in building a bamboo rod, writing:

> A wooden rod is worked down from the outside, tested, sandpapered here and there to get the proper curve under a strain, and that ends it. But the split bamboo, which our trans-Atlantic friends call a "built cane rod," must be so worked down from the inside of each of its strips that it will be perfect after they are joined, for there can be no taking down of the outside enamel, where the strength and resiliency lie.[16]

These remarks would seem to be revealing and definitive, but it's important to know that Mather made them in

1901—a time when makers had learned considerably more about bamboo rod construction than was understood in the particular period to which he refers. We'll explain our statement in what follows, noting for the moment only that it seems Mather's recollection innocently conflated later building practices with those that were common when he first conversed with Murphy. (In fact, Mather's mistaken account of Murphy's 1865 bamboo rod-making practices describes what Tom and I mean by the "modern" fly rod.)

First, an incidental point: The "enamel" of which Mather speaks is actually of no value whatever in a split and glued rod and is not preserved. Technically, the term describes only the thin, paint-like deposit along the outermost surface of a culm. But Mather and others used the word both innocently and loosely in those days. Apparently, they really didn't mean to indicate that outer "skin," as such, but rather, the tough rind of "power-fibers" (as we now call them) lying just beneath the enamel.

Rod-makers soon learned to preserve those outer fibers, but how much that need was appreciated back in the 1860s is open to question. Recall especially: Up until the very late 1870s, all rods were delivered with fully-rounded cross-sections, and the rounding process necessarily required both the enamel and the strong, outer fibers to be shaved and pared down.

Nevertheless, the importance of retaining outer fibers was not entirely disregarded, for it seems certain that when six-strip rods evolved from their four-strip predecessors, it was not so much because of any structural superiority lent by two additional strips, but because makers knew the effect of rounding would be less severe on a hexagon than on a square. And less rounding means more of the bamboo's power-fibers can be preserved in proportion to its inner pith. So, there are these observations after all, and while Mather was not on target, neither was he entirely mistaken about early concern being directed to a bamboo rod's outer surfaces.

Building practices during Murphy's and Phillippe's time—and the question of a rod's action—remain our focus. We mentioned Morrell's writings on how to derive a taper, but Thaddeus Norris (*American Anglers' Book*, 1864) probably offers the clearest evidence of early makers' shaping techniques. Although Norris preferred "composite" fly rods (with butt-sections of ash and mid-sections of hickory), for the tips, he recommends four, "rent and glued" strips of cane. Here, Norris specifies the tough, Malacca cane—used in umbrellas and walking sticks—rather than the more common Calcutta bamboo. In building his tip-sections, however, Norris describes a series of steps equally applicable to any of a rod's three sections. Murphy, Phillippe and a few others were building all-bamboo rods shortly after the mid-1860s, and because they were aware of each other's techniques, there's little reason to think that (whether four- or six-strip construction) their methods would have varied significantly from Norris' description. In fact, most fishing-tackle historians believe Norris learned his craft directly at the bench of Samuel Phillippe.

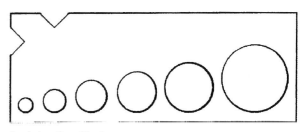

Steel plate from Norris

Norris explains how to split a culm to obtain the four strips, then how to shave each strip into a triangular cross-section with a 90-degree angle at its apex. The outer, enamel side of each strip would be oriented to the top, and the lower (inner) surfaces would be drawn, repeatedly, across a small plate of steel into which a 90-degree "V-groove" had been cut. Strips for each of the rod's different sections were proportioned accordingly.

Apparently, each strip was also tapered somewhat in the process, but with what particular care, and with what "design" considerations in mind, Norris does not say. We would have expected that, since Norris emphasizes other important details in the construction process, he would have called attention to the importance of the taper as well. But, like Morrell, Norris makes no mention whatever of that most-critical element, and the likely explanation is that the usual, straight taper was simply assumed. The strips for each section were then glued together—first,

Those Pesky Phillippes

forming halves, then, when dried, filing their inner surfaces flush, and mating these halves to each other.

Lastly, but most revealing to us, Norris explains that both the rounded shape and the final taper for each glued section would be formed along its *exterior* surface. The first steps were to file and sand the corners off entirely, then to draw various areas of each section through a series of round dies of decreasing circumference. As with the notched grooves mentioned above, these dies were made from a steel plate into which a set of holes (graduated in size) had been cut.

Norris' building techniques, while not easy to perform, seem straightforward, and because he, Murphy, Mitchell and Phillippe (and perhaps others) knew well of one another, it's not likely that their procedures would have differed. In any case, all bamboo rods in those days were given a more-or-less straight taper with both the rounded shape and the final taper being formed later on the *outside* surfaces. This process makes no difference with hardwoods, but with bamboo, the rounding and shaping necessarily destroys many of those most-valuable fibers lying nearest the outer surface.

So, early rod-makers did not carefully preserve the bamboo's outer rind as Mather has written, nor were shaping techniques capable of yielding the precisely tapered strips he describes. Mather claims that individual, bamboo strips were given their taper by being "worked down from the inside" because subsequent external shaping cannot be allowed. Although this is exactly what rod-making soon came to mean, it seems clear that the practice was not employed by Norris and others in the late 1860s—that is, not at the time of the Phillippe rod in question.

Today, rod-makers can look back and converse endlessly about the tapers of those older rods, but the point we wish to make is that Phillippe's generation of makers seems not to have been having that same conversation. Controlling a rod's taper with the sort of precision Mather describes had not yet been conceived, and the simple explanation is that the wheel of time hadn't rotated to that position—but it was about to. The idea itself had to wait for the three objectives we described earlier.

In our journey to locate these discoveries, we return momentarily to Morrell and read once again from his article of 1883. Morrell, writing 20 years after Norris, is no longer speaking about the four-strip tip, but about six-strip construction through the entire rod. In what follows, we encounter still a different process to prepare bamboo strips:

> I first sawed the bamboo in two strips with a fine sharp handsaw; then I took a board with a perfectly straight slit sawed the length of a joint of the proposed rod. Laying the flat part of one of the strips (I had just sawn asunder) on this board over the slit, I carefully placed it so as to get the requisite taper, and then tacked it at the edges firmly to the board. Then with a rule and pencil I drew on the bamboo a straight line, being careful to taper it right, and sawed it out; then taking out the tacks replaced the strips so as to saw out the other side. I sawed six pieces exactly alike in size and taper for a joint....
>
> The board on which I sawed the strips has grooves cut so that I can easily plane the inside of the strips; any inequality I finish off with a file.[17]

Here, Morrell advises against splitting one's strips, and insists, instead, upon the need to saw a rod's taper directly from the bamboo culm. One wonders why he was so finicky in his attempts to saw those tapers, because, regardless of how much care might be taken, Morrell's method could never yield but the crudest of outlines. Not even the finest jewelers saw can cut a bamboo strip to the tolerances needed for a fly rod—that is, *unless* the maker only required a roughed-out, straight taper. Morrell could saw initial tapers of some sort, of course, but it's important to note that his following paragraphs call for additional steps to determine the rod's action; these, to perfect his joinery, to round the outside surface, and then to sand (or file) the rod's final taper. So, the results of Morrell's building practices turn out to be old-fashioned after all.

But, hidden at the end of Morrell's prescription for sawing is that planing board he describes—a most interesting detail. Here, it appears he found the means to achieve a measure of precision for his internal joinery. Morrell offers no particulars in his description of the planing board and its grooves, but perhaps a later, derivative version is shown in the accompanying drawing from Wells' *Fly-Rods and Fly-Tackle*.[18]

None of us knows who first devised the board Morrell describes (or when), but with it, apparently he discovered a way to obtain precise, 60-degree, internal bevels. Morrell's planing board promises some of the accuracy we're seeking to discover, but it's also important to remember that, for Morrell (as for Phillippe, Norris or Murphy in the later 1860s), beveling that 60-degree angle into the strips was not regarded a means to determine the final taper.

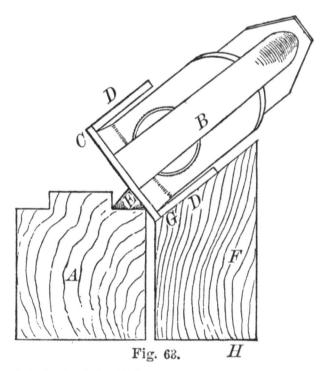

Wooden beveling-jig from Wells

Of course, Morrell's hand-sawn strips couldn't have yielded final tapers either, but apparently, his intention (in sawing those tapered strips) was only to establish an outline, somehow trusting that his planing board would reduce that taper proportionately as he shaped his 60-degree bevels. And that's something, after all! Actually, this was a prime moment, ripe with potential. Our hindsight recognizes that final, precision-tapering could have been devised on Morrell's planing board in some manner: The idea was right there, just waiting to be realized, but evidently Morrell did not see it and he completed the rest of his building process with Norris' older shaping techniques in mind.

Approaching the end of our search for the modern rod, we shift attention back to Wells' book from 1885 and the particular advice he offers amateur makers. As readers begin his two chapters devoted to rod construction, they see that (as with Norris some 20 years earlier) Wells, too, recommends building the composite rod with wooden butt- and mid-sections, and including a four-strip, bamboo tip. Additionally, Wells specifies the same, straight-tapered sections implied by Morrell, but provides additional assistance (in the form of an illustrated, measuring template) to aid the maker in determining those proportions directly.

Also similar to earlier writers, Wells implies that an initial choice of ferrules will bring a rod's taper into the ball park, but again, with the expectation that its final action will be determined at the end of the building process—that is, on the rod's **outer** surfaces. Finally, Wells advises fine-tuning the rod's action by cutting the length back on one or another of its sections, or sanding and shaving a little here and there—all, a repetition of that old "by the seat of the pants" business.

But, then comes the surprise we've awaited. When Wells turns his attention from building conventional, four-strip tips to the newer fly rods (those having all three sections built of bamboo and in the six-strip format), an entirely unanticipated and different set of concerns appears. Suddenly, we learn of the need to preserve the rod's full, hexagonal cross-section. Here, too, we read Wells' insistence that precision-planing must be done only on the strips' **interiors**, emphasizing that, at all costs, the entire outer rind (power fibers) of each strip must remain untouched.

In explaining how to obtain the strips' 60-degree bevels, Wells requires that "...the rind side of the bamboo, which rests on the bottom of the rabbet...must in this, as in all the steps of rod-making with this material, by no means be touched with the plane...." And, just a few pages later, Wells also explains how to construct a V-grooved, wooden form for planing these strips. With this device, makers are

Those Pesky Phillippes 103

instructed (and, we believe, for the first time) to plane a taper only on the *inside* of the strips, and to do so both to preserve all outer fibers and to establish the rod's final taper.[19] Indeed, in what follows, readers will see that Wells' advice has suddenly leaped completely beyond the techniques and expectations described by Morrell just 3 years earlier.

> For since a joint of this kind cannot well be altered after it is glued together, it is plain the taper and consequent action of the rod must be determined at the same time with the angle, and this without the opportunity for trial and local modification which a wooden rod affords. Therefore some definite rule for this must be established at the outset. Perhaps, all things considered, a true taper for each joint promises the most certain result—at all events for the middle joint and tip. The butt may be modified a little, to diminish its stiffness near the handle.[20]

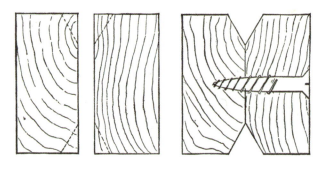

Wooden planing blocks from Wells

How interesting…! Just like that, here we have the quantum leap we've been seeking. It was probably not Wells himself who made it, but at some point between the time of the Phillippe rod and Wells' book, some remarkable thinking took place. Wells is so matter-of-fact, even casual, in his prescription for the hexagonal, bamboo rod that (as with modern rod-makers) he almost seems to take the connection between action and taper for granted. But, because Wells' requirements for the six-strip rod are presented in such a very different context from all earlier explanations, Tom and I do not take that connection for granted at all!

Recall: When writing of wooden and four-strip bamboo rods, Wells describes how action is a function of choosing materials, selecting the ferrule sizes, then experimenting with length, external shaving and sanding. With the six-strip bamboo rod, however, action is established as a ***first*** step—one that's determined by planing that final taper into the strips' inside surfaces. When Wells specifies that "the taper and consequent action of the rod must be determined at the same time with the *[60-degree]* angle," his clear meaning is that a bamboo rod's final action is now a function of its initial taper. Further, the taper must be designed before beginning to plane ("some definite rule for this *[the taper]* must be established at the outset"). Wells does not advise the maker how to devise a good taper for a six-strip, bamboo rod, but there is no mistaking his insistence that the internally-planed taper must now be responsible for a rod's final action.

It is especially interesting to notice Wells' new phrase, "a true taper." Wells says "perhaps a true taper" may be best for the tip- and mid-sections, but he allows that the butt might be modified somewhat. In any case, "perhaps" is conditional and suggests he's aware there could be alternatives. So, the context of Wells' statement no longer confines makers to a taper that runs "true" (straight) from end-to-end, but (in "establishing *some* definite rule") invites a consideration of tapers whose trajectories accord with whatever proportions the maker wishes to devise. This latter notion is entirely different from what makers had been thinking in Phillippe's day, and here emerge the most important consequences in our "search for precision"—the recognized need for predetermined and precisely controlled tapers, and the ability of one's new planing techniques to yield those tapers.

We see that, in several significant ways, while Mather's earlier-quoted remarks would not have applied to the work of Murphy, Norris or Phillippe in the mid-1860s, they surely applied to the best makers shortly before Wells was published. Indeed, if one reads the first sentence of our quote from Wells closely, it would appear that Mather's 1901 explanation of Murphy's 1865 work may have been borrowed nearly directly from Wells' 1885 book. But our point is that Wells' description is meant to describe the new methods, and is not at all applicable to those earlier techniques from the 1860s.

Surprisingly, Wells seems not to have recognized the significance of "his" leap (or, perhaps, even that there *was* one), for the implications had to ferreted from his scattered statements. On the other hand, perhaps this lack of perspective becomes understandable if readers consider the disclaimer offered earlier in his book: "Up to the present writing I have never seen a professional rod-maker at work on a rod of this kind, nor have I ever heard or read any description of the method by them employed...."[21]

But this is a most puzzling statement, for it implies that Wells was writing almost in a vacuum and was not aware that other makers were already using these same methods for six-strip hexagonal construction. Such naivete seems highly unlikely, however because the "production age" was well under way by the date of Wells' 1885 book and it's certain that many makers were building exactly as he prescribes. Perhaps he only meant to say that he hadn't collaborated with other makers on the particulars of their methods—that, on the contrary, he was simply passing along a general set of procedures he assumed to be common practices of the day. Whatever his context, by the time of Wells' publication, those practices *had* become common, though Wells seems to have been the first to describe what suddenly came about.

At some point shortly before Wells' book, rod-makers had started down an entirely different path, both in their deeper understanding of bamboo and in their construction techniques. Building the modern fly rod was now possible. Beginning with the Phillippe rod, Tom and I moved quickly from Mather's recollections of Murphy, then to Norris, Morrell and Wells, and although only 20 years separate the writings of Norris and Wells, a world of change occurred in that short time.

No one seems to know when the planing form Wells describes first emerged or whose invention it was, but by the time of Wells' book, the best rod-makers were using versions of this V-grooved board to shape their tapers and to retain the rod's hexagonal shape. Historians do know, however, that the hexagonal shape Wells prescribes began to appear on the market a good 6-7 years prior to his 1885 publication. Tom and I would insist that only a dedicated tapering form could have created such rods, for neither Norris' notched, steel dies, nor Morrell's apparatus (apparently, designed only to bevel) could yield identical strips

The Phillippe grip, reel seat and reel

with their external surfaces untouched and their final tapers formed only on the inside surfaces.

Wells suggests that he did not know professional makers, but Martin Keane tells us in his *Classic Rods and Rodmakers* that it was H. L. Leonard who first retained that hexagonal cross-section, and who first and fully realized the need to preserve those strongest, outer fibers.[22] Among known, professional makers, perhaps this would be true. But, because Leonard, too, was influenced by others, Keane's statements should not be taken to imply that it was Leonard who invented the grooved planing form—still, we suppose, this remains a possibility.

Interestingly, A. J. Campbell, in his *Fly-Fishing Tackle*, adds to the discussion about "hex-shaped" fly rods, saying it was exactly in those same years (the late 1870s) that Charles Wheeler—Leonard's primary competition in nearby Farmington, Maine—also began preserving the hex shape by planing only a strip's interiors.[23] Nevertheless, while the new construction techniques had become common to these two makers, fly-fishers continued to demand round rods, and for a few years both Leonard and Wheeler conceded to the marketplace by rounding the corners of their rods (though minimizing this effect as each year passed). Apparently, by 1880, the two men were no longer willing to accommodate that public preference and rejected their compromise entirely. Quickly, the full and true hexagonal shape became standard on all their rods.

Historians may never know which of these two makers was first in discovering the new planing methods, but it's apparent that hexagonal cross-sections would not have been possible had these makers been relying on the older methods of external tapering. It simply is not possible to bring one practice for tapering a rod to a halt unless, for other reasons, you've discovered another, different practice.

Regardless, our point is that the rod-making methods Wells describes in 1885 actually began several years before that book's appearance, and the quantum-leap to the modern fly rod seems to have come about quickly between the c.1869 date of the Phillippe rod and the mid-1870s. The earlier discoveries of bamboo and the innovation of six-strip construction were themselves crucial, but the lasting success of the six-strip fly rod was entirely a function of learning how to design a taper and how to plane it precisely into the strips' interiors. With Leonard and Wheeler, a new range of ideas emerged about length, weight and how to predict different actions during the initial, designing phase—no more, that old "by the seat of the pants" stuff!

In 1876, and with the ability to plane final tapers directly into each triangular strip, Leonard and his nephew, Hiram Hawes, designed one of the first mechanical, tapering devices for that purpose. Once again, however, it's A. J. Campbell who suggests that Charles Wheeler may have beat Leonard to the punch in developing the first machine.[24] Campbell admits the possibility is a matter of some conjecture, but even if Wheeler hadn't preceded Leonard, the two devices made their debuts almost concurrently. Historians know little about the relationship of these two men, but it seems clear that Wheeler and Leonard were keeping very close watch on each other's work, and with something other than a friendly interest. Within another year or so of the Leonard/Wheeler machines, Chubb and several other makers quickly followed suit, building tapering machines of their own. The Industrial Revolution was already at hand in other quarters, and by 1880, the "production age" of bamboo fly rods had begun with abruptness and ferocity.

Readers might think that fly-fishers would have reveled in the rewards of modern construction techniques, but it's likely the general public never realized the differences—the hex shape was assumed only to be a six-cornered affectation based on its rounded predecessor. And, too, because most fly rods were still long and heavy (by present standards) and meant for casting a brace of wet flies, the average fisherman may not have appreciated the new benefits.

In fact, the wisdom of preserving a hexagonal cross-section remained in contention even 20 years after Leonard and others had established the practice. The following, peculiar statement comes from James Henshall's 1902 *Outing* magazine article:

> While this *[the advantage of a six-sided rod]* looks plausible enough it has no foundation in fact. The hexagonal rod is not a true six-sided figure, but rather a round figure with six angles; for the face of each section is of course slightly rounded, or convex, as it originally existed in the cane, and the extremely small amount of outside surface that is taken off at the angles to make the rod round does not amount to much, or weaken the rod a particle. In my opinion a round rod will cast truer in every direction.[25]

We mentioned some of Henshall's questionable opinions earlier, but he sticks his neck out very far on this one—wishing to oppose the notion that, by virtue of retaining more of the strong, outer fibers, a hexagonal rod would be superior to its fully-rounded counterpart. Apparently, Henshall had not studied his geometry, nor given much thought to the objectives and advantages of the new construction practices. Perhaps, like so many other fly-fishers of his day, he thought the conversion from rounded to hex-shaped rods was only an aesthetic eccentricity and remained unaware of the actual building practices. Still, Henshall's contention does prove one thing—old and useless ideas often die hardest.

Although contemporary writers may quibble about this and that, no longer conceding to Leonard his earlier position as the "father of the split-bamboo fly rod," Leonard certainly was responsible for fathering a revolution in thinking that, by the late 1880s, transformed the "smith" age of chancy and cumbersome rods into a modern era of precisely tapered and versatile instruments. Tapers, lengths and weights were refined subsequently by Leonard (and the generation of makers trained in his shop) to accommodate the coming craze for casting the dry fly, but it seems to have been Leonard and Wheeler who first accomplished the three necessary objectives stated earlier, leaped past all the old ideas and eventually awakened the public to what a bamboo fly rod really could be.

In circa 1869, the Phillippe rod that Marinaro and Robb discovered some 75 years later, stood as a culmination of everything rod-makers had learned—by no means, the only rod of its kind in this regard, but certainly both rare and one of the finest examples. Within 6-8 short years, and standing of the shoulders of Phillippe's contributions, the change to the modern fly rod took place. And with that change, H. P. Wells, Perry Frazer, George Parker Holden, Robert Crompton, Everett Garrison, Claude Kreider and Marinaro (and the hundreds of other independent makers) inherited exactly the legacy that continues today. Taper preferences and aesthetic taste would vary through the years, of course, but our entire point has been to demonstrate how and why rod-makers arrived at the time when, at last, they could control such choices and build the modern, bamboo fly rod.

At the outset, Tom and I intended only to describe the Harrisburg Fly Fishers' 1954 ceremony, but for us, the story of Marinaro and that remarkable Phillippe rod became an invaluable excursion back in time. The path led through impossible distinctions between facts, assumptions and mistakes, and seemed a great deal more like a maze fraught with briars than a trail. We tried to distinguish between what we came to believe and what we were left only to suppose, and we hope readers would be able to note those differences. Finally, because we know that Tom Kerr, a passionate fly-rod historian and collector, is in the midst of exhaustive research into primary documents and records from the Phillippe era, the full history of six-strip fly rods may soon be set aright.

The Phillippe rod

Chapter Five

News From Other Makers at Mid-Century

Sparse Grey Hackle and Marinaro were the best of friends for many years, sharing a large circle of fishermen, writers and fly-tying colleagues throughout the northeastern states. Working in New York for the *Wall Street Journal,* Sparse grabbed every opportunity he could to escape to his first loves, the Catskill streams. But he also made occasional sojourns to Pennsylvania's limestone country, meeting with Vince, Charlie Fox and others. Perhaps they fished together only irregularly, but Vince and Sparse maintained a close relationship through their frequent and lengthy correspondences. Sparse, especially, would carry on with page after page of news from his other friends, his own tying, fishing, publishing concerns, and often advice for Vince's health an endearing habit since college days, earning him the nickname, "Deacon," or "Deac," for short.

Sparse was one of fly-fishing's greatest advocates—his long and distinguished career promoting fly fishing and its literature, particularly after the 1940s. Yet his published work represented only the tip of an iceberg, for Sparse was even more influential behind the printed word, functioning as a hub or clearing house through whom vast numbers of anglers, fly-tiers, authors and craftsmen passed their information. Just as many of us collect reels, fly rods, coins or books, Sparse collected people, corresponding daily with a long list of fishing friends and colleagues. Very little of his correspondence with Vince has been preserved, but what remains in the PFFMA collection reveals Sparse's expansive and gregarious personality and gives evidence of his deep involvement with the rod-making industry.

"Sparse Grey Hackle" (Alfred W. Miller)

THE HOLDEN ASSOCIATES

It is in Sparse's behind-the-scenes work that we encounter the least-known, but perhaps most interesting of his endeavors. Throughout the 1930s and '40s, he had been fascinated with the craft of rod-making, having carried out lengthy research into the operations at H. L. Leonard, the Hawes brothers and Everett Garrison's shop as well. Sparse was not a rod-maker himself, but in 1947 he undertook a

...and sometimes Vince smiled.

very special project that had been on his mind for many years: Along with his good friend, Dan Brenan (a rod-maker living near Syracuse, New York), Sparse sought to organize a rod-maker's guild. Initially, this was to be called "The Holden Associates" in honor of George Parker Holden (the author who offered so much encouragement to amateur rod-makers), but Sparse and Brenan seem to have dropped that name.

Their guild would focus on small, independent makers, professional or amateur, whose work exemplified the highest standards within the craft. The organization's purpose was to provide a forum for makers to learn of one another and to facilitate discussions among them. In the past, conversations between builders had been as rare as hens' teeth, but Sparse's hope was that, free from public scrutiny or the need for personal promotion, his rod-maker friends might feel free to compare notes. He would serve as the guild's coordinator and editor, ask questions of the members and periodically collate their responses into a newsletter.

The project must have seemed akin to herding cats, but remarkably, and entirely due to Sparse and Dan's winning ways, these several craftsmen eagerly welcomed each other in the common goal to improve the quality of their work. The guild became successful (though only for the briefest moment in time) and provides the sole occasion, saving the present, when we see an exception to the otherwise proud, grumpy and insular world of rod-making. Marinaro, however, preferred not to get involved in discussions on rod-making and declined to join. As always, Vince worked alone and, except for the research on *A Modern Dry Fly Code*, he usually avoided comparing notes—that is, he reveled in his proud, grumpy and insular world.

Dan Brenan, the guild's co-founder, was worried about the amount of time his good friend, Sparse, would need to invest in the new venture and wrote the following letter, expressing early concerns:

> Your suggestion that this rodmaker's Guild be called, eventually, the Holden Associates, is okay; but that connotes a raft of amateur makers ranging, inevitably, from the finest artisan of the Crompton type down to the crudest hencoop carpenter. You couldn't dodge it.... Where could you draw the line? Nowhere. The intent of the enterprise is nominally mutual helpfulness; but in effect it would mean that your life would be made a nightmare by the entreaties for help and enlightenment. You will have created a monstrous Frankenstein that would eventually swallow you whole.... I'll bet right now that you have put plenty of time into it that should have gone into your personal affairs. HAVEN'T YOU?
>
> Right now I can think of several qualified amateurs who could pull their weight, as you phrase it. There's Dan Shepard... who makes superb rods via his sliderule *[sic]*, like Ransom. And Harry Eriksson of ALCOA, engineer... C.E. Decker, Casein Co. Of Amer., expert on adhesives.... And my old files contain many other names I could dig up. Each one you let in will have more or less of a list of cronies; and it is surprising how many folks are tinkering with bamboo in their basements. Must be hundreds of them we don't even know about. But, sooner or later, they would all be on your mailing list and most of them would want special advice on one subject or another, It would drive you crazy; to say nothing of the expense involved.... [1]

We don't know how Sparse resolved these issues, indeed, if he ever did, but despite Brenan's fair warning, he and Sparse went ahead with the guild. They were its initial conveners and appointed themselves as directors. Nearly at once, others joined in and the larger group then ratified all future memberships. While the collection of letters relating to the guild spans only the years from 1946 through 1949 (the majority, written in 1947) they offer a rare look into bamboo rod-building of the day. Sparse's guild is interesting to modern readers for historical reasons, of course, but its true importance is demonstrated within the newsletters and the extensive correspondence from the members themselves. These were preserved by Sparse, then passed to Hoagy B. Carmichael, who recently donated the collection to The Catskill Fly Fishing Center and Museum in Livingston Manor, New York.

During the years Sparse and Dan managed the guild, Brenan was selling sporting books, although from the 1930s through the early '40s, he had been something of a professional rod-maker himself. Dan's was a one-man shop and it functioned on a rather small scale, selling mostly to central New York clients and Brenan's many well-to-do fishing friends.

In an article appearing in *Rod & Reel*, we learn that in 1939 Brenan moved his family from Syracuse to nearby Fayetteville, New York, where he took a job as a machinist. Among his other interests, however, Brenan was both a literary man (writing occasionally for various magazines) and a cellist of some talent. Perhaps his greatest love was for classical music--particularly playing and repairing stringed instruments--but perhaps, too, within his sensibilities, the appeal of these was not so very different from fly-fishing and rod-making. At some point, his bamboo rod business became only a hobby again and Brenan's son, Bill, carried the small business along until the late 1940s. [2]

Writing to Sparse on one occasion, Brenan reported that, over the years, D. C. "Ducky" Corkran had courted him often to join Orvis' revived fly-rod operation at Manchester, Vermont. The shop had been piloted since the late 1930s by Wes Jordan, and Brenan says that he and Wes corresponded frequently. Jordan was rightly proud of his accomplishments at Orvis, but in one of Brenan's later

HOTEL ROBERT TREAT
NEWARK 1, NEW JERSEY
A Knott Hotel

March 29-57

Dear Sparse,

Sorry we didn't have more time to talk at N.Y. sport show. When I get back to Manchester I'll drop a line to Mrs. Atherton.

I have a brook trout that Jack painted for me and of course prize it very highly.

My rod making started in spring of 1919. Made hand made rods and then developed my own milling cutters and machines. The company known as Cross Rod in Lynn, Mass. South Bend Bait bought the Cross Co. and moved it to South Bend where I was Supt. From 1926-1937. Came back east to work for Orvis. The Orvis Co. Went bankrupt and a Mr. Arkel *[sic]* of Beechnut Co. hired me to build rods for the new stock company. Am now V.P. *[in]* charge of all mfg.

While at South Bend I designed some very good high speed splitting machines and millers. Our production in 37 averaged 5,000 bamboo rods a week. The present Orvis rods are nothing more than the old Cross actions impregnated and bonded with phenolic resin. This is one of three patents I hold on rods and archery bows.

I have great respect for Payne Leonard & Thomas but I felt Hiram Hawes was the best. I may be wrong and maybe the few rods of his I came by were exceptionally good but wish that it had been possible to have met him.

Sewell Dunton of the old Montague Co. Is a swell guy and could give you a lot of information on that old Co. The Orvis Co. goes back even farther than 1883 but it wasn't know *[sic]* by that name.

I really believe that Montague put out a better bamboo rod than Orvis previous to 1940. I had to throw the ferrules reel seats and rod stock out and start all over with my own machines and stocks.

Well I have a date to cast at *[Bambergera?]* so will cut this short. Hope you pay us a visit this summer.

Best personal regards.

Sincerely Yours
Wes Jordan

letters to Sparse, we learn that Jordan was not entirely pleased with the company's management team, and privately advised against making the move to join Orvis' operation.[3]

In Sparse's correspondence, we get a glimpse of makers' concerns, questions and a range of appropriate remedies. Topics included heat-tempering, sawing strips, gluing and binding, and locating the best sources for materials. But the members' greatest worries seemed to be directed at securing high quality mill-cutters and mastering sharpening techniques. There were also discussions on dip-varnishing procedures, and of course, the endless crusades to find good nickel-silver tubing and the right man to construct ferrules. Tom and I were particularly amused to note these same troubles beset rod-makers today. It's true; the more things change, the more they stay the same!

By the mid-1940s, Sparse had befriended nearly all the best rod-makers east of the Mississippi, but locating a guild membership roster proved impossible. Still, the newsletters and correspondence identify Everett Garrison, "Pinky" Gillum, George Halstead, Lyle Dickerson, Dan Brenan, Robert Crompton and Nat Uslan. We also came across references to Paul Young, Bob Ransom, Lew Stoner, Walt Powell and Wes Jordan, men who, although they did not become members of the guild, nevertheless remained in frequent contact with either Sparse or Dan. Marinaro, too, stayed in touch with Sparse, but while Vince was well aware of the other makers, apparently only Crompton, Young and Lew Stoner were personally acquainted with Vince. Other letters suggest that the range of Sparse's efforts extended far beyond those makers who agreed to join the guild—correspondence that include the U.S. Forest Products Laboratories, Charles Demarest, F. A. McClure, and a number of commercial suppliers of glue, varnish, milling cutters, snake-guides and nickel-silver tubing.

Both Sparse and Brenan attempted to solicit participation from additional makers, and in another selection from Brenan's letter of February 23, we read his account of somewhat earlier communications with Walt Powell and Lew Stoner:

Powell (Marysville, Calif.) nibbled but did not commit himself; wished us good luck and gave us his blessing. Stoner said NO with loud emphasis. Of all the makers in the country, he had the least to fear from competition; so that wasn't the reason for his view. He is a lone worker by instinct and choice. He developed the hollow rod, put it into Marvin Hedge's hand at St, Louis in 1935 (?) And smashed all records for distance casts.... He answered all my questions without reservations; but he did not fancy the idea of broadcasting such stuff far and wide. He believes that any man who has it in him to make a rod is better off in the long run if let alone; says that Holden (much as he admired him as a man) was responsible for more bad rodmaking than the record shows.... He finally set down and wrote such a searing, scathing, vitriolic denunciation of the methods and standards in mass rod making that I would have been afraid to use it. I thought it was loaded with actionable libel; but I also thought it was true, if unprovable. It is in my files at this moment—and it is going to stay there....[4]

This tale of Brenan's earlier correspondence with Stoner attests to the customary preference among makers of the first order to remain private. Stoner had become legendary as a rod-maker, but he was also a tough cookie. What a shame we're denied the opportunity to read his "scathing, vitriolic denunciation" of mass-produced rods. It's curious to note, also, Stoner's high regard for Dr. Holden, despite the negative comment about his influence. We take Stoner's remark not as a slur on Holden himself, but only on the quality of rods coming from amateur makers who followed his writing. Stoner may seem unfair or excessively high-minded about this, but he was interested in precision at its highest level, insisting that his own rods must demonstrate nothing short of perfection. He believed that any rod-maker unable to turn out first-quality work only devalued the currency. Harsh, perhaps, but in Stoner's mind, this was what Holden's influence upon amateur builders had brought about.

Sparse, too, tested various early prospects for the guild and late in 1946, he made a long trip to Michigan to visit Lyle Dickerson in his shop. Dickerson, despite initial reserva-

Feb 1 1947

Dear "Sparce"

There is some hope for your friend Garrison. I personally am not men enough to take care of the work I have to do and it appears that I am not getting any younger so I am trying to find and develop sources for some of the gadgets that take so much of my time. Among these items are ferrules and we have a small machine shop interested in turning out some high grade ferrules under our direction; just getting under way with the necessary dies, etc. I will still be obliged to draw the tubing for the first number of ferrules and there will not be a heavy production right away. However as these boys get under way I think they will be able to supply ferrules for a limited number of accounts. I am going out there again Monday and see how they are getting along. They have already made some very satisfactory samples and if you will get in touch with Garrison ~~I will do my best to keep him making rods~~ and see what sizes and the number that he needs for immediate use I will try to get them thru during the next month if it at all possible. The big producers in the rod business are grabbing everything in sight; guides, reel seats, ferrules, tubing and what not from regular suppliers and so special sources must be developed.

Just got back from Florida where we fooled snook, sea trout and bass with fly rods -- the tarpon were not in the mood when we were, so didnt connect with them this time.

Will be much interestd ⟨in⟩ with the grinder-- I had to develop a couple myself for war work-- I just wonder if we had the same ideas. I truly hope your eye trouble may not prove too bad--at any rate I hope they leave ⟨you⟩ enough to spread the bull with your typewriter.

With kindest regards,

Dick

tions about joining the guild, subsequently became one of its most enthusiastic contributors. In his following letter, written to Sparse in 1947, we get another glimpse at the rod-makers' general state of isolation:

> You must understand that I am quite a clam and do very little unnecessary talking, but I do use what wisps of information I can gather to further the making of quality rods.... Can you tell me more about who Gillum is and what kind of a set up he has. Also, can you outline what he had to say about the impregnated rods.... As to telling Gillum what you saw in my shop you are quite at liberty to do so and if he needs any... information that I can supply he may feel free to ask me. From your comments on his work I would think that he might be the kind of a rod-maker that I would like to trade procedures with.
>
> Please get the dope on dip-varnishing—I have been going to do that for a couple years but haven't had the... time to monkey with the process, but I am going to have to right away.
>
> Cutters—will always be a pain in the neck—even carboloy gets dull too soon. I am using 18 tooth high speed and have tried many other, but came back to the high speed because they are easier to sharpen than carboloy, and grinding heat doesnt impair the hardness, like it does on high carbon steel; which incidentally is very good.... Do I know who Halstead is—I guess not....[5]

How curious to learn that, even as of 1947, Dickerson had not heard of Gillum or Halstead! We can only wonder how many other independent makers at the outset of this venture were similarly unaware of one another. Even Dan Brenan (deeply involved with rod-making in earlier years), confessed in one of his early letters that he did not know Gillum. While Sparse knew all the makers, it was exactly their unfamiliarity with one another that fueled his effort to found the guild. By contrast, however, it's particularly interesting to note that at one time or another nearly all members wrote in concurrence that Marinaro's friend and mentor, Robert Crompton, was the most knowledgeable and exacting builder among them. Here, in a wonderful letter to Sparse on March 12 of 1947, we read Crompton's early acceptance of the invitation to join the guild and learn of his humble beginnings as a maker:

> Your letter of the nineteenth with the Guild Newsletter are both very interesting. Thank you.... I accept you invitation to "join up" with pleasure. I like the idea.... I was first infected with the flyrod virus when I was about ten years old. I knew nothing about making rods nor anyone who could show me how. Since then I have met many who could—if they wanted to do so—but none was over anxious. When I asked questions they evaded. Some purposely misled. As a result I made many grotesque mistakes. But I finally arrived at the conclusion that the rod fraternity is, was and likely always be, very secretive—tho they have NO secrets. Long ago I decided that when *[anyone]* asked me a rod question which I could answer I would do just that—ANSWER! I well remember how MUCH I wanted answers I didn't get, along with snubs and evasions.[6]

Surely, the most influential of Crompton's early mentors was Dr. Holden. While Crompton was already building rods prior to their meeting, there's little doubt that the collaboration was responsible for his great desire, as he attests, to help other makers. A frequent contributor to the newsletter, Crompton held powerful opinions on a great many matters, not least, the intricacies in locating the best metals for cutting-saws and sawing techniques themselves. In the following selection, taken from one of his undated letters, we read his views on finishing procedures:

> A good varnish application DEMANDS a dust-free room (which few craftsmen enjoy), a shop temperature that is high, plus a Polly-Anna temperament and an extensive cuss-word vocabulary. Varnish is NOT waterproof. It checks and cracks with little age, even the best of it. It is frail, easily scratched and chipped. It ALWAYS severely handicaps the rod! A much better result is more easily obtained, and infinetly *[sic]* quicker by using a good "Sealer" (not "Filler") as per the following routing.

(1) Fit all ferrules over clean bamboo.
(2) Remove all ferrules and set aside.
(3) Swab the sections liberally with Sealer from end to end. Let Sealer "soak in" for fifteen minutes. Sealer penetrates rapidly.
(4) Wipe off all surplus Sealer with clean rag.
(5) Replace and fasten ferrules.
(6) Put on silk (or other) windings.
(7) NEVER use ANY color preservative. Varnish windings.
(8) When varnish is througly [sic] dry wax, if desired. Caution. Use no wax except as an absolute- final operation. Wax can be used OVER varnish OR Sealer. Neither varnish OR Sealer can be used OVER wax.

Sealer penetrates! The film left ON the bamboo is practilly [sic] nil. Varnish film is ON the rod and from .005" to .015" thick. Sealer does NOT "slow up" a rod. Varnish strangles a rod no end. Sealer is nearly "water PROOF"! Varnish is anything but. Sealer does NOT darken. It does not mar easily, chip or crack. Sealer application time is less than a tenth the time required by varnish. Sealer is not a dust catcher....[7]

A great many other makers chimed-in with their opinions on the best finishing techniques, but then as now, no consensus was reached. Overall, it was always Crompton who earned the members' highest respect, but how ironical it is that this man who won such acclaim within the industry simply slipped from memory. It's true that Crompton did not produce a large number of rods, published little more than half-a-dozen articles, and left behind neither letters nor records. Nevertheless, despite his physical disabilities, Crompton was a highly active man, and considering the breadth of his reputation it seems surprising that makers, collectors and historians alike have not preserved the story of his career.

Opinions raged among the members on a wide variety of issues—questions of how to produce the best strips; how to manipulate one's milling machine; which varnish or glue is preferred; how to avoid glue-lines. Of particular concern was what to do about ferrules, locating suitable materials, designing the best product and, especially, finding a reliable shop to supply the product. There were no reliable, commercial sources for first-quality, nickel-silver ferrules in those days, so each maker had to deal with that problem on his own. Dickerson attempted some permanent, professional arrangements as did Crompton, but in both cases, the men were unable to resolve production problems. George Halstead was generally regarded as the best metal-smith in the industry, but he could hardly supply everyone's needs. Interestingly, it was Dickerson who initially raised this issue for the guild members, even though Sparse had previously attested that Dickerson himself made some of the best ferrules in the group. The March 6, 1947 newsletter includes a rather lengthy series of responses to the question of one-piece, swaged ferrules:

Dickerson says: 'Am serious about the best design for a ferrule because I don't believe the 3-pc is the answer in spite of the tradition. Too much wood has to be cut away in fitting them. Not long hence I may make up a set after my own idea and send them to you. They will still be made from hard drawn tubing but they will be made and fitted correctly.'

Brennan says: Leo Benkler, a tool engineer with IBM specializing for the past 25 years in dies of various types, says that such ferrules are very poor stuff. Says that Granger uses such ferrules; and that it is a shame to put such rubbish on the really high grade sticks they make (or used to make). All cheap rods—Horrocks-Ibbotson, Union Hardware, Montague City, etc.—use such ferrules of course.

Gillum says: If one of my customers came in and picked up a rod of mine with such ferrules on it, he would lay it down and walk out. They are so well connected with cheap rods in the mind of the angler that I would not want to use this type.

Garrison says: The disadvantage of the swaged ferrule is that none of them are properly made yet. They must be made with stock enough for hand fitting, but they try to punch them to fit. The metal in a Heddon pre-war swaged ferrule was actually thicker than that in their 3-pc ferrule of the same size, but the 3-pc ferrule was noticeably heavier. The sloping swaged neck distributes the stresses; bamboo works at 15,000 pounds per square inch, with complete reversal of stress, and it is very difficult if not impos-

TROUT RODS   Since 1919   SALMON RODS

H. S. GILLUM
Finest Custom Made Rods
Manchester, Vermont

Ridgefield, Conn.
February 3, 1947.

Mr. Alfred W. Miller
55 Liberty Street
New York, N.Y.

Dear Mr. Miller:

Sorry that we were not in yesterday when you called, but as usual that is the case-when we are out for a few hours, someone whom we wish to see, usually drops in. But if I don't drag my husband out a few hours he would be working constantly.

It was swell of you and Mr. Garrison to drop in for a little visit-we both enjoyed it very much for Pink is always ready to help a friend out. But one thing he would like to ask is that the ferrule situation be kept confident between you, Mr. Garrison and Pink, himself. The reason for this is that Mr. Halstead is such a peculiar person that he may get a little peeved. Pink feels certain that he can keep this from him by just ordering the extra ferrules along with his own supply.

As for the cutters, Pink is aware that they are not just right. He has approached Mr. Halstead several times on this very subject but there is no changing his mind or opinion. An agreement was made between Pink and Mr. Halstead (who designed and constructed the milling machine) whereas Pink could reject or accept the machine, whichever he saw fit. As he did not find it to his liking he certainly has no idea of taking it. But in order to get out our rods this year, we have no other choice but to use this machine as we are also running through one hundred and twenty five rods for him-so as to give him an opportunity to work on the ferrules.

Pink would certainly appreciate any information that you could advance on the designs and angles of cutter blades which you think would be the proper design for milling bamboo segments.

We are looking forward to seeing both you and Mr. Garrison at an early date.

Very truly yours,

Mrs. H. S. Gillum

sible to get a nonferrous metal which can withstand such stress and reversal without ultimately crystallizing and breaking. That is one reason why ferrules should be oversize in diameter, compared to the body of the rod. Heddon has the best design I have seen except that it is not made to be hand-fitted. The mouth of their female ferrules are reamed to seat on the sloping shoulder, which is right, and important. Gillum recently told the editor he had heard that in fitting ferrules at the Leonard factory, the last thing they do is give the male ferrule a good hard squeeze in a three-jaw chuck.[8]

Significantly, it was the late Lewis Feierabend (working with Nat Uslan in the latter half of the 1940s) who developed his new, "Super-Z" ferrule. Feierabend's initial purpose, however, was not to redress the dearth of good hardware available to bamboo rod-makers, but to devise a suitable ferrule for the new fiberglass, fly-rod industry. All existing ferrules were of the "step-down" design, but fiberglass rods required a ferrule with uniform internal dimensions on both the male and female parts. Feierabend did not obtain his patent until in 1952, although the new ferrules had become commercially available several years earlier. Through Sparse's letters we learn that, at once, many bamboo makers, including Crompton, Garrison, Young, Bill Brenan, Wes Jordan and Gillum, converted to their use. Vince, too, wrote to Sparse, advising that the "Super-Z" was simply the finest ferrule available.

Additional newsletter topics included metallurgy, tooling and other technical issues, but these discussions often became highly specialized or existed as fragments within some larger context. Nevertheless, the example that follows is of interest because it reveals the makers' concerns for tapering bamboo strips and the machines dedicated to that purpose. The discussions are compelling, but because each maker's own machine for sawing, beveling or tapering was a "one-off" design, the several conversations rarely connected to a common problem. Some machines employed tiny, circular saws; some used cutter heads; some were built to move the cutters across the bed; others were designed for the bed to travel under fixed cutters. Some used templates for each taper, and some had beds that were adjustable. Since each machine engaged the cane in a different manner (or at a different rpm), opinions differed on the best kind of steel to use. And, of course, no two makers offered the same advice for the best sharpening procedures. Typical of these discussions, is the following summary, found in the February 19, 1947 newsletter:

> *Gillum* says: Is using Halstead's equipment and does not think the cutters are properly designed but can't get him to alter them. Cutters are stellite, he thinks No. 4, about 3 inch diameter with 16 inserted radial teeth 1/8 inch thick. Run about 3,000 rpm for roughing and 2.600 for finishing; Halstead insists on light depth of cut, .025 inch per pass.... Feed is 42 inch strip in 40 seconds. A gummy substance forced from the bamboo by heat and pressure gathers on the teeth back of the cutting edges....

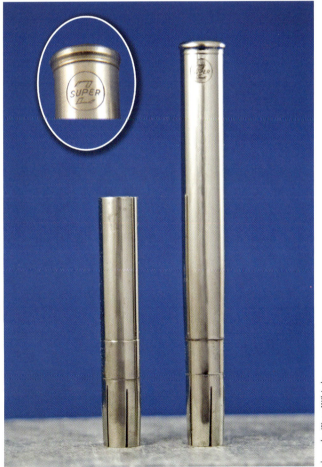

"Super-Z" ferrule

photo by Tom Whittle

News From Other Makers at Mid-Century 119

All Gillum's data point to wrong tooth angles and shape. He is getting clean cuts but with far too much pressure and friction. His strips get so hot they are unpleasant to handle. I think that so far Dickerson seems to have the most practical set-up with his high speed cutters and permanently set up heavy equipment for rapid and easy sharpening. What the rodmaking profession needs is a good cutter sharpener who does business by mail. Brenan sent some chi[p]s from his high speed cutter; none available from the carboloy. He did not state depth of feed, but they were almost as fine as dust. His feed is about 30 seconds per joint. He says chips from his carboloy cutter were larger. As I hazily remember, Dickerson cut a strip to show me how his mill worked, in a single pass, and only took 10 to 15 seconds to put it through. Maybe not even that long. I can't see well enough to tell whether it was roughed or finished, but it was fully shaped and felt and looked good as far as I could tell. Don't remember inspecting his chips for size, but the [m]achine sure threw them around to beat hell.⁹

As we read through the many letters written to Sparse, it's especially curious to note the absence of disagreement or controversy. It's not that the makers would reach consensus, but rather that each seemed to be engaged in a private discussion with Sparse instead of conversing more openly with each other. In most of the letters, members only barely acknowledged others who may have volunteered opinions on an issue. We're guessing the reason for this would be due to an inherent time-lag in the logistics of the guild's operation. Apparently, makers were asked sets of questions by Sparse, and each person would respond as time permitted. Of course, there was only mail service in those days, and because all correspondence flowed only through Sparse's office, members had to wait for a subsequent newsletter to learn what the others were saying. In the meantime, perhaps not everyone had weighed-in on an issue, but, by then another set of questions had been raised.

Brenan's letter to Sparse, quoted at our beginning, seems to suggest that Sparse's initial idea for the guild was to create something similar to our modern "chat-room," yet, based on the evidence of the letters, the give-and-take of communications doesn't appear to have worked out quite that way. As to the guild itself, while apparently successful, it seems not to have survived more than four newsletters. Still, because we find no signs of discontent whatever, we can only surmise that Sparse's energies for managing the project must have become taxed to the limit. Evidently, Brenan's early warnings finally came home to roost, and in 1948 the guild ceased to be.

In Praise of The Humble Panfish

Although a great trout fisherman, Sparse was also in love with smallmouth bass, traveling often to south-central Pennsylvania to fish for both "smallies" and brown trout. Vince never showed much enthusiasm for warm-water fishing, although on occasion he, too, would try his hand at bass. In the 1940s and early '50s, Pennsylvania's trout season ended in July, and because a guy has to do something, from time to time Vince would be found on the Susquehanna or Juniata Rivers.

In the PFFMA "Marinaro Collection," Tom came across a wonderful set of letters between Sparse and Vince, dated October, 1949, about a year after the guild's demise. Sparse begins his nine-page, single-spaced, typewritten tome by thanking Vince for a "bully" letter with "bully news." Apparently, in a previous letter, Vince had reported that G.P. Putnam's Sons intended to release new books by both him and Charlie Fox in the coming new year. Marinaro's book wouldn't have been news to Sparse because Vince had circulated an early manuscript of *A Modern Dry Fly Code* at the first FFH banquet in the previous year—when Sparse and Edward Hewitt were in attendance as guests. But, together with Fox's new book, *Advanced Bait Casting*, the two publications coming from the same publisher in the same year may have been a surprise. (Sparse, later, wrote the preface for Fox's work.) Sparse then jabbers on for many more pages about his health, work, the publishing industry, friends, bass fishing and plugs, bamboo, casting rods and rod-makers.

Working open water on the Susquehanna River

Of greater interest, however, is Sparse's mention of a most surprising gift from Vince—and Fox, too, becomes implicated in the episode to follow. Trout or not, fishing is always fun, and while Vince often grumbled to me about Charlie and his "damn plug-fishing," he often accompanied Fox to the better smallmouth streams. Charlie was as mad about bass as Vince was about trout, and had a mission to convert Sparse and Marinaro to a new form of casting, called "midget-plugging." Fox's *Advanced Bait Casting* highly touts this recent and little-understood idea of sportfishing for smallmouth, and in his introduction, we read about some of the techniques:

Strange it is that four generations of casters have produced so little popular change or accepted advancements in the field of bait casting. It is the opinion of some anglers, this writer among them, that bait casting as it is commonly practiced today is crude and ineffective as compared to what it could be and what it should be. There is a specialized method, a variation of common plugging, which is a delight to employ, effective to the highest degree, and satisfactory in every respect. It is the use of the 1/4-ounce lure and the specialized tackle that handles it perfectly.

I am of a firm conviction that the small lure properly handled will take many a fish that the large lure cannot touch, and I am positive that practically every bass that took a large lure would also have taken a small one....

The refined sport involves: a long, light rod, a light line, a casting leader, and a free, light running reel along with the midget lure. It meets the fancy of the most sophisticated. I have observed ardent dry-fly fishermen go all out in their pursuit of this sport once they were introduced to it. I have never seen anyone reject this method of angling once it was given fair trial. Why? The answer is obvious. Here is something that affords more pleasure, it is more interesting and more effective....[10]

A side channel

"Smallie" with Clouser minnow

Actually, Fox's new book, although enamored with light-lure casting and midget-plugging, was in some respects a mirror of Marinaro's *A Modern Dry Fly Code*: Both books focus on specialized equipment, new casting techniques, stalking strategies, lure or fly selection, feeding patterns through the changing seasons and the importance of learning to read the water. Some of the finest smallmouth bass fishing in the East was available almost at Fox's doorstep—on both the Susquehanna and Juniata Rivers. These are broad, rocky rivers, holding many deep holes and runs, inaccessible except by boat. Yet, much of the best bass water can also be waded just as one would do for trout. Local fishermen have always been aware of the great sport to be had on these rivers, and at mid-century, Charlie Fox was one of the chief instigators.

During Sparse's trips to the Susquehanna River, he and Fox often spent time fishing with some of Charlie's other friends. Sparse appreciated the opportunity to learn new techniques, cast more lively rods and use the new, lightweight lures just coming onto the market. Vince, meanwhile, never took to bait-casting. He opined—for reasons of his own—that trout held more interesting secrets, and that casting a dry fly was the more beguiling game. In Sparse's letter, however, we learn that, in some earlier correspondence, Vince had volunteered to give Sparse a set of bamboo blanks so he could assemble a bait-casting rod. Despite Vince's disdain of bass fishing, he'd been successful in designing a couple excellent casting-rods for Fox and himself. While it seems doubtful that these would have occupied a place close to his heart, Vince was proud they performed so well and was eager for Sparse to give one a try.

Back to Sparse's letter... two pages address Vince's offer to supply the bait-casting rod:

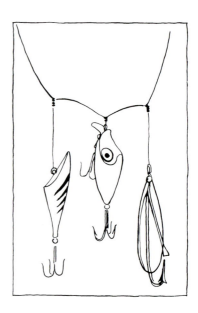

When I asked for the calibrations of your casting rod, I had it in mind to commission one of my rod-making friends to make one up for me; but as that would run into money, I figured to wait until I had a financial windfall which I could use for the purpose.

Your offer of a set of sticks is therefore a very grateful surprise, and I cannot find it in my heart to refuse—assuming, of course that I am not depriving you of anything you were intending to use for yourself. I certainly can finish up a set of sticks; but there is one thing about it. <u>I wish you would cut them to exact length</u>. I can more or less make out with fly rods, but bait rods are unknown territory to me....

Other than that, you don't need to do a thing, even clean off the glue, if they are still rough. I will get my friend Gillum, who is the best man I know at setting ferrules, to do that part for me; the rest I can either do myself or get Garrison to do. Merely a matter of getting or making up the kind of reel seat I want and putting it and a cork handle on the rod.

I have never been able to cast a 1/4 oz. the way I would like nor get anything like the distance you fellows do. I have always been satisfied that the rod was partly to blame, I having used a series of home-made jobs constructed out of dry fly salmon tips, etc. I can see where it is a whole lot of fun, when everything is working right, though.

When you send me the sticks, let me know the top weight of plug or lure this rig will handle and I will put everything I have on the scales and eliminate everything overweight. I assume that 1/4 oz is the top mark. That will not bother me as my favorite is the Johnson Silver Minnow, with or without a little pork rind; casts fine, does not snag up when allowed to sink, and takes many fish in my waters. I still have in the back of my mind the recollections that you recommended the Bugaboo Baby and whenever I see one I'll grab it. I think the Baby Popper and smallest size Oreno are OK, also, and I have a 1/4 oz Jitterbug which does not seem to be made any more, if I read their ads correctly. I think that the Popper and the Jitterbug for topwater, the Oreno and maybe a little River Runt for midwater, and the Johnson spoon for any depth are enough to test the possibilities of any water I may find. [11]

There's little doubt that Sparse knew his bass fishing, and it's a wonderful trip back in time to be reminded of those favorite old lures from the 1940s. We have no verification that Vince's "sticks" were actually delivered, but there's no reason to think otherwise. Vince was a man of his word, happy to accommodate his friend, and in quick response to Sparse's letter, Vince writes:

> I am glad that you will take the sticks and make them up. Really, I ought to apologize for not making them up myself, but I have no idea when I might get them done, and anyway, I have never put a grip on a rod that anyone else liked.... I have been using the sister to that rod for two seasons and I have quit experiments for anything better. I like to remember how skeptical Fox was about that design and then last year when he and I were up on the Juniata together, I put that rod in his hands and told him to cast. He took the rod and fiddled around with it for a few minutes trying to get the hang of it and then suddenly started throwing them to the middle of the river as flat as and straight as a yardstick. You should have heard him rave. He talked about that rod the whole way home and for days afterward. I am not bragging, I don't have to. I don't sell rods and don't want any orders.... [12]

Although it was "only" a bait-caster, it's surprising to learn that Vince would part with one of his rods, something he did on perhaps only a couple other occasions in his life. We'd love to know what became of Sparse's rod or what he thought of it, but that doesn't seem to be in the offing. Fox, however, wrote about his own rod from Vince in *Advanced Bait Casting*:

Vince's old bait-caster from 1947

> Most fishermen do not realize that there are convex and concave tapers in a rod. That is, the builders can set the planing molds so that the diameter of the stick at different points increases or decreases to bring about certain effects in action and strength. Cane casting rods vary more in design and workmanship than is the case of reels, lines, and leaders, the last three having become standardized....
>
> Unfortunately some of the great builders, who are expert fly-fishermen, are not artists with the light-lure bait-casting rod, hence, they depend upon theory and advice, with the resultant wide variation. The common faults are too thin a butt and too thick a tip.... The sport is so young that the best specifications have not as yet been formulated and standardized.
>
> The best rod I ever employed for casting the 1/4-ounce lure was designed and constructed by Vince Marinaro, a top-flight amateur rod-maker. I intend to have a commercial builder duplicate it as closely as possible...
>
> I also intend to have a maker of five strip rods translate these specifications into that type of construction in order to secure similar rods of both types. Such sticks should possess backbone without clubbiness, and the special tapers should put strength where it is needed the most, yet a lure as light as seventy-five grains should bring out the action of the rod.[13]

We suppose this rod would have been the same design that Vince and Sparse were discussing in their letters. But the surprise is to see that, following his strong endorsement, Charlie then publishes precise dimensions for Vince's rod—only to be topped by the announcement that he means to have both five- and six-strip versions of this rod reproduced by still another maker! What's going on here? Certainly, there would have been no mistake, for in those years Charlie and Vince were the very best of friends, constantly reading and offering critiques of each other's work. We don't know what the explanation may have been for releasing that taper information and assigning the rod's construction to another maker, but whatever it was, it would certainly seem to fly far from the ordinary.

One more "wrinkle" to this bait-casting rod—and then an amusing tale.... The wrinkle is this: We note again the existence of that single, bait-casting rod found in PFFMA's "Marinaro Collection"—a rod that was built in 1947. Might this be the "sister" that Vince mentioned in his letter? Marinaro does say in that 1949 letter that the sister rod had been used for two seasons, so its date would be about right. He also says that he had "quit experiments for anything better." It seems more than likely that we have a match here, for surely (considering Vince raved so about the rod) he would not have discarded it in favor of some other, built perhaps at the same time.

The entertaining tale, however, returns us to fly-fishing—but not for trout. While Marinaro was a dry-fly purist with brown trout coursing through his veins, perhaps he was not the most pure of his breed. A fish, after all, is a fish, and lots of 'em eat bugs. So, with July's end to the trout season on the one hand, and Vince's boyish streak of mischief on the other, one of his delights was fly-fishing for panfish. Especially memorable, were a few occasions during the 1970s when Vince and I traveled east to Lebanon, Pennsylvania for an afternoon's bluegill fishing with our good friends, Dick Henry and Frank Loehle. Middle Creek (a small, recently-built reservoir, with drowned, but still-standing trees) was our destination. Dick told us it was chock-full of fat, spunky bluegills.

Frank Loehle and Vince

I'd guess that, apart from the brook trout, no fish is more likely than the bluegill to call back our days of an earlier innocence. Maybe this is just me, but they almost seem happy to see us. Anyhow, driving along, each of us told his own version of a first "sunny" fishing adventure—an old rod, some garden-hackle and a pond. Each story was different, yet the same.

We parked the car, geared-up and made our way to the reservoir, talking about the best flies to use and which areas to try first. Now, Dick has always been happy to help out and, among us locals, is every bit as legendary as was Vince in his knowledge and fishing abilities. But Vince wasn't about to stoop to a "rookie's" advice, and besides, he already had his eye on a little cove just over to one side. So, we just spread out and began casting. At once, the fly-question became irrelevant. These fish couldn't have cared less what we showed them, and the old days came rolling back—the whooping and laughter, the needling back and forth and our delight to hook into these scrappy, little fellas. I wouldn't swear we took fish on every cast, but it almost seemed that way. They wanted chow, and a bare hook might have been as attractive as anything else. I'm sure we landed and released more than 100 fish on any given afternoon, sometimes keeping just enough for each of us to fry up a nice meal.

But then, one overcast day, we just couldn't make it happen. Maybe the fish were tired of seeing us, or maybe they had just moved off to different areas. Anyway, after making our way back to the cars and wondering what to do with the few bluegills we had, Vince spotted a young fellow coming along down a path, peddling an old bicycle. He might have been 10 years old, a worm-fisherman, and he had a nice stringer of bluegills dangling from his handlebars. Vince, always quick to recognize opportunity, pounced on the little guy and began complimenting him on his expertise and his nice string of fish, obviously, with an eye to wheedle the kid out of his catch. Pathetically transparent, still, his silver tongue worked its will (although the boy said he was going to give his fish away anyhow).

It was an outrage, really. Picture this poor little farm-boy, shy and innocent, trying to have some fun one afternoon, and he's accosted by a world-famous author, a grown-man,

Vince and Frank Loehle on Blue Marsh—1977

Dandy little bluegills

photos by Dick Henry

A nice fish-fry

renowned fly-tier, rod-maker and lecturer, who skins the kid alive for a few lousy bluegills (which our expert, with his fancy bamboo rod and specially-tied flies, couldn't catch). So, with jeers and sneers at the rest of us timid, Johnny-come-latelys, Vince grabs the kid's fish for his supper while we were left to flip a coin for the measly, remaining plunder. Then, with buckets  of temerity in reserve, he scoffs openly at the more gentlemanly discretion of his friends. And he was a guest in my car! But, didn't we love to rub Pappy's nose in that one.

GRUMBLINGS ABOUT ROD-MAKERS

George Herter, apparently well-known as a blowhard, created his share of gaffes in his *Rod Building Manual*, but in writing of Robert Crompton, he seems to have outdone himself with the following remarks:

> I knew Crompton personally. He lived in St. Paul, Minnesota. I knew what he could do and what he could not do very well. Crompton had a mania on the five strip rod. That was his only accomplishment. This and letter writing at which he was accomplished. He knew very little about bamboo. Never learned even to use dry bamboo to make rods. Had no scientific equipment of any kind. He could make a good five strip rod by hand. He tried unsuccessfully to design a machine for cutting strips for fly rods. He was a poor mechanic and never succeeded. Because I liked his doggedness I backed him financially on one such machine. It was a complete failure as his others have been. He tried making ferrules and had no success with it either. [14]

But enough of Herter's incivilities.... Let's stay with Sparse's letter to Vince just a bit longer. Sparse, too, was highly-opinionated, but always gracious in his remarks about makers. His letter contains several insights into rod-makers' thinking at mid-century, but in its conclusion, Sparse returns to offer high praise for Robert Crompton. One issue causing Sparse to write to Vince with particular passion was that of heat treating—a practice makers have disagreed on since its beginning. The idea is that, after planing the initial 60-degree bevel, the six bamboo strips are then bound tightly together and "baked" in a specially-constructed oven. Schedules for the requisite time and temperature vary widely from one maker to the next, but once the heat-treating process is completed, all excess moisture is driven from the bamboo, their fibers stiffened and the cane deeper in color.

Apparently Sparse felt compelled to vent on the practice of applying heat to cane. Indeed, all his correspondence with Crompton, as well as his many letters from Gillum, Hewitt, the U.S. Forest Products Laboratory and F.A. McClure advised strongly against heat-treatment. From Sparse's letter to Vince, we read:

> What Crompton says about heat-treating is fascinating. Of course he has his facts correct; I got some dope from the Forest Products Laboratory myself on the effects of heat on wood, and Ed Hewitt ran a lot of experiments, years ago, which precisely confirm Compton's findings. Any amount of heat great enough to affect the wood reduces its physicals.
>
> And yet, you know and I know that you can take a rod and cook the hell out of it and make it fast and hard to beat the band—not just after it has been treated, but from then on. We all agree that it shortens the life of the wood but while it lasts, it sure is pretty to use.... I have a cockeyed idea, not even a theory, but it is something no one else seems to have considered. First, heat-treating drives something out of the wood besides moisture, as you can tell by feeling of the "oil" which comes out. McClure says it is broken down cell structural material somewhat resembling pectin, the stuff that makes jelly jell.
>
> Second, we know from the process of seasoning wood that it *[sic]* possible to drive the moisture out of it in such a way that it will not be reabsorbed in the same quantity. Regardless of how damp it gets, seasoned wood never turns as wet as it was when it was green.

> So. Is it not possible that more moosture *[sic]* is driven out than is reabsorbed? And furthermore, is it not possible that cell structure material is broken down and driven out – and of course does not come back?
>
> If so, let us see what we now have. The cells which have been broken down are not those of the hard resilient fibers but of the binder which holds them together. I believe it is the gradual failure of these binding cells which eventually makes a rod "wear out" and take a permanent set. In other words, the heat-treated rod is as resilient as ever but its life has been shortened.
>
> But the main point is that we have considerably <u>lightened</u> the wood. This makes a hell of a difference in the action of a rod, particularly as it occurs in the upper end.... Crompton himself says that the substitution of floor sealer for the conventional varnish makes an amazing difference in the action of a rod.
>
> Is it possible that the improvement in action through heat treating is merely the lightening of the wood? [15]

The topic of heat-treating remains equally controversial today and will be discussed at some length in Chapter Seven, for Vince, too, believed that all forms of excessive heat severely damage bamboo's power-fibers and that any darkening of the cane is evidence of cellular damage. But Sparse's letter had not yet exhausted its store of strong opinions—he also held a few notions about both the amateur use of the "shooting-board" planing form and the commercial use of a "beveling saw." Recalling that Sparse was not himself a builder, the following opinions are his own reflections on the experiences of his rod-maker friends:

> Of course, I can't see where anyone can make a really accurate rod with that damn steel shooting board that both these fellows *[George Herter and Claude Kreider]* endorse. I just don't see how they can make their various short sections of straight tapers (that's what it amounts to) of exactly the same length on all six strips. They give themselves away when they talk about fitting the "finished" strips together and then going to work on them with a file to take down any "irregularities"— in other words, places where they don't come together.
>
> I just don't think there is any substitute for a full length mold, fully adjustable thrughout *[sic]* its length. I am talking about hand planing, of course. With cutters, a full length template or its mechanical equivalent is equally a necessity.
>
> I don't think Garry *[Everett Garrison]* and I will ever get out a book; for one thing, I know too many rodmakers, and if I said what I thought, I would lose some friends. I just simply don't believe, for instance, that any circular saw, even if only 2" in diameter, can follow the grain of a stick of bamboo accurately, particularly when it "kicks" out of line at the nodes; those bends are sharp angles. I don't believe that the beveling saw is accurate enough to be dignified with the title of a tool; it is just a toy and I marvel that they get out strips with it that even approximate fits. I don't see how any rotary milling cutter can produce a flat surface, devoid of small ripples. But I would lose friends if I said so in print. [16]

Sparse's intention to work on a rod-making book with Garrison is particularly interesting. The two men became very close friends, and Sparse had nothing but the highest praise for Garrison and his rods. It's a shame the project died aborning, but Hoagy B. Carmichael wrote the book the public needed in 1977 and we doubt anyone could have trumped that effort. Hoagy, we also note, had the benefit of reflecting on Garrison's entire career as a maker, so perhaps some things work out exactly as they're supposed to. Still, think how interesting it might have been to read both works.

Hoagy B. Carmichael

Sparse's letter of 1949 concludes with his fond regard for Robert Crompton, and in appreciation of Vince's particularly close association with the man, Sparse offers the following:

> I have often wondered why Crompton never wrote a book. He is indeed the Grand Old Man of rod building, amateur and professional alike, and I don't think there is a serious professional who has not learned something at his feet. Every angler is indebted to Crompton, and some day there ought to be a memorial of some kind to this big-hearted man who resolved in boyhood that if he found out anything, he would share it freely with anyone who asked. He is really a noble character.[17]

It's heartening to read such testimony to Crompton. Ironically, however, Sparse's high praise in August, 1949 turned out to be homage to a man who had passed away just two months earlier at age 61. Sparse and Vince, evidently, had not learned of Crompton's demise, yet his last letters to the guild speak of his failing health and how he was becoming less active.

Despite George Herter's strange and denigrating opinions, Crompton's contributions to the world of rod-making were thought to be almost without bounds, and both Sparse and Vince regarded him as the most helpful, innovative and influential maker of his day. And they were not alone: Other members of the guild also spoke of Crompton as "the best among them." Vince and Sparse concurred with nearly everything he had to offer—especially his strong warning against "flaming" and other heat-treating processes. The list of discoveries and advice coming from Crompton's shop could go on and on, and Marinaro vowed to me that almost everything he knew (excepting his choice not to build the five-strip rod) came from the man.

In our years of friendship, I often heard Vince express disgust at the practice of "undercutting" the center apex on a rod's strips, and in another of Crompton's letters to the guild, he, too, complained about that practice—explaining that, while undercutting those inner, 60-degree angles may help reduce some unsightly glue-lines, the technique can only result in weaker, glued joints. Glue-lines, Crompton argued, would never become a problem in the first place if the strips were only properly planed (or milled); or again, if the maker completely understood his gluing procedure. In both cases, he believed that undercutting was the last resort of a maker to disguise poor craftsmanship—whether he quite realizes this or not. Certainly, all modern makers agree that proper planing and gluing schedules will always be critical in a good rod, but because modern glues have mechanical properties that are very different from the glues used in Crompton's and Marinaro's early days, there's good reason to challenge the notion that undercutting produces a weak joint.

Crompton had long believed that problems during glue-up result either from carelessness or from inadequate equipment. In his letter to Sparse (mentioned above), Crompton wrote with conviction that his new "buggy-whip," binding

Vince's binding machine

130 *Split & Glued by Vincent C. Marinaro*

machine would resolve all such issues. Crompton taught Vince to build this same device back in the late 1930s, and a later version of the little machine was offered in Herter's catalogue from the late 1940s through the '50s. Similarly, the widely-used "Garrison binder" (as shown in Carmichael's book), is also derivative of Crompton's first version. Many improved iterations of this binding machine have evolved in recent years, but the basic principle of Crompton's original design remains almost as a standard in the industry.

Marinaro also held strongly to Crompton's opinion that the common practice of applying multiple coats of varnish will kill the flexing action of a rod—a view Vince insisted upon throughout his decades of building. Once primary sealing is accomplished, any added varnish only increases weight, making the rod "loggy." But, excess weight aside, multiple coats of varnish also form a flexible, resinous sleeve that functions as a kind of shock absorber, and for this reason as well, varnish quickly dampens the (otherwise crisp) action of a rod.

Although none can dispute Crompton's reasoning in this, few makers to this day have followed the advice. Aesthetic considerations enter the picture and, for better or for worse, the marketplace has always demanded a rich, glossy finish. The first thing a customer sees on a rod is the varnish, and although this is a most unreliable indicator, a beautiful finish frequently becomes conflated with an assumption of excellent craftsmanship lying within. It's true, these two will coexist in the best rods, but makers and customers alike would do well to remember that they are, inherently, unrelated.

Kim Mellema

Mid-century marked a rapid and sharp turn in the rod-making industry. For one thing, the revolution in fiberglass fly rods had just begun, while for another, the recent popularity of spin-casting was also sweeping through the industry. In the early 1950s, an entire generation of fishermen began converting to this inexpensive and highly-efficient method of casting. But as a final nail in the coffin, the 1950 China Embargo brought Tonkin cane imports to a halt. With no prospects for future resumption, the larger companies hedged their bets and turned rod-production to the wave of the future—synthetic materials—and nearly in the blink of an eye the bamboo, fly-rod market was brought to its knees.

Readers having a deeper interest in Eastern U.S. rod-makers through the first half of the 20th century could do no better than to pick up a copy of George Black's *Casting A Spell* (2006), relax one evening with three fingers of a favorite single-malt and enjoy this remarkable work—its prose style, interviews and information delivering in spades what its title promises.

At once, commercial competition among tackle manufacturers grew fierce and the race was on to capture a new market. Among the larger and older manufacturers of bamboo rods still standing by the 1960s, profits resulted from their quick changeover to fiberglass, and stashes of bamboo were simply abandoned. On the other hand, independent bamboo rod-makers needed only small amounts of raw materials and survived the Embargo by scrounging cane from the big companies where it could be found. Because their products always offered quality of the highest order, each of these smaller makers was able to retain a following of loyal customers. Still, in less than a decade, bamboo fly rods constituted little more than a niche market, and by the 1960s, the heyday of the bamboo fly rod was drawing to its end. Vince, of course, carried on because he had plenty of cane in reserve and had no market to consider, building solely for his own use.

At the beginning of the 1960s, commercial bamboo makers included Winston, Orvis, Leonard, Payne, Garrison, Gillum, Carlson, Dickerson, Uslan, Young and Powell,

photo by Dick Henry

Not even Marinaro saw everything

Vince on Big Spring in front of the old Barrel Factory

plus several, excellent, but lesser-known independents. While this may appear to be a substantial list, the first two are larger companies whose profits derived, not from bamboo rods, but from the full range of fishing equipment. The other, smaller makers barely survived the changing market, but none more than briefly. Within a few short years, most ceased production –Leonard, the first in the game in the early 1870s, being the last to fall just over a hundred years later.

In the 1970s, the small and independent makers on our list were replaced by another generation of perfectionists: Gary Howells (who left Winston), Bob Summers (who left Young), Glenn Brackett (later, joining Winston), Charlie Jenkins, Per Brandin, Mario Wojnicki, Jon Parker, Tom Maxwell and Tom Dorsey (soon to form Thomas & Thomas) and several others. And, from the ruins of the Leonard Rod Company, an additional group of superbly-skilled independents emerged: Bobby Taylor, Ron Kusse, Walt Carpenter and Mark Aroner.

Each of these, laboring alone to generate his own clientele, was just able to survive, but none of the larger companies ever again produced more than a handful of bamboo rods per year. Continuing even to the present day, Orvis has tried hard to maintain something of its old tradition of New England-built, bamboo rods, with Charlie Hisey now in charge of its shop. But at the other end of the spectrum, Winston abandoned its fine old heritage a year or so back when their new gang of bean-counters clamped down and capitulated to the global economy, Pacific Rim manufacturing and the idea of efficiency-at-all-costs: A move, apparently, that caused their entire team of bamboo makers (the legendary "boo-boys," Glenn Brackett, Jerry Kustich, Wayne Maca and Jeff Walker) to resign in dismay and set up a shop of their own.

CHAPTER SIX

*GOOD TIMES
BEYOND THE
CUMBERLAND VALLEY*

Vince traveled a good bit during each fishing season, but except for excursions to New Brunswick to fish for Atlantic salmon and a single trip to England, he rarely traveled far. On another occasion, his path led him to Montana, but apart from these sojourns, nearly all his fishing was in Pennsylvania, Michigan and, from time-to-time, the Catskill streams of New York.

From the early 1970s onward, a favorite expedition was his annual Memorial Day camping trip to Poe Paddy State Park along Penn's Creek. A few miles downstream from the small village of Coburn, Pennsylvania, Penn's offers a prime, 4-mile stretch extending from Poe Paddy down to the end of the "Winters Project." This area became a hallowed beat for Vince and a few friends who gathered there each year for a week's fishing to the Green Drake, Pennsylvania's largest mayfly. Known to bring grown men to their knees, its emergence causes fishermen to lose control with even greater certainly than do the fish. Locating prime water on any given evening and fishing to that fly is not unlike the lunatic frenzy occurring in late June during Michigan's *Hexagenia* hatch. Differing from those *Hexagenia* jack-pine savages, however, Pennsylvania's lovely *Ephemera guttulata* at least shows the civility to emerge and fall during hours when good gentlefolk are apt to be about.

Vince works a slow pool on Penn's

photo by Dick Henry

Penn's is magnificent water, more river than creek, and is one of Pennsylvania's best-loved trout streams. The creek begins as a collection of underground springs coming together in Penn's Cave, near Spring Mills. This is Pennsylvania's ridge-and-valley country—land dominated by southwest-to-northeast mountains and spanned by fertile, limestone-rich valleys. From its source, Penn's follows an agricultural valley for perhaps 7 miles to the little village of Coburn, then cuts through a mountain gap to the south and flows eastward again for 50 miles before meeting with the Susquehanna River. At first glance, a newcomer to Penn's might assume that it's a freestoner, yet it is actually the state's largest limestone stream, the upper quarter supporting wild trout and prolific hatches.

Above Coburn, however, Penn's uppermost stretches remain troublesome. The steam is largely inaccessible near its source due to private club postings, then becomes warmer and sluggish through the patches of treeless farm country—until Coburn. At Coburn, Penn's is rejuvenated by a powerful infusion of cool, limestone water from Elk Creek and other spring-fed tributaries. For the next 10 miles down past the Cherry Run tributary, Penn's flows through Poe Paddy State Park and Bald Eagle State Forest where it truly becomes a "Class A" fishery, an alkaline flow, rich in nutrients, authoritative, shaded and broad. Here, live wild trout—wily, strong and mocking the sorry ineptitude of their stocked brethren—and a profusion of insect life including the famous Green Drake.

ROUGHING IT AT POE PADDY

Fishing the Green Drake is never quite the same from one year to the next, and whatever your expectations, they're always likely to be a tad off the mark. It's maddening to wile away the late-afternoons, wondering if you're at the right pool (do we want the head or the tail?); rehearsing what you'll say when some bozo barges in to spoil your options; teasing early fish with nymphs, but just waiting out the duns. In some years you'll find gentle pools where the Drakes seem to emerge in swarms, but it can also happen that the fish only want to feed below the surface. You

Are the drakes on?

Elwood Gettle, Vince and "Gutulatta"

Cabin at Poe Paddy. From left: Tom Maxwell, Vince, Frank Basehoar, Maxwell's son, and Frank Thompson

can fool them with a nymph or an emerger, but it's just no damn fun when you've spent months dreaming about this moment and perfecting your dry pattern. Catching fish is always good, but catching them when they're looking to the surface is what we're really after.

Then, in the evening, it's also possible that spinners may coat the water so heavily that competing with the naturals seems an exercise in futility. The trick, of course, is to walk away from that pool, find a spot upstream or down where the odds are more in your favor, then work the pockets and eddies in search of some fat "slurpers." But who has the discipline to turn his back on a feeding frenzy when time is running out—shrugging off prime water just at dusk to scout other areas more sensibly?

Over the years, many brothers of the angle drifted in and out at Vince's Poe Paddy gatherings (camping at first, later taking a cabin), but the core was always Vince, Tom Maxwell, Frank Thompson, Rick Robbins and sometimes Ted Sutsos. Many, too, were the stories emerging from Vince's outings, tales of lucky hook-ups, lost trophies, rain-outs, and lies and arguments over flies and equipment.

Frank Thompson loves to recall a yarn he calls "Vince And The Venison." Evidently, on one of the trips, instead of camping, the group rented a cabin, and for one evening's fare, planned to make a meal of a beautiful venison roast. Vince took charge at once, of course, for he knew exactly how to deal with the beast. After thawing, the roast was placed in a large pot and covered with vinegar, salt and pepper, herbs and a dash of sugar, for apparently Vince had some sort of Bavarian, sauerbraten dish in mind.

The pot was placed near a window for a day, awaiting the morrow when the meat would be removed from the marinade, braised, then smothered in onions, carrots and potatoes for roasting. But, by the next afternoon, the meat had formed a nasty film and the vinegar was fermenting into a stinking, bubbly froth. "Not to worry," Vince assured the company, "this is Mother Nature's process," and into the oven went the not-so-savory roast. Some hours later, the cabin became overwhelmed with a foul odor, and when the dish was removed to be served, Frank reports that everything about it reminded him more of his septic system than anything he might contemplate for dinner. No one, including Vince, could touch the dish—who, quite without winning concurrence, would allow only that the meat must have spoiled in the freezer.

Vince and I hit the earlier Hendrickson hatches on Penn's pretty hard during the middle and late 1970s, but other fishing arrangements kept me from attending the Memorial Day camp-outs. Between the Hendricksons of mid-to-late April and the Green Drakes at the end of May,

Vince, Elwood Gettle and Dick Henry at Poe Paddy cabin—1980

Good Times Beyond The Cumberland Valley

Vince was spending a good bit of each fishing season on Penn's—nearly always favoring one or another of his 9-foot rods. He built several long rods during these years, and many were meant for the broad water and larger flies.

I'm certain I'll never forget one such trip to the "Winters Project" early in 1975. I had along my very first rod (an 8-foot, three-piecer for 5-weight line) and was about to initiate it. We parked the car and were walking the long, sloped trail down to the stream when Vince asked to see my Hendrickson ties. I showed him my little stash, of course, although his response was exactly what I expected. "Junk!" he said, "You won't catch a fish with those." Little more than a serviceable fly-tier, I could neither argue the case nor take offense. But then he reached for his Wheatley box and pulled out a half-dozen of his own cut-wing, thorax ties, and without ceremony, he plopped them into my hand. "Try these," he muttered, "you'll do better."

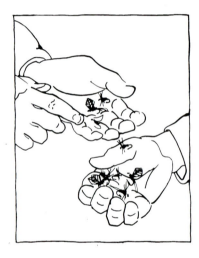

We'd known each other for nearly two years, but I wasn't aware that Vince simply did not give flies to anyone. On the contrary, because my experience had been that fishing companions regularly offered flies to one another, I thought little of the matter and took Vince's gift happily. I had six, perfect Hendricksons, sparsely dressed and as perfectly proportioned as one could imagine. With their "X-ed" hackles turned over the thorax ball at mid-shank, each one cocked so gracefully—holding tail fibers high in the air—that it was enough just to watch them dance downstream. I almost felt bad when one would be hit by a fish. Almost.

Thorax pattern on the water

What a perfect treat it was to indoctrinate my first rod with original Marinaro ties. Only months later, when I learned how out-of-the-ordinary was Vince's offer, did the point of his gift finally dawn on me. That's what he had meant. A more unsuspecting version of myself in those days, I thought only that I had some dandy flies given to me by a good friend. But, one by one, the flies disappeared over the next week or so, lost to fish, rocks, tree-limbs and what have you. Still, while the little Hendricksons are long since gone and I am sorry not to have kept one as a memento, I'm also glad to know they were used for the purposes Pappy intended. Actually, I know he would have been greatly disappointed had I tucked some of the flies away and told him so.

Amusingly, not all at Penn's was grace and magnanimity. Frank Basehoar, another of Vince's friends, attended a few of the later trips to Poe Paddy and recalls one wonderful occasion when Vince took to lecturing his fellows at length about the proper care of one's bamboo rods. Apparently, he had become fixated on the topic, so various of its nuances became regular (if tedious) items for each evening's agenda. Still, in deference, one endured.

On the last day of fishing, however, after the waders were off and the rods broken down, Basehoar, Vince and a couple others were driving the short distance back to the cabin when Vince suddenly recalled that he had left his rod on the roof of the car. Back they went to the expected spot, and there were the sections of the rod—lying in the grass just where they had fallen, undamaged. Appropriate gratitude was expressed, but not another word was spoken for a very long time. Finally, after more than a couple drinks back at the cabin, Frank bellowed to the group that he probably hadn't grasped certain of Vince's finer points and would like to hear a little more discourse on how to take care of one's equipment. Silence again.... Then, chomping his old cigar butt and in no mood for jollity, a chagrined Vince harumphed, "I don't believe I care to comment on that...."

All of which, we think, goes to show there's a God.

SPECTERS ON THE HAMPSHIRE DOWNS

Very early in 1976, and immediately upon completing his work on *In The Ring of The Rise*, Marinaro began making arrangements to pay a long-overdue visit to England. His intention was to arrive in mid-June to fish the fabled chalk-streams of Hampshire just to the south and west of London. Surely, there was never a book written about fly-fishing in England that Vince had not read, nor a treatise on the old flies he left unexamined. From the time I first met him, Vince spoke often about his desire make such a trip, so we all knew this was to be as much a pilgrimage as an opportunity to fish the famous waters. Chief among his interests, of course, was the chance to learn how well those rods and flies of his own design would work on waters long studied and fished by the old masters. Vince also felt that, although he was of pure Italian extraction, his journey to England would be a return "home" at last, with news from the colonies. Indeed, he could hardly wait to receive his first check from Crown Publishers to begin his plans.

Through an introduction from his good friend, the late Datus Proper, Vince contacted Roy Darlingtorf (a prominent member of the Fly-Fishers' Club of London) to see about the possibilities for this visit. At once, Marinaro was welcomed with enthusiasm, invited to dine as a special guest of the members at their quarters in London, then to drive to the Hampshire meadows for a week of fishing and sightseeing. Vince was enormously flattered by the invitation to be feted at a venue of such renown, but he was a middle-class bloke and not entirely comfortable rubbing elbows in such exclusive circles or dressing for dinner. Still, he was as delighted as a schoolboy at Christmas, and in the months leading to his departure he could speak of nothing but the upcoming trip. Everything was made ready at home, while in England, several invitations to fish private stretches along the Test and the Itchen had been extended.

Stalking a spooky fish on an Itchen carrier—1976

Good Times Beyond The Cumberland Valley   139

Alas, travel difficulties and foul weather would conspire to spoil the plans: Vince's flight landed very late and he was forced to make his own way south immediately upon arriving. Certainly, he had mixed feelings about this because, while he was spared the awkwardness of a dinner party, he also had become greatly inconvenienced. Adding to the difficulties, when he reached his destination, he learned that his host and fishing guide for the first few days had become ill and could not accommodate him. Less-than-satisfactory lodgings were arranged in a nearby village, and Marinaro was not a happy camper; the weather remained wet, cold and miserable, and the wind howled inland off the English Channel. How would he get about to try the waters where he had permission to fish? Taxi service seemed the only solution, so Vince arranged to be picked up and delivered to the stream on his first day—finding his ride back only by walking great distances through wind and rain to the nearest telephone. Sodden, morose, and wondering if he was having fun yet, Vince made a phone call to Mr. Darlingtorf. Fortunately, he and Gordon Mackie were able to get free, as, apparently, they only had to advance their arrangements by a day. So, down they drove to the rescue, spending the remainder of the week with Vince.

In *The Flyfishers*, a periodical of The Fly-Fishers Club of London, Darlingtorf writes that Vince was eager to spend the rest of that week staying at the storied St. George Hotel in Winchester where Halford, Marryat, Skues and so many others had gathered back in the day.[1] But this, too, was not to be, Darlingtorf reports, because some years earlier, the facility had been converted into offices for a Barclay Bank.

Inauspicious beginnings with so many disappointments, but the problems were soon put right and Vince was made comfortable in a nearby hotel. And it helped that Darlingtorf and Mackie jointly leased a length of water on the Itchen at St. Cross, so the matter of fishing prime beats was also resolved. Most particularly, though, Marinaro had been eager to fish Halford's and Skues' favorite sections of the Itchen at Abbotts Barton. Darlingtorf, ever to the rescue, also happened to hold the lease on that stretch and recounts treating Vince to a most memorable day of fishing:

Vince stretches a long line on the River Itchen

We collected Marinaro the following morning and took him to Abbotts Barton where we were privileged to see him fish for the first time. His observation and precision in delivering the fly to the trout was awe-inspiring. He seemed to understand totally just how the fish expected to see the natural fly drift into and across its field of view, and was uncannily able to cause his artificial to do likewise. It was at once obvious that he felt at home on our chalk-streams. His native Pennsylvania has many fine limestone streams and the tiny flies which he had developed there worked equally well on the Itchen. He outwitted some large and difficult trout in the tricky Abbotts Barton carriers, all of which he returned.

I particularly recall one fish which had, already, been subjected to a succession of fly patterns, despite such an early stage in the season, and consequently was extremely shy. Because of a multiplex of bank-side obstructions in the form of young trees and weed-beds the fish was unapproachable from the opposite (right) bank.

With quite the most beautiful casting I have ever witnessed, Marinaro dropped one of his beautiful little dry-flies with leader curled, sweetly, in a left-hand bent so that the artificial fly, not any part of the leader, was the first element of the deceit to be presented to the trout.

Darlingtorf assures us the fish was netted and released unharmed, but not without noticing Marinaro's "smug, self-satisfied look of a man who knew he had impressed his spectators." Oh yes, Pappy was like that. Many were the times I was treated to that same smirk stealing across his face. He knew well when he had accomplished some special little feat of expertise and he dearly loved an appreciative audience. With us, however, his little victories were never entirely without compensation—a good dose of needling was always the price to brighten our trips back home.

Later in that same article, Darlingtorf quotes his fishing companion, Gordon Mackie, who, writing for a different magazine, reports witnessing Vince's famous "puddle cast:"

Further downstream, a trout was rising against the bowl of a large willow on the far bank whose many fronds fingered the surface. It was an impossible position for the quick millstream current, suggesting immediate drag. The cast would have to be made six yards or more ahead of the lie in order to avoid the trailing branches. Here I was to witness a preview of Marinaro's incredible "puddle cast...."

Pulling off almost twice the line needed to cover the distance, he pitched it high into the air and allowing it to fall in a loose, dreadful-looking heap (his own words) across the river.

Miraculously, as the current took the overlapping coils out of the line, the fly perched high on the slower water close to the bank, sailed on, and on, and on, without drag. I could hardly believe my eyes, so long was that drift.

It was 1 inch from the trout's nose when the line finally straightened, the trout half-rose and the fly whipped away across the surface of the stream.[2]

Serendipity is a most delightful ally when the odd piece of information comes tripping along. Tom and I recently discovered that Vince himself pitched a slightly altered version of Mackie's story. In an unpublished, 11-page manuscript (now part of PFFMA's "Marinaro Collection") Vince recounts his memories of the trip to England's chalk-streams. The memoir is written with a reading audience clearly in mind, so it's likely he intended to publish the

An aristocratic, Itchen brownie

A nice afternoon's work in England—1976

piece one day as an article. Interestingly, Marinaro and Mackie differ remarkably little in the important details of that "puddle-cast" episode—all except for the outcome. According to Vince, it happened like this:

> At the Halford water on the Manor fishery *[downstream from Winchester, and leased by Mackie]* I had an odd experience with an aftermath that could happen once in a million chances. Gordon and I fished there one bright day when the wind was still blowing, and when there was a fine hatch of fly that was beautiful to see, a real dry-fly day. I am sure that the ghost of Halford smiled and approved.... It was on this same Manor fishery that I did my best piece of fishing on the Chalkstreams. Most of these rivers flow through open country and only rarely, do you find a lonesome tree on the bank hanging over the water. There was one such tree at the lower end of the Manor fishery very close to the famed thirty-two arches that span the valley. Underneath the low overhanging limbs there was a very fine trout rising repeatedly. Gordon and I watched him for some time and when I suggested that it was a fishable piece for the dry-fly, Gordon offered the comment that it was an impossible situation. Nevertheless I was determined to try. I had an American trick for that English fish. I went upstream and made a puddle cast, an extremely high soft pitch on the upstream side of the tree and let the cast collapse in a compact, series of loose snaky coils. The fly separated itself from the coils as it is supposed to do and floated sedately downstream under the low branches where it was taken confidently by the trout. Gordon was delighted with the maneuver and so was I. It was a great pleasure for me to make something so chancy come off right, in the presence of my English friend."

Well...! Shall the truth of the trout ever be known? Dare we venture a guess? Consider carefully, now, for this is a tough one. Pappy was an honest man, but he was a *fisher*-man, and as we all know, that prefix has carried many a good man to his ruin. On the other hand, Mackie, while he was only the reporter, was also an English reporter, perhaps sodden with ancient and ugly, anti-colonial resentment. Okay, time's up....

For some reason, Vince's manuscript was left unfinished, but in one of its early recollections, Vince confesses to some ghostly impressions upon first encountering a meadow along the River Itchen at Abbotts Barton:

> As I opened the last gate to the water-meadows a strange mixture of sensations assailed me. I knew that I was stepping into a bit of history and onto a stage once peopled by some great performers.... But I did not really feel like a stranger in these meadows. Everything seemed familiar to me as though I had been there before, yes many times before. The turf felt good underfoot; the cry of nesting plovers seemed like a hearty welcome and even the hostile stare of a huge cob swan guarding his brood on the river bank appeared right to me. Nevertheless I was continually conscious of an atmosphere reeking with trout fishing history and great fishing personalities: G.E.M. Skues who fished this water for fifty-six years and founded the world wide practice of nymph fishing. I stood and fished on the same spot where he first discovered the importance of nymph imitation; Frederic Halford, historian of the dry-fly whose first confrontation with Skues, occurred in this meadow ... Francis Francis, Author, editor and the only fisherman other than Izaak Walton who has been memorialized in the Great Cathedral at Winchester; Major Hills who wrote the finest history of fly-fishing that has ever been done; Edward Hewitt fished with the major on this same stretch of water and recorded his perplexity and vexation caused by his failures with these shy trout.... I am no mystic but there were times in my late wanderings along the river, I am sure, when I looked around involuntarily for strangely clad ghostly figures casting ghostly fly lines in the long English twilight.

Vince used nothing but his own rods during the trip and was deeply gratified to learn that the aristocratic, English trout bore no grudge against commoners from the New World. Knowing those meadows would require substantial rods to clear the tall grass and to cast across distant weed beds, Vince reports in his manuscript that he took with him one 8-foot rod for a 5-weight line and two 8-footers. Of these latter, one was for a 6-weight line, and the other (built back in 1944 and supplying the power needed to overcome winds blowing from the coast), a very strong rod built to handle a 7-weight line. All three rods were taken out for regular exercise, and just as Vince had hoped, his mayfly and terrestrial patterns, too, were a great success. Delighted with the opportunity to fish these ancestral streams, Vince was even happier to have found the same "problem fishing" he loved so much at home—a perfect match across the pond, for his equipment and expertise. Of course, all this might have been assured, for his decades of experimentation along the Pennsylvania limestoners presented fishing difficulties that differ but little from those found on the chalk-streams and carriers of the Hampshire meadows.

Vince had no interest in collecting souvenirs, but he did have a special interest in odd things of practical use. On one of his explorations through the town of Winchester he came upon a little implement the English call a "marrow spoon." It's a very narrow, double-ended instrument and the scoops are used to tease delicacies from the hollow of bones, either in food preparation or at table. Vince knew immediately this would be perfect, so he purchased the spoon and carried it home; not to enjoy bones, but to disgorge the stomach contents from trout before returning them to the stream.

Marinaro demonstrates his marrow-spoon

The practice may seem a little rude to some fly-fishers, but Vince assures us the English have done this for a very long time and the procedure brings no harm to the fish—straight in, gently, a quarter-turn, then straight out. I watched Vince perform the little operation countless times, the trout swimming off chastened but otherwise in fine condition. Having interviewed very few of his out-patients, however, we can only hope they were as comfortable after as before. In any event, ever the investigator, Vince carefully rounded the edges of his spoon and carried it in his vest ever after, regularly filling little bottles with stomach samples and taking them home to be examined.

The pilgrimage to England represented a deeply revered moment in time, and in an act of special tribute prior to his departure from the Hampshire countryside, Vince filled two, small, pharmacists' bottles with water drawn from the Test and the Itchen. These, he tucked into his pockets to be transported back to Pennsylvania. Somewhat later in that same summer, Vince held a little stream-side ceremony on his meadow along the Letort, marrying the august contents of these vials to the waters of the New World. A sentimental sort of gesture, perhaps, but those of us who joined Pappy on that day felt moved, for we always believed those rivers rose from the same springs. Less an expression of sentiment, the ceremony was one of deep respect for the traditions and kinships flowing on both sides of the Atlantic.

Darlingtorf, musing over Marinaro's departure from this world, closes his piece with the following testimony to a man sorely missed, "I would like to think that perhaps now and again, he sits in the smoking room of the George Hotel, that he was so disappointed not to have seen, among those other great innovators of fly-fishing for trout: Halford, Marryat, Hall, Skues and their contemporaries, for he was equally one of angling's greatest exponents."[3]

Vince "marries the waters" on the Letort—1976

Fishing is a tough job

Another Camp David Accord

In November of 1980, President Jimmy Carter invited Vince and several other friends for a weekend visit to Camp David in northwestern Maryland. President Carter, never much of a city-boy, often used Camp David for purposes other than the affairs of state, frequently being drawn there by his great love for natural settings, hiking and the fly-fishing that he and Rosalynn had taken up. As perhaps the best-known of our fishing statesmen, there weren't many places around the world Jimmy Carter hadn't wet a line, but upon taking up fly-fishing, one of his favorite spots was Spruce Creek in Huntingdon County, Pennsylvania—another rare and superb limestoner. From President Carter's *An Outdoor Journal*, we read:

> [We] helicoptered in, to a field adjacent to the water. Our hosts met us, then graciously left us alone to fish. Before we left to return to civilization, Wayne Harpster, who owned the land, came to invite us to return at any time. So began one of the most cherished friendships of our lives. Thereafter, whenever it was possible, we went back to Spruce Creek, landed in Wayne's pasture near the stream, stayed overnight in an old but comfortable house, and enjoyed some of the best fishing in the eastern states.[4]

It's hard to imagine today what sorts of security issues would be involved for a President to go tooting off to the countryside for a few days of fishing and relaxation, but times were different back then, and apparently it was possible. The private lodgings on Spruce Creek (now rented to the public) are tucked in an open and beautifully kept farm valley, but just across the stream on its eastern bank there is a very high, forested bluff. Along this ridge—so the local grapevine has it—groups of security officers would camp out during the President's visits, having the advantage of an excellent view of the lodgings and meadows below. On the other hand, if this were true, who could have known...?

President Carter, eager to stay current with his sport and to learn more about its recent developments, arranged for Vince and a dozen or so fly-fishing dignitaries and friends to join him and Rosalynn for the Camp David weekend. The occasion may have been all the more therapeutic, for the President recently had lost his bid for re-election and was, no doubt, eager to gather some non-political friends around him. It was Tom Maxwell who had befriended President Carter, coaching him on fly-fishing, casting, and the finer points of entomology, and it was Maxwell, too, who was requested to help with the Camp David arrangements. Tom would speak about taper design and the wide variety of fly rods available, while Rick Robbins, an excellent maker from Virginia, would demonstrate bamboo rod construction. George Harvey was to offer two presenta-

President Carter's hideaway on Spruce Creek

President and Rosalynn Carter with Vince—1980

President Carter and Vince inspect Rick Robbins' rod-work—1980

President Carter watches Barry Beck tying—Ed Shenk at his side, Tom Maxwell standing—1980

photo by Frank Thompson

tions, one on leader construction and the other on fly-tying, and "Bucky" Metz would do an informal session on his new, genetically-improved, rooster necks (*sans* proprietary secrets, of course). Vince was scheduled to present a special slideshow on the history of fly-fishing and its many famous personalities.

This event was actually the second such occasion for Vince and friends to visit with President Carter. The first had taken place much less formally and earlier in the summer of that same year—not within Camp David, but just outside its gates at the Superintendent's house in adjacent, Catoctin Mountain Park. Unlike the more heavily-scheduled arrangements at Camp David, this earlier meeting was just a one-day affair (called "The Corn Roast"), and meant for more casual purposes of socializing, fishing and instruction. Again, it was Maxwell who gathered together the fly-fishing friends. Vince was on hand, of course, but also present were Ed Shenk, Frank Thompson, Eric Leiser, Jim Gilford, Barry and Cathy Beck, and several other guests.

The weather was perfect, so Barry, Vince and Maxwell offered casting demonstrations and tips for the group, while Leiser, Shenk and Thompson set up their fly-tying tables—laid out with the usual array of materials, but to present ideas for some new patterns and tying techniques. It was on this occasion, too, that President Carter was presented with one of Maxwell's handmade, bamboo fly rods, specially designed, wrapped and inscribed. Unfortunately, the rod was barely used by the President, for when he left the White House only a few months later, Tom's gift and many other valued, personal possessions were never seen again.

Reports from Barry, Ed and Frank confirm that President Carter is actually a very good caster, but with scant leisure time, apparently his flies leave a little to be desired. Modest and gracious, President Carter turned out to be both knowledgeable and accomplished as a fly-fisherman, and the Camp David sessions wouldn't have been needed for more than enjoyment of the sport and the camaraderie he sorely missed. Again, from President Carter's *Journal*:

> These were the kinds of fishing expeditions Rosalynn and I squeezed into the interstices of a busy presidential life. They were always too brief but especially welcome. For a few hours we enjoyed the solitude we badly needed. Or, if we were fishing with expert companions, we were able to learn more and more about how to fish effectively under different conditions.⁵

Barry Beck, Ed Shenk and President Carter: Vince and Tom Maxwell in front of the car—1980

photo by Frank Thompson

SALMO SALAR

Atlantic salmon fishing, too, was in Marinaro's blood, but like the salmon itself, the fever was sometimes there and sometimes not. In the 1970s, Vince and friends would fish Maine's lower Penobscot (briefly, and if only in homage to better days), then carry on to Cape Breton's Margaree River. The Margaree is a perfect gem of a stream, set in idyllic surroundings, but it doesn't drain a particularly large watershed and the better salmon pools require anglers to share the resource, using the "rotation" method. The Margaree is often a productive river, but because of its great beauty, popularity and easy access, there isn't much opportunity for lovers of solitude to feel comfortable. Vince always called the Margaree, "the Letort of salmon rivers," but as salmon populations declined all along the East Coast and fishing pressures increased, the group traveled, instead, to New Brunswick's "Mighty Miramichi."

The Miramichi river system, by contrast, covers an enormous spread of wild real estate—its two main streams and their several branches and tributaries offering a few hundred miles of good water. Despite its falling numbers of fish, the Miramichi has always enjoyed a reputation for being the Atlantic Seaboard's most prodigious salmon fishery. Larger salmon will run up the Restigouche and

Vince fishes the Penobscot with his "Penobscot"—1980

photo by Dave Williams

Good Times Beyond The Cumberland Valley

Larry Little and Vince along the Penobscot

Grand Cascapedia rivers, but neither of these can equal the sheer numbers of returning fish found in the Miramichi. Even so, 60,000 salmon in a watershed the size of the Miramichi may not reward the angler like 5,000 fish in a stream a fifth its size. And, too, in the end, everything depends upon whether you, a spate of water, and the salmon happen to be at the same pool on the same day—an assumption when pursuing *Salmo Salar* that's never safe.

Over a three-year period, Vince built three different salmon rods. The first, named "Salmo," was finished in 1976 and is a 9 1/2-foot, two-piece rod, designed for 8-weight line. The second, named "Salar," was built a year later, and is an enormously powerful, two-handed rod, 14 1/2 feet in length and carrying a 9-weight line. This rod is just incredible in its ability to deliver the goods, but because of its great weight and length, only the most experienced casters

Salmon and flies on the Miramichi

A foggy morning on the Margaree—Vince with salmon

"Salmo"

"Penobscot"

can handle it. I wrapped and varnished this rod for Vince, and when complete, he asked if I'd like to join him in his back yard for a little test-casting. I really wanted to put this monster through its paces, but though I tried and tried to get the feel of the brute, I simply couldn't lay line. When I passed the rod back to Vince—who was certainly not a large man and nearly 30 years my senior—he stripped his reel of most of its line and instantly got a good 60 feet of it airborne. Then, a couple false casts to build speed and when he was happy, he just reared back, waited, and with his two-handed grip, he cranked the rig forward and let the line go. Straight as an arrow, Vince sailed the leader and half of his line right up and over the roof-beam of his house (admittedly, a ranch-style). Taken to school with such alacrity, I could hardly lay my problems to the rod, and didn't Vince just love elaborating on that point!

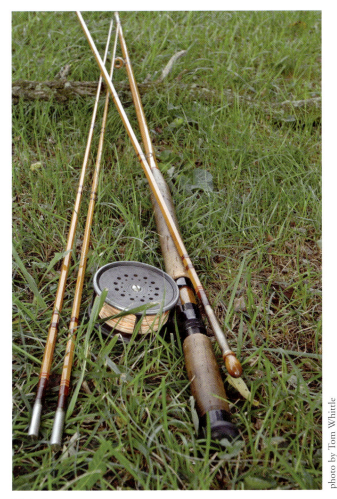

"Salar"

photo by Tom Whittle

excesses of off-shore netting, earlier damming of the rivers, logging, contamination from salmon aqua-culture, deteriorated spawning areas, and, who knows, perhaps global warming itself. All seem to have conspired to take their toll on the salmon—at present, decimating the entire Atlantic sea-stock across to Ireland, England and Scotland.

Back in the 1930s, the Miramichi River was reported to have seen something like a million spawning fish annually, but by the 1960s the annual run had fallen to less than half this, and during the early 1980s, only 80-120,000 adult salmon returned to the river to spawn. As with all estimations, much depends upon who is counting and how (many reports doubling or halving one another), but in more recent years, these numbers would be reduced still more severely.

Vince made several salmon expeditions to the New Brunswick area, even into the early 1980s, and nearly always joining with local friends, Don Ebright, Larry Little or Terry Tatarus. Departing in early morning hours, they would spell each other, driving straight through to the river. A week on the Main Southwest Branch was usually the plan, and although the group traveled around a little, the pools surrounding their own lodge seemed to be as productive as any others. Fish or no fish, Vince would return home exhausted, but never disappointed. As he often told Ebright, "Boy, there's no shame in not catching Atlantic salmon!"

The third salmon rod, called "Penobscot," was built in 1979. Like "Salmo," it is also 9 1/2 feet, but designed as a three-piecer with a fighting butt, and meant to carry an 8-weight line. It's another powerful rod, but with a stronger butt than "Salmo" and rather more up to the task of dealing with Atlantic salmon. This rod became Vince's favorite weapon when he didn't need the persuasiveness or reach of his two-hander.

Declines in salmon populations over the last 50 years have affected the entire Atlantic fishery, and Vince's last trips to the Miramichi River in the early 1980s took place just after the reduction in numbers was becoming truly alarming. Any number of possibilities may explain the phenomenon, including the

Vince heaves "Salar," his 14 1/2-foot rod

Marinaro on the Mriamichi

"Penobscot" rod and a pretty little grilse

A mid-day snooze

TELLING TALES OUT OF SCHOOL

Vince was blessed with the rare gift of brilliance, and over a lifetime of innovations and accomplishments, he used it well. It's perhaps a strange thing (given his enigmatic personality), but while I never felt intimidated by Vince in any other way, I knew that he was, by a good stretch, anyone's intellectual superior. Both of us had the good fortune to be formally educated, but Vince—and largely on his own—had become both wise and learned. In addition to his own profession in law, he'd acquired a deep understanding of the history of several cultures, architecture, photography, Native American lore, the fine arts, biological studies, politics, geology and a surprising range of formal philosophy. There weren't many topics one could discuss with Vince without soon being left in the dust. The deeper you probed, the more he seemed to have in reserve.

As early as age 10, Vince had grown to love the violin and, while Vincentia says the family remembers he was quite accomplished, later friends said he had become something of a virtuoso. But Vince never admitted to that (and there's no doubting he would have, had it been true), so we regard the claim as typical of the embellishments that became part of the "Marinaro mystique." Vincentia also reports that, although his violin lessons came largely at the insistence of his father, Vince enjoyed them and soon was performing regularly with small orchestras all around the Butler and Pittsburgh areas. His interest in the violin faded, however, as Vince entered adolescence, and his pursuit of the instrument and classical music did not survive much beyond late childhood.

Actually, except for one occasion when I asked, he never brought the topic up—or the subject of music at all, for that matter. Most of us gathered that, for whatever reason, he simply didn't wish to discuss the issue, and we assumed the old fiddle would have gone the way of his early fly rods. But during a visit with Vince's daughter-in-law, Maggie, a year or so ago, Tom and I spied the violin and its bows displayed in a lovely, oak bookcase—one of several that formerly held his legal library. Perhaps Vince always regretted giving the instrument up, but if so, he kept that very much to himself. None of us would have suspected there remained any particular tie to this early part of his life, yet there the instrument was, still in beautiful condition and still strung.

Maggie then related that she recalls earlier days when, from time to time, Vince would be heard from another part of the house, playing softly to himself. It couldn't have been simply to rehearse the finger-exercises.... But, how interesting. How unlike his more public demeanor. Now, for some reason, whether because of Vince or myself, that image sticks in my mind. It's been said that Marinaro was not sentimental, and overall, I would have to agree. Yet through the years of our friendship, I always believed there

Vince's old violin

photo by Tom Whittle

Good Times Beyond The Cumberland Valley 155

was another, entirely private side that tapped deeply into loneliness, beauty and loss, and although no one would have heard it from his lips, I know there was a large part of Vince that did not pass through this world with ease.

Foreign languages came easily to Vince, and it's said that he could speak 10 of them fluently. But here again, perhaps we find more symptoms of "the mystique" than fact. His daughter, Vincentia, seems to have inherited Vince's love for foreign tongues, and she, too, took courses in several languages. She says they used to have a favorite game—taking turns to think of a word, then challenging each other to see who could translate it into the greatest number of additional languages. Though still "youngish," my own abilities with foreign languages were already fast slipping away, and Vince, regretting that he, too, had forgotten much, often admonished me like a disappointed father for not trying harder to stay current. Pappy did love to tease and would often give me hell, ranting away in a barrage of foreign phrases, so I could tell that he retained a great deal more than passing familiarity with Italian, French and German.

Nevertheless, while he did have a love for languages, passing familiarity does not mean fluency, and fluency in several languages is hardly possible for one not living within the cultures and using those languages daily. Vince grew up in a community of immigrants from several ethnic groups, and his own parents were natives of Italy, so it's easy to understand how he became attuned to foreign cultures and languages. Recent memories from the Old World and native tongues abounded among the older generations in these small communities and Vince said he always had a fascination for European traditions. Still, to assert that he actually attained fluency in 10 languages would be an altogether different matter—not that he couldn't have accomplished this, but it's unlikely.

But cooking! I can't begin to recall how many times I read (or heard it said) that Vince was all but a gourmet chef—a veritable culinary wizard. *Au contraire!* You already know about Vince's venison roast at Poe Paddy, but I can report, on the basis of a meal he prepared for Hoagy Carmichael and me, that his cooking was... well... just edible. Vince had invited Hoagy down for a visit to his home a year or so after *A Masters Guide* was published, and because Martha was away for the weekend, Vince asked if I'd like to come along as well for an evening's repast and an exchange of lies.

A lovely salmon fillet was purchased at our local farmer's market, some fresh asparagus, wine, and the makings for a beautiful salad. Vince thought he might sauté the salmon lightly in olive oil with sprigs of dill and wisps of lemon zest, while the asparagus was to have a nice Hollandaise sauce. You see? He really did know how to do things nicely. But, Lord! The oil must have been some rank, old off-brand, certainly not extra-virgin, because the poor, damned fish nearly blackened in the pan and tasted as much like salmon as my socks. The asparagus was fine, but the Hollandaise had curdled and the salad dressing was that same nasty, foul oil with vinegar.

Pappy was in heaven, of course, toasting us and ringing praises down upon the old-country, culinary arts. But I recall (although I cannot speak for Hoagy) that I may have been rather elsewhere. Now, it's not at all becoming to tell tales out of school like this, and it's also possible that other of Vince's friends may have had other experiences on other occasions—but I just thought the world should know more of the facts in this matter of Vince's *haute cuisine*.

Frank Basehoar recalls our last tale from the Marinaro mystique. Fly-tying had always been one of Vince's passions and for some reason, during the mid-1970s, he became particularly enamored of the Tups Indispensable, both in its dry and nymph configurations. Never really a nymph fisherman, still, Vince sometimes dipped below the surface when conditions invited a more systematic probing of certain runs.

Fashioning a Tups?

The Tups was first developed about 1900 by R.S. Austin, a tobacconist living in Devon, England. He and his daughter are said to have tied the fly "secretly" for many years, but after Mr. Austin's demise, his daughter finally divulged the mystery materials—with G.E.M. Skues soon writing at length about the pattern. The original Tups pattern required the fly's body to be made from a dubbing mixture of seal's fur and the soft wool taken from the scrotum of an adult ram. (Let's see... a ram was called a "tup," so was it the fly itself or the scrotum-fur that was "indispensable"— and indispensable to whom, the persnickety fly-tier or the mortified ram?)

Well, seal's fur wasn't much of a problem, but (can you see it coming...?) how about those other bits? Most modern tiers would quickly find an appropriate substitute, but Vince was Vince, and everything had to be just so. After putting out some inquiries, he learned of an Amishman in nearby Lebanon County who kept a herd of black-faced sheep, including a few rams—precisely what Austin's original pattern called for. So, off went Vince to make his arrangements.

The Amishman was both thunderstruck and amused to hear such an outlandish request, but he agreed, nevertheless, to help. So, one hot summer's day, into the pasture they tromped—the Amishman, with his boy and a strong rope, and Vince, with his cigar, barber's shears and a plastic bag.

We hope old, Mr. Austin and his daughter would have had an easier time of it, but after our latter-day shepherds chased this ram and that through the pasture, they finally cornered and captured a victim. Trying to avoid the kicking and butting, Vince kept his distance while the Amishman roped the ram, wrestled it to the ground and tied off the flailing hoofs. When all seemed safe, gingerly, Vince approached with his shears, spread the hind legs and was met with a stench that nearly bowled him over.

Steadfast! Vince held to his task. The Amishman was laughing so hard he could barely keep his grip, while his boy stood bug-eyed in disbelief at this loony "English" from across the river. "Snik! snik!" went Pappy's shears all 'round the humiliated ram's nether-parts, the fruits of his urine-stained glory falling into the waiting baggie. Nasty business, this, but if you mean to catch a trout, a man's gotta do what a man's gotta do....

Good Times Beyond The Cumberland Valley

Chapter Seven

At The Master's Bench

I don't know how things may have worked out for other makers, but my first bamboo fly rod took about a year-and-a-half to build, and nothing seemed quite so interminable. Vince, too, took his sweet time before agreeing to teach me—wanting, I'm sure, a better estimate of whether I could carry through. Would I be a fair-weather friend, a dabbler, or would he have a student worth his effort? I doubt I would have appreciated the matter at the time, but Marinaro had a reputation to consider and the last thing he needed was to waste his time on a whippersnapper whose only purpose was to parade the local streams, boasting he'd built a Marinaro rod. But that wouldn't have happened in any case because Vince had no intention to show me his tapers—something he never did.

Shall We Dance...?

Our relationship was an interesting two-step, for while I always had great respect for Vince (both in teasing and in more sober conversation), he loved to test me as if I were his errant, bumbling progeny. I was a generation behind Vince, and I'm sure he delighted in the chance to rub my nose in the many things I did not know. We certainly enjoyed ourselves, but considering the number of folks who've regarded Marinaro as morose, irascible and opinionated, I think it's interesting that what I remember most is laughter and discussions with great doses of give-and-take. It has been said, too, that he was tough-minded, fatalistic and stubborn. All true, but I saw as many demonstrations of sentiment and optimism. I witnessed his grumpiness, but it was the easy, good-natured side of Vince's personality that best described our years.

Those who knew him would vouch that either Marinaro liked you or he didn't. In either case, you saw only one side. In an article written for *The American Fly Fisher*, Gordon Wickstrom suggests Vince's dualism was like the ancient, Roman god, Janus—depicted with two faces, each looking out in an opposite direction:

Vince plays him gingerly

At The Master's Bench

> When Marinaro writes of the past, of Halford, Skues and Harding, of Gordon and the early Americans, he uses language and imagery hinting of their time and place; language that is richer in metaphor, more expansive, classical in its resources, more "romantic," one might say.... He wants communion with the giants of angling history whom he so greatly admired.
>
> But let him shift in a single paragraph, turning 180 degrees, to thoughts about the present and the future, and his style quickly takes on a different tone, dryer, more economical, analytic, and scientific.... The reader feels and hears the emotion of ideas in his writing—this Janus standing pivotal in the twentieth century....
>
> To face off with Vince Marinaro was to experience a genuine and original thinker, restless and on the intellectual prowl. One had either to stand to the pressure of his personality and ideas or get out of the way. If one wanted to compete, it meant competing with the champ.... Still, my own experience was always with Marinaro the gentleman, expert in the graceful traditions of his European heritage....[1]

All this had been my experience as well, yet I was to swallow my pride, forget my profession and submit to this new teacher. I thought I was done with that, but apparently not, and didn't Vince just *love* his new role! We teased about this as about nearly everything else, and he relished the banter. We had a favorite ritual, carried out upon each of his early morning phone calls in the spring. Not knowing who may be on the line, I answered in my usual manner, but without even a "hello," Vince would complain dryly that, from his bedroom, he'd been roused from his sleep by a commotion of Hendrickson nymphs shucking-out up on Penn's Creek. With matched, acerbic tone, I would ask if he knew anyone who could tie a dun imitation that was worth a damn, offering to provide him with a few of my own if he weren't familiar with the pattern. Stupid, but typical of us. I don't know why, but we laughed every time. So, if I could get free, off we'd go, spying along the way for old antique barns or rummage sales, smoking impossibly stinky cigars and telling great lies. At each little creek or drainage ditch we'd cross, Pappy would cup a hand to his ear, wink, and venture, "Yessir, today's the day!"

Our chapter is called "At The Master's Bench," but when Vince moved across the river from Harrisburg to Mechanicsburg in the early 1960s, indeed, he had neither a bench nor a shop at all. What he had at his new, Mechanicsburg home was a screened-in porch that overlooked a large back yard, and it was there, during the summer months, that his rod-building was carried out ever-after. On the porch was an old picnic table for his use, and to this he would add a rickety, wooden, ironing board. Then, he dragged his stuff out from amongst a stash of cardboard boxes in the furnace room, and there you had it—his shop!

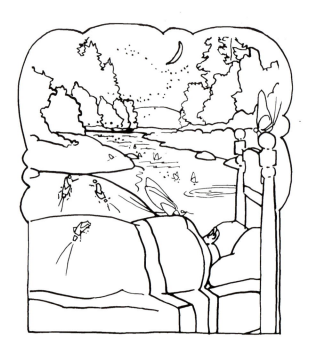

We can't even begin to list the number of things wrong with this arrangement and still have a hard time imagining how he turned out so many precise rods amidst the makeshift mess. But he did. Modern-day makers may be shocked to read of Vince's primitive techniques, the shabbiness of his workplace and the dearth of tools around him—disappointed, even, to learn that he did not have two of the best of everything. Our culture teaches that the

A Handful of Vince's rods

photo by Tom Whittle

At The Master's Bench

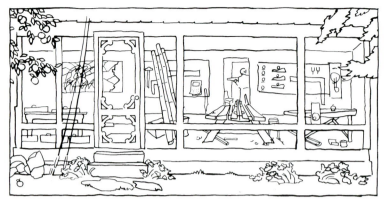

Vince had no interest in "things," and this extended to the craft of making fly rods as surely as it did to everything else in his life. From his own early experiences, he knew that the only requirements for excellent craftsmanship were one's hands, eyes, the most fundamental of tools and a finely focused mind that can anticipate later implications of some present task. All these, he honed to perfection and I never heard him wish for any improvement in his working conditions. Certainly, he could have provided himself with whatever he wanted, but with equal certainty, that's just what he did. Vince had the ability to distinguish between what was needed and the fluff that's superfluous, exercising a crusade to champion the former while rejecting the latter. This was simply part of his personality—an incisive and articulate way of living that was reflected in his professional life and speech just as in his fly-tying, fishing and rod-building.

best products derive only from a highly sophisticated technology, with the misguided implication, conversely, that a fine array of tools assures fine results. Indeed, we all know makers who seem more concerned to equip their shops than to practice their craft. Rod-makers love to marvel at machinery and procedures that are complex while looking past those that need not be so, and the focus is quickly sacrificed. But Vince was adamant in his desire to keep things simple, and became famous for saying, "Boy, you shouldn't try to overwhelm the fish with technology!"

An absolute master of minimalism, Vince owned nothing but the most basic equipment, and he performed every part of the rod-building process by hand. There were no

Some of Vince's equipment

power tools whatever. He would use an old Stanley plane to hog the first bulk of cane from his strips, but had no special iron for it, and he took the last wisps down to perfection with a small, palm plane. He referred to this as his "violin-maker's" plane, reminding me a hundred times over that Samuel Phillippe had built violins. In truth, that's rather what it looked like, but his was only an inexpensive, hobbyist's modeling-plane. Its iron, however, took a fine edge, and because the body was very small and had an unswept palm rest, he obtained exactly the control he wanted.

His planing form was placed upon wooden blocks and clamped to the picnic table; similarly, his binder would be fixed to the ancient ironing board. With these, plus a couple mill-bastard files, a center gauge, paint scraper and sandpaper, he built some of the finest rods one could imagine. This is not to suggest that rod-making is uncomplicated, but that for Vince, expertise did not derive from fancy tools. Reel seats, grips and ferrule stations would be prepared on his "lap-lathe," using his left hand to roll the material back and forth across his thighs, and his right hand to hold either a file or sandpaper to the material. One might expect his results to be crude, but rod-makers would be hard pressed to find more precise cane-work or more accurate dimensions. The point simply is: If you're good, you're good—and if not, no tooling will help.

As it happened, I became the only person Marinaro successfully taught to build fly rods, and while I remain endlessly grateful for that, the arrangement was probably as much circumstantial as anything else—largely to do with the mix of compatible personalities and the two of us being at the right place at the right time. We had great fun over the years, but if I were to build a rod, rules were required and I was to abide by them exactly: 1) I was to do things *only* his way with no challenges or doubts; 2) I was to follow his schedule to the letter, neither questioning an assignment nor asking to jump ahead; 3) I was to submit my "home-work" at each stage before being allowed to progress to the next, and; 4) I was never to request his taper information. These conditions agreed, Vince directed me to begin by constructing a planing form according to his own design—an adaptation of the original device as designed by Dr. Holden.

There was no alternative to making my own form because in those days commercial versions simply did not exist. Vince's design, while something of an improvement over Holden's, remained crude in its setting capabilities, and to obtain the convex shape he sought in a tip section, his

Vince's binder on the old ironing-board

form called for a special feature filed into the grooves through its uppermost areas. Vince used 7/8-inch, cold-rolled, steel bars instead of our more usual 3/4-inch, and while the larger bars bent nicely enough to accept all the general contours of a rod taper, they were not sufficiently supple to form the critical, convex shape needed for the upper 15 inches or so of a tip—the area of greatest concern. Vince's solution was to file the groove through that area, such that a measure of the needed convexity would be lent directly by the shape of the groove itself.

Vince's planing form and tools

There being no local machine shop with a milling bed capable of dealing with 5-foot lengths of steel, nor one willing to guarantee tolerances of plus-or-minus one-thousandth of an inch, my only recourse was to file the grooves by hand. Vince had done this in making his own form, but while the work is straightforward, it's also time-consuming, exasperating and boring as hell.

In addition to filing grooves down the length, Vince's design called for holes to be drilled and tapped directly through the bars at locations corresponding to three, steel, anchoring plates. By means of the through-holes, these plates could be affixed either to the upper or the lower face of the form (depending upon whether one intended to build a butt or a tip-section). The desired width of the groove would be given its rough adjustment merely by sliding the bars open or closed across the plates, then tightening the bolts.

Vince always designed his rods with "control stations" located at 6-inch intervals, so, after locking the plates roughly in place, these 6-inch stations would be adjusted by inserting a variety of shims, washers, cardboard and whatnot between the bars, then securing each area with little "C-clamps." I didn't build my form with Garrison's threaded, adjustment bolts because, at the time, I was unaware of that improvement. Once Carmichael's book appeared, however, Vince accounted for his earlier instructions, saying he just didn't see the need to change an arrangement that had worked so well for so long. That is, he simply chose not to tell me about Garrison's threaded bolts. In the early 1980s, however, I discarded my steel anchor-plates and installed pairs of push-pull bolts at 5-inch increments—an improvement that reduced my set-up time from nearly a day to just an hour or so.

Filing the grooves was simply a matter of fixing the bars in a somewhat opened position to accommodate an 8-inch, 60-degree, triangular file; thus making it possible to shape the inner corners of both bars at once. Triangular files are tapered down their lengths, so, to avoid binding, the idea was to separate the bars just enough to allow the narrower end to drop through the gap with only the file's mid- and rear-areas making contact with the bars' corners. The file needed to remain stable within the gap, however, and this was assured by brazing a 2-inch length of key-stock across the upper surface of the file's thinner end. This key-stock would glide across the surface of the form as I made my strokes, maintaining the file's 60-degree orientation while also preventing its narrow end from dropping and binding between the bars.

The object was to file a groove that would increase in depth at a rate of 0.005" for every 6 inches of length. Well, I began one evening near the tip, making great progress for a few hours, and I recall thinking I would be finished with the task in short order. Full-length strokes were taken down the form with each pass, and after every series of eight or ten strokes I would stop a couple inches shorter. I soon came to realize, however, that while the groove's depth increased at a linear rate, the exposed surface-area to be removed was growing exponentially. Finally finished, after more than two weeks of sweating and cursing, I drew the bars almost together and dressed the groove with triangular stones of increasingly fine grit.

Vince, of course, had forewarned none of these difficulties, merely giving me my marching orders and sitting back to await the report. I'm sure he thought that would be the best way for me to learn, and once again he was correct. But I know, too, that Pappy was looking forward to a hearty laugh, and I was the marked man. Once inspected, Vince found the forms to be good, their surfaces flush and true.

Back and forth we went, either to Vince's home in nearby Mechanicsburg or to mine in Carlisle, as I progressed through my various assignments. I had the binding machine to build once the planing form was completed, taper designs to discover, and after that, I needed to learn how to recognize the best culms for rod use, how to split and straighten the strips, to plane and to glue.

My binding machine was modeled after the Crompton "buggy-whip" design, for we knew of no other. Vince had built his binder as instructed by Crompton himself, and I would build mine according to a few updated twists that Vince had in mind. So, off to the machine shop and hardware stores I went, in search of proper materials. Again, the project was straightforward, but this time the work also progressed quickly. A little fussing and more foul language soon did the job, and again Vince was pleased. I even pressed a ball-bearing race into the hub of the turning crank to assure smooth operation—useless overkill, as Vince was only too happy to point out, but I thought I was pretty damn clever.

Locating some cane was the next step, and in a stroke of great luck, our mutual friend, Bill Fritz, came across a good stash. He had become acquainted with Tom Maxwell and Tom Dorsey just at the time these two bought the entire holdings of the Sewall Dunton company and put Thomas & Thomas on the map. Dunton, long before them, had purchased everything owned by Montague, including probably the most enormous supply of cane in the East. Vince had become friends with Maxwell and Dorsey when

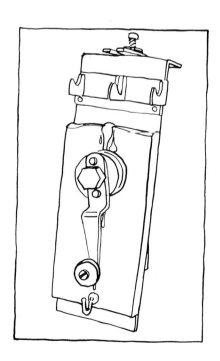

At The Master's Bench 165

Bill Fritz, ably assisted by Vince

Bamboo net built for Bill Fritz

Inscription on net

the two were still located in the Chambersburg, Pennsylvania area, but it was Fritz who made arrangements to obtain the bamboo.

Much of Montague's old cane supply had been used by Dunton or sold, and the rest would be kept by Thomas & Thomas, but 100 or more sticks were set aside as rejects because they'd been cut to 4 1/2-foot lengths and many were too crooked to produce good, sawn strips. These culms were passed to Fritz, who, although he had no need for them, imagined Vince might. But Vince already had plenty of cane, so the culms came at once to me. Still, between the worm holes, mold spores, indentations from force-bending, confused stress-splits, 15-degree node kinks and so forth, I immediately assigned more than half of my treasure to the burn barrel. What remained, however, was a substantial supply of good bamboo for three-piece rods. I would learn still more about selecting cane, but not until later when Vince said it was time.

Deciding on the best adhesive became a problem for us because Vince finally grew disenchanted with hot hide glues. I had no experience working with these and could offer no suggestions, but Vince grumbled that he was no longer able to obtain the kind and quality he'd been accustomed to using. Those who are unfamiliar with hot hide glues should know that the term has become rather generic, for there are many varieties and grades available—those made from the skins of rabbit or fish to other formulas prepared from hoof, bone and cartilage. It's true that the best quality hide glues are not available through one's usual, local sources, but commercial supply houses have always offered a wide range of types and strengths. So, I think Vince was probably looking more for an excuse than a reason.

I also remember him complaining about animal-glue's offensive smell, shelf-life issues, the gooey mess, and the trouble he would have in teaching me how to handle the product in application.

Hot, hide glues indeed do present the rod-maker with difficulties, and good results require a fair measure of operator familiarity. These glues are not the least forgiving of one's miscalculations in open-time, mix-ratio, viscosity or operating temperature. Despite all this, however, we should add that there has never been a more tenacious glue for non-exotic woods—saving, of course, resorcinol. But Vince had his quarrels with this latter product as well. Not least, were the distasteful, purple stains defining each glue-line.

Most of us object to resorcinol's discoloration on aesthetic grounds, but Vince was even more concerned about what those stains suggested. Back in the early 1950s, Marinaro prepared two articles for the *Pennsylvania Angler*, focusing on the special difficulties of gluing a bamboo fly rod. In the second of these articles, he reflects on the advisability of giving the cane surfaces an initial swabbing with a 10% caustic soda solution—a procedure recommended by the U.S. Forest Products Laboratory to remove resinous or oily residues and to improve adhesion. While this seemed an excellent practice when working with acidic oaks (or "oily" materials such as cedar, redwood, teak and certain other tropical woods), Vince worried about the caustic effect on bamboo fibers, writing:

> I do not especially like these strongly alkaline solutions even though they allegedly make a stronger joint. I have a suspicion that they weaken the wood fibers and shorten the life of a rod. In some of my rods treated in this manner, I noticed an alarming brittleness, particularly, in top joints where there is not enough thickness to buffer the penetrating action of the destructive alkali. I feel the same way about some of the synthetic glues, which usually have powerful caustics in their formulas. *Any glue which stains the bamboo ought to be regarded with suspicion.* [italics added] ²

Looking back, I'm sure there was little cause for such concern, for certainly thousands of perfectly good fly rods, glued with resorcinol, are in service. But Vince was skeptical, so in 1974 we decided to run a little experiment with half-a-dozen locally available glues. Admittedly, we were not entirely scientific in selecting our products or in controlling the procedures. What we wanted to learn, simply, was if any commonly-available glue would be satisfactory when applied to bamboo under ordinary working conditions. We chose an off-the-shelf hide glue, an epoxy from a local boatyard, Casein, Weldwood, and a then-new product from Elmer's, called "Carpenter's Glue." Several test-sections, about 18 inches in length, were prepared. These were glued, bound and allowed to cure at 90 degrees for a month or so in my little drying cabinet. Our working hypothesis was that, after splitting the glue-lines apart, those joints that showed the greatest shredding of fibers probably also offered evidence of the strongest bond—and we hoped we would be able to distinguish some differences.

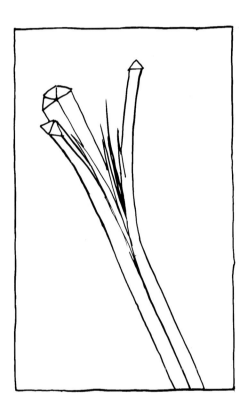

When we were sure the various glues had reached maximum cure, we split our samples open and examined the results under magnification and a very strong light. I won't review all the findings because, frankly, I cannot recall them, but I do clearly remember the best and the worst: Our worst results came from the epoxy, no doubt, because that particular formula was never intended for our purposes. (Had we known about "Epon" or "Nyatex," our results would have been vastly different.) Best, however, was the

Elmer's Carpenter's Glue, straight off the shelf from our local hardware store and as common as mud. The difference in fiber-shredding between this glue and all the others was in no way subtle, for even the naked eye could detect torn and damaged surfaces. In most areas the glue-lines remained intact while destroying, instead, the surrounding fibers. So, that's what we used ever after.

Vince built the remainder of his rods with Carpenter's Glue, and I continued with the product into the mid-1990s when Whittle encouraged me to switch to "Urac." This glue is perfect for our purposes, especially if "kicked" with simple ammonium chloride. It cures to a strong, clear, waterproof bond, has excellent working properties, and it allows just the right open-time for alignment, binding and straightening. Tom continues to use Urac, as do probably the majority of makers, but I'm not a patient man, and became unhappy because it seemed a little too sensitive to heat when straightening a section (though it's not as temperamental as Carpenter's Glue), and without refrigeration, its shelf-life is limited.

Then, a few years back, fellow maker, Bill Fink, suggested I try an industrial, epoxy product called "Epon." Bill first became interested in rod-building back in the 1960s, and at once, he too, found himself in a quandary over the gluing issue. Back then, he had been an electrical engineer for RCA, so he prevailed upon a few colleagues in the chemical laboratories for advice. Bill says their quick and unanimous recommendation was Epon (a family of resins and hardeners used for the company's NASA projects), and he's used it ever since. As Bill told me recently, "I've seen no reason to change: It's space-worthy and rod-worthy."

But, let's return to those two, odd, *Pennsylvania Angler* articles that Marinaro wrote in the early 1950s. For one thing, it seems most peculiar that the pieces came to be written at all, because apart from these two instances, Vince simply did not discuss rod-making. Why would he have chosen to do so at that time—and why would he have **begun** with the gluing stage? Perhaps he was influenced by Sparse, who, although his rod-makers' guild had since seen its demise, nevertheless remained deeply involved with independent makers across the country—including, of course, Marinaro. Or, perhaps it was done at the behest of Charlie Fox, who had been the editor of the *Pennsylvania Angler*.

Our curiosity is piqued further when we read Vince's puzzling conclusion to the second of those two articles. He writes: "Maybe if some long suffering editor will let me, I may be

Bill Fink at Spruce Creek—2003

photo by Chris Bogart

tempted to write again and tell some pretty little secrets about making your splines to melt-and-marry, and working out a first class design for your rod."[3] Did Marinaro actually believe there would be enough amateur rod-makers out there in the early 1950s to justify continuing the series? Vince writes almost as if he were standing before some appreciative brotherhood of amateur makers—folks who knew one another and had developed a fair measure of expertise. We have that now, but where was such an audience during the 1950s?

Most peculiar, however, is Marinaro's teaser that he might, in the future, offer help in "working out a first class design." Of all things that Marinaro guarded jealously, design information was inviolate! On the other hand, perhaps the tease wasn't meant as a promise to reveal any particular taper, but only the principles of the convex design (as he finally did in 25 years later in *The Ring*). In any event, the series of articles faded away at once and no further installments appeared. Vince never offered an explanation of that episode to me, dismissing the project by saying only "it was a mis-guided idea."

There remains, however, one last selection from his article before moving along. Admittedly, Marinaro's observation in what follows is of no particular relevance to our purposes, but it's one of the more charming rod-makers' anecdotes and we simply couldn't resist its inclusion. While speaking of hide glues and their susceptibility to mold-deterioration, Vince writes:

> But strange to relate, this poor resistance to molds that animal glues have, has been of enormous advantage to me over the years. I like to glue all of my experimental models with hot glue and if, after I have first tried them, I do not like them for some reason I simply coat the bare joints with mold, lay them in a dark damp place and let the little devils eat out all of the glue, allowing the strips to separate as beautifully clean and flat as though freshly planed. Then I apply an antiseptic or expose them to ammonia fumes, redesign my rod and use the same splines over again. It certainly saves a lot of work and bamboo.[4]

Perhaps this explains what became of all those earlier rods no longer suiting Vince's needs. They were simply recycled by exposing their glue-lines to "the little devils," with each former rod attaining final incarnation in the current PFFMA collection! Butts became mid-sections; mids became tips; and tips became fly-tying bodkins. Anyway, apocryphal or otherwise, there we have it—a peaceable kingdom with perfect harmony between man and beast.

We Build A Rod: Part I

(Here, and through the following sections, the reader may find it helpful to refer to our Primer on rod-building, located just before Chapter One.)

For Vince, teaching me to build a fly rod also meant instructing me in designing my own tapers, the idea being to address both at the same time. As mentioned earlier, Vince did not believe one could call himself a rod-maker unless he had made his own equipment and developed his own tapers—the old-school idea of submitting to an apprenticeship and paying one's dues.

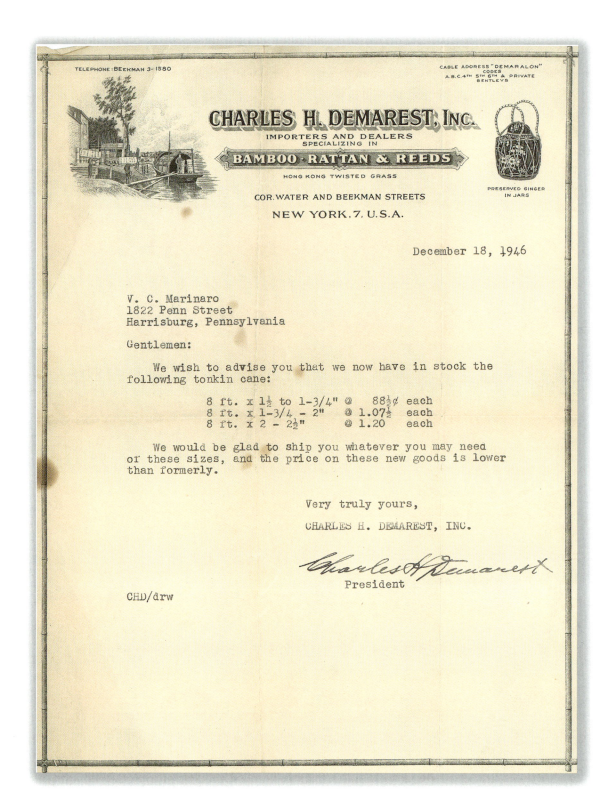

A 1946 invoice from Charles H. Demarest, Inc.

While his design principles were passed to me, in my own limited way, I was to "discover" them again through trial and error. Vince provided endless advice over the many months, and because of his help I built a first, pretty-good rod after only a year or so. Of course, I thought the rod was superb, but "pretty good" was about all Pappy could allow of it. Still, at that point I could see the target, and various tweaks to refine problem areas for future rods seemed manageable. We'll get into Marinaro's design criteria in the following chapter.

Vince offered critiques of my designs while they were still on paper, but unless something were radically off, he rarely predicted if my sections might be satisfactory. Instead, I was to build them for myself to find out. Often, I grew impatient and sometimes disheartened to complete tapers that were obviously not good. On occasion, I even wondered if Vince were playing games with me. Certainly, he could have known a rod wouldn't be successful without bothering me to build it. But it wasn't just my patience that was being tested: It was my ability to discern on my own where changes needed to be made, why, and in what measure. All the trial-and-error was a way for me to understand what I was doing, and Vince knew that protecting me from my own mistakes was no way to learn the craft.

Selecting a good culm of cane would be our next step. Much has been written, advising us in the matter, and there's little need to review that information here. Vince had no secrets, but while his standards were high, they were not different from those of other builders. He, too, searched for a culm with the greatest relative weight ("heft"), for this would be early evidence of a densely-packed layer of outer fibers. Density (compactness) is always the most important feature when selecting cane for mids or tips, but of equal importance for larger butt sections is the overall thickness of that layer. Rods smaller than 7 1/2 feet (and for less than 5-weight lines), however, will be no better for having been built from culms with an especially thick layer, and the same remains true for mid- and tip-sections—even of larger rods. Rod-makers usually think it's best to build a rod from a single culm, but because bamboo with a particularly thick layer of power fibers is not easy to come by, and because it seems a shame to waste such cane on rod sections that cannot benefit from that thickness, Vince always reserved these special culms for his special projects.

Vince did buy a little bamboo, but more often it was scrounged from one or another of his friends in the industry. He maintained a goodly stash because, in the end, more than half of it would be rejected. When purchased, the order always went to Charles H. Demarest, Inc., the first (and still largest) US importers of *Arundinaria Amabilis*. Since the founder's death, this company has been managed by Harold and Eileen Demarest, the most gracious and supportive benefactors one could hope to meet. Until the sad news of Harold's own death came in July of 2007, he had remained actively involved in the business, and year after year he and Eileen would travel the country to attend the many rod-maker's gatherings—sharing their optimism, Manhattans, good cheer and wonderful tales from earlier days.

Eileen and Harold Demarest at the 2004 Catskill Gathering

Upon receiving a supply of cane, if the culms were new and not previously split, Vince would run an opening down one side, tag the lot and stash it in his attic for as many years as possible before he actually selected a stick. Of course, there was no certain way to know how long would be long enough, so when the time came to pull some culms out for building, he simply assumed the oldest would be the best. His first tests were to determine their relative heft and then to give them several good raps along their lengths with a hardwood stick. Like a luthier, Vince was listening for a certain ringing sound that promised good density and dryness.

One learns these distinctions only upon comparing a great number of culms, and because bamboo is a natural material, wide variations will be found. Some cane may be used to build good tip sections, but would yield poor butts, while many other culms, though lovely in all respects, may be unsuited for any rod-building purpose. One may also find cosmetic blemishes on the surface, but except if one wishes to build a "flawless," blonde rod, these do not ordinarily indicate much (notwithstanding worm-holes, mold, deeply scared enamel, blackened nodes and the like). Vince was not particular about minor cosmetic issues, however, and he regarded a few superficial blemishes as a natural part of a natural material—"beauty-spots," so to speak, much like grain irregularities found in an interesting piece of wood. I feel the same, and always prefer my rods to show some of the cane's own character.

The next step of splitting a culm into strips is no easy task, but, again, Vince's techniques were not different from those explained, say, in Carmichael's book on Everett Garrison. Some of Vince's oldest culms were 8 feet in length, but following the China Embargo, cane became available in 12-foot lengths. These, he would saw into 6-foot sections and split each in half, lengthwise, with a broad hunting knife and a mallet. In similar fashion, each half would then be split into thirds. Next, he chiseled-out the inner dams at each node location and marked the six, larger segments for final splitting into the smaller strips. Beginning mid-length, Vince obtained these narrower strips by driving a somewhat broad and beveled screwdriver into a node. A second screwdriver would be inserted into the opened slot, twisted, and in this manner he would begin prying toward each end, leapfrogging his screwdrivers, node-by-node, along the opening crack. Faster and more accurate splitting techniques have since been devised by other makers, but this was the accepted method that Vince learned, and this was what he continued to do.

Before splitting the full number of strips, however, one needs to determine a culm's ultimate suitability to become a fly rod, and for this, Vince relied upon one, last, all-important test. He would take an initial strip from a culm, perhaps 1/2-inch in width, then file its outer nodes, remove the inner dams, and subject that strip to a series of very careful bending tests. It happens, unfortunately, that nature does not always grow a culm with uniform resilience between the nodes, and if a relatively weak, inter-nodal area should be found, that culm cannot be used. Indeed, even some of the most promising-looking cane can reveal local weaknesses, and one simply cannot determine this without putting a strip to the bending test.

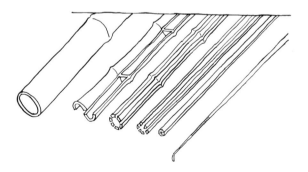

Vince gripped his sample, enamel-side-up, placed each hand on a neighboring node and slowly bent the strip downward to determine its resistance. Then, he would release quickly, and move to the remaining inter-nodal areas, testing in like manner. A good strip should feel "steely" (certainly, a relative term) between its nodes, rebounding sharply toward its initial, straight shape. By contrast, any inter-nodal area that demonstrates a certain "mushiness" and does not want to spring back will implicate the entire circumference of the culm at that location. Makers who build "nodeless" rods simply cut out and discard the offending inter-nodal area, but nothing can be done by the maker who builds rods in the traditional, "noded" format.

The bending test is important because, unfortunately, inter-nodal weaknesses are not likely to be cured with any heat-tempering regimen. Whatever the growth irregularity may be, it's not one that will be overcome merely by baking out the excessive water-content. Interestingly, it's not only the cane that's being put to the test, but also a maker's willingness to reject an otherwise beautiful culm. Nobody likes to discard a culm that looks wonderful and appears to have great potential. But worse, nothing is more disheartening than to cast a new rod and notice that a mid- or tip-section has taken a "set" position—or that it can be bent by hand to remain in almost any other position. Certain, older rods will exhibit this characteristic, should the fibers have broken down through decades of hard use, but even some new rods will show the same problem. Vince believed, as do Tom and I, that this condition in a new rod is simply the price the maker pays for failing to check his strips for local weaknesses.

So, assuming the culm is good and the remaining strips for the rod have been split, Vince would dress the outer nodes with his rasp, stagger these into a pattern (sometimes spiral and sometimes random) cut the strips to length, and begin "squaring" them in preparation for the next stage of rough beveling. It is also at this point that Vince, like other makers, would perform the necessary heat-straightening. But he did so entirely by hand, with no jigs or tools and using only the open flame of an alcohol lamp. He argued strongly against the more common practice of applying a heat gun, believing the forced, hot air to be too dry and risking fiber damage. By contrast, he thought the alcohol flame (being gentle and producing water vapor as it burns) could help prevent excessive drying and scorching.

Similarly, he vigorously opposed the practice of straightening nodes in a vise, for the mechanical advantage of that tool is far too great and cannot sense the fibers' readiness to yield. Certainly, each maker has experienced a few, odd nodes that seem to resist the effects of heat (under equal application), but a vise will crank down upon all just the same and with no regard for whether the material is ready to bend or not. The risk, here, is that fibers can be crushed into conformity without the maker even being aware of it. Vince believed that only with one's hands could one sense when the fibers had become sufficiently "plastic," and in this manner one accomplishes node-straightening with a minimum application of heat and a minimum risk of damage.

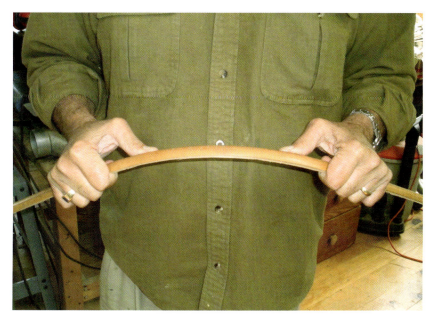
Testing a sample strip for stiffness.

Excessive heat is potential trouble in other steps of the building process, too, and this leads us to another of Vince's contentions. Like Crompton and many other independent makers, Marinaro believed that all heat-treating regimens ("tempering") are a mistake and will cost dearly in the longevity of a rod. There may be something to it, after all, but more recent studies suggest that a great deal depends upon how the procedure is carried out. Other than makers' continuing quarrels about the best glues and varnishes, probably no discussion rages with greater variance of opinion than that of the "best" heat-treating regimen.

At The Master's Bench

Because we still lack a complete understanding of bamboo's botanical/chemical properties, and because one maker's tests do not necessarily bear out those undertaken by another, it's difficult to know how to settle the issue.

There are makers, too, who do not want to worry about questions of longevity, being satisfied that heat-treatment *does* yield the short-run advantage of stiffer strips—perhaps telling themselves if a rod can hold up for a decade or so, that's good enough. Probably the best information a reader could find on the topic of heat-treating is published in R.E. Milward's book, *Bamboo: Fact, Fiction and Flyrods* (2001). In this study, Milward takes great care to explain both the physical properties and the structural behavior of bamboo, offering both visual evidence and testing results. Milward explains that bamboo is a heavily lignified, cellulose structure, and that the application of high heat will cause the sugars in that structure to become caramelized:

> We are all familiar with caramel; when compared with cellulose, it *[caramel]* has no significant strength. The sugar molecules in cellulose form extremely long chains, hence the enormous strength and flexibility. The slight discolouration of the early stages of heat-treating causes caramelization of the sugars and causes the long fibres to break into shorter fibres. Further heat-treatment destroys more cellulose, causing progressively darker colouration and ever shorter cellulose fibres until, ultimately, it starts burning, if oxygen is present. The structural element of bamboo is cellulose. Lignin only modifies its behaviour, so *any discolouration of the bamboo represents some loss of strength.*[5]

Robert Crompton, similarly, believed that, although heat-treating stiffens the fibers of bamboo, this extra "springiness" must come at the expense of durability—possibly, similar to the way that toasting a slice of bread will cause it to become stiffer and darker, but also more brittle. Vince, too, believed that discoloration should be regarded as evidence of fiber damage (toasting), and he refused to apply any form of heat other than the minimum needed to straighten nodes and "sweeps." Neither Crompton nor Marinaro had undertaken systematic studies of the matter, but in both cases their intuitions seem to be borne out by Milward's work. Milward does not recommend against heat treating, but his study does explain its likely effects on the cellular level. In any case, if excellent cane were required to build a rod, Vince preferred to discard two or three good culms in search of the one that possessed outstanding qualities rather than to subject his strips to flaming or heat-treating.

The heat-treating oven

Tom and I have no quarrel with Crompton, Hewitt, Sparse, Marinaro and the many other old masters on this topic, for their reasoning seems sound. Nevertheless, nearly a century has passed since heat-treating was first introduced by W. E. Edwards (in 1914), and except for certain cases of abuse, moderate heat-tempering does not seem to have had an adverse effect on the older rods. Indeed, and most puzzlingly, even rods that have been heavily flamed (such as those built by Paul Young) have held up well for half a century. We hasten to point out, however, that the operative word here is *seem*, for none of us could have sufficient time or opportunity to examine all those older rods. Neither could we know with certainty how they had been heat-treated, nor, through the years, what care may have been given to them.

In the end, we believe that although no heat-treating regimen is able to convert questionable bamboo into good, a good stick of bamboo is usually made better through modest measures of heat-tempering. How "modest" will be up to each maker to determine, always remembering that it's possible to devise heat-treating schedules that stop short of discoloration—perhaps the key consideration in this discussion. As a last note on the topic, however, we should say that all the above is only our own prevarication on the matter, and is not necessarily meant to overturn Marinaro's own view of tempering—which was, simply: "Don't do it!" To Vince's credit, certainly none of his rods exhibits any need for greater "crispness." For ourselves, however, although we believe the jury is still out on the issue of heat-tempering, its judicious application does not appear to damage cane as inevitably as Crompton, Marinaro and others had thought.

WE BUILD A ROD: PART II

The planing form now needs to be set for the desired taper, and to do this, Vince would read the numbers at 6-inch stations on his graphed design and make corresponding, 6-inch adjustments to the groove of his steel bars. Actually, I never witnessed Vince setting his form, for that would have been to reveal his tapers, so what follows is a review of the steps he taught to me.

Prior to fitting my own form with push-pull, adjustment bolts, we obtained taper settings with the anchor-plates, an elaborate shim-system and clamps—springing the bars open or closed to the widths needed. But we lacked the good sense to use a depth indicator to take direct readings from the V-groove, and relied instead on sets of "feeler-gauges" to measure the gap between the bars. These sets consist of a couple dozen metal leaves, each with its graduated thickness marked in thousandths-of-an-inch.

Our system was clumsy and indirect, but it worked. First, however, we needed to know the exact dimensions of the groove itself as our starting point. To obtain this, we locked

Vince adjusts his planing form using the thickness gauges: Notice, the form is elevated to provide space for clamps below

the bars tightly against one another and planed a bamboo strip to fill the groove precisely. This strip served as a sort of "master pattern," allowing us to know, in thousandths-of-an-inch, the dimension of the V-groove at any location we wished to measure. With this information, we could determine how far the bars needed to be spread at any given, 6-inch station. Readers possessing a lively sense of geometry will anticipate a problem, however, and we'll get to that in just a moment.

To establish our settings, we determined where the rod's section would begin and end along the form, then assigned the 6-inch stations directly on the bars. The master strip's thickness would be measured at these stations and recorded on a little chart. From there, it was simply a matter of subtracting our readings from the corresponding numbers at each, 6-inch station on the graphed design. The numerical differences, of course, would represent the distance the bars still needed to be separated at each station. The proper combination of "leaves" was then selected from the feeler gauges, slipped between the bars, and the anchor-plates could be locked into place.

Once the proper gap between the bars had been established at a strip's larger end, the width for each subsequent station was determined merely by subtracting its graphed dimension from that of the one just set. So, it was not a strip's actual measurement that we used to set the forms, but only the graphed, numerical difference between each station. These numbers represent a "rate-of-drop," and for this, our feeler gauges measured the gap just fine.

Readers who've been successful in following this may congratulate themselves if they guessed that our 6-inch stations probably wouldn't fall at those spots where the anchor-plates happened to be located. That is, while the anchor-plates could fix the larger trajectory of a taper, they were never in a proper location to establish the 6-inch stations. These were brought into accord by sliding an array of shims between the bars and fixing the whole mess with small C-clamps applied from the underside—followed, of course, by the inevitable re-setting of certain plates.

The system, however clumsy, may seem to be sound in its logic, but it is not. Well, the logic is okay (as logic goes), but the implied geometry is not. Mathematically-minded readers will have noticed that we've disregarded the shape of a triangle. Consider: Our graphed designs are created to establish the thickness of each strip as measured from its outer flat to its inner apex (the "chord" of a triangle), and those measurements must be reflected in the depth of the planing form's groove. But our settings have just been accomplished as if spreading or narrowing the bars would yield the depth measurements we were after. They won't. That is, you can't expect to adjust a triangle's side (the width across the groove) by some particular measurement, thinking that its chord (the depth of the groove) will register a change in that same amount.

Rather than mucking about with mathematics and more feeler gauges, however, the faster and more reliable way was simply to take a scrap piece of cane and plane a full-length, test strip. We'd mike the resulting strip at our control stations, then tweak the form to obtain the final settings we needed. Because it's always prudent to run test strips before beginning the actual planing anyway, preparing a couple of these at the same time we fine-tuned the form gave us both efficient and accurate results.

So, the old, empirical methods won the day once again and we did get our settings. But what a mess! What with all the shims and clamps, my forms looked more like a junk-yard than anything else. Vince didn't seem to mind the process, but Lord, the moment I converted to push-pull adjustment bolts, switched over to 5-inch increments and began using a depth-gauge, life suddenly became sweet.

After a few years of fiddling, I finally evolved some tapers that pleased me, so in an effort to avoid the lengthy set-up rigmarole, I prepared pattern-strips for each rod section. These were tagged, stored, and appropriate ones pulled out for each rod I wanted to duplicate. Vince, on the other hand, always working in the experimental mode, didn't bother with this because it's doubtful he ever built the same rod twice.

But it's summertime now, and Pappy would be out on his screened porch in the oppressive heat and humidity of our south-central Pennsylvania climate, perspiring and planing happily away on some new rod. Ordinarily, rod-makers take every possible precaution to keep their strips away from the combination of heat and humidity, and many folks (especially those without air-conditioning) even store their strips in a descant, resisting the urge to build until the dry, winter months. Vince, however, did not believe that properly seasoned cane would retain the adverse effects of ambient humidity.

Basically true, this statement requires a few important explanations. Being a natural, cellulose structure, bamboo "breathes" and will, indeed, adapt to atmospheric, moisture content, absorbing whatever the ambient humidity has to dish out. And it's true, too, that in the short run, our humid, summer months can cause cane strips to become somewhat "mushy," robbing them of the crisp, flexing action we want. Vince's argument, however, was that well-seasoned bamboo does not retain that particular form of moisture, and once the weather dries out, so does the cane.

Vince planes a strip

It's worth going into this matter still more deeply. Vince acquired quite a bit of literature from the U.S. Forest Products Laboratories on the subject of seasoning wood and he knew that the moisture contained within all fibrous, cellulose vegetation exists primarily in two forms: "hydrating" (or "bound") water, and "free" water. In unseasoned bamboo, the hydrating water is actually bonded on the molecular level *within* the tougher lignin structures of the "power-fibers." The so-called free water, on the other hand, is not molecularly bonded at all, and it comes and goes within the pithy structures amongst and between the power fibers.

Adequate seasoning over time will have the final effect of driving both forms of moisture from the bamboo, leaving the lignins in the power-fibers shrunken, toughened and more tightly meshed. Thus, the bound water is removed and the resinous power-fibers will have become stiffened and rather permanently sealed against its re-entry. (Heat-treating both accelerates and exaggerates this same process, but with the added benefit that certain molecules also undergo the process of polymerization, called "cross-linking.")

By contrast, the free-water potential will always vary according to changes in ambient humidity, passing in and out of the more "spongy" structures in the bamboo. Nothing in the world can seal the cane and prevent this absorption and release of humidity (breathing), although final varnishing greatly retards the process. Realizing all this, Marinaro felt confident that a well-seasoned culm would take up only free-water during the summer months, but he also knew this would not remain a problem later in the building process, or indeed, in the final, glued and varnished rod.

So, summertime or not, Vince would build his rods on the screened porch when he was able, but he always stopped the process short of fitting the ferrules, mounting the hardware and finishing. His rod sections were planed on the old picnic table, glued, the string removed, and the sections cleaned and sanded. Then, they would be hung from hooks in his furnace room until our driest winter month when he returned to mount the ferrules and complete the building process. This overall schedule seemed to work perfectly, because after several months in the dry house, all the moisture had left the cane, the glue had more than ample time to reach full cure, and his sections would become light and crisp—ready for ferrules, wraps and varnish.

Now, there is a very old quarrel among rod-makers—the question of which of the six sides should receive the snake-guides. In bringing the issue up at this point, readers will think we're jumping rather far ahead in the building sequence. And we are. But the steps we were just about to discuss (Vince's planing procedures) have an important influence upon guide-placement, so we'll indulge our digression briefly and return to the planing in just a moment.

At The Master's Bench

Some makers will say a rod's guides should be placed on the side opposite the "spine," while others insist they should be wrapped on the same side. What we mean by the term "spine" is that a given rod section may feel stiffer when flexed across one pair of flats than another. The choice in locating one's guides, however, is only a matter of deciding whether one wants to take advantage of the differing stiffness on the back-cast or the forward delivery. But notice: In this debate, there is the foregone conclusion that a rod *will* have a spine. If there were no spine, of course, any side of a rod would perform as well as its neighbors and there would be no discussion,

This quarrel drove Vince absolutely buggy. He wasn't at all concerned about choosing the "right side" because, for the life of him, he couldn't understand why a bamboo rod should have a spine in the first place! He insisted that, while most bamboo rods do, indeed, have spines, their presence is neither desirable nor inevitable. Now, all fiberglass and graphite rods will exhibit spines in some measure, but these are a necessary result of the construction process. Not so, the bamboo fly rod. Vince argued that the only reasons a bamboo rod might have a detectable spine would be if strips had been obtained at random from different culms and introduced into the same section, or again, if the strips themselves had not been planed to identical dimensions.

But amateur makers have no reason to build sections of a fly rod with strips taken randomly from different culms, so this potential for trouble needn't concern them. On the other hand, planing precisely uniform strips is quite another matter. Still, it's exactly here that the amateur maker has the advantage, for the process of hand-planing can yield greater accuracy than could be obtained in any production shop—that is, *if* the maker is willing to expend the necessary time and care.

One may think that if a spine were the result of mating strips of differing dimensions, its presence would be revealed simply by measuring across the three pairs of flats on a finished section. Yet, it's possible for a spine to be felt even though the flats may yield consistent dimensions down the rod's entire length. What we must realize is that, while a given strip's outer surface may have been planed to the appropriate widths, its inner surfaces could still be quite off. Planing, itself, is not a problem, but planing exactly equilateral triangles is damnably difficult. It's all too easy to roll the plane ever so slightly to one side or the other while working a strip down, thus creating inner faces with something other than a perfect 60-degree apex along its center. Upon gluing, however, it's the strips' outer surfaces and corners that regulate the measured dimensions of the hexagon. So, from the outside, all may appear to be well. Hidden within, however, certain thinned or misaligned inner faces remain, and there's your spine—the result of strips with built-in dissimilarities you probably didn't even know were there.

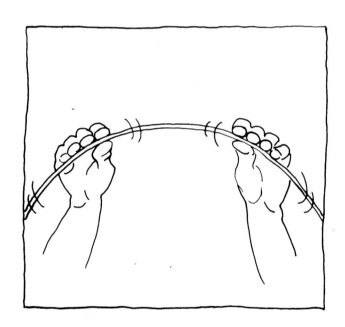

There are several ways to check for a spine, but tips are most likely to exhibit the problem. Perhaps the quickest test is to hold the section with one hand near the tip-top, while placing the other 10 inches or so down the shaft. Then, give the section a slight bend between the hands and, while bent, roll the section back and forth between the fingers. If all is well, the bent section should rotate with silky smoothness. The presence of a spine, however, will cause the section to "bump" slightly on each rotation. This little test should be repeated by moving the hands 8 to 10 inches down the section, and repeated again until one arrives at the ferrule end.

Mid-sections, though more difficult to manage, can sometimes be checked in a similar manner, but the presence of a spine in a butt section will be hard to discern because its greater thickness will obscure detection of the sorts of subtleties that cause spines in the first place. How seriously a spine may affect one's casting is only for each fly-fisher to say, but Vince's point remains: Spines in a bamboo rod are evidence of a fault, and since these can be avoided, they must be. Period.

So much for that issue. Before departing on this rant, however, we were talking about Vince building in the summer, and he was about to plane his strips. For Vince, once his planing form had been set, every step to follow was focused upon obtaining precisely identical strips. He would have set the forms, dressed and staggered the nodes and cut the strips to length. Nearly ready to plane the initial, 60-degree bevel, the final steps were to square and heat-straighten the strips. These last operations may strike the unsuspecting amateur as a matter-of-course, but doing them properly is crucial if one expects to obtain uniform strips in the later, tapering stages. Or, seen in reverse, final accuracy depends upon the relationship of objectives established during preparatory steps. Vince insisted that only a properly straightened strip could be planed accurately, but that only a properly squared strip could be heat-straightened accurately.

Most professional rod-makers do not worry about these steps, however, because of time constraints and the difficulties of heat-straightening. Instead, for more than a century, production shops have merely sawn their strips directly from a culm and fed these into the beveling or milling machines. This process yields straight strips, ready to be glued, but showing grain run-out surrounding each node. Production makers have argued that grain run-out is only an aesthetic issue anyhow, and causes no harm to the action of a rod. Whether their case has merit or not, the matter certainly *does* remain an aesthetic issue. But grain run-out also provides a tell-tale sign, separating the careful craftsman from those who prefer (or need) to save time and trouble.

The amateur who splits and planes by hand, however, cannot skip these steps. A hand-split strip will be crooked and must be straightened to conform to the V-groove, but for trouble-free planing, it's also necessary that the blade not encounter angled grain.

What's a properly "squared" strip? The term is used loosely, for although the strip needn't necessarily be square in cross-section, it should reveal 90-degree angles between its enamel surface and its sides. The purpose of squaring a strip is to bring the (probably crooked) fibers into clear, visual definition, thus, making it possible to heat-straighten with accuracy. But of greater importance than the strip's overall straightness, all fibers within must run straight from one node to the next. To attain this, the maker needs to study the fibers' actual orientation upon squaring—and their direction is not always as obvious as one might think.

Here's the point: The process of splitting-out strips often creates the illusion that we've obtained a straighter stick than we actually have, for splitting itself brings uncertain results. Bamboo grows to its full dimensions within less than two months, but "matures" slowly through the four years prior to harvesting. During this period, the culms often develop internal stresses, and as a result, when the maker splits his strips, the advancing crack may wander somewhat across the fibers. Of greater importance, however, fibers within a node are always a tangled mess, and they often enter and exit the nodes at some odd angle. Typical patterns reveal a bell-shaped curve riding up and down the outer surface of each node, but after splitting, it's just as common to see similar curves when viewing down on the lateral plane—kinks that extend an inch or so on either

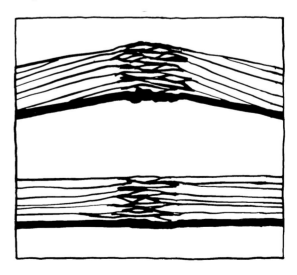

side of a node. Internal stresses have formed here as well, and where there is a crooked node, the splitting has probably torn somewhat across the angle of those fibers, with the result that the strip may appear straighter than the fibers themselves would reveal.

As preliminary steps in squaring, Vince always prepared his strips by scraping an inch or so of enamel on either side of the nodes, followed by reducing the inner pith from his mid- and tip-section strips. These steps allowed him to see the orientation of the fibers clearly. Next, he planed the sides of each strip (focusing especially on the node areas) to ensure these new outer surfaces would run exactly parallel to the course of the fibers. Seemingly counter-productive, this process actually created kinks, bends or sweeps where, earlier, the strip may have appeared to be straight. But only by doing so would the heat-straightening to follow yield a strip that ran true, both in its overall length and with regard to the fibers lying within.

So, his strips, now squared and straightened and their enamel sides dead-flush, Vince's next step was to establish the initial 60-degree bevel. Some makers like to use a special form for the beveling step, but Vince found he could accomplish the process just as efficiently by manipulating the strips directly in his basic planing form. Again, he preferred to avoid any unnecessary complications. Each strip was to be transformed from a four-sided cross-section into one that's triangular (although without the taper), and the three corners soon matched the 60-degree shape of his V-groove.

Beveling completed, the corners of each strip would be checked full-length with his center-gauge, corrected for accuracy if necessary, and finally, the actual tapering could begin. Planing the taper is, itself, straightforward, but each bamboo strip seems to hold a few, surprise complications for the maker and the overall process rarely goes off without a hitch. Most especially, nodes present problems, and Vince, too, found that the fibers of certain nodes want to "lift" without warning, causing minute tear-outs along a strip's outer corners. Once a node demonstrates this tendency, the difficulty is likely to continue with each pass of the plane. To resolve the problem, Vince would plane the offending area in reverse direction, or, if this didn't work,

he simply angled his plane out of its cut just before reaching the node, addressing that area with his file each time thereafter.

As all makers know, apart from dealing with nodes, the most critical part of hand planing is what we call "chasing the apex." We mentioned earlier that maintaining a precise, 60-degree, inner angle can be difficult, and without frequent checking, one risks creating unequal inner faces. The inaccuracy is likely to become worse and worse with each pass of the plane until, finally, a strip approaches its target dimension and the maker can no longer afford to remove enough material to restore that apex. You think you're doing well because, to the eye, everything looks just fine—only to discover (often too late) that the strip has been planed with some areas that are not truly equilateral at all.

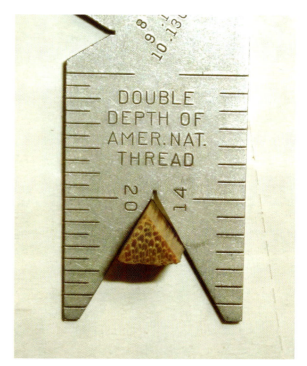

Inner apex is off-center

Even subtle differences may involve errors of several thousandths-of-an-inch, and the gluing process may fill the inner gaps and hide everything from view, but the mistake remains. Should such errors be in a tip strip, it's likely the section will reveal some uneven flexing—a spine. And, should one double or triple small errors of this sort in as many different strips, you'll have a rod that cannot realize its design potential, never becoming more than ordinary. Some makers are happy enough with a rod of this sort. It *is* bamboo, after all, and it ***has*** been made entirely with one's own hands. While that's certainly something to be proud of, such rods never satisfied Vince. What would be the point of fussing for so many decades to evolve just the right tapers if his work were not capable of delivering what he designed?

Vince's fastidious attention to detail was a regular habit in his work, and the snail-like pace of his planing was no different—a result of his obsession constantly to check his strips against the 60-degree center gauge. He would plane three or four passes on one surface, pause to "read" the inner apex along its length with the gauge (dressing any problem area before continuing), then flip the enamel to the opposing face in the groove and carry on. Irons were sharpened by fixing them in a simple roller-guide and stroking the device across a Norton combination-stone. For honing, however, Vince used only hard Arkansas, lubricated with kerosene, then a hard strop. A pair of irons would be sharpened at the same time, and as each took on wear he would stop for touch-up honing.

Little by little, each strip was worked down to within 10 thousandths-of-an-inch (or so) of its target dimension, and finally the strip's enamel side would be rotated to the top of the groove for removal. Vince liked to leave the enamel in place until nearly the last moment. I don't know why, because there's no particularly good reason I've ever come across not to remove it at the start. Still, I've always done the same.

At the other end of the spectrum, even some of the best makers will leave the enamel in place until after the strips have been glued, to be removed later with a scraper, sandpaper or file. The problem with this, however, is that the thickness of the enamel has already participated in the target dimensions for the strips—even if these were intentionally overbuilt. But there's no way to predict how thick that enamel may be, and depending on how a culm happened to grow and the vagaries of one's scraping, the maker may remove anything between 0.003" to 0.006" along each outer flat (the effect doubling in cross-section). But, even in removing the minimum necessary, the rod's final dimensions become uncertain and are almost bound to differ somewhat from its design. Thus, Vince insisted the most accurate results are obtained only by scraping the enamel at some point prior to establishing each strip's final dimensions.

The strip, now lying in the V-groove with its enamel side just above the form's surface, is scraped along its length with long strokes. An ordinary paint scraper did the job for Vince, sharpened to a slight angle on 600-grit sandpaper, then burnished and hooked to a keen edge. The enamel would fly off with each pass, barely exposing the fresh power fibers beneath, but Vince scraped gently and worked only down to the "ghost." This last hint of enamel would be draw-filed with his mill-bastard file and the result would be a smooth, outer surface with all power fibers intact.

With the enamel removed and the outer surface flush and true, Vince returned to dress the last licks from the strip's inside surfaces. Here, he switched to his violin-maker's plane, set the iron to its finest cut and made no more than two passes on each side before checking with the center gauge. Finally, the strip would nestle neatly into the groove. With barely a thousandth or so to go, he would inch his way down the form, using his left forefinger to press the strip firmly into the groove while running his right fingers obliquely across the surface to feel for irregularities. High spots would be noted with pencil marks and final passes over the inner faces of these areas would be made with his file.

Lastly, in preparation for gluing, Vince re-established the sequence of his strips in each section, aligned their ends, and fixed their positions with strips of masking tape across the outer surfaces. Then, he placed each set, inner-apex-up, on his picnic table, and using 400-grit sandpaper wrapped around a block of wood, he knocked the apex down equally on all six strips at once. Only a few thousandths would be removed—just enough to relieve the strips from having to compete for that theoretical point of "dead center" within the hexagonal shape. (Dead center, by the way, is indeed very dead because the stress loads of compression/tension cannot accumulate appreciably here.

Sanding the inner corners before gluing

Consequently, because the center point in a fly rod does not contribute to is strength, minute amounts of material sanded from each apex will not be missed, and the strips will be free to mate as intended all along their surfaces.)

GETTING IT ALL TOGETHER

And now, to the moment of truth—that final step in the construction process when glue is applied. In earlier days when the only really good adhesive was hot hide glue, this was always the stage of greatest anxiety for a maker. Hot glue presents a fast-ticking clock that turns the process of marrying six, long, willowy strips of bamboo into a nightmare. Actually, in addition to its fickle handling properties, there are two other objections—a tendency to delaminate under heat and humidity and its vulnerability to damaging bacteria and mold. Nowadays, however, both these problems can be overcome by mixing certain additives into the glue. (There's no need to go into the issues at this point, only to say that, for the maker who wishes to experiment, hide glue can be made both moisture-resistant and immune to bacteria. So, this leaves us only with the physical battle.)

Returning to Marinaro's "Part II" of his early articles on gluing, we read of the problems and the solutions he encountered in working with animal glues. If hot glue is applied with a brush, the danger is that cooling will take place before the strips can be positioned properly and fed through the binder. Once its temperature dips below a critical point (and with such a thin film, this happens fast!), the glue begins to gel, and even heavy binding pressure will be unable to penetrate the adhesive amongst the tough cane fibers. Excess glue merely squeegees out—just as one would expect to see anyway—and the rod may appear to be a success even after the string is removed. But if the glue has gelled to any degree before binding, the rod will surely be subject to delamination.

As an alternative to brushed application, Marinaro recommended what he called the "closed assembly." A minimum amount of equipment (and a little fussing) is needed to construct an apparatus, but this amounts to no more than two tubes; the first, maybe 2 1/2 inches in diameter and sealed at its bottom end; and the second, about 1 inch in diameter and also sealed at the bottom. The larger tube functions as a water-jacket, into which the smaller tube (a glue-reservoir) is inserted. This glue reservoir must be a few inches longer than the water-jacket to prevent water contamination. Lastly, a small hose supplying hot tap water is inserted down into the jacket, and in operation, the whole device is placed over an open drain. Constant circulation must be maintained through the jacket to hold the glue at its ideal operating temperature, the overflow water merely running away to the drain. Marinaro, in that same article, describes how to put the gluing apparatus to use:

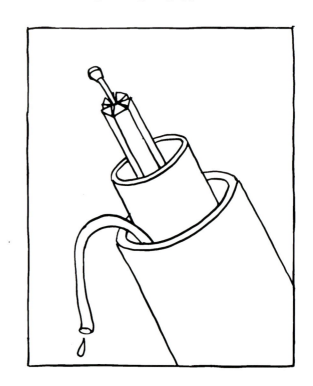

To operate the closed assembly merely bring together the strips of your joint and hold them with rubber bands at each end. Insert a round toothpick or matchstick in the ends to keep the strips separated. Dunk the whole joint into the copper tube which contains the glue and remember that your joint may displace a considerable amount of glue, therefore, do not fill the tube completely. If you like, you can dunk the joint into the tube, cork the open end of the tube, then turn it upside down to be sure that the entire joint is covered. It is a good idea to tie a string to one end of the joint in order to withdraw the joint. Lift the joint a couple of inches out of the tube, wrap a piece of rubber sponge around the joint and around the mouth of the tube. Hold firmly and withdraw the joint completely. This procedure will remove excess glue from the outside of the joint, and return the excess to the tube at the same time. Remove the toothpicks and pressure wrap without delay.... In this way the glue remains hot and fluid. No chill air strikes the inner surfaces and the temperature of the wood is brought up to the proper level.[6]

For the amateur who might want to give Marinaro's process a try, it seems a good idea to soak the rod section in the glue reservoir for a few minutes, for the introduction of cool strips will require a little time before everything returns to optimal temperatures. Secondly, rod sections should be inserted with their thicker ends facing upward, toward the tube opening. In this manner, the squeegee-withdrawal will favor the reduced direction of the taper and avoid snagging corner fibers. Still, the process is not easy, and one is left with almost no time to straighten joints after binding. Consequently, the maker would do well to rehearse his working schedule thoroughly—understanding his binding machine inside and out and tuning it to produce straight sticks from the get-go.

With his sections glued, wrapped and hung in the furnace room, there was nothing to do but wait a few days until the adhesive had taken a good initial set. Hide glue would require additional weeks to reach full cure, but there would be plenty of time for that before late winter when it was time to mount the ferrules and wrap the guides. Carpenter's Glue, on the other hand, needs very little time to complete its curing process. But in either case, after a week or so, Vince would peel the binding string off and lay

Vince runs a glued section through his binder

At The Master's Bench

R. L. Winston Rods

Telephone SUtter 3979   684 HARRISON STREET, SAN FRANCISCO 7, CALIFORNIA

June 20/47

Dear Mr. Marinaro:

    Am happy to enclose a list of the rods we now are able to make. In the fly rods, those are all custom built as nearly to the ideals of the patron as we can be made to understand those, with literally hundreds of possible variations. We start with the specification of the line to be cast, the fishing to be done, the kind of casts required, and all possible other information. Any wanted length of rod, amount of power, and variant of action, can be supplied. Total weight of rod, dependent on these factors, must be whatever is necessary to best embody them. In general the Fluted Hollow rod is about 30% lighter than any comparable solid rod, much faster, and with far greater "expectancy of life".

    Our new ferrules were a development forced upon us by post-war conditions, when we could get none anywhere. They proved to be so much better than anything ever "hand-made" or drawn, that we shall never use any other. They are machined from solid bar stock of enough over-diameter to allow complete removal of all metal crystalized by rolling or drawing, are precisely reamed and turned. The external part of the male has plenty of bearing on the full diameter of the cane, so it is wholly independent of the entering part in its full support of the rod top. We do not serrate them, but thin them so that when driven onto the cane within a driving bushing, they expand to completely hoop, at their open end, the full hexagon of the cane. This affords the needed flexibility there, without detracting from the length of bearing on the wood in this part. We have been wholly free of "ferrule trouble", since using these.

    I at first made the needed tools and made them myself, but since turned their making over to a very fine mechanic who bought the needed equipment and installed it at his home. Working only after hours and on weekends, he finds it hard to supply our needs, and unless we can get the job done on Swiss slow-speed automatics which embody the needed accuracy, we may have to get another lathe and another man in our own shop. Until one or the other eventuates, we can't sell any of them.

    Please give my best to Chas. Wetzel. I hope he is getting on with his new book, and that we shall see it before too long.

    I'm figuring on getting away, within a few days, for an extended vacation such as my health and my years demand. Maybe a couple of months or so on the McKenzie River, in Oregon. While I'm away, Doug. Merrick will probably care for the correspondence.

                                     Thanking you, yours,

                                          Lew Stoner

"THE PERFECTED BAMBOO ROD"

Letter from Lew Stoner to Vince—1947

the sections on his picnic table to remove excess adhesive. Working along one flat at a time, he took nearly full-length strokes with his 10-inch, mill-bastard file—a quick and easy process that shaves through the mess smoothly and without disturbing outer fibers. Then, a light sanding with 400-grit paper, and the sections were hung once again to cure until later in February.

Well, Labor Day, Thanksgiving, New Years and Valentine's Day have all come and gone and it's time to take the sections down from their hooks and turn the sticks into a fly rod. The first steps would be to heat-straighten each section, then to set the ferrules. These are available in tube-diameter increments of sixty-fourths of an inch, so the idea is to measure across a section's flats where the female ferrule is to be mounted—then to select a ferrule of the nearest, larger size. In preparation for mounting, the serrated tabs on each ferrule part must be filed to a feather edge.

Vince favored a mounting technique he learned from Lew Stoner in the mid-1940s. The process called for an almost too-tight fit between the ferrule and the cane. Then, the ferrule would be heated to expand its inner diameter and pressed onto the rod section. First, however, the rod's ferrule stations needed to be dressed. Stoner would have used a lathe for this operation, but Vince did everything by hand. He began with a 6-inch, mill-bastard file, taking equal numbers of strokes across each corner and checking his newly-created flats against reflected light to be sure he was maintaining concentricity. The diameter of these new flats would be measured in pairs and knocked-down until each of three pairs was barely one thousandth-of-an-inch larger than the internal diameter of the ferrule.

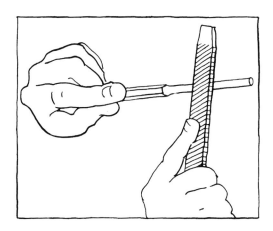

At this point, the once, six-sided ferrule station now had 12 sides, but only the six that were just created would bear against the ferrule's inner diameter. All 12 corners needed to be rounded, however, so Vince laid the section across his lap, and, holding fine sandpaper to the station with his right hand, he rolled the section back and forth under the palm of his other hand. This softened the sharp corners, but without compromising the bearing surfaces. The next-to-last step was to create a slight taper at the very end of the rod section—only enough for the ferrule to get a clean start. Finally, but most importantly, Vince would clean the ferrule with acetone, heat it to expand its diameter, apply glue to the inner walls, heat again, align the serrated tabs with the section's flats and drive the ferrule home—with the excess glue squeezing out in little burps. Quickly, the tabs were bound with string, and the whole was left to cure for a few days.

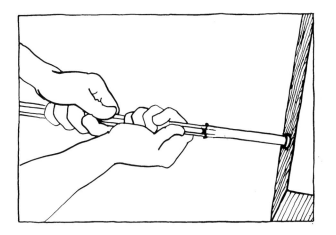

Soon, he was ready for the final fittings; the grip and reel seat, the guides and varnishing. As a means of minimizing weight, Vince used his rasp and file to remove excess cane under the cork and reel seat, rounding the hexagonal butt to a dowel measuring something like 5/16 inch. The tapered transition from the hexagon to the smaller, dowel dimension would occur under the first two corks of the grip, and except for a butt that now weighed perhaps 3/16 of an ounce less than before, nobody would be the wiser.

The cork grip was fitted next, and for this, Vince simply reamed the center-hole of each ring and slid these down the butt-shaft. The rings were then glued, both to the shaft and to each other, and the assembly was clamped tightly together. Shaping was done with the rasp, file and sandpa-

At The Master's Bench 185

per, and as before, his lap became the lathe—a somewhat tedious process, for cork is soft, works quickly, and concentricity is tricky to maintain. Vince often produced odd profiles for his grips, but, he never made a cork grip that could be distinguished from one turned on a lathe.

Reel seats for his trout rods were frequently made of balsa, or if not, then simply cork. On larger rods, Vince preferred Hardy's lightweight, locking hardware, but for the smaller rods his choice was simply to fit the reel seat with a pair of sliding bands (usually, very thin rings of aluminum). If a cork real seat, it would be turned at the same time as the grip, and in the same manner, but if the filler were wood, it would be shaped separately. Here, he resorted to the only power tool—a borrowed drill to bore the center-hole in a block of wood. Next, the block was mounted temporarily on a longer dowel, then whittled, rasped, filed and rounded on his lap. Lastly, one area would receive a somewhat flattened radius to accept the foot of the reel, and when finished, the filler would be cut to length and mounted on the rod shaft. The final touch usually included a "button" of cork or wood attached to its end.

Notice, in all, that weight was constantly on Marinaro's mind. We've spoken about this issue in earlier sections, but, truly, Vince's desire to minimize weight was an obsession. He could sometimes forgive other shortcomings in a fly rod, but any rod that seemed heavier than necessary would be rejected, summarily, out of hand. Actually, he couldn't have cared less about how his rods looked, just as long as they were as light as he could possibly get them, and except for hollow-building, Vince overlooked nothing. He told me that he always wanted to give hollowing a try, but could not think of a way to create the unique, fluted shape that Lew Stoner developed for Winston back in the early 1930s. To Vince's mind, Stoner's fluting method was the only truly effective way to hollow a rod, for the "U-shaped" channel down each strip removes large amounts of material from its core while still preserving strength along the broader gluing surfaces. But accuracy would require additional jigs and power tools of one sort or another, and Vince simply did not wish to start down that road.

Once the grip and reel seat were complete, Vince turned his attention to guide-placement. His method was very simple, but it differed from the usual preference of other

Hollow-fluted strips ready for glue

rod-makers. Instead of employing one *more* guide than the foot-length of the rod, Vince chose one *fewer* guide. For him, once again, weight was the issue. Of course, in themselves, a couple snake-guides weigh next-to-nothing. But they need to be wrapped, and once wrapped, the thread becomes saturated with varnish. Consequently, Vince believed that a surplus of guides quickly becomes detrimental—and especially to the action of a tip-section. On rods of 7 1/2 feet and more, the first guide would be placed a good 6 inches down from the tip-top, and the stripper would be located 28 to 30 inches up from the end of the butt section.

Locating the rest of the guides was determined on the basis of the rod's action. To discover approximate placement, Vince started at the tip and calculated a constant increase in separation, then taped the guides only temporarily in place. Next, he threaded a line through the guides and induced a bend—"loading" the rod with a steady, fixed pull on the line. The objective here was to measure the resulting distance between the taut line and the bent rod just at the center-point between each set of guides. Because a rod will flex more through its upper sections, the gap between rod and line becomes larger as one approaches the tip-top, but that increase should be proportionate and uniform from one guide to the next. Any noticeable variance will mean that certain guides need to be shifted to distribute the loading more evenly.

This simple, visual exercise quickly indicates how well the guides are sharing the rod's varying strengths along the length of its taper. After all, it is only because of the guides that a rod is able to transmit its flexed energy to the line. Conversely, it's also only because of the guides that the weight of the line is able to load the rod properly upon casting. So, from either perspective, all areas along the taper, in progressive increments, need to be accessed by the guides. Finally, Vince would test his placements by casting, and depending on how well certain areas seemed to be performing, he made his final refinements and spotted the guides permanently.

That done, the rod was ready to be wrapped and finished. But, here, and unlike all other considerations in the building process, Vince had no real interest in how his rods

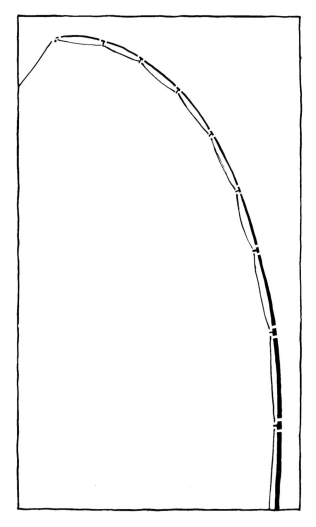

looked. In later years, he only wanted them Spartan and free from embellishments. Actually, once a rod was ferruled, had its grip and reel seat mounted (and guides located), he considered his work to be finished. To him, the rest was just a bore. Things needed only to be thoughtfully designed, carefully built, and they needed to function as precisely as possible. Period. Everything else was fluff. So, in finishing his rods, Vince filed the guide feet and wrapped them in place with silk of almost any color—again, on his lap. The spool would be tossed to the floor, and wrapping tension was maintained simply by closing the pages of a book upon the thread as it exited the spool.

Vince's finishing work was neat enough, but no particular care was taken. His only objective was to get the job done. Just four coats of varnish would be applied to the wraps, then the rod would be set aside for a week before sanding

It's perhaps a strange thing, but I never heard him comment on the appearance of any rod, no matter how stunningly it may have been carried out. That part just didn't matter, almost as if his general sense of aesthetics had never developed at all. But the same could be said for his choice in cars, decor, and fashion of every other sort. Always neat and presentable, he simply wasn't tuned-in to style. Amusingly, Vince's last car was a sleek, silver Mustang with a maroon interior—exactly the opposite of what you'd expect to see him driving. But, actually, it suited him perfectly because the car was really nothing but an old "beater" that he bought on the cheap. To him, all cars were hopeless encumbrances, but more than that, he actually hated to drive. So, silver Mustang or no, all he really wanted was to get to the stream or the grocery store (in that order), and he held the old beast in the contempt it probably deserved.

the "fuzzies" that always seem to show up. Lastly, sometimes using only a crude, ballpoint pen, he would inscribe his name on the butt and sometimes a moniker for the rod itself. Well, "scrawled" is perhaps closer to the mark, for Vince's penmanship left more than a little to be desired. Lastly, he would brush a single coat of varnish over everything, again taking his cue from Crompton who was similarly critical about loading a rod with varnish. But, sometimes, he would just buy a can of spray varnish and blast away. For Vince, any old varnish would do. Cut the crap! Just get a little of it on, get it dry, and get fishing!

We wouldn't go so far as to say that Vince's rods look dreadful, but neither are they likely to win any beauty contests. Tom Maxwell, Hoagy Carmichael and I each finished (or refinished) some of Vince's rods, but only after constant teasing. Perhaps, on some secret level he might have cared that his finishing skills weren't the best, but again, probably not. On a few occasions, he actually asked if I would wrap and varnish a rod for him—again, the instructions were for only four coats on the wraps plus one on the rod. I never knew if he asked for help because he was hoping for a nicer job than he could manage or if he just want-

It's not that he didn't practice....

ed to avoid a chore. Anyway, on the first rod, I cheated, putting seven or eight coats on the wraps as I usually do, but sanding them well back for smoothness. The rod itself received three coats, again, sanded between. When I returned it, Vince was genuinely happy and gracious, and he thanked me for my efforts. But when I purposely needled him about the rod's appearance, he refused to look up, barely stopped munching his cigar butt and muttered, "It's okay, I guess, if you like that sort of thing...."

That was Pappy. He knew perfectly well I wanted to yank him around a little, but on that day he didn't feel like giving an inch. I'd get him later, the old fart—nothing is free!

photo by Tom Whittle

Chapter Eight

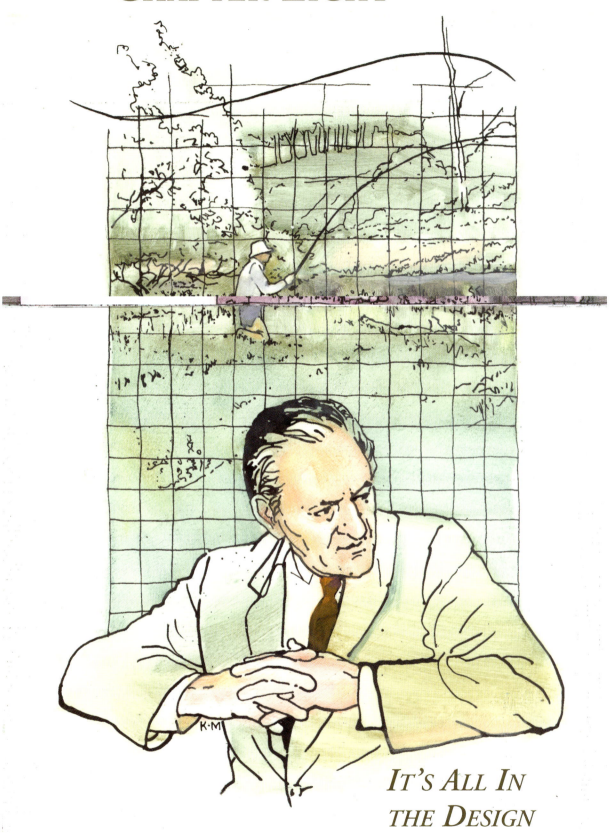

It's All In the Design

Marinaro had a great, intuitive understanding of the mechanics of a fly rod as it's being cast, the result of experience that could come only from decades of fishing, building and querying. As readers would have gathered, Vince was anything but an occasional fly-fisherman. He lived and breathed it, constantly thinking about how to resolve this problem or that. As it was for his fly-tying, so was it for his rod-making. Marinaro had an intensity about him that led to shelves-full of reading material—anything he thought might be helpful—and he ransacked everything in his search for the dry-fly taper that suited his needs. While he came to understand several relevant principles of physics, however, his practice in designing and building fly rods was entirely trial-and-error. It was a matter of preference. Vince knew how his mind worked, what it could understand best and why.

Although Marinaro finally came to insist exclusively upon the principles of the convex taper, we all know there are dozens of superb fly rods whose tapers describe nothing like a convex curve. Both Tom's and my fly rods also employ convex tapers (this is what we have come to understand and prefer), but I'm sure neither of us would argue for some inescapable superiority in the design. Indeed, upon picking up certain Paynes, Dickersons, Edwards, Grangers, Heddons or what have you, I always find myself both delighted and grateful that they cast so beautifully; grateful, because good rods always provide a shot of reality just when, like Vince, I too, start believing too exclusively in convex theory.

Of equal significance to the quarrels over "the best taper," it's important to realize that, because all casters impart energy to a rod in ways that are very different from one another, certain rods will suit one fly-fisher, while other, equally-excellent rods simply will not. And these differences exist even among the best casters. As with a golfer's swing, principles of physics may be able to describe how the sequence of movements needs to be executed, yet all golfers on the professional circuit will demonstrate slightly different form as they get that theoretical job done. The result is that every player has good reason to prefer one set of clubs to another.

Most of our ability to cast a fly line is based upon a learned (but then, instinctive) ability to feel bending stresses as they accumulate in a rod. This information is sensed, then translated into appropriate muscle motions and timing, all meant to maximize the action of the rod and to convert those loads back into a good cast. Understandably, we're all very different in our abilities to sense and to respond, but in suiting a rod to the individual fly-fisher, we do believe these factors are **at least** as important as the differences among taper designs themselves. Still, regardless of how compelling this case may be, I know that Vince would have disagreed, and most energetically. For him, what was right in designing a rod was right, and should remain so for any caster if he were really aware of what's going on. Vince was many things, but "humble" was usually at some remove from the top of that list.

Earlier chapters related Vince's origins as a rod-maker, a few of his fishing experiences and his many acquaintances. We reflected, too, on his building practices and offered a few thoughts about taper design. But to understand Vince's own tapers, a great deal more explanation is needed. What follows, then, is an account of the particulars of Vince's convex-taper theory—including his own procedures in designing fly rods. Tom and I have talked all

It's All In the Design

around the topic, but have not addressed it directly. Readers may breathe a sigh of relief, however, to learn they will not be burdened with complicated theorems, software programs or applied mathematics. And this is as it should be, for Vince, too, lacked familiarity with these.

No doubt, much of what follows could be analyzed by structural engineers whose mathematical language and computer models might render our explanations with greater scientific precision. It's just possible, too, that these same folks might disprove some of Vince's notions—or at least poke a few holes. While Tom and I hope that any ensuing, technical discussions would carry on just as they should, we point out that our purpose is only to present Marinaro's thinking, and that the fruits of his process are borne out in the quality of his rods. Whatever questions one may have about his working-hypotheses or procedures, his results speak for themselves. Some may argue that a more scientific approach would have been helpful and could have saved a great deal of time. It's not that Vince, Tom or I would necessarily dispute this, only that we don't see things that way.

FROM THE SHOOTING-BOARD TO A ROOF-ROD

As we begin our discussion, let's have another look at the most important piece of equipment in the rod-maker's shop—his planing form. We begin here because, from the 1930s forward, this single device and how it operates remained the focus for all Vince's rod-design considerations. You can't design a bridge unless you know, first, whether you'll be building it with hammers and saws, welding torches and rivets, or trowels, mortar and stone. Similarly (as we discussed in Chapter Four), you can't design a fly rod unless you first understand the techniques used to transfer that design into a reality and what tolerances your methods and equipment can deliver.

Following this, we'll explain the principles of the convex-taper as Vince himself came to understand them, attempting to speak his mind in the same terms he used. Lastly, his design methods themselves will appear, together with an explanation for the special character of Marinaro's rods.

A miscellany of rods by other makers

While it's certainly true that Vince was a first-rate maker, the excellence of his rods lies within the tapers. Admittedly, there are now many dozens of first-rate makers, but while they would never minimize the need for excellent craftsmanship, they would also affirm that without a great taper a great rod is simply out of the question. Indeed, it's just possible that a first-rate rod may emerge even without first-rate craftsmanship.

One need only look at certain fly rods built by Heddon, Montague or Granger—"second-flight," production rods perhaps, sometimes showing glue-lines, poor cosmetics, mismatched strips, spines, and other indications of less-than-perfect work. Nevertheless, among these same rods we will also find a few models whose actions are simply wonderful! Fly-fishermen might wonder how much better they would feel had they been built to higher standards of craftsmanship, but the point here is that without an excellent taper, nothing of value can follow. The point also would be that, among those of us who do not need to meet production schedules, there's no excuse for skimping on either. Just as Marinaro required, every maker should insist on both a great taper and great care in its construction.

Our purpose is to discuss both, and upon beginning, George Parker Holden's adjustable, steel-bar planing form (first made public in 1920) is the focus. Its capabilities, together with certain later refinements, allowed amateur rod-makers to obtain truly accurate results for the first time, and the increasingly specialized taper requirements for dry-fly fishing came to be within reach. Precise and subtle design adjustments could now be realized, and this precision would make all the difference between an ordinary, merely-serviceable rod, and a great one.

Until recent years, however, Dr. Holden's steel planing form was never available commercially, so amateur rod-makers had to choose between building one for themselves or simply buying the more primitive, multi-grooved, planing board (or "shooting-board"). These latter had been recommended by Perry Frazer, George Herter and Claude Kreider in their books, and from the late 1940s through the '50s, Herter's mail order catalog offered an improved, steel version. It was George Herter's acquaintance, Robert Crompton, who developed the steel model, and because Crompton was also the champion of "penta" rod construction, it seems likely that it was he who also convinced Herter to add a five-strip version to the catalog.

Over the decades, thousands of serviceable fly rods were made with such shooting-boards, but an inherent problem plagues the device that simply cannot be overcome with any measure of consistency. Basically, to obtain the taper one is after, "target" dimensions are determined in 5- or 6-inch increments (as preferred), and corresponding index-marks are then penciled across the outer surface of each bamboo strip. A chart containing these dimensions is prepared and kept close at hand, and as the strips are reduced in dimension, the maker repeatedly applies his micrometer to check progress against the data. Each strip is shifted about in various grooves and gradually tapered until the desired dimension for each index mark is reached.

A little thought, however, will reveal some obvious and consuming problems. With all the slipping and searching up and down the grooves, it's only with extreme difficulty that one may arrive at an accurate measurement for each mark. And this same searching must begin again for each successive strip, with the inevitable result that the exact taper of any given strip could only approximate that of its neighbors. (Recall from earlier, Sparse's similar denunciation of the shooting-board.) Worse, however, the taper *between* the indexed marks would remain relatively uncontrolled and uncertain. Thus, when brought together to form the hexagonal section, even if the resulting flats should measure accurately at the indexed marks, almost anything else may obtain through the several inches between these stations. Finally, because this clumsy process of building a fly rod is tedious and chancy almost beyond description, a maker could hardly restrain himself from becoming prematurely satisfied—talking himself into accepting, too soon, that his work was close enough.

All these difficulties and inaccuracies were rendered obsolete, however, with Dr. Holden's steel-bar planing form—a device that actually operates as a full-length "mold." In constructing the steel planing form, Holden calls for two, 4-foot bars of 3/4-inch, cold-rolled steel, with each of their four corners beveled (or chamfered) at a 30-degree angle. Each bevel is to be milled with a larger, exposed surface. The smallest would measure 1/32", and the next three, 1/16", 1/8" and 3/16", respectively. When setting a taper, the two bars would be rotated to a matched pair of bevels and sections of any size could be built.

Holden then specifies that the bars are to be attached to a sturdy, fixed base by means of a series of angle-brackets—these, to be located at something like 10-inch intervals. One angle, or leg, of each bracket is bolted to a selected side of the steel bars with a simple machine screw. The bracket's other leg, however, remains adjustable on the fixed base and is secured in place with a bolt that passes through a milled slot.

These angle-brackets might seem to be an incidental matter, but it's chiefly due to the slots milled into their lower legs that the genius of Holden's device is brought home. The whole point is that the steel bars, being somewhat flexible, are meant to be spread or narrowed, such that any desired taper can be formed within one of the four possible grooves. The bars are then locked in place with the brackets' lower legs. Finally, each 5- or 6-inch control station would be adjusted by inserting shims and locking these with C-clamps along the form's underside. The shape of the taper is now fixed within the bars and will be replicated exactly in each strip as it's planed flush with the top of the groove.

Taking one strip after the other and holding each to its index mark on the form, the maker planes first one inner surface and then the other, flipping the outer enamel from side-to-side. The triangle is kept uniform, and soon the strip nestles, full-length, into the tapered contours of the groove. No longer required to shift the bamboo strip about from one groove to another (as with the shooting-board), a maker using Holden's form can plane the full length of a strip's taper in a single V-groove. Every strip is formed the same way, and with care, each will be identical to its neighbor. All target dimensions for the various stations have been determined by the adjustment of the form, and the areas between those stations will be held uniform as well. Now, this is the way to get reliable results.

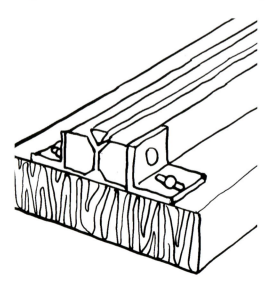

Adjustable, push-pull bolts in the modern planing form.

It was Holden who taught Everett Garrison to construct such a form, but at once Garrison made a few, significant improvements to the design. First, he dispensed with Holden's four, beveled edges—milling, instead, just two grooves along the top and bottom surfaces of the bars. Also differing from Holden's device, Garrison tapered the depth of those grooves from one end to the other. Thus, butt sections could be built in the deeper groove on one side of the form, while mid-sections and tips would be built in the shallower, tapered groove on the other. Most significantly, however, Garrison also discarded Holden's slotted angle-brackets in favor of a series of differentially-threaded bolts. With these, he established new adjustment points (control stations) at 5-inch intervals down the length of the bars. So, placing a machinist's depth-indicator in the V-groove, and working from one set of screws to the next, Garrison was able to "dial-in" exactly the tapers he wanted—a simple and remarkable improvement!

Notwithstanding Herter's persistence in offering the old shooting-board, the best planing forms from the first half of the century onward have always employed Garrison's basic arrangement.

At the other end of the rod-building spectrum, commercial makers had been using either mechanized mills or bevelers for nearly four decades prior to Holden's 1920 publication. But, because these machines were one-of-a-kind, heavy and custom-built to meet the demands of high production, no amateur was going to construct something as extravagant as that. Holden's steel bars (particularly with Garrison's improvements) gave the amateur exactly what was needed.

Vince told me that once he built his own flexible, steel form, he immediately saw promising results in his fly rods. But Vince also said that, although he had all the dimensional control he needed, the perfect dry-fly taper remained elusive. Tapers for casting the dry fly were still very much in the developmental stages in the 1920s, and not even Holden's book offered a great deal about their particulars. Nevertheless, as Vince explained, it was because of Holden's description of the convex taper that Vince, too, anticipated it was the design principle holding the greatest potential.

Bill Arend's old milling machine

It's All In the Design 195

In an earlier chapter we explained that it was not Dr. Holden, but his friend, Robert Crompton, who first worked with the convex taper—experiments that probably were responsible for Holden's strong endorsement of the design in his *Idyl*. In the following quote, we read Holden's recommendations for that taper:

> To secure the nicest action for fly-rods, do not have the diameter at the butt-joint any oversize (unless deliberately so for special, dry-fly work); the same caution applies with even more emphasis to the top end of the middle-joint; but be sure to have the butt end of the top-joint fully up to the measure, and to lighten the outer half of this section as already mentioned. The reason why the delicate top-joint of a properly-proportioned rod that is skilfully *[sic]* handled is sufficient to withstand all legitimate stress, is because a steadily-increasing strain is continuously thrown back upon the stronger parts of the rod. But when the butt of the top-joint is too slender and joins with a middle-joint small end that is too stiff, then the strain on the top is not progressively and properly transferred to the middle-joint, which is the prime factor in the rod's action.
>
> We spoke awhile ago of giving a double-taper to light fly-rod top-joints.... Another way to achieve practically the same thing is by a swelled taper obtained by *springing the mold apart a bit when setting it for getting out the individual strips of the joint*.... In getting the exact desired width for setting the small end of the mold, it sometimes is convenient—when double-tapering joints in this way—to use a certain number of pieces of tin or cardboard of a definite thickness and to bring the halves of the mold tight up against these 'shives' *[sic]* when placed between their ends. [1]

Of greatest significance here are Holden's explanations of: 1) the manner in which flexing stresses accumulate through the smaller areas of a taper; 2) how these are "continuously thrown back upon the stronger parts of a rod," and; 3) how the "double-taper" should be devised in the upper portions of a tip section. In these, together with Holden's emphasis upon the different flexing requirements for each of the three sections in a rod, Marinaro seems to have heard his marching orders echoing loud and clear. Indeed, all these concerns dominated his thinking even through the 1970s. Holden, who died in 1934, could not carry Vince further, however, so it was Crompton himself who remained his mentor through the many early years of development.

Just as Dr. Holden had explained, Vince, too, accounted for his design objectives in terms of how much (or, more to Vince's particular quest, how *little*) strength would be required at any given point to support those smaller areas distributed farther down the length of the rod. Conversely, he also considered how the flexing induced through thinner portions of a rod would load the larger "shoulders" along the thicker areas. Always, *always*, Vince held firmly to the belief that unnecessary weight, wherever it may be located, was the fly rod's greatest enemy, eventually becoming convinced that only the convex taper could yield the optimal strength-to-weight relationship he was after.

Mathematical calculations might be made to predict other kinds of tapers, but because the operative, flexing strength of a convex taper does not seem to reveal itself simply by calculating the cross-sectional sequences of its dimensions, Marinaro realized there must be some additional, complicating factors—something cumulative deriving from the effects of solid geometry. But the peculiar "buttressing" strength of a convex shape (as with Greek columns, ships' spars, flagpoles and arrow-shafts) seemed to imply a set of formulae that Vince's limited familiarity with mathematics could not fathom.

Marinaro had no training as an engineer, so he knew no scientific discipline to help with convex taper designs. Trial-and-error was the only way for him, and the only relevant tests were empirical. How lightly could he build the rod, and how does it feel in one's hand when casting? Can it be fished effectively both near and far? And how well does it hold line in the air or turn a tippet over? That is, could he comfortably cast it for hours on end, fishing under all conditions, and would he be able to call it a "roof-rod"—one capable of shooting line over the roof-beam of his house, his ultimate test. Vince reports trying a great many ideas, but always came back to his elusive

Jack Hunter (l) and Vince on Boiling Springs lake

expectation that a convexly-tapered shaft holds within it "a geometry" capable of yielding a fly rod stronger and lighter than any other tapered shape. A more complete explanation of these principles will emerge in our next section.

Reading Holden, Marinaro, too, came to realize the value of building the "double-taper" into upper portions of a tip section—particularly important for a rod to "hold line in the air." Marinaro never adopted Holden's term to describe the shape of his tips, but preferred instead to consider a tip's entire length as a single, convex taper, and with its most rapid reduction occurring just along the last foot or so toward the tip-top. "Convexity," as Marinaro later determined, is not necessarily a uniformly distributed curve, although, from end-to-end, the trajectory must be drawn smoothly and without interruption (without dips, sudden changes or reversals), and the tip is the most critical part of a rod. Consider Marinaro's thoughts about tip design from *The Ring*:

Sketch 4 *[shown on his page 56]* shows a joint with the peak of the swell near the thick end and its influence is carried forward more gradually toward an extremely fine point.

The top half of the top joint is the most critical area in any rod. It is that part that delivers the final impulse or thrust that determines the character of the cast. I have agonized longer and more often over the construction of that last one or one and a half feet of a rod than any other part. The great blessing of the convex design lies in the possibility of controlling the amount of bend or tip fallover so that it remains just about the same on short weak casts as with the powerful thrust of a long cast. This control is not possible with straight tapers. [2]

Readers can't help but notice the similarity between Marinaro and Holden as each expresses his concerns about proper tip construction, but when Vince speaks here about "the peak of the swell near the thick end," he creates confusion. I know that Vince had special meanings attached to the terms, "peak" and "swell," but in the quote above, his use of these words doesn't conform to his more usual applications. Apparently, what he meant was simply that the thickest dimension of the overall taper is to be found at the ferruled end. But, because that's only as one would expect, his explanation is not edifying. Let us describe more accurately what the convex shape of such a tip actually means, applying Marinaro's terms in his own, more customary way.

When tracing the convex trajectory of his tip-section forward from the ferrule, one sees a gradual, curved taper carrying down the section's length toward its tip. The curve of this line begins its path along the shaft with extreme subtlety until reaching a foot or so from the tip-top. There, however, the shape assumes a more rapid "roll-off" in its trajectory. Looking at the section's entire taper from end-to-end, it is actually this point (the roll-off) that should be called the "peak" or "swell" of the convex taper. This application of Marinaro's terms corresponds to his own thinking—his more precise way of describing the "swell." And it's this same, swelled area that equates to the "double-taper" of which Holden speaks. But the devil's in the details, and managing its exact position and proportions came to be part of the magic of Vince's rods to fish up close as well as to hold the leader high—even to shoot line over his roof.

To the naked eye, Marinaro's convex tapers are barely different from other fly rod designs, but since no rod's taper can be determined merely by looking at the finished product, visual inspection will be of no use. Indeed, even though side-by-side comparisons with other rods will reveal differences, it's not possible to tell if those differences are themselves evidence of a convex taper or some other design consideration. Readers may wonder, "So, what's the big deal if we're talking about something you can't even see?" The resoundingly simple answer is that the differences between a good and a great fly rod are always measured in subtleties too fine for the eye to detect. It's in the nature of what a great fly rod is—regardless of design principle.

You can't tell by just looking

THE WELL-TEMPERED TAPER

Early on, as Vince and I grew to be friends, we began our long discussions about design, but I was not to work with his tapers. Neither did I want to. Marinaro had evolved the principle of the convex taper and this was what I would learn as well, but with none of his numbers or data. Instead, he showed me how to design my own tapers using large-format (11" x 17") graph paper, lined with quarter-inch squares. It's an easy and highly accurate method—one that we pass along in detail here because the remainder of this chapter depends on its particulars.

Vince's practice in designing a fly rod was always to think in terms of its individual sections, and he created the largest, graphed version for these that his paper could allow. His design process is not meant to be mathematical, but altogether visual, and for purposes of seeing the whole rod at once, each of its sections is "stacked" directly above the other on the same sheet of paper.

In all the following explanations it's important to note, too, that the design process shows just one strip to represent each, respective, rod section. A single strip actually equals one-half of any section's total thickness, and six such strips finally emerge from the planing form to become our hexagonal shape. So, all the resulting thickness measurements on the graphed taper are half-dimensions of the finished rod. Here's how the drill goes:

First, a grid needs to be created on the graph paper, and to begin this, we draw a horizontal axis just above the bottom of the sheet. This line corresponds to the desired length of our sections, with each quarter-inch square representing 1 inch of a section's actual length. The vertical axis is drawn next, but will represent each strip's thickness in thousandths-of-an-inch. This is shown by extending lines upward, from both the right and the left ends of our horizontal line, then marking their scales. Start with "0 thousandths-of-an-inch" at the bottom, and mark each quarter-inch square upward to represent an increase of 10 thousandths-of-an-inch (as 0.010", 0.020", and onward to perhaps 0.180").

Although the common practice nowadays is to work with 5-inch station settings, Marinaro, like so many other amateur makers in the earlier years of the 20th century, always used dimensions obtained along 6-inch increments. If only for purposes of consistency in our demonstration, then, we'll stay with Marinaro's method. (In later chapters, Vince's tapers will be shown with our 5-inch stations.) So, on the horizontal axis and starting at its far right, "0-inches" will indicate the strips' smallest ends, with each 6-inch interval to the left numbered as "6 inches," "12 inches" and so on. Now, at each of these 6-inch station marks, we draw a vertical line up through the open area soon to be occupied by the rod's sections. These lines are the "control points" for the tapers we will devise in a moment, but more to our final goal, the lines also correspond to actual mechanical settings distributed along the planing form itself.

(Note that all our accompanying illustrations are for purposes of demonstration only and do not represent the proportions or details of actual graph paper.)

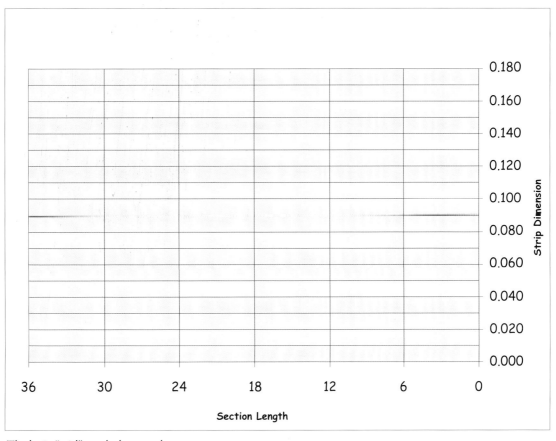

The basic "grid" marked on graph paper

It's All In the Design

As one can imagine, once the actual design is created, the resulting, graphed "picture" will reveal a greatly exaggerated and foreshortened view of the taper (represented in its half-dimensions). The thickness of each strip (in thousandths-of-an-inch) is shown in an enormously magnified scale, while the strip's length (in inches) will be miniaturized. But this is the just picture the designer needs to see because without these exaggerated proportions, he couldn't possibly control the details of a trajectory whose actual progression must develop by mere thousandths-of-an-inch. Convex tapers, as Marinaro worked out their proportions, reveal the swell with blatant clarity on the foreshortened grid, even while the actual shape in the finished rod is realized with extreme delicacy. That is, to create the smooth and uniform, convex shapes Vince had in mind for his rods, it's necessary to have clear and precise visual control over the graphed dimensions at each control station. The planing form, in turn, will yield the resulting measurements with equal precision.

It's the large scale of the resulting "picture" that's important, and we would contrast this design method to the several computer programs currently available. Software programs are precise and valuable in what they offer (charted dimensions, stress curves and a variety of conversion options), yet none yields a graphed, pictorial view adequate to reveal all those rises and dips in a taper that actually exist. The graphs are very small in scale rendering a rod's entire length across the width of a computer-screen "page," and each graph depicts a rod's full, cross-sectional dimensions. The visual results of such graphs suggest that there really aren't any local, taper anomalies of significance, and that if one builds the rod according to the accompanying station measurements, the resulting sections will yield nice, smooth trajectories. They probably won't. It's not because the charted numbers would be unreliable. They're not at all. It's because these small-scale graphs simply can't render accurate, visual representations of the numbers, and such "pictures" are insufficient for our purposes here.

Nevertheless, despite their inability to display design details in a useful scale, computer-assisted programs do offer a wide range of useful information. Their greatest strengths lie in a highly flexible data-base (essential when comparing one rod design to another) and in their ability to crunch numbers when asked to alter some given design. The numbers for each taper will be as true as possible to the rod in question; the stress curves will be representative of the rod's overall flexing characteristics; and any program options intended to convert a given taper into some alternate version will yield reliable results. You may or may not like the results you've requested, but the data will be dependable and the software will tell you what you ask.

In Vince's day, of course, there were no home computers, but even stress-curve calculations were of little significance to him. For Vince's method of design, the large-format, visual experience was actually everything—of far greater importance than any listing of numbers. Only by using his graph paper and looking directly at the exaggerated scale of his half-dimensions could he know how the local details of his taper were developing.

Back to that design process.... After lining-off and marking the basic grid, the last step prior to devising a taper calls for three additional lines to be drawn—these to define the hypothetical, straight-taper slope for each of the rod's three sections. Slope lines establish the basic, overall, thickness-to-length ratio, and in design, their primary function is to

It's about fishing... remember?

provide a critical, visual reference when devising the swelled shape of the actual taper. Each slope line begins at a given strip's maximum thickness to the left of the grid and is drawn directly to that strip's minimum dimension at the right.

But, how are their proportions determined? We can't draw these lines from any old, arbitrary height, or to describe any old, downward angle. I can't imagine what the first person designing the first rod may have used as his starting points. Indeed, if ever there was such a person, he must have thought he'd just landed on Mars. In our more fortunate circumstances, however, the maker simply resorts to a selection of existing rods whose lengths and actions seem more-or-less promising. There will be no intention to work with their tapers for, in themselves, these are of no value to us. Our only interest in the sample rods is to derive a limited set of "givens." What's needed is an initial choice of thickness dimensions—these to be taken at the start of the grip, the ferrules and the tip-top.

Choosing in this manner may seem somewhat arbitrary, but the choices are meant to serve only as foundations for the graphic work to follow. Lord knows, a world of differences exists amongst a gaggle of rods, all built to same-sized grip dimensions, ferrules and tip-top! Accordingly, because a rod's slope is actually a critical decision, the designer also knows that his choices here are only provisional. A great many factors are yet to be determined, and the maker remains free either to retain his initial slopes or to alter them later.

Often, the angle of a slope line may be common to all sections of a rod, but it's just as likely that this angle may vary slightly from one section to another. Typical slopes yielding a softer action will increase in thickness at an averaged rate of 0.028" per inch of a section's length, while stronger actions are obtained with a slope of 0.032" per inch. Still, one does not need to build very many rods before discovering a few, basic, thickness-to-length ratios that suit his own casting style best. In subsequent designs, various iterations of these ratios can be assigned to rods of different lengths and line-weights.

So, having made his choices and taken measurements, the designer divides his results by two (we're working with half-dimensions, remember), places a mark on the left- and then the right-hand, vertical scales, and draws a line between the dots to represent the slope for each strip. At this point, all has been made ready to design the taper, and we begin with Vince's recommendations for the optimum location of the swell along each section.

The particulars of Marinaro's preferred shapes are understood only by referencing a graphed "picture," and we call attention to the accompanying illustration. Again, we emphasize that the entire process is one of refining a visual concept, and in carrying this out, our eyes will be focused on the details of a taper line as it contrasts to the straight, slope line drawn immediately adjacent. Both lines are tapered, of course, but the convexity we're after is always conceived as one sort of departure or another above the neighboring, straight, slope line. It's from the particulars of that visual relationship, only, that we derive meaningful information.

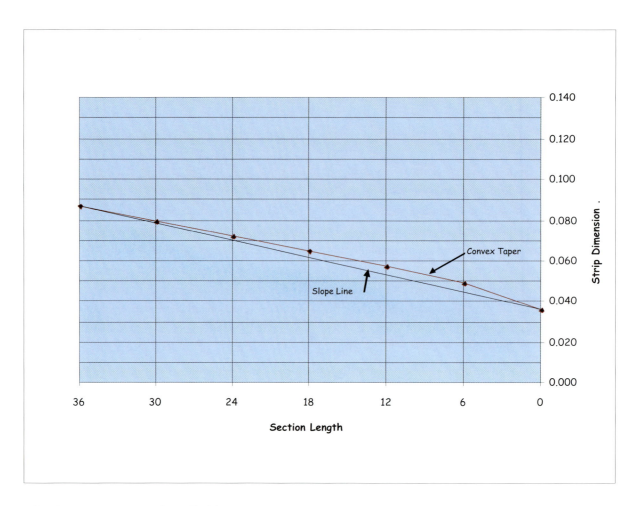

Slope line in comparison to the swell of the convex taper

Our accompanying graph is only generic and its scale is very small, but it demonstrates how a curved taper begins very subtly from the male ferrule forward, while by contrast, the slope line falls away directly to the section's smaller end. Then, at some point down the shaft (depending on which rod section is being designed), the convexity begins to develop more rapidly. The "swell" of the convex taper is always that area where the taper line achieves its greatest distance from the straight slope—its location and its proportions to be manipulated differently in the various rod-sections.

At long last, Marinaro worked out his recommendations for the ideal shape in each rod section. As explained to me, a tip section should have its greatest swell located approximately 10 inches back from the tip-top, with a uniform curve dropping forward to the tip and a considerably "flattened" shape carrying gently back toward the ferrule. A mid-section should realize its greatest swell less than a third of the measured distance back from the female ferrule—with that shape being held high above the slope line (rounding only slightly) until one reaches the last third of the section's length near the male ferrule. There, the curve rolls off again to meet the ferrule station. The design-portion of a butt section, however, extends only between the ferrule and the beginning of the cork grip. This area will show a rather shallow curvature between the two points with its greatest swell a third of this confined distance behind the ferrule.

In all cases, the magnitude of the swell (measured between slope and taper lines) will depend upon the length of the rod in question, the line it's meant to handle, and the caster's preference in action. The usual range for a swell's height above the slope line will fall between 2 and 5 thousandths-of-an-inch—never less, but for larger rods and heavier lines, often more. This may not seem like much, but remember that the measured effect of these dimensions actually doubles once the 6 strips are assembled. Lastly, it is important to note that Vince's principles serve as guidelines only, and each maker will want to vary the suggested proportions according to his own casting preferences.

Surprisingly, the experienced maker could design and build, say, a single 7 1/2-foot rod for 5-weight line, and whether the rod were successful or not, he would learn volumes about future designs. The great advantage of Vince's pictorial method is that, after a period of trial-and-error, one quickly visualizes how various changes in a taper will affect a rod's action. You can *see* your rod on the paper and know from previous experience how it's likely to perform. The disadvantage, of course, is that trial-and-error is an empirical process of undetermined duration. It knows no science. One needs to be willing to build a number of sections, try them out in different combinations and always be willing to go "back to the drawing board."

This suited Pappy and me perfectly because neither of us understood much about mathematics anyway and really responded only to visual representations. For myself, I can barely determine the cocktail hour by looking at a digital clock. What I need is a big, round face that says, "when the little hand is on 'Martini,' and the big hand is.... " Similarly, the numbers representing a rod's stress curve aren't nearly as significant for me as looking directly at the half-dimensions of a plotted taper. For Vince and me, our most valuable tools were a bright light, a sharp pencil and a large eraser; our most precise tests were weighing sections, measuring flats and casting.

While chuckling at our methods, readers should also bear in mind that every maker who's in earnest to perfect a set of tapers will need to go through some kind of trial-and-error in the design process, for very few rods built according to computer software programs (mathematically-derived tapers) will suit the discriminating caster "out of the box." That is, even though designers may find computer-assisted data helpful to gain a start, the empirical process of trial-and-error should never be regarded as out-dated or amateurish. Indeed, in the end, it's the only way for a fly-fisher to learn what really works best for him.

The need to visualize his tapers was writ particularly large in Marinaro's case because, from the start, he was exploring a design theory as yet undeveloped. Several useful notions were derived from Dr. Holden's book, and more particular advice came from Robert Crompton, but no known rendering of "convexity" pleased Vince in any way. For him, the problem was always one of determining where to locate the point of greatest swell along the length of a rod section. Should it be established uniformly across the entire rod, or should it be conceived somehow with respect to the separate sections? There were these questions, plus the need to determine how steep the swell should be and which particular areas it should occupy.

It's also about smelling the "roses"

THEORETICALLY SPEAKING....

Just here, it will be useful to consider a few principles of theory—those applying to the flexing characteristics of any fly rod—for these precepts are fundamental to our explanation of the convex taper. The explanations through the next few pages (as promised, without math) may tax the reader whose interest in rod design is casual, but they will be necessary for those who desire a more complete understanding.

As mentioned before, there was just one primary objective in Marinaro's efforts, and that was to obtain the very strongest rod at the very lightest weight—factors that ordinarily become mutually exclusive. In what follows, "strength" will mean a rod's relative ability to resist the forces of bending (induced "stress-loads"), while "weight" means... well... weight.

Structural engineers know that, all other things being equal (itself, usually a silly proposition), when the flexural strength of any solid, equal-sided beam or shaft is estimated it must be done through a consideration of its material and calculations of its cross-sectional mass. Put simply, for any given material, increased resistance to deflection derives from increased mass. But mass is weight, and in a fly rod, any increase in weight risks becoming the enemy. So, it would appear that if strength is always some proportionate function of mass, we're stuck, and there's just no getting around basic physics. Or, is there? Maybe, if we mix in a couple other wrinkles, we might come to a different set of possibilities.

There's something of a dilemma here, but it will be tempered by understanding that, in casting, a fly rod does not function as a simple, cantilevered beam (which the strength-analysis just above would have assumed). That is, this means of calculating a rod's flexural strength would be relevant only if the rod were assumed to be in a state of static repose—fixed at one end and with some known, steady load imposed on its outer end. But these assumptions are inadequate to describe a fly rod as it's used. On the contrary, a fly rod's relative ability to withstand the stresses of bending functions, not in static repose, but dynamically, with differing kinds (and degrees) of loads being induced successively at each of its ends. Actually, then, a fly rod would behave more like a spring than a simple beam, and in consequence, all ordinary calculations (or predictions) of strength-to-weight ratios now become greatly complicated.

If we were to capture a "freeze-frame" depicting the final moment of a back-cast, we'd see a rod bent somewhat to the rear with its line fully extended and floating in the air. This momentary condition constitutes a load (of some magnitude) on the tip, and any subsequent casting motion induced through the butt will begin in opposition to that partially loaded tip. Not immediately, but very quickly, the energy imparted through the butt will overcome the loaded tip—loading it still more and setting the line into a forward motion. The energy needed to cast a rod derives only from the motion of its butt, but that motion is always begun in response to the partially loaded tip; is always greater than that load; and is always initiated in advance of its final effect on the tip.

To explain this delayed effect, all fly-fishermen know that (during a cast) the rod does not merely rotate through a uniform, back-and-forth arc. Instead, part of the rod's movement includes a subtle "whipping" stroke—almost as if the caster had flexed a spring at its end. But this load on the butt is not simply "there." On the contrary, it's sprung into the lower shaft and sent traveling down its length as "linear waveforms"—not a static load, now, but a dynamic pulse of energy. Thus, the casting motion has created a moving target flowing toward the tip, and its progression causes the differing strengths along the rod shaft to participate, not in unison, but in rapid sequence. The result is that any mathematical means to predict the rod's optimal "strength requirements" now become almost impossible to estimate.

Finally, because the timing of the casting motion is executed differently by each fly-fisher, we can expect these waves of energy to move with varying speeds and magnitude. Ideally, upon casting, the induced energy (waveforms) should travel uniformly down toward the end of the rod and leave no residual bounce at the tip. (Poor rod design, however, causes some waves to rebound from the ferrule stations or tip-top toward their point of origin, creating "harmonic vibrations"—a highly undesirable condition because that measure of available energy becomes, not simply wasted, but actually counter-productive. In such cases, although the rod has been loaded, it will also have been "shocked.")

When a rod is cast, our "spring" wants to uncoil, uninterrupted. But there *are* interruptions, and the energy of the linear waveforms will be absorbed by a range of opposing factors (loads). One such factor, of course, is the rod's resistance to deflection as derived from the sequenced distribution of its own mass. A second load is contributed by the ever-changing weight of the extended fly line. Yet a third load is wind-resistance, acting upon both the rod and its line. This last factor is real, significant and ever-present, but because its practical effects are almost beyond reckoning (being imposed by weather conditions and the varied motions of the rod), the particulars of wind-resistance do not participate in most design considerations. Rods meant to be used in windy conditions are easily built, but the maker simply "cranks-in" a stronger action for a heavier line.

In any event, the energy of the waveforms will be taxed while traveling down the rod's taper, but with just enough power in reserve to overcome the load of the fly line and to create the needed line-speed. Then, if a forward cast, the leader, tippet and fly will all travel high, straight and true, alighting on the water just as the last bit of available energy is sapped by wind-resistance and gravity. It should now be apparent that the "strength" of a fly rod is far from an absolute term, and becomes, instead, a function of exactly where our strength is located, and how (or when) it is asked to come into play.

We also see that the engineer's, cantilevered-beam theory (even with the caveat of "all other things being equal") is of extremely limited help in fly rod design. In design, it's barely possible to determine what all those "other things" may be, much less to hold them equal while addressing just one. Consequently, any effort to predict a fly rod's action with numerical calculations alone is chancy at best. It's often done, but the question of whether the resulting rod will please any given caster remains wide open.

In design, we know that a rod's relative strength comes from the trajectory of its taper, but because this is always manipulated in some way, the rod's mass will not be distributed in anything like a uniform progression. Instead, it will be moved about here or there as desired. Thus, we obtain strengths of different measure in different locations on the shaft according to our preference for a rod's action. (Not least, in design manipulations, will be the effort to defeat harmonic vibration, or waveform "bounce-back").

Finally, however, it's important to note that, while there is much to be considered in designing any fly rod taper, and while the general shapes of convex tapers were described earlier, we still have not identified the operative principles that distinguish the convex design from that of other rods. In pursuit of this, we might consider the graphed (thus, exaggerated) trajectory of nearly any conventionally-tapered rod. Typically, these will reveal a series of dips and

Kim Mellema

bumps that roll down their length. Vince called such tapers "step-and-dip" because of the telescoping reductions along each rod section—a sort of irregular sequence of waves. Certain rods have noticeable steps and dips deliberately designed into the taper, while others (even the so-called "straight-tapers") will reveal subtler variances.

Marinaro insisted that the necessary consequence of such fly rods must be that, at each location where the taper takes a dip (where its graphed trajectory momentarily turns "inside-out" as compared to the adjacent, straight slope-line), relatively weaker spots in the rod will be found. Just in these areas, the concavity of the taper line offers comparatively less resistance to bending stresses, and when casting, this condition results in something of a "hinge" effect.

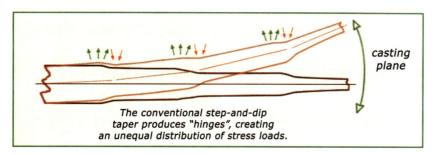

The conventional step-and-dip taper produces "hinges", creating an unequal distribution of stress loads.

Conversely, at every nearby rise (a humped, or locally convex area), a stronger effect will be found, with increased cross-sections of cane providing relatively greater resistance to bending stresses. The effects of all the steps and dips upon a rod's action may be great or they may be very small, depending entirely upon the shape of the taper through the areas in question and their location along the length of the rod. But all will determine, in some cumulative measure, how the smaller portions of a taper will be supported by the larger when casting.

To appreciate the effect of such local variances, we note that, particularly in a tip section, a change in taper of only 0.004" (the thickness of a single sheet of paper) can alter its action—a matter of just 0.002" in our half-dimension design. And should this rise or dip be distributed over an area of, say, 5 or 6 inches, the action of our tip may be changed greatly— especially if it occurs anywhere through the tip's upper half. But numbers alone do not tell the whole story, for a change of this same magnitude would affect a mid-section or butt much less. The issue is one of proportion, and changes of greater magnitude are required to affect cross-sections of greater mass.

In any event, Marinaro reasoned that all local dips and rises are equally and necessarily problematic—each for a different reason, both needing to be eliminated. One predicted result of a taper built along a smooth trajectory, free from all such steps or dips, was that it should reward the caster with a more uniform transition of power down the rod (a more efficient flow of linear waveforms with less risk of bounce-back).

Kim Mellema

206 *Split & Glued by Vincent C. Marinaro*

But Marinaro was hoping for another, even more important, result, one that might help him beat the "weight game." The expectation here was that a smoothly drawn, convex taper might be built to finer, overall dimensions than its conventional, step-and-dip counterpart. Marinaro's hope for reduced weight was only a hunch, but if it were to come about, this would be the result he was really seeking. For, only by obtaining equivalent strength at less weight would he be on the path to developing tapers truly worth pursuing.

Just here, and exactly to this point, is the special contribution Marinaro thought might be obtained from the geometry of a convex shaft. Now, whether this "geometry" could actually benefit something as subtle as the tapered sections of a fly rod remained to be seen. Here, it's necessary to consider still more matters of theory and to make the distinction Vince believed would render the flexing action of a convex taper different from that of any other.

The geometry of a convex shaft has been the darling of engineers for a very long time, for its very shape seems to lend a kind of "buttressing" effect against forces of bending—providing an inherent strength that functions somewhat differently from the otherwise, straightforward analysis of cross-sectional mass. Ancient Greeks and Romans first employed the convex shape in constructing their columns (although in these cases, its application seems to have been more for visual than for structural reasons). Later, when shipwrights and fletchers wrestled with the strength-to-weight conundrum, they discovered that if they shaped their spars and arrow-shafts with convex profiles, they would be both stronger and lighter than their straight-taper counterparts. So, the theory certainly was not new. Marinaro, however, even after long conversations with Crompton, had to discover for himself how that theory could best be applied to a fly rod.

Let's have a look at what actually happens when one flexes any ordinary, round shaft (not tapered, just for the moment). The bending creates forces of compression along the inner (now, concave) surface of the bend, while forces of tension develop along the outer (convex) side. Put simply, the materials, or molecules, on the inner side of the bend will be forced to squeeze as they adapt to a new and tighter radius, while those on the outer surface are forced to stretch and extend as they adapt to an expanded radius. But, because of the way certain molecules are bonded together, they really don't like having to accommodate these stresses, and the resulting forces on both surfaces constitute the "stress-loads" discussed above.

The bamboo in a fly rod doesn't want to tolerate distortions of bending either. In growing, the culms developed long and strong fibers to protect against such stresses, and particularly in seasoned bamboo, the structure of their cells is highly resistant to both tension and compression. The fibers just can't wait to spring back to their straight position. Still, the solid, bent shaft (bamboo fly rod or otherwise) will resist forces of bending only to the extent that the thickness of its materials can provide. Greater diameters demonstrate greater resistance to stress-loads, and in this manner the thicker areas of a tapered fly rod are called upon to accommodate the flexing actions induced by thinner areas down the shaft. When designing a rod's taper, the maker is always thinking in terms of how stresses in the smaller diameters will be supported by ("thrown back upon") the somewhat larger diameters just behind.

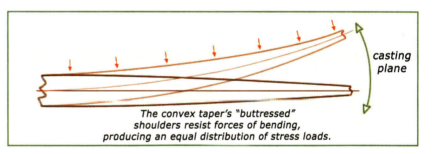

The convex taper's "buttressed" shoulders resist forces of bending, producing an equal distribution of stress loads.

Next, let's transfer these principles to the convex taper as recommended by Marinaro and consider the unique distribution of its cross-sectional diameters. Beginning at the smaller end of a convex rod-section, it's apparent that each inch along its length grows thicker. By definition, of course, this is what "taper" always means, but the convex taper also reveals a curved profile in its overall development. This growing thickness does not occur in a simple, linear progression, but develops (in comparison to its adjacent, straight, slope line) according to a sequence of exponential factors. It's this rounded profile that provides the "geometric-buttressing" strength (known by shipwrights, archers and architects), and that shape, particularly through the swell of a rod section, suggests a visual effect that Vince called "shoulders."

Despite the tangle of words, the best way to describe the contribution of the swell would be: In tracing the convex taper from its smaller end to the larger, the "buttressing" first grows at an exponentially increased rate, until this effect reaches its maximum potential to resist compression and tension (in relation to its mass) at the peak of the swell. After passing that peak, while the taper's overall dimensions continue to increase, the buttressing effect itself begins to diminish at some exponentially reduced rate until the ferrule end is reached. In the convex taper, then, it's the geometric contribution of the swell (and its distribution) that provides an overall resistance to bending that operates differently from the conventional, step-and-dip taper.

Even rod-makers have a life

To put this explanation into operation, we point out that, unlike other tapers, when a convex shape is flexed, the outer side of its shouldered curvature (or swell) is able to contribute exponentially greater thicknesses of bamboo to resist the stretching forces of tension. At the same time, the bend along the shaft's inner side will force against the counterpart of this same built-in, shouldered curvature. Here, the swell offers similarly increased resistance but this time, to the forces of compression. Also, as might be expected, the geometric effects of buttressed resistance reach their greatest potential (relative to mass) where the sections contain the greatest swell. Through these areas, the cumulative effect is almost like a beam that's been pre-stressed to resist deflection. It's the smooth distribution of this "shouldering" down the length of each rod section that seems to create greater resistance to bending than might be available through the sequenced interruptions of step-and-dip tapers (when designed to the same slope line). And it's this factor, too, that seems to provide an explanation for why the convex taper—having its own, geometrical strength—can be built to finer overall proportions. Equivalent resistance to deflection; less mass.

Accordingly, if we may put words into Marinaro's mouth, we might say his hypothesis would be this: "If the strength of a convex shaft derives in some measure from the geometry alone of its rounded profile, then, to the extent this may be true, proportionately less strength needs to be contributed by its overall, cross-sectional mass." Put simply, in contrast to a step-and-dip taper, the overall mass (weight) of a convex taper could be reduced while retaining comparable resistance to the stresses of compression/tension. Here was the objective in a nutshell, and if Marinaro could find a way to apply the hypothesis, he could build fly rods with a more efficient distribution of strength—they would cast more smoothly, but also be lighter in weight than their step-and-dip counterparts.

Even though Marinaro's rods seem to meet all these objectives, it's difficult to demonstrate quantified comparisons to other rods, for the question of what's meant by "counterparts" remains troublesome. In a ship's spar or the archer's arrow, the counterparts to a convex taper would be either a straight, un-tapered shaft of some length and girth, or some uniformly-tapered one—either case yielding manageable comparisons of strength-to-weight ratios. But among fly rods, the counterparts to a convex taper turn out to be almost every other, existing, tapered shape. The variables are suddenly out of control, thus putting a strict comparison of design-principles themselves beyond reach.

Surely, it's easy to weigh a bunch of rods of a certain length and line-weight, but how shall we compare their strengths, with the questions of a rod's "strength" and its casting characteristics themselves in such disarray? Shall we confine our comparisons to line-weight, stress-curve and slope line, or do we need a more complete range of design and casting factors? And which step-and-dip "counterparts" will we consider—only the extreme and obvious ones, or any and all? In short, although Vince's objectives indeed seem to be realized, perhaps each fly-fisher will need to make the final evaluations according to his/her own casting style. Even so, regardless of how one evaluates the strength-to-weight issues, the smooth and crisp casting characteristics of the convex taper alone are enough to validate its design objectives. Fly rods are instruments of extreme subtlety, so we call back the shipwright, the fletcher and the architect as expert witnesses to convex theory.

READING THE GRAPHED ROD

Vince liked to fish longer rods. He also liked the handiness afforded by the three-piece format, and unlike many rod-makers, he didn't mind having a second set of ferrules. Some builders (myself included) would say that ferrules are good for nothing other than making a rod portable. Ferrules add weight exactly where you don't want it, and their stiff, physical properties interrupt the movement of linear waveforms, again, exactly where you don't want it—risking double harmonic vibrations in a two-piece rod and triple harmonic vibrations in the three-piecer. But Marinaro came to value ferrules in a three-piece rod, if only because their presence served to focus his attention on the flexing requirements of the individual sections. To him, this was an entirely justifiable trade-off. He believed he could control the action of a long rod more perfectly by designing the whole as a three-part system, exactly as the designer of an automobile transmission transfers an engine's power by devising geared stages. We'll make use of the analogy a bit later, only observing here that Vince meant to assign a different "job" to each section of his three-piece rods.

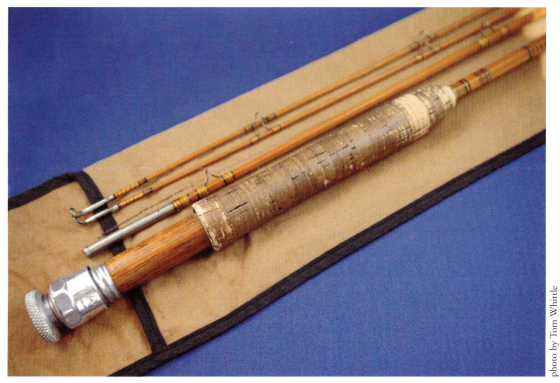

Marinaro's 1944, 8 1/2-foot rod for 7-weight line

photo by Tom Whittle

It's All In the Design 209

Marinaro built a few longer, two-piece rods, but he considered their actions compromised because of the need to "average" flexing requirements and to distribute these through only two components. On the other hand, he believed that rods of 7 1/2 feet and shorter perform very nicely with the flexing action being shared by just two sections. These observations need not be regarded as dogma: They're only Vince's opinions, and based upon his own preferences.

In this final section, we will present an applied demonstration of Vince's design ideas. We'll devise a fly rod taper just as he would have done, but reverse the process by recreating one of Marinaro's own rods—an existing, 8 1/2-foot, three-piece rod for 6/7-weight line. The steps of the design will be described just as Vince went through them, and as the rod's shape emerges on paper, we'll offer an evaluation of the casting characteristics contributed by each section.

This particular rod dates back to 1944, and is one of three, favored rods Vince took along on his trip to England. A strong rod, it is also somewhat unusual, but because this is Vince's earliest, surviving, convex-taper design, the rod becomes an especially interesting example here. Vince called for a line of either 6- or 7-weight, but Tom and I like it best with a WF-7.

We're only recreating an existing fly rod here, and as one would expect, the exercise will be a very different matter from designing a rod from scratch. Still, Tom and I hope the following demonstration will provide an understanding of the basic considerations. With very little practice, the designer soon learns how to compare tapers to their slope lines; how convex curves need to be developed; how the different rod sections should perform, or indeed, how their shapes may need to be altered. Let's do the drill:

First, a grid is established on the graph paper (explained above) with its horizontal axis drawn to the 34-inch length of the rod's sections, and with each 6-inch station marked and lined. Following this, the scale along the vertical axis is marked with an increase of 0.010" per square. Next, we draw slope lines to represent the individual strips (half-dimensions for each rod's section), and stack these on the grid—the tip at the bottom, the mid-section next, with the butt on the top. The greatest thickness of each slope is located on the left-hand, vertical axis, and the smallest dimension is located at the right. Our chart tells us that the maximum slope for the tip-section is 0.090", while its tip-top end is 0.038", so those two points are marked accordingly. Similarly, for the mid-section, the slope marks are located at 0.138" on the left, and 0.090" on the right. The two points for each slope are simply connected with a straight line.

The slope through the butt, however, is determined a bit differently from the other sections. The reasoning is that, while the "lever-arm" of a butt section functions over its entire length, the flexing action provided by its taper does not. Effectively, flexing stops at the cork grip. Depending on other factors, it's always possible for a rod to have some action through its grip, but because the cane in this area will be rounded somewhat and have both cork and a reel seat glued to it, it's of no use trying to develop (or predict) design information here. Accordingly, the dot indicating the thickest end of the butt's slope (0.168") will be located just at the point where the cork grip begins—the 24-inch station, 10 inches in from the butt's end. The dimension at the smaller end of the butt will be marked at a height of 0.138" and, again, the dots are connected.

There's not a lot of information on the graph as yet, but what is present is vital. Already, the intended rod sections reveal their thickness-to-length ratios, and this information is just as fundamental to a rod's action as any subsequent taper-manipulations along those slopes. But, how did Vince determine the slope he wanted for this rod?

Station	Butt	Mid	Tip
0	0.138	0.090	0.038
6	0.144	0.101	0.051
12	0.154	0.111	0.059
18	0.162	0.120	0.067
24	0.168	0.127	0.076
30	0.173	0.134	0.084
34	0.176	0.138	0.090

Charted half-dimensions for each section, representing Vince's 6-inch stations

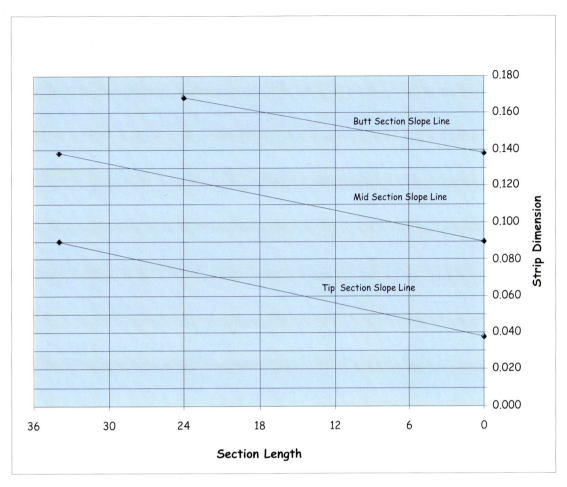

Slope lines for the three sections

Well, trial-and-error.... He may have built some experimental rods before deciding, or he may have cast a few 6- and 7-weight rods already in existence. Either way, he chose the slope dimensions that came closest to his needs—making his own adjustments up or down later. Once Vince's basic design principles had been established, it was a matter of tweaking a little here and there until he found a slope that did the job. It all sounds pretty casual and off-hand when we put it in these terms, but once Vince knew what he was about, this was how the process worked. ***Getting to*** that level of understanding, as we've tried to explain, was the difficult part.

So, back to the drawing board. Three, straight lines are shown, each representing the slope of the three, different strips. Next, we draw the taper lines, and these will represent the shape of each completed, rod-section's outer flat. The taper for Vince's tip-section will be drawn first.

Our chart indicates the half-dimension at the tip-top as 0.038", and from that point back, the convex shape begins to increase at once. Marinaro said a tip needs to have its area of greatest swell placed something like 10 inches behind the tip-top, but this location will vary from rod to rod as suits its length and line-weight. In the rod we're plotting here, however, Vince apparently wanted to carry the tip's strength farther forward, and in a moment it will be clear that its maximum swell is located only 6 to 7 inches or so from the tip-top.

In our earlier step, a dot was placed on the right-hand, vertical scale at a height of 0.038" to indicate the smaller end of the tip's slope. But because this dimension also represents the end of the taper, our attention moves to the left—the first 6-inch station. Reading again from the charted half-dimensions, this control point calls for a thickness of 0.051". A dot is placed on the station-line at that height,

It's All In the Design   211

and in similar fashion, dots are located on the remaining 6-inch stations until, at the far left, the last, half-dimension measurement merges with the section's maximum slope of 0.090"—also located in an earlier step.

When finished, the dots at each control station are connected with as much care and accuracy as a bright light, ruler and a fine, drafting pencil will allow, and the proportions of the taper emerge. Particular care must be taken when locating the dots and drawing the taper because, on the scale of our graph, even the finest pencil line will represent something more than 0.001"—with any errors being doubled in the finished section. The resulting taper shows its convex proportions as a vivid contrast to the section's straight slope immediately adjacent, and its trajectory represents the actual (though foreshortened) shape of each outer flat on the tip section.

As a most helpful exercise, one should pick the graph paper up, hold its edge to the eye and "sight" down the taper and slope lines. The relationship of these lines jumps out with even greater clarity, making any needed "smoothing" refinements obvious. The area of greatest swell in Vince's tip seems to be a good 0.004" above the slope line, but it's located only 6 to 7 inches back from the tip-top, and that's several inches closer than we might have expected. Apparently, this is exactly what Vince wanted for this rod, but its location is unusual. Moreover, the shape carrying back to the ferrule is so subtle that a curve really can't be discerned at all. The shoulders (as Vince called the broader areas across a swell) can be seen only through the first 15 inches or so of the tip.

(A comment on our illustrations: The very small scale of the following graphs can only generalize actual dimensions as they were plotted, and cannot reveal the accuracy we would see in full-sized versions.)

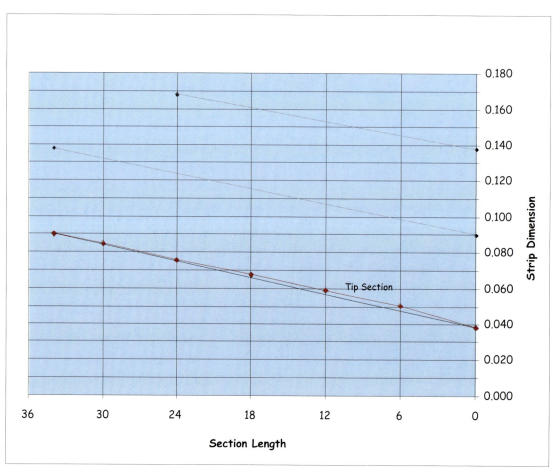

Graphed tip section

Considering the overall shape of this section, one can expect it to yield smooth action, but without pronounced resistance to forces of bending through its lower half. On the other hand, the broadening shoulders through its upper third (viewed in comparison to the slope line) are quite strong, and should provide a good "kick" at the end of a cast. Actually, we might have worried that such strength near the tip-top might send shock-waves rebounding back through the section toward the ferrule area. In casting the rod, however, this doesn't happen, and the reason seems to be that the swell dissipates so very uniformly back toward the ferruled end that stress-loads are absorbed proportionately, thus preventing any particular area from setting up harmonic vibrations.

Turning our attention to the area extending from the swell to the tip-top, we can expect the rod to deliver fine presentations when needed—that is, fine for a 7-weight line. Vince said he agonized longer over the upper quarter of his tip sections than over any other part of a rod, and the reason is that the taper through this area contains the rod's final means of transmitting its casting energy to the line and its leader. Other areas of a rod are able to average (or "share") their flexing characteristics to some extent, but the last 8-10 inches of a tip communicate with the line alone. These last several inches must be delicate enough to effect a smooth transfer of energy between the stiffer bamboo and the more supple line, yet strong enough to create a tight loop with the leader held high. Long and powerful casts are just as important as short, delicate ones, and getting the shape of a tip section just right is part of the "magic" of Vince's designs. But it's a taller order than one might suspect.

The same plotting procedures are repeated to draw the other two sections of Vince's rod, but notice how very differently their convex swells have been managed. Particularly in the mid-section, powerful proportions are

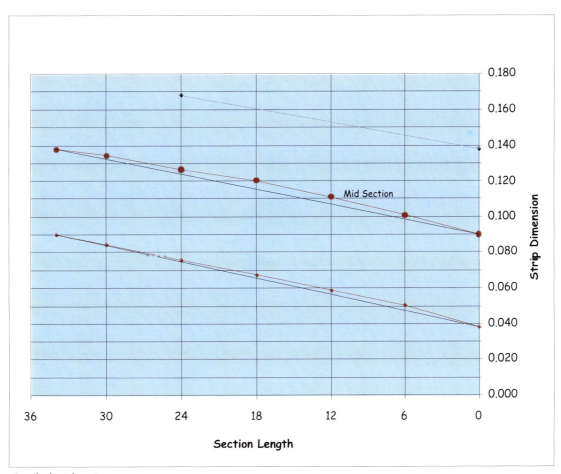

Graphed mid-section

It's All In the Design   213

maintained throughout its length, but the maximum swell develops between the 12- and 18-inch stations—rather closer to the middle of the shaft than Vince's usual position. Additionally, the size of that swell is very large, being placed a good 0.005" above the slope line and spread across a broad area, then rounding-down toward both ferrule ends. The shoulders, as Vince called them, can be seen with great clarity through much of this section—from its 6-inch station right through the 24-inch station. An elongated swell such as this will provide great resistance to whatever forces of bending may be thrown back upon it by the tip section. Or, conversely, upon casting, it's easy to imagine how that shape would stand up to strong strokes—transferring powerful waveforms up through to the tip section and "kicking" the line out with that last foot or so near the tip-top.

It's the middle area of any bamboo rod that is called upon to do the greatest amount of "work," so if one seeks to design a powerful rod, it will always be the mid-section that needs special attention. We mentioned earlier that Vince sometimes thought of the three sections of a fly rod (when casting) as similar to an automobile's transmission: Generally, the butt is a "first-gear" and is meant to overcome inertia and get the vehicle moving; the mid-section is "second-gear" and it powers the car nearly up to speed; while the tip section is the "third-gear," both sustaining the speed and delivering us down the road with subtlety and smoothness. (Carried further, our analogy breaks down in all sorts of ways, but it'll serve up to this point.)

Finally, the taper for the butt is plotted in the same manner as the other sections. Upon completion, however, we see that its trajectory is quite unusual. The shape barely demonstrates any convexity at all, even showing a subtle dip where the taper line passes through the 6-inch station. Overall, the basic slope is consistent with the rest of the rod, but the taper line nearly traces that same trajectory and is weakly developed in comparison to the powerful mid-section. Why?

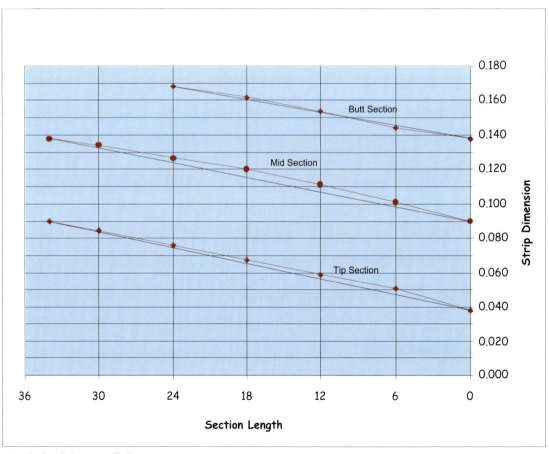

Graphed rod showing all three sections

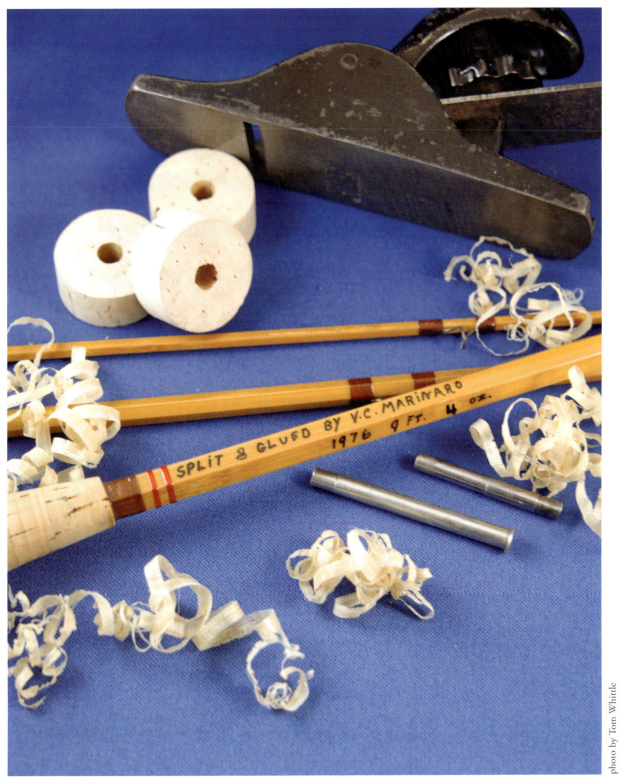

One of Vince's 9-footers

It's All In the Design 215

First, readers might reason that this rod is an example of Marinaro's earlier work with convex tapers, and as such, maybe he hadn't yet formed clear ideas of what to do with the butt—especially considering that most of this rod's power was meant to come from its mid-section. But I can vouch that Vince did not keep rods that didn't please him, and I recall seeing this rod often, especially on our nastier days fishing up on Penn's Creek. So, to whatever extent its butt section may depart from his usual convex shapes, I'm sure Vince built exactly the rod he meant to build.

It's ironical, but what is seen in the graphed version of the butt section is precisly what one would expect *not* to see in any of Vince's rods—a small "hinge." Yet its presence seems to be a way of dealing with the rod's weight, while taking advantage of the lever-arm of its 8 1/2 foot length. The butt would appear to bend rather easily and quickly, transferring the flexed energy of his casting stroke to the powerful, middle area of the rod, then out to that strong tip-top.

In short, the butt's graphed shape seems to suggest something almost like "parabolic" action. But this is particularly surprising to see, for there was no rod design Vince came to dislike more than the parabolic taper, sneering at the concept and calling such rods "paregoric." Although this hinged effect isn't felt at all when casting Vince's rod, still, that's what seems to be shown on the graph. Actually, we doubt that Vince would have heard of the parabolic design back when this rod was built in 1944 because Charles Ritz was only just beginning to refine that concept in France at the time.

Instead, and on his own, we think Marinaro simply meant to devise a butt that would easily accept a casting load without offering a great deal of resistance—without tiring his wrist and arm. This is a long and strong rod, but one must also be able to use it for hours on end. So, the trick was to find a way to allow the caster to relax, slow down and let the rod's length do the work while still imparting powerful casting strokes. The results here are especially interesting because this rod turns out to be both strong and delicate at the same time. Seems a paradox, but it's one Vince was well aware of, often insisting, "Boy, to achieve delicacy, you need power!" That said, however, everything depends on where the power is distributed, and how (or when) it comes into play.

Returning to our earlier analogy, this butt section would be a relatively short "first-gear" with tremendous torque. The caster gets the rod bending quickly and easily, and without requiring a great deal of energy. The mid-section becomes a long and strong "second-gear" that responds to the flexed butt and powers the rod nearly up to full speed. The tip is a relatively weaker "third-gear," but with an all-important "overdrive option" at its end. Actually, the tip

Using the dial-indicator to set the planing form

216   *Split & Glued by Vincent C. Marinaro*

almost seems to function on its own—like sprung catapult, or like a water-skier in a sharp turn, "cracking the whip." Indeed, that's the way the rod casts, and perhaps now the graphed designs for these three sections would seem able to speak for themselves. So, just as was stated earlier, Vince's prescription for a three-piece rod forms a system. The parts have been managed differently, but it's clear that he explored these compartmentalized options to address an overall objective.

The only thing remaining now is to set the planing form according to the design, and for this, the builder merely prepares a chart containing the strips' half-dimensions and takes this to his workbench. The information for each, graphed section will be charted separately, so he begins at a strip's smaller end and records thickness readings from every 6-inch, control station (just where the taper intersects the station line). Each of the sections is prepared in similar manner.

Vince's elaborate set-up procedures were described in the previous chapter, but because all modern planing forms are built with adjustment screws at 5-inch intervals, our own set-up becomes greatly simplified. Also, of course, if the builder were designing his own taper, he would have lined-off his grid to depict those same 5-inch stations.

A dial-indicator depth-gauge (fitted with a 60-degree point at its end) is "zeroed-out" on top of the bars, then simply dropped into the groove at each of the 5-inch stations. The corresponding adjustment screws are turned in or out, and the dial-indicator will register those changes as they're being made, showing when the groove's depth matches the charted data. (It's always necessary to go back and forth a couple times, however, because each adjustment seems to alter, slightly, that of its neighbor.)

Finally, the groove will correspond exactly to a strip's design, and after a bit of grunting and some sliced fingers, the greatly foreshortened information on the graph paper will be realized, full-scale and precisely, in the dimensions of all six strips. And if one works as carefully as did Pappy, the maker can lay his micrometer across each control point on the glued sections to read cross-section measurements as perfectly executed as they were designed.

Chapter Nine

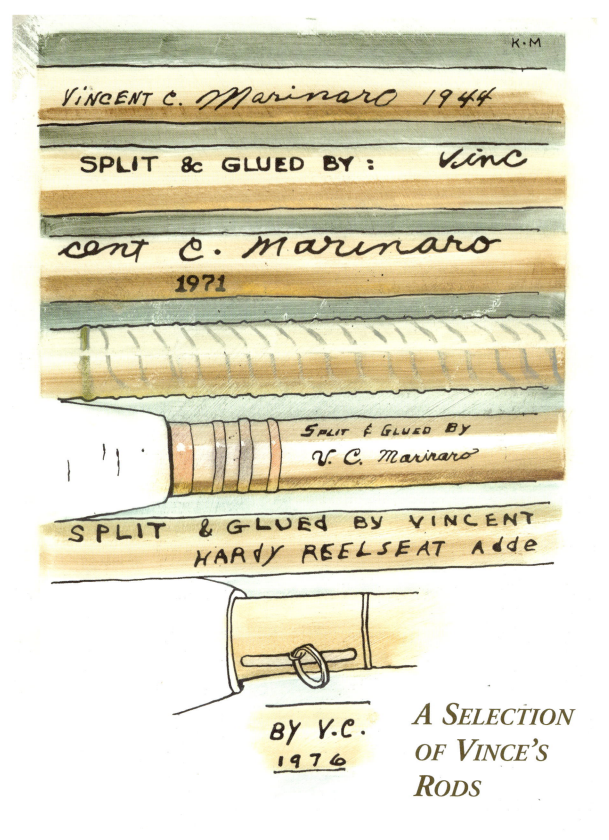

A Selection of Vince's Rods

A few years ago, in a New Jersey bar, one of my good friends overheard a fellow from Boston boasting loudly that he owns a Marinaro fly rod. That seemed highly unlikely to me, so I did a little detective work to trace the information back to its source. I got just one chance, by email, to explain what I had heard and why I was interested. But just as quickly, my source "went away" and I was never able to raise him again. Surprise, surprise.... Folks emerge, seemingly from nowhere, with one story or another about some Marinaro rod—or saying they have one of his tapers. Lord only knows how many other tales are still to come. While we'll never be able to explore the range of these claims, we expect most would only be part of the Marinaro mystique—a sort of piscatorial equivalent to Elvis sightings.

Vince's rods simply did not come before the general public and only three ever left his possession—one bait-caster to Charlie Fox and another to Sparse Grey Hackle, plus an experimental, 7-foot fly rod to Barry Beck. Vince didn't build all sizes and configurations and except for specialty fishing, he really preferred the longer rods. Oddly, the other extreme is also well-represented with three examples falling between 6 and 6 1/2 feet and for 2- through 4-weight lines. Between the large and the small rods, we find just one rod of 7 1/2 feet (built in 1971 and retained by Sebastian's widow, Maggie Marinaro), with all the others coming in at 8 feet and longer. The experimental rod mentioned above exists as well, first belonging to Barry Beck and now to a collector in the Pittsburgh area. This latter rod is most unusual, with an oddly-turned grip and an especially large tip-diameter, but we've been unable to determine when it was built or why. Barry tells me he thought the rod cast very nicely even though Vince absolutely hated it.

It is also the case, at least to the best of my knowledge, that Vince never built quite the same rod twice. An exception, perhaps, would be the small series of 9-footers we examine below. Occasionally, when a rod no longer suited his tastes, he would build an altered version, but most of Vince's rods were one-off designs and he never developed "models." It is

An assortment of Marinaro's grips and reel seats

A Selection of Vince's Rods

difficult for us to say if any rods received his stamp of final approval because Vince was rarely satisfied in his search for the perfect design. I can say that the rods I saw him using most frequently were his 7 1/2-foot, two-piece for a 5-weight, the 8 1/2-foot, three-piece for a 7-weight (from our previous chapter), and a 9-foot, three-piece rod for a 5-weight line. On the other hand, while he often mentioned how proud he was of his 6 1/2-foot "Guppy," I never saw it being fished. That notwithstanding, this rod remains one of our two, personal favorites from the collection.

Our Picks

Together, the seven rods presented below offer a good sampling for makers who would like to build a Marinaro replica for themselves. In this, however, we repeat the restrictions of the Marinaro Estate and the Pennsylvania Fly-Fishing Museum Association: The appearance of Vincent C. Marinaro's name (and all variants) on any fly rod is strictly forbidden, and no commercial transaction may benefit by claiming his taper information.

Marinaro's rods differ only slightly from one another in their casting characteristics, but as a group, they provide an opportunity to comment on the range of his design objectives. Vince often railed against "that old saw about letting the rod do the work," explaining in *The Ring* that a fly rod, even as it's being cast, is never able to do its own work. In the strictest sense, of course, this is true but the "old saw" is just a figure of speech—an attempt to describe a rod whose action is so smooth and gentle that only minimum effort is needed to maximize the results. Vince must pardon our gaffe, but this is exactly what his rods offer.

We note yet another remark from *The Ring:* Vince states on page 41 that all his rods have been designed "to carry only one weight of line, a 5-weight." We don't know why he would have said this because the results of our casting tests (below) show that his rods actually carry a variety of lines—ranging from 4- to 7-weight. Admittedly, his system sounds like a very good one, but it appears to have been more an idea than a reality.

In what follows, Tom and I will describe seven Marinaro rods—those seeming to represent his best efforts (with charted information for all his rods appearing in the Appendix). More truthfully, we made our selection according to what we thought most likely to please other fly-fishers. There are, in all, just 15 surviving rods—13 in the PFFMA collection and two others in the hands of private owners. We point out again that neither has there been any way to know how many rods Vince built during his life, nor do records exist that might guide us through the history of his experiments—and he did experiment a great deal. On the evidence of my conversations with Vince (and his daughter, Vincentia), we're certain a great many more were built in earlier years, but while we don't know what became of them, we feel confident the survivors would be those he came to favor.

Marinaro's trout rods are our focus, but in his later years, Vince again became fond of salmon fishing and built three, stout rods: "Salmo," a 9 1/2-foot, two-piece rod, was built in 1976; "Salar," a powerful 14-foot, three-piece, two-handed rod followed in 1977; and "Penobscot," another 9 1/2-foot rod (but in three-pieces) was made in 1979. Just for fun, will offer a brief evaluation of these rods as well, and for the intrepid piscator who still finds charm in chucking salmon flies with bamboo rods, the details of their tapers can be found in the Appendix.

Measuring The Tapers

Marinaro's own data have never been available, so we need to explain that Tom prepared all the following charted and graphed information from measurements taken directly on the rods themselves. This could only be done over the varnish, but Tom obtained readings at one-inch intervals down the full length of each rod—measuring all three flats and averaging these readings. Vince's varnish is quite thin, but usually not neat, and in subtracting a typical 0.004" from each measurement, Tom's graphed results sometimes showed minuscule, localized bumps or hollows. These could not have been part of the designs, nor could Vince's steel planing form ("miking" smoothly through 1-inch increments) have created such oddities, so the tiny irregularities were either averaged or ignored in preparing the charted data. Additionally, because there was no way to obtain measurements under the tip-tops, guides and ferrules, Tom simply projected adjacent taper-lines across these locations. None of this is cause for concern, however, because Vince never made sudden changes in his tapers and Tom's projections always carried through smoothly.

Lastly, we point out that, although Marinaro designed and built his rods using older, 6-inch, control stations, the charted information included here has been transposed to our more common, 5-inch stations. This is not always a safe practice with other rods because, in establishing stations that differ from those according to which a rod was designed and built, one will pass over certain, local, taper changes and the new profile may vary slightly from the original. Vince's tapers, however, were designed without local changes, and even when graphed in 1-inch increments, their trajectories remain identical, whether viewed along the 5- or the 6-inch stations.

Letort brownie: 1971

photo by Marinaro

But now, something of a caveat: All of us who build bamboo fly rods know that we will have been fortunate, indeed, if our completed results agree precisely with the design information. Alas, it's almost always the case that, here or there, flat-to-flat conformity in the finished rod (or accuracy at control stations) may vary from our ideal by as much as plus-or-minus 1-2 thousandths-of-an-inch. Inconsistencies from flat-to-flat typically indicate planing imperfections, while irregularities found at the control stations usually implicate settings on the planing form itself.

We always hope that whatever anomalies may be found, these would never range from one extreme to the other, for this could create an unacceptable swing of 4 thousandths-of-an-inch or more. One may still obtain an excellent rod, but probably not quite the one that was intended. Accordingly, we want to emphasize that, although the data provided in this chapter accurately represent Marinaro's finished rods, we can never know how closely our measurements conform to his actual designs. Realizing how fastidious Marinaro was, we would say: "As closely as mere mortals can get." But, because no assurance of ours can set that question to rest, rod-makers will have to be satisfied that at least the charts and graphs do document his rods as they were built. It's all we have.

By the time he taught me to build, Marinaro had become an "absolutist" of convex-taper theory, but upon evaluating Tom's measurements of the rods, we were surprised to learn that a few of Vince's own applications depart somewhat from the ideal shapes he prescribed in *The Ring*. Most especially, we note the sweeping, reversing curve seen in the tip sections of his two-piece rods. This seems to be a special feature of Vince's two-piecers, and Tom, in particular, wonders if those "reversed" areas were meant to approximate the shape the rods would have were they designed, instead, as *three*-piecers. I think that's an excellent and revealing call, though it's impossible to know what Vince may have had in mind.

On a related issue, readers will see that the small graphs we offer below show rather perfect convex curves, even while a rod-maker's own, full-scale renditions might not yield the flawlessly smooth shapes he had expected to see. Questions arise and we wonder what such departures from the norm could mean. At one extreme, they could mean Vince wasn't actually as precise a builder as we might have thought. Or, at the other extreme, perhaps something went wrong with our data or with your ability to plot. All these are possible, even in combination, but we suggest that, while deflections of +/- 0.001 can be ignored (and smoothed-out), any notable irregularity in a convex trajectory is probably evidence of Vince's effort to resolve some particular issue—either in redressing a "problem-area" found in an earlier rod, or in creating a rod meant to satisfy some new casting objective.

But, even if so, where would this leave us? Here, we have Marinaro insisting upon one thing in *The Ring* (and endlessly to me), but then designing certain of his own rods a little differently. Imagine that—a man who experimented and did not always do what he finally came to recommend! We wish we could offer Vince's own account of the history of his work and the particulars of his thinking, but because that was never possible, the occasional gap between "Do as I say...not as I do!" lingers without explanation. Nevertheless, Tom and I emphasize that although we remain curious about Vince's own journey, in our designs, neither of us has found the need to compromise the continuous, convex shapes Marinaro finally recommended.

Meet Our Experts

Each of the selected rods below, is documented and described with as much technical information as we could provide, but to demonstrate the rods' actual casting characteristics, we enlisted the help of some fellow rod-makers and collectors. We scheduled two test-casting sessions—the first, with Wayne Grauer and Tom Smithwick casting together, and a second session with Bob Selb at a later date. As we introduce our volunteers, we'll offer an account of each person's preference for fly-rod action—the length, line-weight, and kind of fishing he usually prefers. We fully expected Vince's rods to receive mixed evaluations from our casters because, regardless of expertise, every fly-fisher we know has different tastes, casting strokes and ways of sensing (and explaining) how a rod is performing. And so, we also invite readers to consider each caster's personal preferences as a "check" when pondering his opinion of one rod or another.

Wayne Grauer

Wayne and his family live in Baltimore, Maryland—pretty much limiting his local fishing options to the Gunpowder River north of Baltimore and Big Hunting Creek just outside Thurmont, Maryland. Wayne says his favorite fishing is for native, mountain brookies, using little 6- to 6 1/2-foot rods and a 3-weight line, but he also spends his days fishing New York's larger, Catskill waters

Wayne Grauer

photo by Tom Whittle

where he and a few friends share a small place on the Beaverkill. As a fly-fisherman for more than 40 years, Wayne purchased his first rod back in 1962 (an 8-foot Sewall Dunton for 5-weight line), and has been collecting bamboo rods ever since—financing his obsession for cane with a small business that trades in both new and collectible rods. Wayne handles bamboo rods by a few contemporary makers and is also a factory representative for both Winston and Cortland.

As a certified casting instructor with Cortland, Wayne frequently conducts classes for beginning and intermediate fly-fishers. The beginner, Wayne says, will do far better with a rod that has smooth, "progressive" action, and he warns against tip-action rods with strong butts. He explains that the progressive action seems to be more forgiving of a caster's less-than-perfect timing, loading deeper and deeper as more line is extended and requiring only minimum effort from the caster.

Wayne is almost exclusively a dry-fly fisherman, and says he stays with it "even when I know I'd do better fishing nymphs." At a minimum, Wayne insists that a good rod "should be able to cover the full spectrum of trout fishing—short, accurate casts as well as long, accurate casts." When asked about the fewest number of cane rods the accomplished fly-fisher should have, Wayne chose a 6 1/2-footer for 3-weight, a 7 1/2-footer for 4-weight, and an 8 1/2-foot rod for 5-weight line—generally giving up on bamboo rods as they approach 9 feet. The call goes out for graphite when fishing conditions become more rigorous—slinging weighted nymphs, fighting wind, or pitching streamers to the surf.

Tom Smithwick

Tom and his wife live just outside Philadelphia on the New Jersey side of the Delaware River and recently began enjoying one of life's greatest pleasures—retirement. Tom has been fly-fishing for trout for nearly 4 decades, and is surely one of the finest casters we know. His first love is fishing big water with a large rod and a dry fly, although Tom says he has also come to appreciate the more subtle limestoners. (We add, however, that a few years ago he was seen using his 12-foot Spey rod on Pennsylvania's little Spruce Creek. Now, there's a nut-case!)

Perhaps earlier than most fishermen, Tom fell in love with bamboo almost as soon as he took up fly-fishing, soon beginning a small collection of his own and restoring some of his older cane treasures. Despite his modest and self-effaced ways, Tom is widely recognized as one of the most knowledgeable and gifted rod-makers among us, and over the last couple decades has designed both rod-building equipment and several tapers. Among many other things, it was Tom who first worked with Letcher Lambuth's recommendations for the spiral rod, and it was also he who popularized techniques for building the two-strip, "poor man's quad" (the PMQ).

As to a rod's behavior, Tom insists above all else that the most important quality is "lightness in the hand and a responsive feel." It should be able to form a tight loop in close, but Tom says it should also be capable of stretching over a good distance "without casting heroics." We surely can't argue with those requirements, but the proof in that pudding is wherever one finds it. When asked which rods he would insist upon if reduced only to a handful, Tom says his list would include a 6-foot rod with fast action for small streams; a 6 1/2-to-7-footer for a 4-weight line with progressive action for midge fishing; an 8-footer for 4-weight line with progressive action to handle wet and soft-hackle flies; an 8-footer for 5-weight with "moderate progressive" action for all-around dry-fly fishing; and an 8-9 foot rod for 7/8-weight line for bass fishing, grilse or slinging big streamers. Tom adds, "I could be talked into a parabolic taper for this work."

Tom Smithwick

photo by Chris Bogart

A Selection of Vince's Rods 223

Bob Selb

Bob lives in Lansdale, Pennsylvania just north of Philadelphia and is the proprietor of The Classic Fly-Fisherman. Bob's interest in bamboo fly rods started with his grandfather nearly 35 years ago, and his love-affair with the history of the sport (and fly-fishing paraphernalia) began at once. Happily, Selb's family was able to depend upon his automobile repair center for incidentals like the mortgage, food and clothing, but his collection of fly-fishing gear also grew into a small business. This was run for many years from a small room adjacent to his garage, but a couple years ago Bob dumped the cars, moved his shop, and turned full-time attention to buying and selling collectable fishing gear and books. He says that although he still loves the old, classic rods and reels—trading in them regularly—his own fishing preferences will always favor bamboo rods built by contemporary makers. "They're simply made of better materials, more precisely crafted, and they cast more accurately."

The quintessential "Type-A" personality, Bob fishes as hard as he works, and in keeping pace with him along the stream, one can hardly tell the difference between the two. I don't care who you are, given the same period of time, Bob will cover twice as much water as you, put his fly over twice as many trout as you, and in the end, hold twice as many fish accountable for their folly.

Bob is a strong guy and certainly does not baby his rods. He says they must be "crisp" in action, capable of "doing their own work," and be willing to shoot a good length of line. He does not care for rods relying on tip action because their upper portions lose control of the line by the time the stronger, butt section becomes loaded. Nor, as a rule, does he care for the other end of the spectrum—parabolic tapers.

Over the many years, Bob has become a superb caster and regularly takes on anything from fussy, limestone trout to Alaskan salmon, Costa Rican tarpon or bonefish in the Bahamas. We tried to pin him down on a minimum list of rods, but he couldn't stand even the thought and refused to budge from his entire arsenal. His favorite fishing, however, is on the Catskill streams with a dry fly, and he particularly looks forward to the early Hendrickson hatches. Bob prefers medium-to-large streams, larger flies, and nearly always chooses a 5-6 weight rod, 7 1/2 to 8 feet in length, and with balanced, progressive action.

Bob Selb

photo by Tom Whittle

Let's Cast Some Rods

Casting-tests are always subjective, but we tried to be as methodical as possible and to hold the procedures uniform across both the rods and the casters. By "methodical," we do not mean scientific because, in all, our desire has been to gather personal reactions. We wanted opinions from accomplished fishermen with decades of experience casting bamboo rods—guys who know how to evaluate a cane rod's performance.

We stretched a 100-foot tape to its full length and set targets at distances of 25, 40 and 55 feet—leaving the tape in place. At the outset, we wanted to maintain some consistency in the tests, so each participant was asked to "aerialize" identical lengths of line when false-casting, and without using the haul. At once, this became unreasonable because, regardless of distance, our casters were all accustomed to using a quick haul (a tug, as they call it). Casting our way felt awkward and unnatural and judging the rods' performance was uncertain—so back they went to their own styles.

After evaluating each rod at the target distances, our volunteers were invited simply to "mess around," trying whatever little exercises they thought appropriate. Finally, our experts were asked to respond to a set of questions about each rod's performance. Of greatest interest to Tom and me was that, despite very different personal preferences and casting styles, our volunteers' evaluations did not differ by much—and these were accompanied by similar qualifications or explanations. Secondly, however, was their agreement than none of Vince's rods really invites casting to distances beyond 70 feet (excepting the 8 1/2-foot rod for 7-weight line and the three salmon rods). In this, however, we remind readers of Marinaro's statement in *The Ring* that the most important test of a trout rod is its complete control from close-up, out to 55 feet. Vince's rods could easily have been designed to haul and shoot line to 80 feet (as some do), but what would be the point if you sacrifice lightness-in-hand to gain something of minimum practical use?

The photography was prepared by Tom, and will reveal the flexing characteristics of each rod—its ability to elevate the line, to form a loop and to deliver a cast. But exact comparisons remain very difficult: There are differences in casting strokes, and shutter exposures could not be timed to capture identical moments. Thus, no set of photographs can be expected to reveal identically-loaded rods. Nevertheless, the sequenced shots of each rod offer a useful range of visual information.

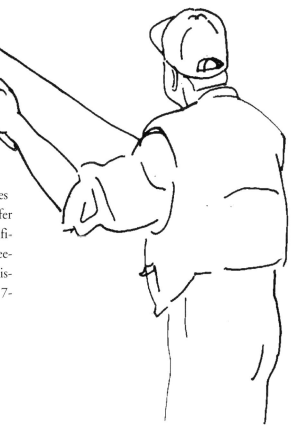

Six-foot Six-inch, Two-piece Rod for Four-weight Line

6 1/2-foot, 4-weight rod from 1976, called "Guppy"

Beginning with Vince's smallest rod, we have his 6 1/2-foot, two-piece "Guppy," finished in 1976. Actually, in the years to follow, he built two rods still smaller (both at just 6 feet), the first called "Guppy Jr.," and the other, "One Crazy Ounce." It's hard to imagine why Vince would have built three such rods, considering that none was fished much, and the last rod (wrapped and varnished in 1985 by Hoagy Carmichael), not at all. Of the three, the rod we feature here is the most desirable from the group and was designed to cast a 4-weight line on the little brookie streams of Pennsylvania. Vince built it with just one tip, and it's one of three or four rods I wrapped and finished.

The "Guppy" is very light and snappy, with a delicate, "Superfine" grip. Its reel-seat is made of balsa-wood with a small, wooden button at the end, and the hardware includes two thin-walled, aluminum, sliding bands intended to be pinched slightly into an oval shape and eased over the reel foot. The rod has a true "Super-Z" ferrule, and the guides are wrapped in rich, light-brown silk with black tipping. Vince said he used nothing on this rod but his Hardy, "Baby" St. George reel.

In our accompanying graph, the taper of the tip section shows that "reversed sweep" (mentioned above) carrying through its 25-inch station. The rod's overall proportions are actually similar to Vince's three-piece rods, and as Tom noticed, had the "Guppy" been built in three pieces, its upper ferrule would fall in the center of that sweep. An unmistakable design feature, the reversed shape through this area reveals a marked departure from the continuous, convex curve described in *The Ring*. But, recall: Vince makes no overt mention of two-piece rods in that chapter, and the drawings he includes are for his three-piecers.

Station	Butt	Tip
0	0.083	0.029
5	0.089	0.043
10	0.095	0.050
15	0.102	0.056
20	0.109	0.060
25	0.112	0.065
30	0.118	0.074
35		0.082
39		0.083

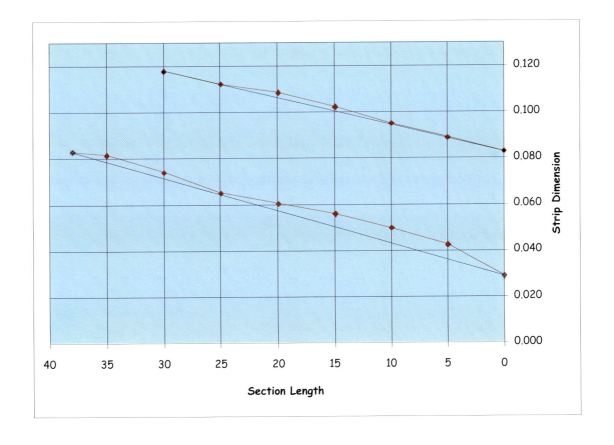

A Selection of Vince's Rods

(Six-foot Rod, continued)

End of back-cast; good loop; no tip-bounce

The results...

In our two sessions, the casters all agreed this is a perfect small-stream rod. Its action is "progressive," flexing ever deeper as more line is extended. Smithwick remarked that even as close as 25 feet, the rod loads easily with a WF-4 and "bangs its target" every time with nothing but a flick of the wrist. You can almost feel that tip doing a catapult on the forward delivery. Interestingly, no one imagined this might be because of a "hinge" effect at that 25-inch station—indeed, a hinge, as such, was never detected. At 40 feet and beyond, the rod works best with just the slightest "tug," loading very easily and casting precisely. All three casters reported that the rod was consistently smooth, effortless and accurate out to 50-55 feet, but added that it seemed finished at 60 feet—just what you would expect of a small-stream rod for a light line.

Grauer described the rod as "medium-fast, forgiving and very responsive," saying that, while the "Guppy" did not seem markedly better than others of its class, "it's surely as good as it gets." On the other hand, both Smithwick and Selb found it to have exactly the kind of progressive action they look for in a rod, and claimed it as one of their favorites from the collection

Start of stroke; no haul; full-flexing

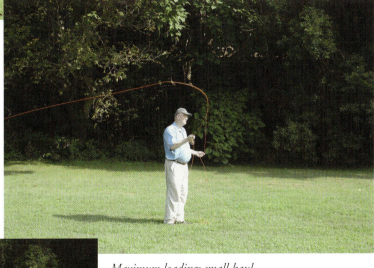

Maximum loading; small haul

Energy spent; good loop

Seven-foot Six-inch, Two-piece Rod for Five-weight Line

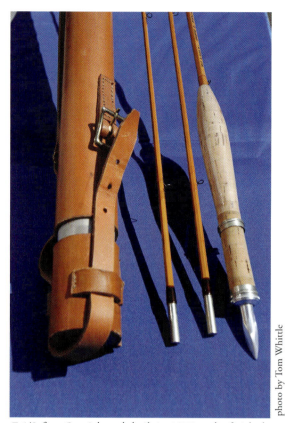

7 1/2-foot, 5-weight rod, built in 1971 and refinished by Tom Maxwell

This next rod is a 7 1/2-foot, two-piecer for 5-weight line and was built in 1971. We've always referred to this as the "Maxwell" rod because, in the very late 1970s, after years of cajoling and teasing, Tom Maxwell finally talked Vince into allowing him to re-wrap and finished it. The rod looked perfectly dreadful with its coarse, brown wraps and a messy, sprayed-on varnish, but Vince didn't care about such minor barbarisms, and he used it regularly on more accessible limestoners like the Tulpehocken and Falling Springs. It was largely because of this rod that Maxwell regarded Marinaro as one of the finest makers he knew—raving about it as the best 7 1/2-footer he ever cast. Vince, too, thought highly of it, but he never capitalized on his success and built no others of its kind.

The shape of its tip-section is similar to that of the "Guppy," but designed on a steeper slope. The accompanying graph also shows the tip to have a more pronounced downward sweep though its 30-inch station than seen on the "Guppy." As a third notable feature, we see a butt section designed to a much shallower slope than the tip, but that gentle slope is "compensated" by an enormous swell in the taper-line from the 15- through the 25-inch stations. In all, the taper shows an odd set of combinations, and we wonder if the swell through its butt may be a bit overdone.

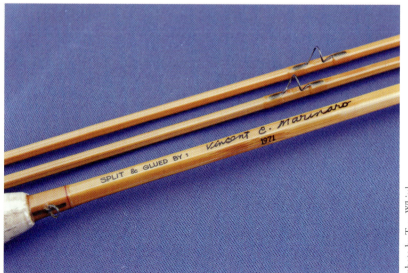

7 1/2-foot rod inscription

Maxwell provided a new, cork reel-seat and grip, identical to the original. The wraps are turned with transparent silk (honey-colored), and the varnish-work is as flawless as can be found anywhere. Vince's own signature was preserved, but Maxwell lettered the rest of the inscription himself, and as icing on the cake, he returned the rod with a leather-covered rod tube. The ferrule is a true "Super-Z," and the reel-seat hardware consists of a butt-cap with a sliding band, but featuring one of Marinaro's favorite accessories—a "bank spear" that can either be tucked away within the hollowed reel-seat or reversed to plant the rod upright in a meadow when releasing a fish or changing tippets. This rod remains in the possession of Maggie Marinaro and is in pristine condition, Maxwell's shrink-wrap still on its grip. Evidently, Vince never fished the rod again.

Station	Butt	Tip
0	0.100	0.030
5	0.107	0.044
10	0.114	0.054
15	0.121	0.061
20	0.127	0.066
25	0.129	0.071
30	0.130	0.080
35	0.133	0.087
40		0.093
45		0.100

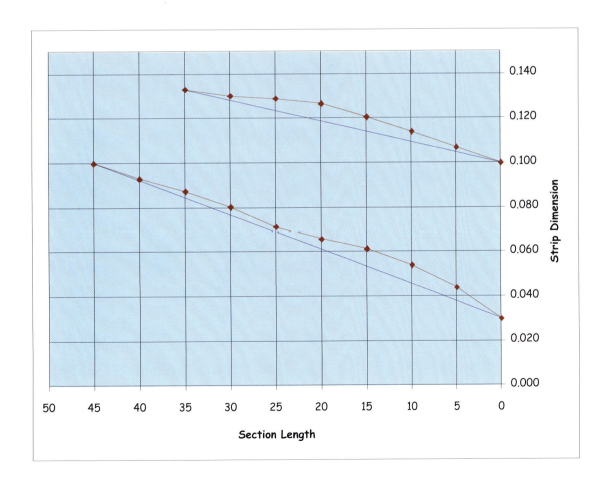

A Selection of Vince's Rods

(Seven-foot Six-inch, Rod, continued)

Good, strong pick-up

Beginning of a strong stroke; good haul loads entire rod

all photos by Tom Whittle

The results...

Here was our biggest surprise on the first day of our tests. Tom Maxwell had sung the praises of this rod, but Grauer and Smithwick thought it seemed a little too stiff through the butt—requiring a good 35 feet of line in the air to load smoothly. Both stated that the rod is an excellent design, but, as a matter of personal preference, neither cared for its faster action. The tip is largely responsible for doing all the work at distances less than 40 feet, but at those modest ranges the front half is about all one needs anyway.

Grauer noted that the rod also casts nicely from 45 feet onward, although it requires strong strokes and a haul to effect bending through its lower third. Smithwick suggested (too late) that we probably should have tried the rod with a 6-weight line "to get that butt bending a little sooner with less pushing." Not suspecting the huge swell through the butt section mentioned above, Tom's guess was that its slope is simply too steep. Tom agreed with Wayne that a strong haul produces casts beyond 65 feet, and both casters remarked that, at any distance, a little tug on the forward stroke is all that's needed to tighten the loop for shooting.

Bob Selb, on the other hand, was greatly impressed with the rod's action when he took his turn, and found no need to "push" to make it perform well. Still not quite his favorite rod from the collection, he had no difficulty casting either close-in or beyond 60 feet, and remarked that the rod "shoots line like crazy" at almost any distance. Perhaps the differences in our casters' opinions could be traced to Bob's habit of imparting strong wrist-action on his forward strokes—something he holds in check when required, but exercises freely when invited.

Upper-third unloading

Nice, tight loop

Strong cast; maximum loading

Eight-foot, Three-piece Rod for Four-weight Line

There's a very nice 8-foot rod in the Marinaro collection; a three-piecer for a 4-weight line. The date, "1977," is marked on its shaft, but the rod appears to be a good bit older. Vince rarely designed his longer rods to carry a light line, and finding one bearing a date so close to the last years of his career seems most peculiar. Adding to our suspicion, I don't recall ever seeing this rod or hearing about it, even though its soiled and polished cork grip shows years of use. A further oddity is contained in Vince's inscription: "Hardy reel seat added." Well, it does have the Hardy reel seat, but so do some of his other rods—none calling for special notation. Why did Vince think anyone would care to know, unless he meant that 1977 reflects, not the date of the rod's construction, but the year it was refurbished?

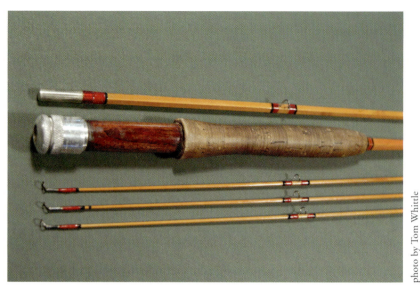

8-foot, 4-weight rod from 1977

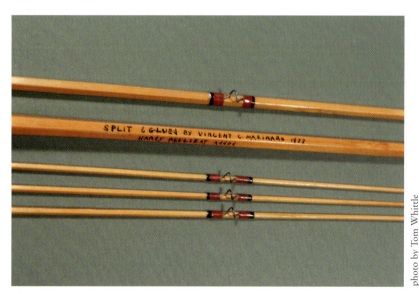

8-footer; 1977

Also, if this were one of his later creations, the rod shows a very strange mid-section: Our graph reveals its swell in a "reversed" position from Vince's more usual shape, being located along the last third of its length instead of the first. The butt, too, is odd for a later rod and its taper follows a very shallow slope-line. Still, the date of its construction doesn't matter greatly. The important thing is that its design gives evidence of the range of Vince's ideas and occasion to wonder how they may have evolved.

This rod sports red wraps with black tipping—very nice, but also a tad loud for Vince's tastes in latter years. The swaged, nickel-silver ferrules are from Herters; the cork grip is a reverse half-Wells, and the reel seat and its aluminum, up-lock hardware were made by Hardy. Vince built three different tips for this rod, the strongest giving our casters the best results. Our guess would be that he wasn't exactly sure how his unusual mid-section might perform, so the sequence of tips probably reflects his search for the best combination.

Station	Butt	Mid	Tip
0	0.119	0.076	0.030
5	0.124	0.083	0.041
10	0.127	0.091	0.051
15	0.128	0.099	0.058
20	0.132	0.107	0.066
25		0.114	0.070
30		0.118	0.075
32		0.119	0.076

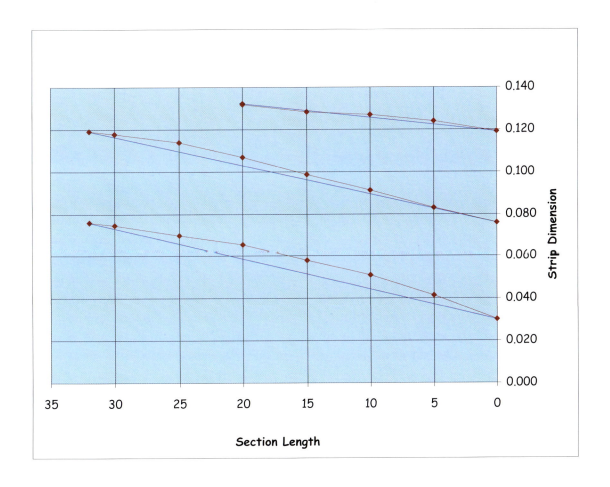

A Selection of Vince's Rods

(Eight-foot Rod, continued)

Strong pick-up

Strong stroke; small haul

all photos by Tom Whittle

The results...

This is a very gentle rod with progressive action, and the WF-4 line loads it quickly and easily. Of its three tips, even the finest of these managed to reach 55 feet, but the strongest tip suited our casters best. Using the preferred tip, casts up to 45 feet were entirely effortless and accurate, and (discounting the need to dry one's fly) false-casting this rod seemed unnecessary at medium distances. Smithwick remarked that he was able simply to "pick it up and lay it down." When Selb tested the rod in his later session, his comment was much the same—"you don't even have to try; just go up and down."

Using the strongest of the three tips, a medium haul produces the line-speed and loop-control needed to cover 60+ feet. This 8-footer is something of a specialty-rod, intended to hold a back-cast high above surrounding grass and to deliver small flies (perhaps not larger than a size 14) delicately. It's a light rod, meant for a light line, and as Grauer pointed out, it's in its glory through all short and medium distances. Smithwick and Grauer noted that the caster must take care not to impose wrist-action on the stroke—overpowering the rod unnecessarily—but affirmed that it performs without effort when the arm is held more stiffly. Selb, whose own preference is for somewhat stronger rods, said in his inimitable way, "Naw, just slow your stroke down and let the rod load itself."

50-foot cast; no haul; full-flexing

Same cast; upper-half unloading

Long cast; tight loop; no tip-bounce

A Selection of Vince's Rods

Eight-foot Six-inch, Three-piece Rod for Seven-weight Line

The only surviving rod of 8 1/2 feet is this example from 1944, whose taper we demonstrated in the previous chapter. In his 1976, unpublished manuscript, Vince mentioned that he took two 8 1/2-footers with him to fish England's chalk streams, but we don't know what became the other rod. Actually, apart from Marinaro's 1947 bait-caster (and possibly the rod described just above), the rod we present here is the only one pre-dating the 1970s.

This is a three-piecer, built for a 7-weight line, and like the 7 1/2 footer demonstrated earlier, this too, sports an English bank spear. The aluminum, up-locking, reel seat and wood filler were supplied by Hardy, and the ferrules are a nickel-silver, step-down design, but of unknown make. The butt shaft shows several decorative wraps in yellow and dark brown just above the grip, plus a long, yellow, spiral wrap a bit farther up. Guides and ferrules are wrapped in that same yellow, tipped with brown. Because the effect is rather garish we thought perhaps Vince hadn't done the wrapping himself, but we also couldn't imagine he would have given a blank check to someone else, not liked the results and still done nothing about it. Vince was a young man when he built this rod, so we suppose his taste was different back then.

As a rule, I find long and strong bamboo rods to be clumsy, tiring and annoying to use. This rod, however, casts with a minimum of effort, does not feel at all heavy, and is a welcome exception to my rule. It's meant to drive a fly through the wind and to shoot line across a good stretch of water,

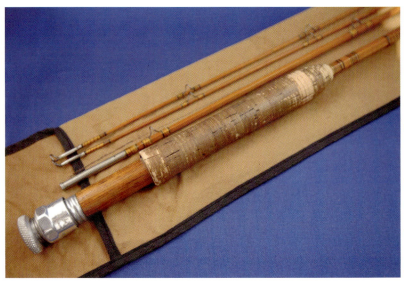
8 1/2-foot, 7-weight rod from 1944

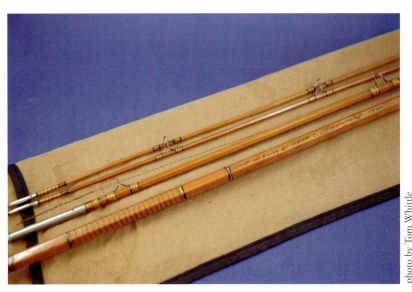
8 1/2-footer; 1944

but I'm thinking that, for my needs, a WF 6-weight version might do the job as well. Scaling the taper back somewhat and hollowing its butt and mid-sections strike me as perfect exercises for a great rod on the upper Delaware River.

Note, once again, how the graph reveals that same flat taper through the butt—just as we saw in the previous rod and perhaps typifying what Vince wanted in earlier years. On the other hand, the tip- and mid-sections reveal rather pronounced convex shapes, with the swell of the mid-section being located close to its center and carrying across a broad area. We also call attention to the slope-lines of these two upper sections, for, unlike Vince's other three-piece rods (with mid-sections designed less steeply than tips), this rod shows identical slope angles through the two sections, and the mid-section in particular promises great strength.

	Strip Thickness		
Station	Butt	Mid	Tip
0	0.138	0.090	0.038
5	0.143	0.099	0.049
10	0.151	0.108	0.056
15	0.158	0.116	0.063
20	0.165	0.122	0.070
25		0.128	0.078
30		0.134	0.084
34		0.138	0.090

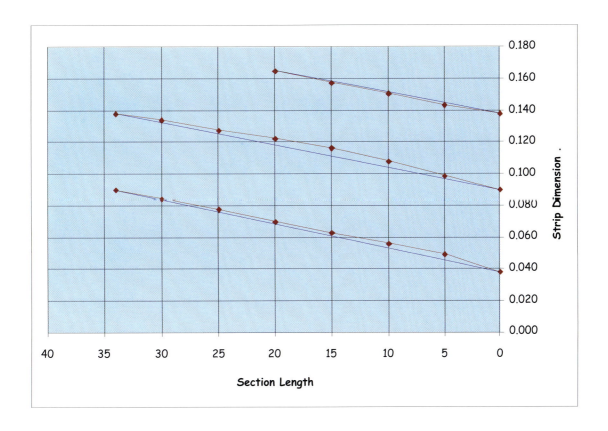

(Eight-foot Six-inch Rod, continued)

Strong cast; full haul; upper-third unloading

The results...

Smithwick's first response was that, for all distances up to 55 feet, this rod lays out its WF-7 line by "just going up and down like a tack-hammer," then blurting, "now, that's *my* kind of rod!" This is a powerful rod, meant for large flies, large water or wind, but surprisingly, its action is not fast; its weight does not "hang on the wrist," and the rod doesn't require strong strokes. The tip is very responsive at distances between 25 and 50 feet, but it also has the strength needed to shoot a very long line.

In the former chapter on rod design, we mentioned that the graphed view of this rod almost suggests a "parabolic" shape, but none of our casters could describe its action that way. Instead, each of them agreed that the rod felt "perfectly balanced and progressive." Grauer and Smithwick quickly learned that the rod's tip allows for fine presentations close-in, but a longer stroke and a haul will punch a tight loop to 80 feet handily. Grauer was especially impressed with the rod's ability to pick line up, even out to 55 feet, and with its ease in forming tight loops at any distance. Smithwick added that the rod's "sweet-spot" seemed to be about 50 feet, and pointed out that wrist-action will not overpower the rod.

This is an impressive rod, so when Selb lined it up in our later session, he was eager to test its maximum range. When asked how it performs at 25-40 feet, however, he predicted, "Aw, this is a cannon. You can't expect it to be good close-in." The look on Bob's face changed quickly when he found it to be as responsive at short-to-medium distances as the other rods... asking, "How the hell does a cannon do that!?" Then, it was back to hauling for distance, just because it's fun and because the rod can get it. Even against a little breeze, Bob punched his line past 85 feet, and the rod won his vote as "overall, the easiest of all the rods to cast."

Full haul; great loop; no tip-bounce

Nice, straight back-cast

Energy spent; beginning of loop formation

A Selection of Vince's Rods

Nine-foot, Three-piece Rod for Five-weight Line

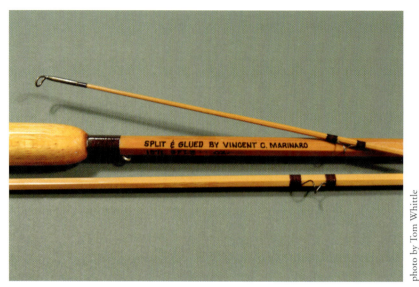

9-foot, 5-weight rod from 1971—note the balsa grip

In 1971, Vince built a 9-foot, three-piece rod for 5-weight line, and weighing exactly 4 ounces. Two other 9-footers were to follow in 1976, but this one was his first effort and it may be the 4-ounce rod he describes in *The Ring* (the latter, two rods come in a tad over that 4-ounce mark). The first of his 1976 rods was built about the same time *The Ring* appeared, but because the book went to press in the first part of the year, we don't imagine that rod would have been completed in time to tout its virtues. Besides, Vince's 1971 creation was already at hand, and seems to match the description found in his book.

In this and the two examples to follow, we'll be evaluating Marinaro's series of 9-foot rods and raising some questions: Namely, we wonder if our volunteers' impressions of the rods resulted from their own, varied, casting style or from inherent design qualities in the rods themselves. Descriptions of a rod's performance will always involve a mix of these two, but in what measures? The three 9-footers presented here form a perfect case-in-point: The rods cast differently from one another, but in subtle ways and without conclusive explanations. We will note differences in their graphed information, but actual casting comparisons were somewhat harder to nail down.

This first example from 1971 is a "plain-Jane" for sure, devoid of all decorative trim and showing only simple, deep-brown wraps. The ferrules are true "Super-Zs," but the rod's grip and reel seat are highly unusual. In his phobia about excessive weight, Vince used a single block of balsa and shaped it, overall, like a miniature baseball-bat—without the customary step between grip and reel seat. The whole was then simply given a couple coats of satin varnish. The reel is held in place with aluminum sliding rings and a cork "stop" fixed at the butt-end.

Certainly, I wasn't always Vince's fishing companion, but I don't believe he used this rod often, preferring his 1976 versions. The later rods are nicer-looking, but of the three 9-footers tested, Tom and Wayne believe this 1971 rod actually makes the better choice. Selb, however, demurred, holding with one of the 1976 versions.

Our graph shows the "classic" Marinaro shapes through the tip- and mid-sections. The swell in the tip is a little less pronounced than we will see in his later 9-footers, but its shoulders distribute across a broader area. Once again, there's that same straight-taper through the butt-section. That's the puzzling part, however, because if this should be the rod Marinaro described in *The Ring*, its butt doesn't demonstrate the convexity that his drawings recommend—while the two, 9-foot rods built in 1976 do. Once again, we just don't have an answer, and only observe that this flattened taper appears frequently on the butts of his earlier and longer, three-piece rods.

Station	Butt	Mid	Tip
0	0.127	0.082	0.038
5	0.133	0.092	0.046
10	0.140	0.100	0.053
15	0.147	0.105	0.059
20	0.153	0.112	0.064
25	0.161	0.117	0.070
30		0.122	0.076
35		0.126	0.081
36		0.127	0.082

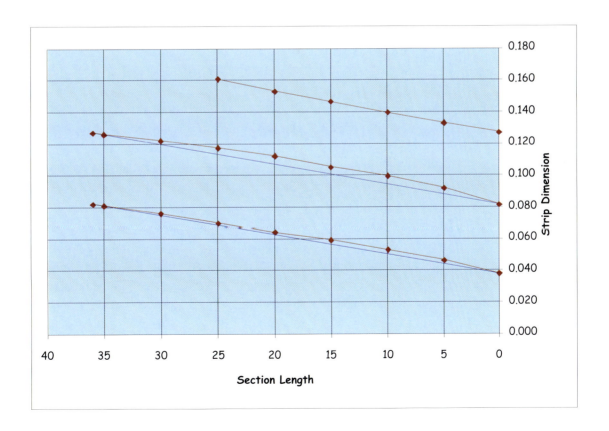

A Selection of Vince's Rods

(Nine-foot Rod, continued)

Great pick-up and start of back-cast

The results...

Smithwick, waxing enthusiastic, said at once, "this is the best of the bunch—now, that's a hell of a rod!" We lined it with a WF-5, and all three volunteers agreed the rod cast with equal ease and delicacy to targets from 25 to 55 feet. Grauer was impressed by its smoothness, pointing out that it remained gentle and accurate at all distances. On the negative side, he hated that thin, balsa grip and felt it slipping around in his hand—something that would grow far worse with wet hands on the stream. Selb, too, thought the thin grip prevented him from controlling the rod as well as he might. Grauer's preference on a longer rod leans to the more substantial, half-Wells shape. Can't argue with him there.

Grauer also pointed out that he's not usually fond of 9-foot bamboo rods, but this one felt very light in the hand, and for casts up to 50 feet, needed nothing more than a single back-cast to pick up, load, and lay the line out again. Smithwick was especially impressed by its efficiency, saying that even without much of a tug, "the line just wants to fly...." Selb, however, wasn't entirely convinced, believing the rod to be a little too slow for his taste. On the other hand, he also remarked that it shoots line very well and the tip provides a nice "kick" on finishing the forward cast. All three casters noted the rod's gentle action—meant for medium-sized line and flies, not casting heroics—adding that they were not surprised to see the rod "running out of steam" beyond 65 feet.

Perfect start of forward cast

Slight haul; rod fully flexed

Rod unloaded; good loop forming; no tip bounce

A Second Nine-foot, Three-piece Rod for Six-weight Line

This next example is the first of two 9-foot, three-piece rods Vince built in 1976. As with the rod described just above, this one was also meant to cast a WF-5 line. Vince inscribed the weight on the butt-shaft as 4 ounces, but my little postal scale shows 4.25 ounces. Of course, there could be differences in calibration, but it's also possible that Vince may have weighed his blanks at some point before finishing the rod. This rod is stronger than our former example, but it's still a very light rod for its length—designed for delicate deliveries, not for powering large flies through the wind. Vince wrapped it tastefully in medium-brown silk and mounted an extremely thin, cigar-shaped grip. The reel seat is shaped from balsa with a small, cork button at its end and, again, we find the thin, knurled, sliding-band hardware.

9-foot, 6-weight rod from 1976

9-footer, 1976

The ferrules are nickel silver, not the usual Super-Z design, but the rolled-and-swagged product supplied by Herter's—certainly more than serviceable. Vince built this rod with just one tip, possibly because he was unsure of the rod's performance. He would often do this, advising me to build modestly as well. But I knew if I didn't make a second tip at once, it wasn't likely to materialize in the future. And, as it usually happened, so it was with Vince. Nevertheless, this rod quickly became one of his favorites, and although he developed yet another three-piece, 9-footer in the same year, this was the rod he carried religiously to the Letort.

A quick look at its graphed profiles again shows "classic" Marinaro shapes, but this time through all three sections and typifying Vince's recommended proportions. We see a large swell through the first 12 inches of the tip, but more modest development through the mid-section and butt. The swell in the butt is a little farther back than might be expected, but provides easy flexing in the area through the first ferrule. Overall, the tip and butt sections on this rod show slightly more strongly-developed tapers than seen in the 1971 rod, and the slope-lines are somewhat steeper. On the other hand, their mid-section swells are similar (not in slope, but in the development of their taper lines).

Station	Butt	Mid	Tip
0	0.130	0.087	0.036
5	0.140	0.096	0.049
10	0.149	0.104	0.056
15	0.156	0.110	0.061
20	0.163	0.117	0.067
25	0.166	0.122	0.074
30		0.126	0.080
35		0.129	0.086
36		0.130	0.087

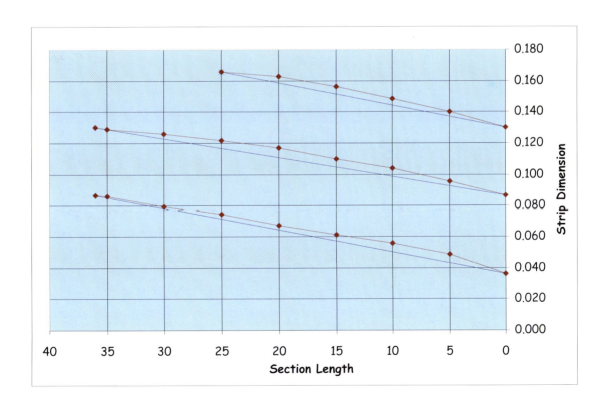

(A Second Nine-foot Rod, continued)

A little "tug" gets a 50-foot cast; full-flexing

Energy spent in lower-half; upper portions unloading

The results...

This rod is a slightly stronger counterpart to the one tested just above, but two of our three casters did not receive it with quite the same enthusiasm. It seemed to load well enough with its intended WF-5 line and delivered a good loop to targets as far as 45 feet, although beyond that, Smithwick and Grauer noted the rod can be overpowered. But, keep your wrist straight when false casting, give the line a little tug, and the rod performs nicely even out to 65 feet. Smithwick remarked that it's excellent for distances up to 50 feet, but he was not able to avoid a tailing loop when pressing out toward the 60-foot mark. Grauer agreed, emphasizing that the rod calls for an easy motion to feel its rhythm. That done, both confirmed it's a very nice rod for a light-to-medium weight line.

Interestingly, Selb, who tested Marinaro's rods on a later occasion, thought this 9-footer simply was not performing properly with the 5-weight line. When he changed up to a WF-6, the rod suddenly came alive, performing all casts with delicacy and grace, and holding a very tight loop through all distances. Again, the stroke needed to be kept slow, but Bob's line-switch eliminated the tailing-loop problem and he did not sense that the rod was in danger of being overpowered. Close-up tasks were performed with less effort and greater accuracy, and even at 60 feet, Bob's tight loop actually pulled clicks off his reel.

The puzzling part in all this is that, when using the 5-weight line, the other two volunteers cautioned against overpowering the rod, while Selb found that a heavier line made the needed improvement in the rod's performance. This is exactly the reverse of what one would expect, but with that change, the rod became Bob's favorite of the three 9-footers. Perhaps Grauer and Smithwick felt the rod

Tip still has enough energy to kick out a tight loop

was on the verge of being overtaxed because, to load the rod with a lighter line, stronger strokes were needed. But these may have "shocked" the rod as much as loading it.

It's a peculiar situation and raises an interesting design question for longer rods: What relation is optimal between the load of the extended line and that created by the casting stroke? Specifically, to load a long and light

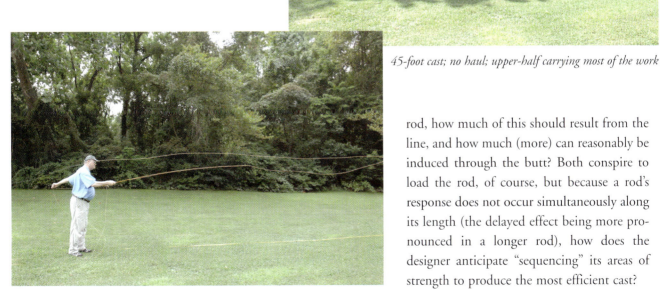
45-foot cast; no haul; upper-half carrying most of the work

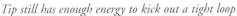
Long cast with a strong haul; good, tight loop

rod, how much of this should result from the line, and how much (more) can reasonably be induced through the butt? Both conspire to load the rod, of course, but because a rod's response does not occur simultaneously along its length (the delayed effect being more pronounced in a longer rod), how does the designer anticipate "sequencing" its areas of strength to produce the most efficient cast?

Nine-foot Two-inch, Three-piece Rod for Seven-weight Line

The third, 9-foot, three-piece rod from the "Marinaro Collection" (actually, measuring a tad shy of 9' 2"), Vince named "Penn's Creek." This was the second of the two rods built in 1976, and his inscription on its shaft calls for a 7-weight line. Vince finished the rod with his typical, slim, cork grip and a balsa reel seat, also mounting the thin, aluminum, sliding-band hardware. Its ferrules are true "Super-Zs," and the wraps are turned in an attractive, forest-green silk.

9-foot, 7-weight rod from 1976, named "Penn's Creek"

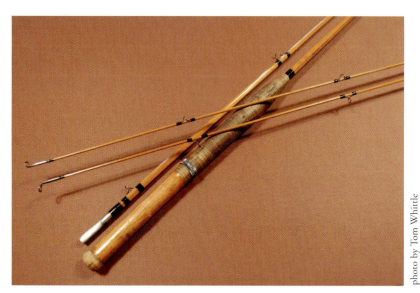

9-foot "Penn's Creek"

Upon simply flexing the rod in one's hand, you'd swear this 7-weight version was gentle like the 1971, 5-weight rod. But long rods are usually deceiving, and you need to line them up to see how they'll actually perform. Vince made some subtle changes from his former 9-footers, apparently intending "Penn's" to deal with larger water and more substantial flies. This rod is meant to handle a larger line, and were it not for its relaxed casting motion, a day of fishing could wear one out—really, a potential problem for any long, bamboo rod. Surprisingly, however, its action is very easy and the rod's power goes unsuspected. But "Penn's" is also a somewhat sensitive and unforgiving rod and seems best suited to an advanced flyfisher whose sense of timing can be adapted to "let the rod do the work."

Our graph of "Penn's" tip-section shows a shallower slope than seen on the other 9-footer from 1976, and with a less pronounced swell through the 5- and 10-inch stations. The mid-section shows still another interesting difference from the former rod: By comparison, it's end-dimensions are somewhat finer, yet its convex shape is more strongly defined and distributed over a greater area. The butt section shows a difference as well, with its swell forming strongly at the 10-inch station and carrying back to the 20-inch station. While the overall dimensions are somewhat finer than seen in Vince's other 1976 rod, evidently he believed "Penn's" would be the more powerful of the two because of the prominent convex swells through the butt- and mid-sections.

Station	Butt	Mid	Tip
0	0.129	0.085	0.035
5	0.138	0.096	0.046
10	0.148	0.103	0.052
15	0.154	0.110	0.058
20	0.160	0.116	0.065
25	0.164	0.121	0.071
30		0.124	0.077
35		0.127	0.083
36.5		0.128	0.084

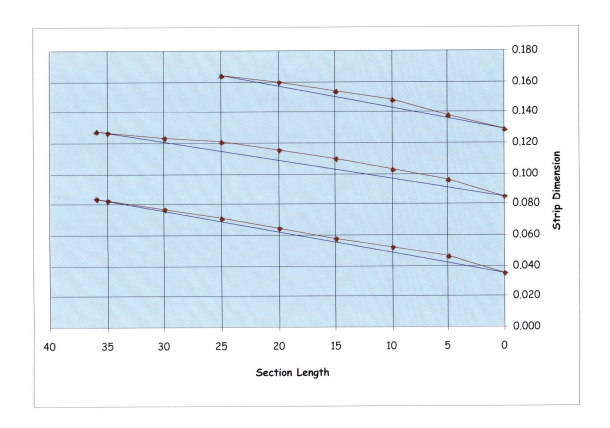

(Nine-foot Two-inch Rod, continued)

50-foot cast; slight haul, full-flexing

The results...

Here was another surprise, for despite "Penn's" designation as a 7-weight rod, all three of our volunteers agreed that a WF-6 line provides the proper match. As with Vince's other rods, this one also casts both accurately and "by itself" through all distances to 50 feet. But with a smooth stroke and a haul, it's also able to shoot line beyond 70 feet.

It's a curious thing, but while the first rod from 1976 needed to be lined-up one size, this second rod needed to be lined down. Our casters found that both rods handle the WF-6 properly, but differently. Smithwick had a hard time deciding which of the 9-footers was his favorite rod—the first one from 1971, or this—finally choosing the former as, "the greater rod-making achievement because of its light-in-the-hand feel for something in that size range."

Grauer, too, was taken by "Penn's," but again its thin grip was a source of annoyance, also noting that (as with certain other rods) one's wrist needs to be kept out of the casting stroke. Without some awareness of how this rod loads and shoots, the average fisherman will overpower it, open the loop and watch his leader collapse early. With a little practice, however, "Penn's" pays you back many times over with its efficiency. The trick to casting this rod is to move it gently, almost disregarding the need to flex the lower two-thirds of its length—then, just "pick it up and lay it down."

Selb, on the other hand, and even considering his habit to cast with a good bit of wrist-action, reported minimum danger in overpowering "Penn's," again saying that a slower stroke is all that's needed. The caster's sensitivity must be directed to the tip section, almost as if that were the only part of the rod you meant to put into action. That done, and without pushing, the rest of the rod loads itself. Or as Selb put the matter, "the line just takes off!" All three agreed that this is a surprisingly light rod (for a 9-footer, after all), but despite its easy action, it also has the power to drive a fly into the breeze.

Tip ready to "kick" a nice, tight loop

Great loop; no tip-bounce

Good line-speed, high and straight; again, no tip-bounce

A Selection of Vince's Rods

Three Stout Salmon Rods

Lastly, we have a handful of Vince's salmon rods. There are just three, all built between 1976 and 1979. First, came a two-piece, 9 1/2-foot rod called "Salmo," carrying a WF-8 line. It's a mystery why Vince wanted to build a large rod like this in the two-piece configuration (having his doubts about these anyway), but that's what he built. Next, came the big, 14 1/2-foot, two-handed rod, called "Salar." This is a three-piece rod, also designed for an 8-weight line, but requiring the long, "rocket" bass-taper. Lastly, in 1979, Vince built his "Penobscot," another 9 1/2-foot rod. Unlike "Salmo," however, this one is in three pieces, has a fighting-butt, and carries the 8-weight, bass-taper line.

"Salmo," built in 1976

"Salar," built in 1977

"Salmo," the two-piece, 8-weight rod, handled very well and shot line easily beyond 85 feet. Grauer and Smithwick thought the bass-taper line might have overpowered the rod a little at those distances, but we didn't have a standard WF-8 with us. Their estimations, consequently, were not made under ideal conditions. "Salmo" has a strong tip and its shortest effective range seemed to be 40-45 feet—about what one expects of a salmon rod. Even so, they agreed the rod was very smooth and responded to the haul just as it was intended to do. Smithwick liked the rod better than did Wayne, but Wayne explained at the outset that he's no fan of long and beefy bamboo rods.

The burly, 14 1/2-foot, two-hander, was bested only by Tom Smithwick. The rest of us tried as we might, but "Salar" is a rod for fly-fishers who've logged a good bit of experience with industrial-strength casting gear. Smithwick, earlier, had been greatly impressed with Vince's other rods, but said he was "blown away" by this one—everything else growing pale by comparison. He was astonished at its ability to hold line in the air, load, then shoot to distances beyond 100 feet. Pick-up works best when the line is stripped in to about 55-60 feet. But then it's up in the air, two false casts, and out she goes...!

Smithwick loads Vince's 14 1/2-foot, two-handed rod for a 100-foot cast. Plenty of power remains in that butt for far greater distances

Most remarkably, "Salar" is flawless in its construction, a seemingly impossible feat when working with such large and unyielding strips. But we also marveled at how Vince might have designed such a thing. You have to start from *something*, so what did he use as his basic parameters!? He couldn't have been greatly influenced by existing rods of other manufacture because our graph showed perfect, convex sections—each strongly developed and corresponding exactly to Vince's own recommendations in *The Ring*.

Next, we took a lesson in the Spey cast, which Smithwick performed beautifully even off the grass. Not much for us to say about this rod but, "Holy Crap!" The rod has two different tips, but because Tom reported that both perform well, the choice would seem to depend only on the kind of water being fished. Smithwick, who has designed and cast more than a few large, bamboo rods wrote later, "it's like the thing came from another planet! If I could ask Vince only one question, I would want to know what inspired that rod."

Unfortunately, the 9 1/2-foot, three-piece "Penobscot" had a loose ferrule at the start of our first session with Grauer and Smithwick, so they were unable to cast the rod. In our second session, however, Selb put the rod through its paces and sailed a tight loop past 85 feet with ease. As expected, this is an extremely powerful rod, meant to deliver a heavy line over long distances, and with a minimum of false-casting. But, without some experience in casting bamboo rods of this size, slinging a big fly can become tiring in short order. Fortunately, "Penobscot" was built with a substantial fighting-butt that can be gripped for two-handed casting if desired. Selb said he greatly enjoyed casting it and believes it to be an excellent rod, but he also pointed out that, for him, graphite always makes the less taxing choice when an appointment with *Salmo Salar* is on the calendar.

Grauer's overall estimation of Marinaro's rods was one of pleasant surprise, remarking, "they were not at all what I expected them to be. I thought Vince preferred fast rods

(Salmon Rods, continued)

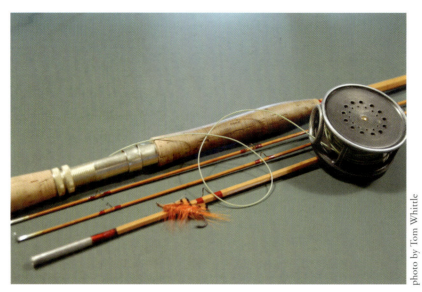

"Penobscot," built in 1979

with tip-action." Instead of finding this, however, Grauer judged the rods to be progressive in their action—working smoothly, flexing evenly and adjusting easily to each casting situation. Just what he likes to see. Although he does not care for longer bamboo rods, he was pleased to find even they behaved far better than anticipated. Grauer's only complaint about the rods was a preponderance of skinny grips, believing that, not only would a larger grip look better on a long rod, but the hand would gain better leverage when casting.

Smithwick agreed and was similarly impressed by Marinaro's rods, but said he found no astonishing surprises other than the 14 1/2-foot, two-handed, salmon example. Explaining, Tom said he came into the casting session expecting Vince to be a first-rate maker, capable of building a first-rate rod, and was delighted to have found exactly that across the range. Selb's overall assessment was that he was most impressed by Marinaro's ability to design rods that remained consistent and versatile, regardless of their length and intended line-weight. Like Grauer, Selb said he'd been under the impression that Vince's rods would be long and strong, and was surprised to find both power and delicacy at all distances—noting, especially, that characteristic, strong "kick" at the end of the forward cast.

Vince's 7 1/2-foot rod making use of its bank spear (before refinishing)

CHAPTER TEN

Picking Up Where Vince Left Off
—*by Tom Whittle*

We have no doubt that many folks will wish to duplicate one or another of Marinaro's tapers, but in this chapter, Bill and I will offer a few, additional options. Both of us, although independently, have been working with convex tapers for many years and have discovered our own little design methods and objectives. These, we will present, together with a few of our favorite tapers and some advice for those who would like to try their hand at designing their own rods. The design process really is not difficult, and because each fly-fisher probably has come to prefer a certain kind of action, convex tapers can easily be adapted to suit their own casting needs and preferences. While, for the most part, both of us have applied these principles to two and three-piece rods of six-strip construction, Bill has extended convex-taper theory to one-piece, 6-foot rods for 3- and 4-weight lines—both in hexagonal and quadrate configurations. There are a few, basic parameters to observe, but in all, designing one's own rod is well within the reach of every person capable of building.

The purpose of this book—in particular, this chapter—is not to promote Bill's or my designs over other successful approaches: rather, considering Marinaro's highly pictorial technique of design, we would offer an alternative to the more usual, complicated calculations. The maker who is mathematically or computer-challenged can jump right in and create his own tapers that may even be better than most known rods. It's something about looking for a deeper level of personal satisfaction and a fuller sense of intimacy with one's craft. The challenge of experimentation is exciting and rewarding, and in the end, there's no substitute for knowing that, through your own efforts, you have evolved the rods that work best for you.

HOW I MET MARINARO....

In November of 1996, a decade after Vince's death, his son, Sebastian Marinaro, exhibited a sampling of Vince's collection at our local Trout Unlimited banquet. Sebastian spoke of his desire to keep Vince's collection together and available for the public. Always interested in the preservation of angling history, I was pleased to learn of the plans the Marinaro family had for Vince's collection, and, as a budding rod-builder, this rare opportunity to see first-hand some of Vince's rods was truly inspiring. Again, in the Spring of 1997, the Marinaro display was among the exhibits celebrating the 50th Anniversary Celebration of the Fly Fisher's Club of Harrisburg. These two opportunities to view just a small part of Vince's collection caused me to dig out my copy of *The Ring* and revisit Vince's description of the convex taper. Not a great deal of practical assistance there, but his ideas seemed to reinforce certain of Garrison's tip-shapes, and I had already been working with these. (When graphed, several of Garrison's tips also show the convex shape—possibly inspired through his early years of work with Holden.) Sadly, Sebastian Marinaro passed away not long after the Spring, 1997 event, with the entire collection being retained by Sebastian's widow, Maggie.

During the first week of January 1998, Jodi Reese, a co-worker, told me about meeting Don Ebright at a holiday party, and of Don's connection to the Marinaro family and Vince's collection. Working with Don, the Pennsylvania Fly Fishing Museum Association was formed shortly after, in large part to preserve the Marinaro collection. Maggie Marinaro, always gracious and supportive of our efforts, granted the museum limited access to Vince's rods and its larger holdings during our early negotiations to acquire the collection. In the summer of 1998, eager to promote the newly formed Museum Association and the "Marinaro Collection," I built a replica of Vince's "Guppy" (a 6 1/2-foot, two-piece rod), and in September, demonstrated it as part of a PFFMA presentation at the Catskill Rodmakers Gathering in Roscoe, New York.

In January 1999, the Museum Association also began the "Guild Rod," a fund-raising project to help purchase the "Marinaro Collection." Twelve builders were gathered, each to plane a strip replicating the taper of Marinaro's 7' 6" two-piece rod (the "Maxwell" rod–see Chapter 9). This rod was then raffled and presented at the Association's Annual Banquet. Almost from its inception, the PFFMA was talking about sponsoring a book on Vince and his rod-building, and as President of the Association, I started twisting Bill's arm about some sort of joint-authorship.

By June 2000, when the Museum Association took possession of the "Marinaro Collection," I had already become a convex-taper practitioner. Although I had limited access to some of Vince's rods and tapers all along (the "Guppy" rod for the Gathering and the "Guild Rod"), I really wasn't interested in copying Marinaro tapers—actually, I was pretty happy with my own convex designs. Two-piece rods were my favorites, but as Bill mentioned earlier, Vince didn't care much for two-piecers and some of his own designs didn't conform exactly with his convex-taper theory. So in a way, my marching orders from Vince were the same as for Bill: "Do as I say, and not as I do."

Throughout earlier chapters, Bill offers apologies that we cannot provide all the answers to what Vince was trying to accomplish with his designs. However, without Bill's insight as a student of Vince, this whole project might have ended up with merely a "listing" of the specifications, measurements, and other anecdotes about Vince's rods—and a gob-lot of speculation about what Vince may have been thinking in *The Ring*. While Bill and I have been working together on this project for a long time, even I didn't fully understand the details of Vince's theory until Bill's dealings with him began appearing in early drafts of this book. Marinaro offered only the broadest explanation in *The Ring*, but the full information had never been circulated. Like most fly-fishermen, I had no real contact with Vince other than to recognize him as one of "the giants." So, perhaps it is ironical that I too became an "absolutist" of the convex taper theory, for my path to cane rod-building developed quite separately from direct assistance from Vince or conversations with Bill.

It has often been said that bamboo rod design really can't evolve much more—that all we can do is insert a couple tweaks here or there to modify some existing taper. In the largest view, perhaps this is true, yet those of us who have fooled around with design know that there are always ways of creating a rod that's a little different and a little better than something we've used before. Even tweaking is highly rewarding. Or, perhaps we hear others say that all possible taper designs already have been developed and that

Tom planes a strip

photo by King Montgomery

we're only re-inventing the wheel, merely adding or subtracting a spoke. Again, to the casual fly-fisher, maybe so, but it certainly is not the case that convex tapers have been fully explored. Once the maker becomes involved in the design process, he soon learns that these dismissive opinions ignore all the discoveries that, indeed, are possible. Can we come up with something radically new and different? No, probably not. But that's not the target ordinarily envisioned by bamboo fly-fishers anyway. Fly-fishing is a sport of subtleties, and the best practitioners already know what they want a rod to do. Finding the ones that deliver just the "magic" they seek, however, is quite another matter.

We explained in earlier chapters that Marinaro believed no craftsman could call himself a rod-maker until he had developed his own set of tapers. While we do not necessarily hold with that, we do believe that the best makers have become deeply involved in design. We often speak about subtleties in a fly rod, and, while these will not mean much to the inexperienced fly-fisher, for the relatively accomplished caster, they soon come to mean everything. So, even if you only anticipate re-inventing the wheel, we would say by all means, *go and do that*—you're in for a wonderful surprise. You will have become a better maker for your efforts, and if you're in earnest, you will also learn why nobody's rods suit you quite as well as your own.

While my first fly rod was bamboo, my appreciation of fine cane rods came much later. I suppose it was in the late 1950s when I first showed an interest in trout fishing and was given a fly rod by my grandfather. It was a very old, inexpensive, 9-foot, three-piece, bamboo rod with half the tip section gone. The ferrules were split, but had been repaired with a wrapping of copper-wire and solder. Heck, you didn't expect Grand-pop to give a nice Granger or Heddon to a ten-year-old! Certainly, that first rod did lit-tle to foster my appreciation of bamboo fly rods. So after a few years I purchased a Garcia, fiberglass fly rod with metal ferrules; and later, two Fenwick, glass rods—those plain, brown jobbies—one, at 5' 3" and the other, a 6-foot model, both for 5-weight lines. These served me well for a very long time, but years later I decided to "restore" the old, bamboo rod Grand-pop gave me when I was a young boy. Before I knew what happened, I had accumulated more than two dozen cane rods, first merely to satisfy my restoration habit, but also to use for fishing.

My grandson fishes Fenwick 5' 3" glass rod

photo by Tom Whittle

In 1995, a few years after the bamboo monkey was on my back, I contacted George Maurer to sign-up for his one-on-one course in cane rod-building. George has since relocated his operation to Cammal, Pennsylvania in the Pine Creek Valley, but at the time he was teaching me, his shop was only about 45 minutes away from my home in the Harrisburg area. George allowed me to schedule my sessions for one afternoon a week (extending over a few months) instead of the normal, intensive, week-long course. The arrangement was perfect for me because, while I was working on my first rod in George's shop, I also practiced his instruction and started additional rods at home.

As mentioned in earlier chapters, amateur builders in Marinaro's day were generally self-taught and didn't have anything like the learning opportunities we take for granted today. Like many others who built their first rods under George's instruction, my learning curve was shortened tremendously, and it's fair to say that the revolution in amateur rod-making is largely due to the hands-on contributions that he and so many others have made. As of this writing, Maurer has taught approximately 120 men and women how to build their first cane rod, and his book, *Fundamentals of Cane Rod Building* (1998), co-authored by Bernie Elser, remains one of the best "how-to" books available today.

It is true that bamboo rods can be built just as Vince had done throughout his years of building—using a planing form and a few, simple, hand tools. However, like other craftsmen and wood-workers, many rod-makers will jump at any chance to add to their arsenal of tools and machines. Perhaps these help us to save time but, more importantly, they also make it possible to fabricate a greater range of rod components on our own. I'm definitely among this latter group of makers. Immediately upon getting my jump-start from George, I purchased a vintage, South Bend, metal lathe to make my own reel seats and ferrules. I wanted my own hands to be responsible for as much as I could manage—including developing my "own" tapers.

My continuing quest for machinery culminated with the purchase of Bill Arend's old milling machine. This monster-of-a-machine was built for Bill in 1930, weighs 2,600 pounds, and is 9 feet long. It's called a "mill," but uses a 60-degree cutter-head (similar to a shaper-bit), fixed in position over a traveling platform. The platform accepts a variety of adjustable, steel forms that, when fed under the cutter, produce finished and tapered bamboo strips. Upon

Working on the lathe

Mill being unloaded through the basement door

Running a strip through the old Arend mill

receiving the mill in July of 1999, the first order of business was to modify those steel forms to accommodate my own standard, convex-taper designs. While the mill does produce strips ready to be glued into a rod blank, setting it up for particular taper is time-consuming. This machine's strength lies in its ability to produce high volumes of the same rod. But, because I don't normally produce several rods all of the same design at once, I get the best use out of the machine by milling large numbers of butt and tip strips slightly thicker than my strongest design, then finishing each particular taper by taking the last licks on my standard planing form.

Don't Know 'Bout The Other Guys, But....

Why design one's own rods when so many dozens of tapers are now readily available—tested through time, plotted, and merely awaiting our execution? Marinaro and other early makers had their own necessities, of course, for they were working in an age when dry-fly tapers were still in the developmental stages and information was generally unavailable. And, too, Vince had his own design objectives in mind. For the rest of us, however, living in an altogether different era (with easy access to information and all tools and materials being available), we ask the question again.

Certainly, one answer is that designing our own tapers provides the same measure of personal satisfaction that we get from building rods in the first place. So, there I was, a fellow who had a degree in Physics, employed as an engineer by day, but obsessed as a rod-builder by night. It makes sense that, immediately, I was drawn to Everett Garrison—also an engineer—and to Hoagy B. Carmichael's *A Master's Guide to Building A Bamboo Fly Rod* (1977). I had no difficulty understanding the stress-curve calculations Garrison provided in that book, and together with my access to the new computer programs being developed, I almost felt professionally obliged to master these high-tech, design procedures.

Nevertheless, technical calculations aside, I seemed to understand more by just looking at the shape of a taper on graph paper than by studying numbers for its stress-curves. The taper for my ninth rod (built a year or so after finishing my first rod with George) was based on Garrison's model 202E, and the most compelling reason for selecting it fairly jumped-out when I drew a large, graphed version of its tip taper. The smooth, "convex" shape for this 7-foot, two-piece rod just seemed to make more sense than the bumpy changes I saw in many of the tapers I had been tweaking earlier. From that rod onward, all my "new" tapers were designed on graph paper, and all employed convex shapes.

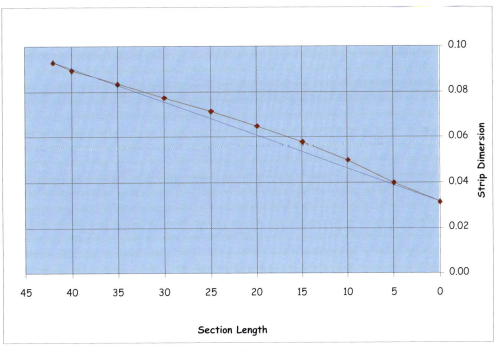

Garrison 202E taper graph, showing tip-section only

Before I began building cane rods, I had expanded my fly-fishing to include saltwater, primarily the surf along Delaware's beaches—using graphite rods—and I came to prefer fast rods. My taste in bamboo trout rods is no different, and these, too, tend to be quick and sprightly. One of the first things I found in employing the convex taper design was that I could add "wood" to some existing taper that seemed a little wimpy and make the rod stiffer. But convex tapers also seemed to provide a kind of quickness or "life" to the rod, and without adding weight. There's a kind of catapulting effect (or "kick") upon delivering the fly, but as Vince and Bill have said of their designs, a correct curve for that uppermost half of the tip section is the most critical part of the exercise. My first designs exhibited a smooth, but somewhat "flattened," convex shape from one end of the rod section to the other, but I quickly came to the same conclusion made by Vince and Bill, and realized that the most important improvement for my tapers would come from attention given to the smaller half of a tip section, from the tip-top back. Interestingly, even back in 1920, George Parker Holden had emphasized that same point.

Soon, I began developing my favorite convex tapers using a combination of shapes "borrowed" from Garrison, as well as those described by Vince in *The Ring*. As my starting point for a new rod, I either modified an existing rod taper or simply selected a generally-acceptable ferrule size for a given rod length and line-weight. From these, I obtained the initial, straight-line taper (slope), expressed as a ratio of the blank's increasing thickness per each inch of its length. As an example, nearly all 6 1/2- or 7-foot, two-piece rods for a 4-weight line will use a 12/64" ferrule, and the completed blank (not including swell at the grip) will typically reveal an averaged slope of 2.8 to 3.2 thousandths-of-an-inch per inch of rod length.

Using only these parameters, we can design a tip-section for a 7-foot, two-piece, 4-weight rod. Before addressing the taper itself, however, we need to establish our slope line on the graph. We start by measuring the inside diameter of the 12/64" ferrule in thousandths-of-an-inch, so we divide 12 by 64, getting 0.188". Next, we can determine the blank's thickness at its tip-top. Knowing that our section's length is 42 inches, and selecting a slope of, say, 3.0 thousandths-of-an-inch per inch of length, we multiply 0.003 x 42, getting 0.126". This number represents the total reduction in the blank's thickness from its ferrule to its tip-top. So, subtracting the 0.126" from the ferrule measurement of 0.188", the thickness at our smallest end will be 0.062" (a size 4.0 tip-top).

Lastly, these thicknesses are divided by two because our graphed version is meant only to show a single strip (half the dimension of any section). The results show a dimension of 0.094" at the ferrule end, and a tip of 0.031", so we plot the slope-line on the graph paper between these endpoints. Following this, we "draw" our desired convex shape above the straight-line slope and, when finished, we extract the thickness-dimensions from each graphed, control station and take our numbers to the planing form.

While I, too, compare the shape of each section's taper to its straight-line slope, my attention becomes a little more "localized" than simply looking at the overall swell (or "deviation" from the straight-slope). I also consider the individual slopes between each 5-inch station. Specifically, my tip designs call for the greatest rate-of-increase between the tip of the rod and the first 5-inch station. The maximum swell is located a "usual" 10-15 inches back from the tip top. But to get the faster rods I like, I carry that convex shape back a bit farther down the section than do Bill and Vince. On shorter rod sections, my maximum swell is likely to rise above the straight-slope by some 5-6 thousandths-of-an-inch, while in my longer sections, it corresponds to the same 2-4 thousandths-of-an-inch Bill suggested earlier. Without having the benefit of sharing detailed information with Bill (until recently putting this book together), it's especially interesting that we both came up with the same approach for designing this most important, front-half of our tip sections. Because I prefer my rods to be a little faster, perhaps, than Bill's and Vince's, it is not surprising that I carry the tip's swell farther along the section, providing somewhat stiffer flexing action.

Beyond Mere Tweaking

Surely, many other rod-builders have "tweaked" tapers of classic rods and been pleased with their results. And, as mentioned earlier, making even small changes can be highly rewarding. But there are also makers who search for design ideas that go beyond the mere tweaking of an existing taper, and it's always exciting to attend the various "gatherings" around the country and discover new concepts that other builders come up with. My "Brookie" rod is a good example of a design that goes a little beyond tweaking.

The hunting camp to which I belong has a small, freestone stream flowing through the property, holding wild browns and native brook trout. Over the years, I had built a few 6-foot rods for 4-weight lines to fish this stream and others like it, and while these rods were okay, they just didn't complete my expectations of what a small-stream rod should be. I believe these little guys need to be accurate enough to drop a fly into any small pocket you suspect might hold a fish, yet strong enough to shoot line with very little false casting (thus, avoiding the ever-present, fly-eating branches). In addition, at least on this particular stream, because the streambed is rocky and in many places, wider than the creek's usual flow, some fairly long casts are needed. Most of the fly line will land on the rocky bed, with hardly more than the leader, tippet and fly actually reaching the water, so I wanted both shooting power and a delicate delivery.

The idea for my "Brookie" rod actually began as a germ—just an idea about a different kind of ferrule. Here's the deal. Rick Robbins (an excellent rod-maker, close friend of the late Tom Maxwell, and a very supportive mentor to me over the years) told me about a ferrule design that Maxwell and Marinaro conceived—one that was quite different from the standard, "Super-Z" style. A Super-Z ferrule requires nearly identical diameters at the ends of the rod-sections where the tip joins to the butt, and the female portion of the ferrule is then fabricated by "telescoping" a larger

Freestone creek at hunting camp

Difference between "Super-Z" and Maxwell/Marinaro/Robbins style ferrules

diameter of tubing over the one in contact with the cane. This larger barrel becomes the socket for the male slide.

By contrast, the ferrule Rick described would still use the conventional, one-piece, male slide for the rod's tip section, but the female socket ("barrel") on the butt section would be formed simply by matching its internal diameter (I.D.) to the outside diameter (O.D.) of the male slide, then gluing that socket barrel directly on the butt—no two-piece telescoping. Interestingly, too, Rick told me that the idea for this ferrule actually came from conversations between Maxwell and Marinaro—their goals being to minimize a ferrule's weight while also reducing its stiffening effect on a rod's action. It's true that their design requires a drastic "drop" in blank dimensions between butt and tip, but their thinking was that the combined effect of a lighter ferrule and a dimensional change might bring about the result, essentially, of taking the ferrule out of the flexing equation.

I thought it might be worth a try, both because of the weight-savings and because the new and different action intrigued me. My "Brookie" prototype would include that unusual ferrule design and become a length of 5 feet 10 inches. Makes sense—that's my height.

(Here again, as Bill has pointed out, the taper-graphs provided in this book are for illustration purposes only—actual graph paper being larger, more finely scaled, and revealing proportions and information more accurately.)

Notice, on the graphed drawing of the tip-section, how the convex shape develops on its path back toward the ferrule end. The charted data specifies that the end-thickness of each strip is 0.080", resulting, of course, in a finished blank measuring 0.160". This dimension will call for a male ferrule-slide having an I.D. of 10/64", but the female barrel to fit over this slide will have an I.D. of 12/64". Now, because this barrel must also fit the cane at the end of the butt section, that ferrule station must measure 0.182" (strip dimensions of 0.091"). Thus, we have the sharp drop in dimensions between the butt and tip sections mentioned above—in this case, amounting to 0.022" across the ferrule station.

In itself, that didn't bother me, but the question remained of what to do with the taper through the rest of the butt behind the ferrule. I really didn't want the entire taper of the butt to develop from a beginning point of 0.182", so I had to figure a way to accommodate that female ferrule.

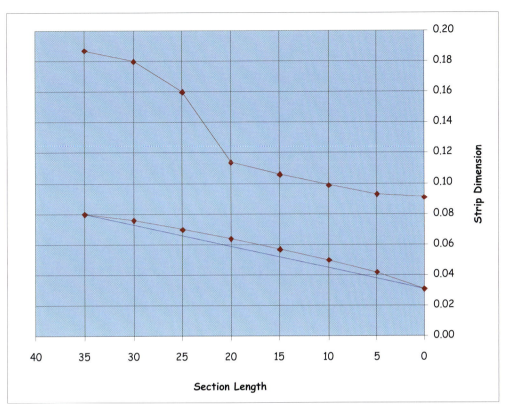

Station	Butt	Tip
0	0.091	0.031
5	0.093	0.042
10	0.099	0.050
15	0.106	0.057
20	0.114	0.064
25	0.160	0.070
30	0.180	0.076
35	0.187	0.080

Graph and chart for "Brookie" rod

Casting the "Brookie" rod

My solution was to minimize the impact of its large I.D. by designing the shape of the butt's taper in my "normal" way, but with its first 4 inches actually swelling to meet the female barrel. Overall, then, my design calls for a male slide identical to any other "Swiss" or Super-Z ferrule, so everything remains standard there. The difference is in the female part. Rather than soldering the usual, Super-Z, step-down tubing into its barrel, the butt's taper (just at its end) was increased to accept the I.D. of the barrel. My thinking was that, essentially, I would be substituting the telescoped, nickel-silver tubing with bamboo, gaining more gentle transition, and I might even reduce overall weight through the ferruled area. Possibly, this design is not as strong as the Super-Z, yet on a short, light-line rod, it's quite strong enough.

I checked several other rod designs and discovered a few that showed an intentional increase in diameter across their ferrule areas. The apparent purpose was to create the faster, tip-action rod that I, too, like, but my adaptation was a little different and I wasn't quite sure what to expect. Rather than increasing my rod blank diameter throughout the entire length of the butt section, I was only adding a localized swell to accept the modified barrel. Maybe what I was designing would have no effect. If so, that would be fine, but at least I'd know what to do on my next attempt. On the other hand, if it were to produce a faster, tip-action rod (like those tapers I checked earlier), this would be what I wanted. Happily, that's exactly what I got, and the rod couldn't perform better.

Now, based on everything we've been taught about smooth transitions and uniform transfer of waveforms, this design should not work. In fact, we'd probably expect the rod's action to "collapse" at the ferrule. But that doesn't happen. To understand why not, first, let's consider the discussion on ferrules in Carmichael's *The Master's Guide* (my "bible" on rod-building in those days). According to Garrison, a ferrule is far more than an instrument to join rod sections together. Garrison explains that both its design and the material of which it is made are crucial to proper functioning—and therefore, to the action of the rod itself. There must be no weak part in the ferrule to bend or move as the butt transmits its flexed energy along the shaft during a casting stroke.

More importantly, however, Garrison also believed that, because the ferrule on a two-piece rod is located in an area that's already rather "stiff" (designed to handle high stress-loads), its presence does not appreciably interfere with the rod's action, particularly in rods up to 8' 9". In short, if my new ferrule design were of adequate strength, and if Garrison's position on the practical effect of ferrules on two-piece rods is correct, then I should expect the ferrule-adaptation on my "Brookie" to work—especially if I were also correct in assuming that building the cane up to meet the female barrel is just as good as building the female barrel down (with a reducing tube) to meet the cane.

In the end, this has turned out to be my favorite small-stream rod, and it deals with that little stream at my hunting camp perfectly. Since then, I've had equal success using this same ferrule design on smaller 2- and 3-weight rods. When the original rod was completed, it was test-cast by several attendees at the 1999 Eastern Rod Builder's Gathering, held in Boiling Springs, PA., and shortly after, Ron Barch wrote a feature article on the Gathering and my "Brookie" in his *Planing Form Newsletter*:

Taking to the lawn at the Eastern Rod-Builder's Gathering–1999

Eastern Rod-Maker's Gathering–1999

During the weekend the weather cooperated and everyone took to the lawn. Rods from midge to giant Speys were on the scene. One rod that stood out in the crowd was Tom Whittle's 5ft.10 inch "Brookie". One aspect of the rod that should be noted is its unique ferrule design which Tom calls a Maxwell/Robbins ferrule. The ferrule is made up of two separate tubes, a 10/64ths and a 12/64ths. This design is used to accommodate a large change at the middle.

During the weekend I spent a good deal of time casting this little gem and found it to be exceptional. The rod can toss a long or short line. What was most impressive to me was the rod's ability to develop line speed, which enables the angler to shoot low and under hanging limbs and sweepers. The specs follow on the next page. Thanks Tom [1]

In preparing this write-up on my "Brookie" rod, I revisited the Maxwell/Marinaro ferrule concept with Rick. While Rick and Maxwell discussed this ferrule design at length and on various occasions, Rick does not believe that Tom ever made rods incorporating the design, and doesn't recall handling a single Maxwell rod with this type ferrule. Bill and I would say the same for all rods by Vince that we've seen.

Rick, however, who knows a good thing when he sees it, has used the Maxwell/Marinaro ferrule on some of his own rods. In his designs, he found it particularly successful on shorter rods with relatively larger line weights—for example, a 7-foot, two-piece rod, for 6-weight line that he calls his "Steeves 726." Rick has also "resurrected" several rods for clients who had broken their rods at-or-below the female ferrule. Using this ferrule design, he was able to repair the rods without needing to undercut the cane to accept a standard Super-Z type ferrule. For some of those repairs, Rick believes the rod action was vastly improved.

What the "Brookie" rod is all about

A Not So Radical Example

Certainly, not all my taper designs are as radical as the "Brookie," and unless you can make your own ferrules, that type of experiment is beyond the reach of many builders. We mentioned that "tweaking" existing tapers can be highly rewarding, but in the following demonstration, I'll suggest something between an original design and the tweak. This project will use a fairly old rod design, one whose data needed to be updated from its original 6-inch stations to the more current 5-inch stations. But more than that, my tweak will transform a "bumpy" taper-line into a smooth, convex curve, and finally, convert a two-piece design into a three-piece model. Each of these alterations is exactly the kind of thing an amateur rod designer can do with a few guidelines and a little thinking.

Several years ago, at the Catskill Rodmakers Gathering, a fellow maker showed me a rod he had built. This was a 7-foot, two-piece design, but when I cast the rod what impressed me most was that, while it was lined with a WF 7-weight, it felt much more like a 5-weight. It's not every day that one comes across a 7-footer for a 7-weight line that actually feels good, and I was intrigued. "Whose taper?" I asked. "The guy says, "It's a Cross 'Sylph' that I got from Herter's book."

Herter's *Rod Building Manual and Manufacturer's Guide* (1953) credits the Cross, "Sylph," rod-taper information to "Harold C. Hollis, famed fisherman and author," who describes the rod as his favorite light, fly rod. However, the rod was originally designed by Wes Jordan while he was still working at Cross Rod & Tackle. From the book, *Wes Jordan–Profile of A Rodmaker* (1992) by Dick Spurr and Gloria Jordan, we know that Cross was founded in 1920 by William R. Forsyth and William Cross, with Jordan in charge of taper design and rod-making.

Jordan was an innovator in two-piece designs, breaking from the traditional, three-piece rods of his time. Apparently, he was trying to find a way to avoid the damage so many three-piece rods incurred at the upper ferrule when those sections were improperly disassembled. Jordan first offered a few 6 1/2-foot, two-piece designs, but these were not commercially successful—no doubt, simply because fly fishermen of the time were not ready for small, lightweight rods. Soon after, however, came the two-piece, 7-foot rod for HDH line, the prototype for the famous "Sylph."

The Cross Rod & Tackle Company's 1925 catalogue describes the "Sylph" as "extreme in power for so light a rod." In 1926, South Bend purchased Cross (acquiring both Jordan and the entire Cross line, including the "Sylph") and moved everything to their new Indiana location. South Bend continued to describe the "Sylph" rod as the lightest and sportiest fly rod in the Cross line in their 1927 catalogue.

Herter's *Manual* recommends an HDH line "even though you may think it too heavy." Sometimes it's difficult to convert the old, three-letter designations to our modern line nomenclature, but most rods built between the two World Wars were designed to use the HDH line—roughly the equivalent of a modern, DT 6-weight line. Because many rods can accommodate two line sizes handily, it's not surprising that the "Sylph," originally designed for a DT-6, would perform equally well with a WF-7.

I wanted to work with Jordan's design, but the taper information in Herter's book is given according to 6-inch station measurements—measured from the larger ends to the smaller. Also, allowing for a one-inch overlap at the ferrule, Herter locates the first stations 7 inches up from their butt ends. This was a mess! If I were to design the rod so it could be built on my modern planing form I'd have to rearrange Herter's information and establish "new" measurements corresponding to my 5-inch stations. Additionally, to express a rod's measurements from the tip down, I also needed to convert Herter's original taper to inches from the tip-top, using overall blank lengths of 42 inches. Therefore, those first, 7-inch stations in Herter's book would equal 42 minus 7, thus establishing that same point 35" from the section's upper end. Now, we're getting somewhere.

After plotting Herter's 6-inch taper information on the graph, we simply extrapolate the "new" strip dimensions at 5-inch stations and create a clean, new table of taper information. My accompanying graph shows Jordan's original taper line, but also reveals the straight-line taper (slope) for each section, drawn from high point to low.

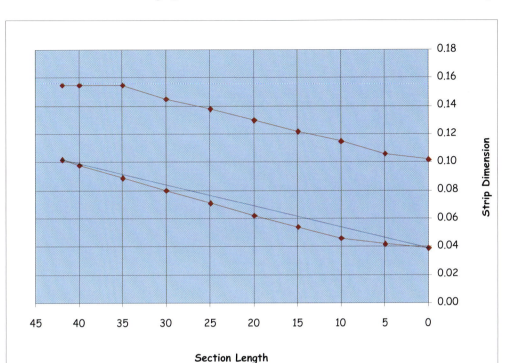

Graph of Cross "Sylph" taper. Converted from original, 6-inch stations to a 5-inch grid

Station	Butt	Tip
0	0.102	0.039
5	0.106	0.042
10	0.115	0.046
15	0.122	0.054
20	0.130	0.062
25	0.138	0.071
30	0.145	0.080
35	0.155	0.089
40	0.155	0.098
42	0.155	0.102

Chart for Cross "Sylph"

Looking at the original Cross taper—now shown in 5-inch stations—I saw a very flat taper line along the first 10 inches back from the tip, but producing a "hinge" just at the 10-inch mark. In fact, the taper actually fell below the slope line, forming a concave "hollow." The shape of this taper is not unlike many other tips I've modified, before and since. My intent in tweaking or revising the taper would be to convert its shape into a convex curve (relative to its straight slope). But there are a couple ways this might have been done: For one, I could have increased strip measurements at various stations, as needed, until all rose above the slope line, but it looked like that was going to create some pretty drastic changes in the section's overall proportions.

Still another way to get a convex taper into the tip (the better way, in this case) would be to start by reducing dimensions both at the beginning and at the end of the tip. By changing the half-dimension, strip measurement at the tip-top from 0.039" to 0.035", and the ferrule-end from 0.102" to 0.100", the entire slope-line would be shifted down on the graph paper. This alteration now revealed the entire taper above the slope-line and would allow me to make smaller and more manageable changes to get the convex shape I wanted. Overall, my reasoning was that, although I had reduced the section's thickness at both ends and slightly steepened its slope line, of far greater importance, I knew the finished rod would suffer no loss in action or speed because its new, convex shape would compensate by offering greater strength of its own than the original taper-line could provide.

The following chart shows the changes I made to the original taper data. Finally (and just for grins), because I remained impressed with the original rod I had cast in Roscoe, I built two tips to evaluate my design changes—one using the original, "Sylph" taper, and the other according to my revised, convex design.

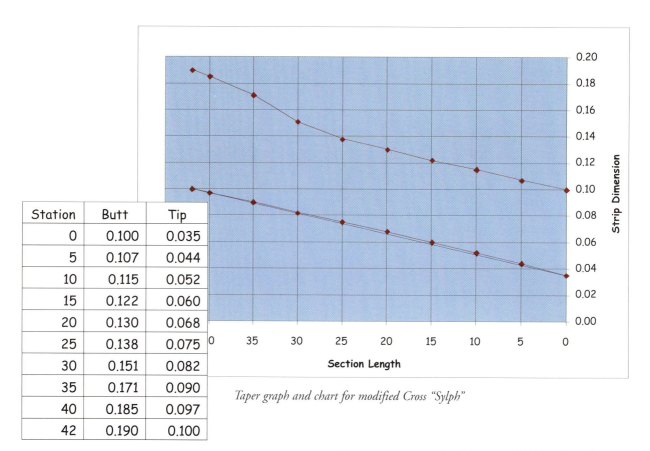

Station	Butt	Tip
0	0.100	0.035
5	0.107	0.044
10	0.115	0.052
15	0.122	0.060
20	0.130	0.068
25	0.138	0.075
30	0.151	0.082
35	0.171	0.090
40	0.185	0.097
42	0.190	0.100

Taper graph and chart for modified Cross "Sylph"

The butt section includes some minor changes from Jordan's prototype as well. First, the ferrule-end of the butt needed to correspond to the reduction at the larger end of the tip section (indicated above), so I down-sized the end of each butt strip by 0.002". Then, to eliminate the "hinge" in the original taper, and to provide a smoother transition of power through the butt and across the ferrule, I added 0.001" to the half-dimension of the first 5-inch station. The measurements from the 10- through the 30-inch stations were left unchanged. Lastly, because I wanted to see a swelled butt, I began this at the 30-inch station (a few inches out from the cork grip). This change wasn't made because I thought I needed to alter the rod's action, but only for its aesthetic effect.

Upon completing the rod, I was very pleased with the action of the new, convex tip. While the original tip also casts well, the new, convex tip develops line speed more easily and has that little extra quickness (and "kick") at the end of the cast that I prefer. My convex tip is more responsive than the "Sylph" original, and apparently allows a much more efficient transfer of energy—not that any of this came as a surprise, but I was highly pleased to see my design ideas borne out.

Other rod-builders may have raised their eyebrows at my reductions to the tip's end-dimensions, still wondering why I didn't just alter a few station dimensions between. But, the longer I work with convex taper design and the more familiar I become with my graphs, the more comfortable I am in making adjustments with predictable results. I started tweaking tapers after completing only a few rods, so the changes I made to Wes Jordan's 7-weight "Sylph" had the benefit of many previous successes and failures—those 44 rods that I made earlier, most of which were converted to convex tapers.

Please don't misunderstand me—I would never have the audacity to put myself up against Wes Jordan as a designer. Although my design is different from his, I am not saying that it's necessarily "better." My changes were meant to address a different preference for the rod's action—certainly better for me, even if not in some absolute sense. But this is what all designers try to do. What's really interesting is that a rod built on a dry-fly taper developed nearly ninety years ago can still be pleasant enough to win attention, and then, with some changes on the graph, become even more responsive.

I'm also thinking how fascinating it would have been to sit in on a discussion between Wes and Vince on rod design. Wes, much like Vince and the rest of us, developed rod tapers through a combination of intuition and trial-and-error. For both men, once a successful design was developed, it was a simple matter to change its action by making slight variations here or there. From *Profile of A Rodmaker* we read Jordan as he explains his somewhat empirical testing methods:

> The tapers that I eventually settled on for use in production were carefully checked, using a graph that charted each rod's reaction to different amounts of weights suspended from the tip. In this manner I could detect flat spots or places where the rod bent at too sharp an angle. These had to be eliminated, for either symptom could cause breakage under strain. I also used this technique to check rods that were sent to me for repair, and it proved to be of great value.[2]

A few years ago, I had my modified "Sylph" rod at a gathering of rod-makers on Spruce Creek. This small, informal, annual event is organized by Tom McDonnell of Pittsburgh, and that year, Jim Abraham (also from Pittsburgh) was in attendance. Apparently, Jim fell in love with my rod, but because he was planning a trip to New Zealand and needed the portability, he asked if I could build the rod for him in a three-piece configuration.

Frankly, when I started the three-piece version, I fully expected to scrap at least one rod before being satisfied, but I told Jim I would try to get one out for him within the few months remaining before he left on his trip. This was a tricky assignment because a 7-foot, three-piece rod doesn't provide much room to develop proper shapes into the sections, and convex curves are especially critical through the tip and mid-sections. Further, the butt section of this little rod reveals only 15 inches of cane between its ferrule and the grip—a pretty limited space to work-up a convex shape.

Station	Butt	Mid	Tip
0	0.123	0.077	0.035
5	0.130	0.088	0.045
10	0.138	0.097	0.054
15	0.146	0.105	0.061
20	0.171	0.112	0.068
25	0.180	0.119	0.074
28	0.185	0.123	0.077

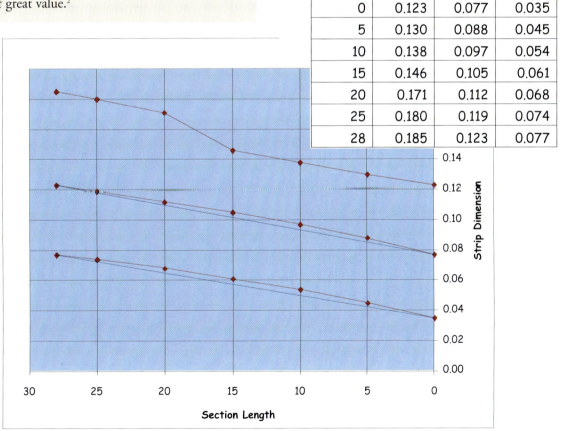

Graph and taper chart for the 7-foot, three-piece version

Herter's Manual and Profile of a Rodmaker with author's rods

Hoping that my three-piecer would perform at least as well as its two-piece predecessor, I was pleasantly surprised to find that my first design attempt produced a rod that was even better. Could it be that Vince's preference for three-piece rods (with each section performing its own job) applies not only to longer rods, but to shorter ones as well? Because of the limitations of my milling machine and dip-tube, all my rods greater than 7 feet had been built in three-pieces, while rods of 7 feet or less were in the more standard two-piece configuration. After my "New Zealand Experiment," however, I think I'd better find time to play around with three-piece versions even for those shorter, two-piece rods.

In all, I've tried to show how it's possible to work with Vince's method of visualizing a rod's taper and to demonstrate that convex shapes can be manipulated in a variety of ways to attain an equal variety of results. Old, "Doc" Holden would have loved the idea, I'm sure, especially because his own enthusiasm for the convex taper remains alive and well, and because we're continuing his advice to become as involved with design as with construction. Crompton, too, held strongly to the convex shape, even though he seems not to have met with the same measure of success as did Garrison or Marinaro. But that's not a reflection on convex design theory, only on Crompton's particular manipulation of it. Readers might be surprised to hear that Garrison's tapers, were largely of the convex design, for his work has never really been described in these terms. Yet, when graphed in the way Marinaro recommends, many Garrison tips will reveal exactly the convex (or "double-taper") shapes that Holden called for back in 1920. And Vince, too, capitalized on all that same, early advice.

My point, throughout, is that experimentation with taper design remains wide open for anyone who wishes to give it a try. It's far from true that the range of possible rod designs is exhausted—and especially so when you start to fool around with the endless variety of fair curves and convex shapes that can be devised. In what follows, Bill and I will offer just a few of our more successful designs, all of which resulted from the pictorial method of design and that old, empirical method of trial-and-error. Don't be duped by our modern age into thinking that only engineering wizards and computer-nerds can design a fly rod. It just ain't so—other nerds can do it too!

Tapers by Whittle and Harms

The following charts illustrate a few examples of some of Bill's and my favorite rods. These are all designed with the convex taper and are either modifications of some existing rod or are entirely of our own devising. The rods may be built by anyone who chooses, but our purpose here is not so much to provide rods for reproduction as to offer a larger selection of starting-points for those who would like to develop their own convex taper designs. With similar intentions, the full range of Vince's tapers is contained in our Appendix.

Whittle: 5' 10" two-piece, 4 weight "Brookie"
(Maxwell/Marinaro/Robbins ferrule)

Station	Strip Thickness		Guides	
	Butt	Tip	Tip	Butt
0	0.091	0.031	4 3/8"	2 1/2"
5	0.093	0.042	9 3/8"	9 1/2"
10	0.099	0.050	15"	
15	0.106	0.057	21 1/2"	
20	0.114	0.064	28 3/8"	
25	0.160	0.070		
30	0.180	0.076		
35	0.187	0.080		

Whittle: 6' 6" two-piece, 4 weight

Station	Strip Thickness		Guides	
	Butt	Tip	Tip	Butt
0	0.094	0.031	4 3/8"	2 3/4"
5	0.105	0.042	9 1/4"	8 3/4"
10	0.107	0.051	14 3/4"	15 3/4"
15	0.117	0.059	21 1/8"	
20	0.128	0.063	27 5/8"	
25	0.132	0.070	34 5/8"	
30	0.158	0.081		
35	0.177	0.087		
39	0.183	0.094		

Whittle: 7' two-piece, 4 weight

Station	Strip Thickness		Guides	
	Butt	Tip	Tip	Butt
0	0.094	0.031	4 3/4"	2 3/4"
5	0.102	0.042	10 1/8"	10 1/2"
10	0.110	0.050	16"	18 3/4"
15	0.118	0.058	22 1/4"	
20	0.125	0.065	27 7/8"	
25	0.133	0.071	35 5/8"	
30	0.146	0.078		
35	0.170	0.085		
40	0.186	0.092		
42	0.189	0.094		

Another rod from Tom's bench

photo by Tom Whittle

Whittle: 7' 6" three-piece, 4 weight

Station	Strip Thickness			Guides		
	Butt	Mid	Tip	Tip	Mid	Butt
0	0.120	0.078	0.033	4 1/2"	1 5/8"	4 1/4"
5	0.126	0.088	0.045	9 3/4"	8 5/8"	
10	0.134	0.096	0.053	16"	16 5/8"	
15	0.141	0.104	0.059	22 1/2"	25 5/8"	
20	0.159	0.110	0.065			
25	0.179	0.114	0.072			
30	0.187	0.119	0.077			

Whittle: 7' 9" three-piece, 5 weight

Station	Strip Thickness			Guides		
	Butt	Mid	Tip	Tip	Mid	Butt
0	0.125	0.088	0.035	4 1/2"	1 5/8"	4 1/4"
5	0.131	0.095	0.046	10"	8 3/4"	
10	0.136	0.101	0.054	16 3/8"	16 7/8"	
15	0.142	0.108	0.063	23 7/8"	26"	
20	0.167	0.113	0.070			
25	0.181	0.119	0.079			
30	0.186	0.123	0.086			
31	0.187	0.124	0.087			

Whittle: 7' three-piece, 7 weight

Station	Strip Thickness			Guides		
	Butt	Mid	Tip	Butt	Mid	Tip
0	0.123	0.077	0.035	4 3/4"	1 5/8"	4 1/2"
5	0.130	0.088	0.045	10 1/8"	8 5/8"	
10	0.138	0.097	0.054	16"	16 1/8"	
15	0.146	0.105	0.061	22 1/2"	24"	
20	0.171	0.112	0.068			
25	0.180	0.119	0.074			
28	0.185	0.123	0.077			

A rod from Whittle's bench

Harms: 6' one-piece, 4 weight

Station	Strip	Guides
0	0.027	4 1/4"
5	0.036	9"
10	0.043	14 1/4"
15	0.050	20 1/4"
20	0.058	26 3/4"
25	0.067	33 3/4"
30	0.075	41 1/4"
35	0.082	50"
40	0.088	
45	0.096	
50	0.103	
55	0.109	
60	0.116	
65	0.124	

Harms: 7' two-piece, 4 weight

Station	Strip Thickness		Guides	
	Butt	Tip	Butt	Tip
0	0.090	0.031	@ferrule	4 1/2"
5	0.098	0.039	9 1/2"	9 1/2"
10	0.108	0.048	18 1/2"	15 3/4"
15	0.117	0.056		22 1/4"
20	0.121	0.062		29 1/4"
25	0.129	0.068		38 1/4"
30	0.133	0.075		
35	0.140	0.082		
40		0.088		
42		0.089		

A couple rods from Harms's bench

photo by Michael Simon

Harms: 7' 6" two-piece, 5 weight (quad version)

Station	Strip Thickness		Guides	
	Butt	Tip	Butt	Tip
0	0.092	0.030	@ferrule	4"
5	0.100	0.038	10"	8 1/2"
10	0.108	0.046	20"	14"
15	0.114	0.054		20"
20	0.120	0.060		26 1/2"
25	0.127	0.065		33"
30	0.133	0.072		39 3/4"
35	0.138	0.078		
40	0.143	0.085		
45		0.091		

Harms: 7' 6" two-piece, 5 weight

Station	Strip Thickness		Guides	
	Butt	Tip	Butt	Tip
0	0.099	0.032	@ferrule	4"
5	0.107	0.041	10"	8 1/2"
10	0.116	0.050	20"	14"
15	0.123	0.058		20"
20	0.130	0.064		26 1/2"
25	0.138	0.070		33"
30	0.146	0.077		39 3/4"
35	0.152	0.084		
40	0.157	0.091		
45		0.098		

Harms: 8' two-piece, 5 weight

Station	Strip Thickness		Guides	
	Butt	Tip	Butt	Tip
0	0.106	0.033	@ferrule	4 1/2"
5	0.115	0.042	11 1/2"	9 1/2"
10	0.122	0.052	22 1/2"	15"
15	0.127	0.059		21 1/4"
20	0.133	0.066		27 3/4"
25	0.138	0.072		34 3/4"
30	0.147	0.079		42 1/2"
35	0.157	0.088		
40	0.165	0.096		
45		0.103		
48		0.106		

Harms: 8' three-piece, 5 weight

Station	Strip Thickness			Guides		
	Butt	Mid	Tip	Butt	Mid	Tip
0	0.126	0.080	0.033	7 1/2"	4 1/2"	4 1/2"
5	0.133	0.090	0.042		11 3/4"	9 1/2"
10	0.137	0.097	0.051		19 3/4"	15"
15	0.146	0.105	0.058		28 1/2"	21 1/4"
20	0.157	0.111	0.065			27 3/4"
25	0.168	0.118	0.072			
30		0.125	0.078			
32		0.126	0.080			

Harms: 8' three-piece, 5 weight (quad version)

Station	Strip Thickness			Guides		
	Butt	Mid	Tip	Butt	Mid	Tip
0	0.116	0.074	0.032	7 1/2"	4 1/2"	4 1/2"
5	0.120	0.083	0.039		11 3/4"	9 1/2"
10	0.125	0.090	0.047		19 3/4"	15"
15	0.133	0.098	0.054		28 1/2"	21 1/4"
20	0.143	0.103	0.061			27 3/4"
25	0.151	0.110	0.067			
30		0.115	0.073			
32		0.116	0.074			

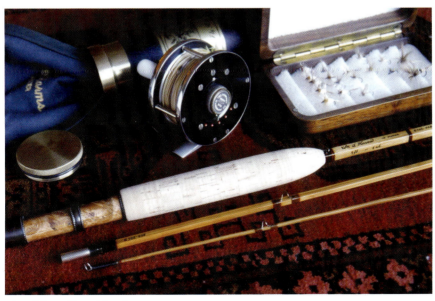

A rod from Harms' bench

NOTES

PREFACE

1 The public was first informed of Vince's rod-making in Charlie Fox's *Advanced Bait Casting* (New York: Putnam, 1950), p. 85. Marinaro's own first account, however, was in his *In The Ring of The Rise* (New York: Crown, 1976), pp. 39-60.

2 *The American Fly Fisher: Journal of The American Museum of Fly Fishing* Vol. 28, No. 1 (Winter, 2002). Schullery's article appears on pp. 2-11; Herd's on pp. 12-17; and Cameron's on pp. 18-25.

3 John McDonald, ed., *The Complete Fly Fisherman: The Notes And Letters of Theodore Gordon* (New York: Charles Scribner's Sons, 1947), p. *ix*.

4 Ibid, pp. *xvii-xviii*.

5 Ibid, p. *xix*.

6 Paul Schullery, *American Fly Fishing* (New York: The Lyons Press, 1987), pp. 90-110.

7 Paul Schullery, "History and Mr. Gordon," *The American Fly Fisher*, Vol. 28, No. 1 (Winter, 2002), p. 3.

8 Ken Cameron, "Rigor Without Mortis," *The American Fly Fisher*, Vol. 28, No. 1 (Winter, 2002), p. 22.

9 McDonald, *The Complete Fly Fisherman*, p. ix.

CHAPTER 1

1 Howell Raines, *Fly Fishing Through The Midlife Crisis* (New York: William Morrow, 1993), p. 155.

2 Vincent C. Marinaro, *In The Ring of The Rise* (New York: Crown, 1976), p. 42, and PFFMA "Marinaro Collection," personal letter to Kevin Leibold, February 3, 1974.

3 Marinaro, *In The Ring of the Rise*, p. 42-44.

Chapter 2

1 Vincent C. Marinaro, *In the Ring of The Rise* (New York: Crown, 1976), p 42.

2 Perry Frazer, *Amateur Rodmaking* (1st edition, 1914; reprinted, New York: Macmillan, 1939), p. 32.

3 Harlan Major, *Salt Water Fishing Tackle* (New York: Funk and Wagnall, 1939), p. 207-208.

4 Marinaro, *In The Ring of The Rise*, p. 45.

5 George Parker Holden, *The Idyl of The Split Bamboo* (1st edition, 1920; reprinted, Lyon, Mississippi: Derrydale Press, 1993), p. 28.

6 Ibid., p. 28-30.

7 Hoagy Carmichael, *A Master's Guide to Building A Bamboo Fly Rod* (New York: Martha's Glen, 1977), p. 33.

8 Holden, *The Idyl of The Split Bamboo*, p. 70.

9 George Leonard Herter, *Professional Glass And Split-Bamboo Rod Building Manual And Manufacturer's Guide* (1st edition, 1949; no publisher), 1958, p. 21.

10 Ibid., p. 22.

11 Holden, *The Idyl of The Split Bamboo*, p. 92-93.

12 Robert Crompton, "The Five-Strip Rod," *1938 Fishing Annual*, p. 61.

13 Robert Crompton, "Measuring Fishing Rod Action," *Sports Afield*, October, 1937, p. 18.

Chapter 3

1 Norm Shires and Jim Gilford, *Limestone Legends* (Harrisburg, Pennsylvania: Stackpole, 1997), pp. 50-51.

2 Paul Schullery, *Royal Coachman* (New York: Simon and Schuster, 1999), pp. 60-76.

3 This little stream, located about 12 miles west of Harrisburg, is among the shortest of our limestone creeks and its flow accommodated only two mills. Both were built in the early 1700s, but their buildings, dams and ponds have long since faded into history. Two limestone houses, however, built by the original property owner, remain in fine condition in a little glade along the stream.

4 Shires and Gilford, *Limestone Legends*, p. 82.

5 Vincent Marinaro, *A Modern Dry Fly Code*, 2nd ed. (New York: Crown, 1970), pp. x-xi.

6 Shires and Gilford, *Limestone Legends*, pp. 93-95.

7 Marinaro, *A Modern Dry Fly Code*, 2nd ed., pp. 52-54.

Chapter 4

1 A. J. Campbell, *Classic And Antique Fly-Fishing Tackle* (New York: Lyons and Burford, 1997), p. 28.

2 James A. Henshall, *Book of The Black Bass* (Cincinnati, Ohio: Stewart and Kidd, 1904), p. 23.

3 Ernest Schwiebert, *Trout* (New York: Dutton, 1984), pp. 924, 929.

4 Genio Scott, *Fishing in American Waters* (1st edition, 1869; reprinted, Secaucus, New Jersey: Castle Books, 1989), p. 155.

5 Campbell, *Classic Fly-Fishing Tackle*, p. 28.

6 George Leonard Herter, *Professional Glass And Bamboo Rod Building Manual And Manufacturer's Guide*, (1st edition, 1949: no publisher), 1958, pp. 7-8.

7 *Charles* Fox, *Advanced Baitcasting* (New York: Putnam, 1950), pp. 89-90.

8 Perry Frazer, *Amateur Rodmaking* (1st edition, 1914; reprinted, New York: Macmillan, 1939), p. 141.

9 Campbell, *Classic Fly-Fishing Tackle*, pp. 28, 33.

10 We want to thank John Zwierzyna, Senior Curator of Military and Industrial History at the Pennsylvania State Museum, who was both kind and accommodating in giving us access to the Phillippe rod. John retrieved all relevant information from the museum's archives, including several photographs, and provided us with a private room and all the time we needed to do our work.

11 Schwiebert, *Trout*, p. 924.

12 Herter, *Rod Building Manual*, p. 8.

13 T. S. Morrell, "Making Split Bamboo Rods–Amateur Work," *American Angler,* Vol. 3. No .17 (April, 1883). The article as we find it is reprinted in *The American Fly Fisher*, Vol. 13, No. 3 (Summer, 1987), pp. 4-7.

14 Scott, *Fishing in American Waters*, p. 173.

15 Henry P. Wells, *Fly-Rods and Fly-Tackle* (1st edition, 1885; reprinted, Lyon, Mississippi: Derrydale Press, 1994), pp. 102, 105 and 161.

16 Fred Mather, *My Angling Friends* (New York: Forest and Stream Publishing, 1901), pp. 163.

17 Morrell, *The American Fly Fisher*, p. 6.

18 Wells, *Fly-Rods and Fly-Tackle*, p. 223.

19 Ibid., p. 224.

20 Ibid., pp. 227-228.

21 Ibid., pp. 217-218.

22 Martin J. Keane, *Classic Rod And Rodmakers* (New York: Winchester Press, 1976), p. 19.

23 Campbell, *Classic Fly-Fishing Tackle*, p. 41.

24 A.J. Campbell, "C. E. Wheeler and His Angling Friends," *Fishing Collectibles Magazine*, Vol. 9, No. 2 (Fall, 1997), p.17.

25 James A. Henshall, "Inventing the Split-Bamboo Rod," *Outing*, Vol. 40, No. 2 (May, 1902). The article as we find it is reprinted in *The American Fly Fisher*, Vol. 13, No. 3 (Summer, 1987), pp. 21- 25.

CHAPTER 5

1 Dan Brenan, letter to Sparse Grey Hackle, February 23, 1947.

2 William N. Fenton, "Dan Brenan: The Forgotten Master," *Rod & Reel*, November-December, 1984, pp. 36-39. Brenan, in a January 6, 1955 letter to Sparse offers a glimpse at his background: "If you plan to give me brief mention, all I can say is that I dabbled as an amateur, following the Dr. Holden doctrines, from 1922 to 1933, when I opened up as a pro, following the imposition of the Roosevelt New-Deal regime, which put the quietus on my old business investments. The Gov't closed me up a few months before Pearl Harbor and I never went back in the business." (Apparently, Sparse was working on an article for *Sports Illustrated* and needed background information on a few contemporary makers. A great number of Brenan's letters also relate the experiences of his son, Bill, who remained involved with the rod-making industry until the late 1940s.)

3 Brenan, undated letter to Sparse.

4 Brenan, letter to Sparse, February 23, 1947.

5 Lyle Dickerson, letter to Sparse, February 9, 1947.

6 Robert Crompton, undated letter.

7 Crompton, undated letter.

8 *Guild Newsletter,* March 6, 1947.

9 *Guild Newsletter,* February 19, 1947.

10 Charles K. Fox, *Advanced Bait Casting* (New York: Putnam, 1950), pp. x-xi.

11 Sparse, letter to Vince, October, 1949.

12 Vince Marinaro, response to Sparse's October, 1949 letter, undated.

13 Fox, *Advanced Bait Casting*, pp. 84-85.

14 George Leonard Herter, *Rod Building Manual And Manufacturer's Guide*, 1958, pp. 70-71.

15 Sparse, letter to Vince, October, 1949. (Our search through the Catskill Fly-Fishing Center and Museum collection revealed two correspondences to Sparse from the U.S. Forest Products Laboratories addressing the advisability of applying heat to wood and other fibrous structures. We found two additional letters on the topic from F.A. McClure—the man who, from the early 1930s onward, first and most completely studied "Tonkin" cane and assigned the species its scientific name, *Arundinaria Amabilis.*)

16 Ibid.

17 Ibid.

Chapter 6

1 Roy Darlingtorf, "The Visit," *The Flyfishers* (a publication of The Fly-Fishers Club of London), Summer, 1991, pp. 28-29.

2 Gordon Mackie (as quoted by Darlingtorf in *The Flyfishers*), p. 30.

3 Darlingtorf, *The Flyfishers*, p. 30.

4 Jimmy Carter, *An Outdoor Journal* (New York: Bantam, 1988), p. 71.

5 Ibid.

Chapter 7

1 Gordon Wickstrom, "Vince Marinaro: On Point of Balance," *The American Fly-Fisher*, Vol. 26, No. 2 (Spring, 2000), pp. 12-13.

2 Vincent Marinaro, *Pennsylvania Angler*, January, 1953, p. 29.

3 Ibid, p. 30.

4 Ibid, p. 22.

5 R.E. Milward, *Bamboo: Fact, Fiction and Flyrods* (Vancouver, Canada: Bob Milward Bamboo Fly Rods, 2001), p. 13.

6 Marinaro, *Pennsylvania Angler*, pp. 23, 29.

Chapter 8

1 George Parker Holden, *The Idyl of The Split Bamboo* (1st edition, 1920; reprinted, Lyon, Mississippi: Derrydale Press, 1993), pp. 102, 110-11.

2 Vincent C. Marinaro, *In the Ring of the Rise* (New York: Crown, 1976), pp. 59-60.

APPENDIX

Included below, are all of Marinaro's known tapers. These are organized by year, from earliest to most recent. All measurements have had the varnish thickness subtracted. Butt sections show tapers only to the first cork on the grip.

1944: 8' 6" three-piece, 7 weight

Station	Strip Dimension			Guides		
	Butt	Mid	Tip	Butt	Mid	Tip
0	0.138	0.090	0.038	9"	2 7/8"	4 1/2"
5	0.143	0.099	0.049		10 5/8"	9"
10	0.151	0.108	0.056		19 1/4"	14 5/8"
15	0.158	0.116	0.063		29 5/8"	21 1/2"
20	0.165	0.122	0.070			29 1/4"
25		0.128	0.078			
30		0.134	0.084			
34		0.138	0.090			

1947: 6' 6" two-piece bait casting rod (Straggered ferrel with a butt of 27" and a tip of 51".)

Station	Strip Dimension		Guides	
	Butt	Tip	Butt	Tip
0	0.134	0.042		9 1/8"
5	0.145	0.052		17 3/8"
10	0.156	0.064		26 1/8"
15	0.168	0.075		36 1/4"
20	0.179	0.084		46 3/8"
25		0.093		
30		0.102		
35		0.110		
40		0.114		
45		0.122		
50		0.131		
51		0.132		

1971: 6' 6" two-piece, 4 weight

	Strip Dimension		Guides	
Station	Butt	Tip	Butt	Tip
0	0.086	0.032	6 1/2"	5 3/4"
5	0.092	0.040	16 1/8"	11 5/8"
10	0.098	0.046		18 5/8"
15	0.105	0.053		26 5/8"
20	0.111	0.060		35 1/2"
25	0.115	0.068		
30	0.120	0.073		
35		0.082		
39		0.085		

1971: 7' 6" two-piece, 5 weight

	Strip Dimension		Guides	
Station	Butt	Tip	Butt	Tip
0	0.100	0.030	6"	5"
5	0.107	0.044	15 1/4"	11"
10	0.114	0.054	24 5/8"	17 1/8"
15	0.121	0.061		24 1/8"
20	0.127	0.066		31 1/2"
25	0.129	0.071		40"
30	0.130	0.080		
35	0.133	0.087		
40		0.093		
45		0.100		

1971: 8' three-piece, 4/5 weight

	Strip Dimension			Guides		
Station	Butt	Mid	Tip	Butt	Mid	Tip
0	0.119	0.080	0.031	10 1/2"	2 3/4"	4 1/2"
5	0.124	0.087	0.041		12"	11 5/8"
10	0.128	0.094	0.050		21 5/8"	19 5/8"
15	0.132	0.100	0.056		31 1/8"	28 1/2"
20	0.137	0.106	0.062			
25	0.187	0.111	0.069			
30		0.115	0.076			
32		0.118	0.078			

1971: 9' three-piece, 5 weight

	Strip Dimension			Guides		
Station	Butt	Mid	Tip	Butt	Mid	Tip
0	0.127	0.082	0.038	8 1/2"	3 3/4"	6 1/8"
5	0.133	0.092	0.046		13 3/4"	12 7/8"
10	0.140	0.100	0.053		23 5/8"	20 3/4"
15	0.147	0.105	0.059		33 5/8"	29 3/4"
20	0.153	0.112	0.064			
25	0.161	0.117	0.070			
30		0.122	0.076			
35		0.126	0.081			
36		0.127	0.082			

1976: "Guppy" 6' 6" two-piece, 4 weight

	Strip Thickness		Guides	
Station	Butt	Tip	Butt	Tip
0	0.083	0.029	3"	6 1/8"
5	0.089	0.043	12"	13 5/8"
10	0.095	0.050		22 1/4"
15	0.102	0.056		31 5/8"
20	0.109	0.060		
25	0.112	0.065		
30	0.118	0.074		
35		0.082		
39		0.083		

1976: 9' three-piece, 6 weight

	Strip Dimension			Guides		
Station	Butt	Mid	Tip	Butt	Mid	Tip
0	0.130	0.087	0.036	10"	6"	5 5/8"
5	0.140	0.096	0.049		14"	12 5/8"
10	0.149	0.104	0.056		23"	21 1/4"
15	0.156	0.110	0.061		33 3/4"	31 1/2"
20	0.163	0.117	0.067			
25	0.166	0.122	0.074			
30		0.126	0.080			
35		0.129	0.086			
36		0.130	0.087			

1976: "Penns Creek" 9' 2" three-piece, 7 weight (A 6-weight line is recommended.)

	Strip Dimension			Guides		
Station	Butt	Mid	Tip	Butt	Mid	Tip
0	0.129	0.085	0.035	10 1/4"	5 7/8"	6 1/8"
5	0.138	0.096	0.046		15 1/2"	13 1/4"
10	0.148	0.103	0.052		25 1/2"	21 7/8"
15	0.154	0.110	0.058		34 5/8"	32 1/8"
20	0.160	0.116	0.065			
25	0.164	0.121	0.071			
30		0.124	0.077			
35		0.127	0.083			
36.5		0.128	0.084			

1976: "Salmo" 9' 6" two-piece, 8 weight

	Strip Dimension		Guides	
Station	Butt	Tip	Butt	Tip
0	0.129	0.036	6 1/8"	5 3/4"
5	0.135	0.049	16 3/8"	12 3/4"
10	0.141	0.058	27 5/8"	21 7/8"
15	0.148	0.067		32"
20	0.157	0.072		42 1/4"
25	0.165	0.079		52 1/2"
30	0.168	0.087		
35	0.170	0.093		
40		0.103		
45		0.113		
50		0.120		
55		0.126		
57		0.129		

1977: 8' three-piece, 4 weight

Station	Strip Dimension			Guides		
	Butt	Mid	Tip	Butt	Mid	Tip
0	0.119	0.076	0.030	5 1/4"	5 3/4"	6 3/4"
5	0.124	0.083	0.041		15 3/4"	13 1/2"
10	0.127	0.091	0.051		26 5/8"	20 3/8"
15	0.128	0.099	0.058			28 1/2"
20	0.132	0.107	0.066			
25		0.114	0.070			
30		0.118	0.075			
32		0.119	0.076			

1977: "Salar" 14' 6" three-piece, 8 weight (Two-handed rod.)

Station	Strip Dimension				Guides		
	Butt	Mid	Tip (1)	Tip (2)	Butt	Mid	Tip
0	0.218	0.150	0.050	0.060	5 1/2"	6"	6 1/2"
5	0.230	0.160	0.062	0.071	17 1/2"	17 1/4"	13 3/4"
10	0.238	0.169	0.072	0.080		28"	21 3/4"
15	0.245	0.177	0.084	0.087		39"	30 3/4"
20	0.250	0.182	0.092	0.094		50"	40"
25	0.257	0.189	0.102	0.101			50 7/8"
30	0.261	0.193	0.112	0.109			
35	0.264	0.198	0.120	0.116			
40		0.202	0.130	0.125			
45		0.206	0.138	0.133			
50		0.210	0.143	0.140			
55		0.212	0.146	0.143			
58		0.213	0.147	0.144			

1978: "Guppy Jr." 6' two-piece, 2 weight (A 2nd version was finished by Hoagy Carmichael in 1985.)

| | Strip Dimension || Guides (Vince) || Guides (Hoagy) ||
Station	Butt	Tip	Butt	Tip	Butt	Tip
0	0.062	0.029	9"	7 1/4"	@ferrule	5 7/8"
5	0.070	0.038		15 1/2"	7 1/2"	11 1/8"
10	0.077	0.045		24 3/8"	14 1/2"	16 3/8"
15	0.082	0.050		33 1/4"		21 5/8"
20	0.086	0.053				27"
25	0.090	0.056				32 1/2"
30	0.094	0.058				
35		0.060				
36		0.061				

1979: "Penobscot" 9' 6" three-piece, 8 weight (Reel seat includes a fighting-butt extension.)

| | Strip Dimension ||| Guides |||
Station	Butt	Mid	Tip	Butt	Mid	Tip
0	0.165	0.105	0.042	8 3/8"	6"	3 1/4"
5	0.175	0.114	0.052		15"	9 1/4"
10	0.183	0.121	0.061		25"	16"
15	0.191	0.129	0.069		35 3/8"	22 5/8"
20	0.197	0.137	0.077			29 5/8"
25	0.204	0.145	0.084			37 1/4"
30		0.152	0.092			
35		0.160	0.100			
38		0.164	0.105			

INDEX

A

Abbott, Tim, 21
Abercrombie & Fitch, 28
aesthetics, 45, 83, 188
alkaline, 74, 136, 167
American Angler, 96, 284
American Fly Fisher, The, ix, 159, 282, 284, 285
Anderson, Don, 19
Arend, Bill, 195, 262
Aroner, Mark, 21, 133
Au Sable, vi, 9, 68, 76, 77

B

bait-casting, 76, 122, 124
    bait-casting rod, 76, 122, 124
    midget-plugging, 121, 122
    plug-fishing, 121
    spin-casting, 31, 132
balance, 21, 37, 39, 47, 49, 54, 286
Baltimore, 59, 60, 222
Baltz, Tom, 11
bamboo
    bound water, 177
    Calcutta, 35, 101
    cell structure, 128
    cross-linking, 177
    culm, 2, 13, 36, 92, 101, 102, 171, 172, 173, 177, 179, 181
    Embargo, 31, 55, 132, 172
    enamel, 4, 100, 101, 172, 179, 180, 181, 194
    free water, 177
    heat-treating, 22, 127, 128, 130, 173, 174, 175, 177
        cellular damage, 128
        discoloration, 167, 174, 175
        flaming, 130, 174
    humidity, 176, 177, 182
    inter-nodal, 172, 173
    Malacca cane, 101
    power-fibers, 101, 128, 177
    pre-Embargo, 55
    seasoned bamboo, 177, 207
    stress-splits, 166
    Tonkin, 30, 35, 36, 132, 285
bamboo shaft, 90, 92
Barch, Ron, 19, 20, 268
    The Planing Form, 3, 19, 40, 105, 165, 175, 176, 199, 200, 216, 217, 221, 264
Barnes, George, 19
    How to Make Bamboo Fly Rods, 19
Basehoar, Frank, 137, 138, 157
Bashline, Jim, 73
Beaverkill, vi, 222
Beck, Barry, viii, 13, 148, 149, 219
Beck, Cathy, 73, 148
Bennett, Bill, 69, 78
Bergman, Ray, vi
Berkshires, 59
Big Hunting Creek, 222
Big Spring, 9, 61, 62, 63, 64, 66, 68, 71, 74, 133
binding machine, 4, 30, 31, 130, 131, 165, 183
    binder, 128, 131, 163, 165, 182, 183
Biondo, Mike, 21
Black, George, 132
    Casting A Spell, 132
Black, Jack, 63
Bokstrom, Jon, 19
Bonny Brook quarry, 12, 13, 71
Boyd, Harry, 21
Brackett, Glenn, 133
Brandin, Per, 21, 133
Brenan, Dan, 110, 111, 114, 116, 285
brook trout, 9, 60, 61, 62, 66, 113, 125, 265
Brooks, Joe, 73
brown trout, 62, 120, 124
builder's notes, xiv
Bureau, Jim, 21

Index 293

C

calibers, 39, 96
Cameron, Ken, ix, 282
Camp David, 146, 148, 149
Campbell, A. J., 83, 85, 89, 91, 106, 284
    Fly Fishing Tackle, 83, 85
Cape Breton, 149
Carlson, Sam, 17
Carmichael, Hoagy B., vii, 19, 111, 128, 129, 263
    A Master's Guide to Building a Bamboo Fly Rod, ix, 19, 30, 263, 283
Carpenter, Walt, 21, 133
President Jimmy Carter, 146
    Rosalynn, 146, 147, 149
casting
    back-cast, 97, 178, 204, 228, 236, 241, 244
    bounce, 204, 205, 206, 228, 237, 241, 245, 253
    casting stroke, 216, 249, 252, 268
    catapult, 217, 228
    haul, 62, 225, 229, 232, 236, 237, 240, 241, 245, 249, 252, 254
    kick, 42, 97, 213, 244, 249, 253, 256, 264, 272
    lightness in the hand, 223
    load, 51, 187, 196, 204, 205, 216, 232, 236, 244, 248, 249, 254
    loop, xi, 213, 223, 225, 228, 229, 232, 233, 236, 237, 240, 241, 245, 248, 249, 252, 253, 255
    pick up, 132, 244
    puddle cast, 141, 142
    shoot, 35, 198, 224, 225, 238, 240, 252, 254, 265, 269
    wrist-action, 232, 236, 240, 252
Catskill, x, xi, 13, 19, 23, 59, 109, 111, 135, 171, 222, 224, 260, 270, 285
Cattanach, Wayne, 19, 20, 21
Cedar Run, 9, 62, 68, 70, 74
Chandler, Leon, 73
Chang, Jimmy, 22
China Embargo, 132, 172
Chubb, Thomas, 17
Civil War, 64, 88
Colorado, 18
computer, 192, 200, 203, 259, 263, 275
Conroy's, 100
Corbett Lake, 19
Cortland, 222
Craighead, Gene, 69, 78

cress-bugs, 12, 74
Crompton, Robert, 31, 39, 42, 47, 107, 114, 116, 127, 130, 174, 193, 196, 203, 283, 285
Cross Rod Company, 17
Cumberland Valley, 8, 9, 10, 12, 46, 56, 57, 59, 60, 61, 62, 63, 65, 66, 67, 69, 71, 72, 73, 74, 75, 77, 78, 79, 134, 135, 137, 139, 141, 143, 145, 147, 149, 151, 153, 155, 157
Cumberland Valley Chapter of Trout Unlimited, 9, 63, 66, 71
Czotter, Ted, 27

D

Darlingtorf, Roy, 286
Datus Proper, 139
delaminate, 182
Demarest, Charles H., 36, 170, 171
Demarest, Harold and Eileen, 171
Dickerson, Lyle, 18, 114, 285
Dietrich brothers, 22
Dorsey, Tom, viii, 10, 22, 133, 165
dun, 61, 78, 160
Dunton, Sewall, 11, 165, 222

E

Eastern Rod Builder's Gathering, 268
Ebright, Don, 153, 259
Edwards, E. W., 17, 28
elodea, 74, 75
emerger, 137
England, ix, x, xiv, 64, 69, 133, 135, 139, 141, 142, 144, 153, 157, 210, 238
    Abbotts Barton, 140, 141, 143
    chalk streams, 59, 238
    Hampshire, 139, 143, 144
    Itchen, xiv, 139, 140, 141, 143, 144
    London, xiv, 66, 139, 140, 286
    Winchester, 140, 142, 143, 284
entomology, xiii, 17, 19, 54, 57, 72, 146
Everett, Fred, 73
external shaping, 102

F

Falling Springs, 7, 8, 10, 11, 44, 230
Feierabend, Lou, 31
Fenwick, 261

Fero, Rosina, 27
fiberglass, viii, 12, 18, 30, 31, 119, 132, 178, 261
Field & Stream, 83
final taper, 100, 102, 103, 104
Fink, Bill, 21, 168
Fishing Gazette, x, xi
fishing hut, 69, 70
five-strip rod, 44, 45, 130, 283
Flick, Art, 73
Fly Fishers' Club of London, xiv, 66
    The Flyfishers, 140, 286
fly-tying, xi, xiii, 17, 19, 53, 54, 59, 69, 70, 109, 148, 157, 162, 169, 191
Foster, Jerry, 19
Fox, Charlie, 8, 9, 57, 60, 62, 66, 68, 71, 72, 73, 78, 90, 109, 121, 122, 168, 219, 282
    Advanced Bait Casting, 8, 90, 121, 123, 282, 285
    Charlie's meadow, 69, 70
    Rising Trout, vi, 72, 78
    The Pennsylvania Angler, xiv, 8, 57, 167, 168
    This Wonderful World of Trout, 72, 78
Frazer, Perry, 29, 91, 107, 193, 283, 284
    Amateur Rodmaking, 29, 91, 283, 284
freestone stream, 265
Fritz, Bill, 9, 68, 69, 165, 166

G

Garcia, 261
Garrison, Everett, ix, 11, 17, 30, 37, 39, 45, 107, 109, 114, 128, 172, 195, 263
geometry, 107, 176, 196, 197, 207, 208
Gibson, George, 60
    American Turf Register and Sporting Magazine, 60
Gillum, "Pinky", 17, 114
Gingrich, Arnold, 73
glue, vi, vii, 4, 43, 55, 92, 93, 114, 117, 123, 130, 165, 166, 167, 168, 169, 177, 182, 183, 185, 186, 193
    adhesives, 111
    Carpenter's Glue, 167, 168, 183
    cure, 167, 177, 183, 185
    Epon, 167, 168
    glue-line, 167
    gluing, viii, 8, 30, 36, 55, 96, 114, 130, 167, 168, 178, 180, 181, 182, 186, 266
    hide glue, vi, vii, 55, 167, 182, 183
    Nyatex, 167
    resorcinol, 167
    Urac, 168
Gooding, Russ, 22
Gordon, Theodore, ix, x, xi, xiii, xiv, 60, 282
    American Fly Fishing, xi, 60, 282
Grand Cascapedia, 150
Granger, 18, 117, 193, 261
graphite, viii, 18, 21, 178, 223, 255, 264
Gray, Dana, 21
Great Depression, 50, 51
    Civilian Conservation Corps, 50
    Depression, 28, 50, 51, 52, 53
Green, Ebenezer, 83
Griffith, George, 9
Grove, "Bus", 69, 72
    Lure and Lore of Trout Fishing, 72
Guild Rod, 260
Gunpowder River, 222
gunsmith, 88, 90, 92

H

Halford, Frederic, ix, xiii, 143
Halstead, George, 17, 114, 117
hand-piece, 90, 91, 92, 93
Hardy, 186, 226, 234, 235, 238
Harpster, Wayne, 146
Harrisburg Fly Fishers, 81, 82, 84, 107
    HFF, 66, 68, 72, 73, 78, 81
Harvey, George, 73, 146
Hauser, Bobby, 11
Hawes, 17, 106, 109, 113
Hawes, Hiram, 106, 113
Heddon, 18, 29, 117, 119, 193, 261
Hedge, Marvin, 114
Hendrickson, 9, 137, 138, 160, 224
Henry, Dick, 10, 11, 16, 47, 78, 110, 124, 125, 126, 132, 135, 136, 137, 144, 159, 166, 257
Henshall, James, 85, 106
    Book of The Black Bass, 85, 91, 284
    Outing, 85, 106, 285
    World's Columbian Exposition, 85
Herd, Andrew, ix
Herter, George, 30, 39, 87, 89, 92, 127, 128, 130, 193
    Rod Building Manual and Manufacturer's Guide, 39, 87, 270, 283, 284, 285
Hewitt, Edward, vi, 70, 121, 143

Neversink, 70, 73
window box, 73
hexagonal, 37, 95, 103, 104, 105, 106, 107, 181, 185, 193, 199, 259
Hisey, Charlie, 133
Hogestown Run, 74
Holbrook, Don and Ed Koch, 72
Midge Magic, 72
Holden Associates, The, 109, 110, 111
guild, 110, 111, 114, 116, 117, 120, 121, 130, 168, 260, 285
Newsletter, 19, 110, 116, 117, 119, 120, 268, 285
Holden, George Parker, 18, 30, 31, 35, 107, 110, 193, 264, 283, 286
Idyl of the Split Bamboo, 35, 283, 286
Honey Creek, 70
Humphries, Joe, 73

I, J

Industrial Revolution, 106
inscription, viii, 8, 166, 230, 231, 234, 250
Jaworowski, Ed, 73
Jenkins, Charlie, 133
Jordan, Wes, 18, 111, 113, 114, 119, 270, 272

K

Kauffmann, Samuel, 87
Keane, Martin, 85, 106
Classic Rods and Rod Makers, 85
Keene, John Harrington, x
Fishing Tackle, Its Materials and Manufacture, x
Fly-Fishing And Fly-Making, x
Kell, Jim, 69
Kerr, Tom, 84, 87, 107
King, Lloyd, 69
Koch, Ed, 69, 72
Kope, Robert, 21
Kreh, Lefty, 73
Kreider, Claude, 31, 42, 107, 128, 193
The Bamboo Rod And How to Build It, 31, 42
Krider, John, 83
Kusse, Ron, 21, 133
Kustich, Jerry, 133

L

LaBranche, George, 73
Lambuth, Letcher, 223
Lauver, Joe, 12, 13
leaders, xi, 75, 124
Leibold, Kevin, 24, 36, 45, 282
Leiser, Eric, 73, 148
Leonard, Hiram, 17, 90
Leonard, Wayne, 9, 11, 12
Letort, 7, 12, 13, 14, 33, 35, 40, 57, 58, 61, 68, 69, 70, 71, 74, 75, 78, 144, 149, 221, 246
Lew Stoner, 31, 85, 114, 184, 185, 186
limestone stream, 136
limestoner, 74, 146
Little, Larry, 150, 153
Lively, Chauncey, vi, 11
Loehle, Frank, 124, 125, 126
Lyons, Nick, 79
Crown Publishers, 79, 139

M

Maca, Wayne, 133
Mackie, Gordon, 140, 141, 286
Maine, 59, 62, 83, 106, 149
Rangeley Lakes, 59, 62
Major, Harlan, 35, 283
Salt Water Fishing Tackle, 35, 283
Margaree River, 149
Marinaro, Alfonso, 26
Marinaro, Carmine, 27
Marinaro, Maggie, 219, 231, 259
Marinaro, Sebastian, xiv, 14, 259
Marinaro Estate, xiv, 14, 16, 220
Marinaro, Vince, vi, xiii, xiv, 7, 24, 40, 64, 66, 72, 90, 124, 150, 154, 160, 285, 286
"Guppy," 226, 228, 260, 289
"Marinaro Collection," 22, 250
"Penn's Creek," 250
"Penobscot," 152, 154, 255, 292
"Salar," 153, 254, 255, 291
"Salmo," 152, 153, 254, 290
"the noble rock," 68
A Modern Dry Fly Code, viii, 8, 9, 11, 69, 70, 72, 75, 78, 87, 111, 121, 122, 283
cooking, vi, vii, 69, 156

Dickinson School of Law, 57
In The Ring of The Rise, vi, vii, viii, xiv, 8, 22, 72, 139, 282, 283, 286
marrow spoon, 143
"Pappy," 12, 14, 127, 138, 141, 142, 144, 156, 157, 160, 165, 171, 176, 189, 203, 217
pilgrimage, 139, 144
puddle-cast, 76, 142
slant tank, 73
surviving rods, 46, 220
Symons, Martha, 51
unpublished manuscript, 238
violin, 50, 155, 163, 181
Marinaro, Vincentia, 54, 69
Marinaro, Vincenzo, 27
Mason, George, 9
mathematics, 176, 192, 196, 203
Mather, Fred, 100, 284
My Angling Friends, 100, 284
Maulucci, Bob, 21, 22
Maurer, George and Bernie Elser
Fundamentals of Cane Rod Building, 262
Maxwell, Tom, viii, 10, 133, 137, 146, 148, 149, 165, 188, 230, 232, 265
McCafferty, Bob, 69, 70
McClane, A. J., 31, 83
McClure, F. A., 114
McDonald, John, ix, xiii, 282
McDonnell, Tom, 273
Medved, Al, 21, 22
Metz, "Bucky", 148
Michigan, vii, 9, 18, 19, 68, 76, 77, 114, 135
Department of Conservation, 9
Grayling, 9
Manistee, 60, 76
midges, 8, 78
Mills, William, x
Milward, R. E.
Bamboo: Fact, Fiction And Flyrods, 174, 286
Miramichi, 149, 150, 153
Mitchell, William, 83
Montague, 17, 18, 29, 113, 117, 165, 166, 193
Morrell, T. S. 96, 284
Murphy, Charles, 83, 87, 96, 100

N

Neumann, Art, 9
New Brunswick, 135, 149, 153
New York
Catskills, vi, 59, 72
Central Valley, 90
Fayetteville, 111
Livingston Manor, 111
Long Island, 88
Manhattan, 83, 100
New York City, 88
Syracuse, 110, 111
nodes, 2, 3, 92, 128, 172, 173, 174, 179, 180
Noland, Al, 22
Norris, Thaddeus, 83, 97, 101
American Anglers' Book, 97, 101
composite rod, 103
four-strip tip, 102
nutrients, 136
nymph, 137, 143, 157

O, P

Oldenwalder, Asher J., 81
Oldenwalder rod, 81, 85, 87, 89, 91, 92, 94
Orvis, x, xi, 18, 111, 113, 114, 132, 133
panfish, 120, 124
bluegill, 124, 125
smallmouth bass, 44, 120, 122
parabolic, 97, 216, 223, 224, 240
Park, Catoctin Mountain, 148
Payne, F. F., 17, 28
Penn's Creek, 7, 38, 135, 160, 216, 250
Green Drake, 70, 135, 136
Poe Paddy, 135, 136, 137, 138, 156
Winters Project, 135, 138
Pennsylvania
Berwick, 13
Boiling Springs, 11, 19, 46, 59, 197, 268
Butler, 8, 27, 28, 33, 50, 51, 52, 53, 54, 155
Cammal, 261
Carlisle, 12, 57, 59, 60, 61, 63, 68, 70, 165
Chambersburg, 10, 166
Coburn, 135, 136
Cherry Run, 136

Elk Creek, 136
Penn's Cave, 136
Poe Paddy State Park, 135, 136
Department of Revenue, 52, 57
Easton, 81, 82, 84, 85, 88, 89, 90
Fish And Boat Commission, 9
Harrisburg, vi, 8, 52, 54, 55, 57, 59, 60, 66, 68, 72, 73, 81, 82, 84, 89, 107, 160, 259, 261, 283
Historical and Museum Commission, 81, 84, 87, 89, 92, 95
Huntingdon County, 146
Lebanon, 124, 157
Mechanicsburg, vi, vii, 55, 160, 165
New Cumberland, 62
Newville, 59, 62, 63, 64, 65, 66
    barrel factory, 64, 133
    Big Spring Watershed Association, 66
    commercial fish hatchery, 9, 62
    Queen Victoria, 64
    Scottish immigrants, 63
    state-managed hatchery, 62
Northampton County Historical Society, 90
Pennsylvania Fly Fishing Museum Association, ix, xiv, 14, 81, 82, 86, 259
    PFFMA, ix, 14, 16, 17, 22, 46, 85, 109, 121, 124, 141, 169, 220, 260, 282
Philadelphia, 59, 83, 223, 224
Pine Creek Valley, 261
Pittsburgh, 50, 51, 52, 155, 219, 273
Poconos, 59
Reynoldsville, 27, 51
Springfield, 64, 66
State Museum, 81, 84, 85, 87, 89, 92, 94, 95, 99, 107, 284
Penobscot, 149, 150, 152, 153, 154, 220, 254, 255, 256, 292
Phillippe, Samuel, 81, 82, 85, 87, 89, 90, 101, 163
Phillippe, Solon, 82, 84, 88
    checkering, 87, 89, 90, 92, 96
    maker's mark, 84, 85, 86, 88, 90
    Phillippe rod, 81, 82, 83, 85, 87, 88, 89, 90, 91, 93, 94, 96, 99, 100, 102, 104, 105, 106, 107, 284
    provenance, 82, 83, 84, 85, 89
    sheathing, 90, 92
physics, 49, 191, 204, 263
Pickard, John, 21, 22
"Poor Man's Quad," 223

Post Mills, Vermont, 17
Powell, Walt, 114
production age, 105, 106

R

Raines, Howell, 14, 78, 282
Fly Fishing Through The Midlife Crisis, 14, 282
Reese, Jodi, 259
Reid, Willis, 21
Reiter, Brett, 22
Restigouche, 149
rent and glued, 101
Richards, Carl, 73
Ritz, Charles, 216
Robb, Mahlon, 81, 83, 90
Robbins, Rick, 11, 21, 137, 145, 146, 148, 265
Rod & Reel, 111, 285
rod-building
    adjustment bolts, 164, 175, 176
    anchoring plates, 164
    apex, 4, 45, 101, 130, 176, 178, 180, 181, 182
    beveler, 22
    C-clamps, 164, 176, 194
    center gauge, 163, 181
    composite, 97, 101, 103
    control point, 211, 217
    cork, 5, 22, 30, 47, 123, 183, 185, 186, 202, 210, 231, 234, 235, 242, 246, 250, 272
    depth indicator, 175
    equilateral, 178, 180
    ferrule station, 185, 202, 266
    five-strip, 44, 45, 130, 193, 283
    flat-to-flat, 221
    four-strip, 89, 91, 101, 102, 103, 104
    grain run-out, 179
    guides, 5, 22, 30, 36, 92, 93, 114, 177, 178, 183, 185, 187, 221, 226, 238
    heat treating, 127, 128, 174
    hollow-building, 186
    master strip, 176
    micrometer, 193, 217
    mill-bastard file, 181, 185
    nickel-silver, 114, 117, 235, 238, 267
    plane, 11, 39, 40, 102, 103, 104, 106, 163, 165, 176, 178, 179, 180, 181, 194, 260

planing board, 102, 103, 193
planing form, 3, 19, 37, 40, 105, 106, 128, 163, 164, 165, 175, 176, 179, 180, 192, 193, 194, 199, 200, 216, 217, 220, 221, 262, 263, 264, 268, 270
planing techniques, 83, 95, 104
push-pull bolts, 164, 194
reel seat, 5, 22, 30, 47, 93, 105, 123, 185, 186, 187, 210, 234, 235, 238, 242, 246, 250
scraping, 180, 181
settings, 59, 146, 175, 176, 199, 221
shooting board, 128
silk, 5, 37, 81, 93, 117, 187, 226, 231, 246, 250
six-strip, 43, 81, 82, 83, 85, 87, 89, 90, 91, 92, 95, 96, 101, 102, 103, 104, 105, 106, 107, 124, 259
sliding bands, 47, 186, 226
snake-guides, 114, 177, 187
spine, 178, 179, 180
splitting, 102, 113, 167, 172, 179, 180
steel bars, 39, 164, 175, 194, 195
straightening, 168, 173, 179, 180
target dimensions, 181, 194
V-groove, 3, 101, 175, 176, 179, 180, 181, 194, 195
varnish, vi, vii, 5, 93, 99, 114, 116, 117, 128, 131, 177, 187, 188, 220, 230, 231, 242
workbench, 42, 217

rod-design
buttressing, 196, 207, 208
calculations, xiv, 196, 200, 204, 205, 259, 263
cantilevered beam, 204
chart, 176, 193, 210, 211, 217, 267, 271, 272, 273
compression, 181, 207, 208
control points, 199
cross-section, 45, 92, 101, 103, 106, 179, 180, 181, 217
deflection, 99, 204, 205, 208
design principles, 16, 22, 171, 211
drawing board, 203, 211
empirical, 36, 176, 196, 203, 273, 275
flexing characteristics, 36, 99, 200, 204, 213, 225
graphed design, 175, 176
graphic, 40, 201
grid, 199, 200, 201, 210, 217, 271
half-dimensions, 199, 200, 201, 203, 210, 211, 217
hinge, 206, 216, 228, 271, 272
horizontal axis, 199, 210
inertia, 49, 214
lever-arm, 46, 210, 216
linear progression, 96, 208
momentum, 49
progressive action, 222, 223, 224, 228, 236
reversed sweep, 226
shoulders, 82, 93, 107, 196, 208, 212, 213, 214, 243
static, 204
stations, 45, 96, 99, 163, 164, 175, 176, 185, 193, 194, 195, 199, 204, 210, 212, 214, 217, 221, 230, 251, 270, 271, 272
step-and-dip, 206, 207, 208, 209
strength-to-weight, 196, 204, 207, 209
tension, 181, 187, 207, 208
thickness-to-length, 200, 201, 210
tip-action, 222, 256, 268
tolerances, 7, 39, 102, 164, 192
torque, 216
trajectory, 99, 176, 197, 198, 200, 205, 206, 212, 214, 221
tweaking, 97, 211, 260, 263, 265, 270, 271, 272
uniform progression, 205
vertical axis, 199, 210

S

Salmon fishing, 149, 220
    Salmon rods, 150, 225, 254, 256
    two-handed rod, 150, 220, 254, 255
Schullery, Paul, ix, 60, 68, 282, 283
    Royal Coachman, 60, 283
Schwiebert, Ernie, 42, 69, 73, 81
    Matching The Hatch, viii
scientific, 68, 127, 160, 167, 192, 196, 225, 285
Scott, Genio, 87, 88, 89, 97, 98, 284
    Fishing in American Waters, 87, 97, 284
Selb, Bob, 222, 224, 232
    The Classic Fly-Fisherman, 224
Shaeffer, Jeff, 22
Shenk, Ed, 12, 69, 72, 73, 78, 148, 149
    Fly Rod Trouting, 72
Shires, Norm and Jim Gilford, 68, 283
    Limestone Legends, 68, 283
Shires, Ralph, 63
Shoemaker, Henry, W. 90
Silver Spring, 61, 74
60-degree bevel, 3, 127, 179, 180
Skilton, Billy, 11

slope line, 201, 202, 206, 208, 209, 212, 213, 214, 264, 271
smith age, 83, 87
Smithwick, Tom, 21, 222, 223, 254
South Bend, 17, 18, 21, 29, 113, 262, 270
Sparse Grey Hackle, viii, 66, 72, 109, 219, 285
    "The Pennsylvania Boys," 66
    Alfred W. Miller, viii, 72, 109
    Journal of the Anglers' Club of New York, 72
spawning, 71, 153
Spey, 223, 255
spinners, 70, 137
spring creeks, 62, 74
Spruce Creek, 146, 168, 223, 273
Spurr, Dick and Gloria Jordan, 270
St. Lawrence River, 88
St. Paul Public Library, 42
    St. Paul Pioneer Press, 42
Stone Creek, 70
straight taper, 46, 96, 99, 101, 102
Summers, Bob, 133
"Super-Z" ferrule, 31, 119, 226
Susquehanna River, 121, 122, 136
Sutsos, Ted, 11, 137
sweepers, 76, 77, 269
swell, 113, 197, 198, 200, 201, 202, 203, 208, 211, 212, 213, 214, 230, 232, 234, 239, 243, 247, 251, 264, 268
"Sylph," 270, 271, 272, 273

T

Talleur, Dick, 73
Talsma, Todd, 22
taper line, 201, 202, 206, 214, 254, 271
Tatarus, Terry, 153
Taylor, Bill, 22
Taylor, Bobby, 21, 133
technical fishing, 74
    problem fishing, 143
terrestrial, viii, 78, 143
Thomas & Thomas, viii, 11, 13, 22, 133, 165, 166
Thomas, F. E., 17, 28
Thompson, Frank, 11, 137, 148, 149
thorax pattern, 8, 138
trial-and-error, 29, 45, 171, 191, 196, 203, 211, 273, 275
Trimmer, Ross, 69, 71
Trout Unlimited, 9, 63, 66, 68, 71, 259

Tulpehocken, 7, 10, 16, 230
Tups Indispensable, 157

U, V

U.S. Forest Products Laboratories, 114, 177, 285
Uslan, Nat, 17, 31, 45, 114, 119
Van Burgel, Dave, 21
Varney, George, 17, 18
Von Lengerke & Antoine, 28

W

Wagner, Jeff, 21, 22
Walker, Jeff, 133
Walton, Izaak, 143
Welch, Robert, 83, 88, 97
Wells, Henry P., 29, 97, 284
West Coast, 18
Wetzel, Charlie, 72, 73
    Practical Fly-Fishing, 72
    Trout Flies, Naturals and Imitations, 72
Wheeler, Charles, 83, 106
Whitlock, Dave, 73
Whittle, Tom, ix, xii, 7, 15, 16, 22, 30, 34, 48, 52, 78, 84, 88, 90, 91, 93, 94, 105, 119, 124, 130, 138, 146, 152, 153, 155, 162, 163, 188, 194, 195, 209, 215, 216, 219, 222, 224, 226, 228, 230, 232, 234, 236, 238, 240, 242, 244, 246, 248, 250, 252, 254, 255, 256, 258, 261, 262, 265, 266, 267, 268, 269, 274, 276, 278, 279, 281
Wickstrom, Gordon, 68, 159, 286
    Notes From An Old Fly Book, 68
Williams, Bob, 22
Winston, R. L., 31
Wojnicki, Mario, 133
Wright, Leonard, 73
Wulff, Lee, 73

Y

Yellow Breeches, 11, 19, 74
Yellow Breeches Fly Shop, 11
Young, Paul, 18, 114, 174

Z

Zern, Ed, 73
Zimny, John, 21

About Adobe Garamond® Font Family
Designer: Robert Slimbach, 1989

Claude Garamond (c. 1480 –1561) was a Parisian publisher. He was one of the leading type designers of his time, and several of the typefaces he designed are still in use, notably the font Garamond, named in his honor. Garamond came to prominence in 1541, when three of his Greek typefaces were requested for a royally ordered book series by Robert Estienne. Garamond based them on the handwritings of Angelo Vergecio, the King's Librarian at Fontainebleau, and his ten-year-old pupil, Henri Estienne. According to Arthur Tilley, the editions are "among the most finished specimens of typography that exist." Garamond's Roman were created shortly thereafter, and his influence rapidly spread throughout and beyond France during the 1540s.

Some of the most popular typefaces in history are those based on the types of the sixteenth-century printer, publisher, and type designer Claude Garamond, whose sixteenth-century types were modeled on those of Venetian printers from the end of the previous century. The Garamond typeface and its variations have been a standard among book designers and printers for four centuries; nearly every manufacturer of type or typesetting equipment has produced at least one version of Garamond in the past eighty years.

Adobe designer Robert Slimbach went to the Plantin-Moretus museum in Antwerp, Belgium, to study the original Garamond typefaces. These served as the basis for the design of the Adobe Garamond romans; the italics are based on types by Robert Granjon, a contemporary of Garamond's. This elegant, versatile design, the first Adobe Original typeface, was released in 1989, and includes three weights, plus a titling font, alternate characters, and an Expert Collection to provide a flexible family of text types.

2150 hardbound copies printed in the United States of America by Jostens Printing and Publishing.

1910

Vince Marinaro born in Reynoldsville, PA, 1911

Perry Frazer, *Amateur Rodmaking*, 1914

1920

George Parker Holden, *Idyl of The Split Bamboo*, 1920

Marinaro's first rods in 1928-'29

Marinaro graduates Butler High School, 1929

1930

Marinaro corresponds with Holden—learns of Crompton, c.1932

Law degree from Duquesne Univ., 1939

1940

Marinaro moves family from Butler, PA to Harrisburg, 1942

Marinaro meets Charlie Fox, 1942

Marinaro and Fox establish Harrisburg Fly-Fishers, 1947

Sparse Grey Hackle and his "Holden Associates," 1947

Marinaro locates a Phillippe fly rod, c.1948